FICTIONS OF
LAND AND FLESH

BLACKNESS, INDIGENEITY, SPECULATION

Mark Rifkin

D1570591

Duke University Press   Durham and London   2019

Printed in the United States of America on acid-free paper ∞
Designed by Courtney Leigh Baker
Typeset in Garamond Premier Pro and Trade Gothic by
Westchester Publishing Services Ltd.

Library of Congress Cataloging-in-Publication Data
Names: Rifkin, Mark, [date] author.
Title: Fictions of land and flesh : blackness, indigeneity, speculation /
    Mark Rifkin.
Description: Durham : Duke University Press, 2019. | Includes
    bibliographical references and index.
Identifiers: LCCN 2018055383 (print)
LCCN 2019013603 (ebook)
ISBN 9781478005285 (ebook)
ISBN 9781478004257 (hardcover : alk. paper)
ISBN 9781478004837 (pbk. : alk. paper)
Subjects: LCSH: African Americans—Relations with Indians. | African
    Americans—Study and teaching. | Indians of North America—
    Study and teaching. | American literature—African American
    authors—History and criticism. | American literature—Indian
    authors—History and criticism. | Speculative fiction, American—
    History and criticism. | Politics and literature—United States—
    History. | Slavery—United States—History. | Indians of North
    America—Colonization. | Race—Political aspects—United States—
    History.
Classification: LCC E98.R28 (ebook) | LCC E98.R28 R54 2019 (print) |
    DDC 305.896/073—dc23
LC record available at https://lccn.loc.gov/2018055383

Cover art: Mark Bradford, *Pickett's Charge (Man with the Flag)*
(detail), 2017. Mixed media on canvas. 353.1 × 1523.9 cm. Photo: Cathy
Carver. © Mark Bradford. Courtesy the artist and Hauser & Wirth.

Contents

Acknowledgments · vii

INTRODUCTION · 1

1. ON THE IMPASSE · 15
2. FUNGIBLE BECOMING · 73
3. CARCERAL SPACE AND FUGITIVE MOTION · 117
4. THE MAROON MATRIX · 168

CODA: Diplomacy in the Undercommons · 220

Notes · 233
Bibliography · 287
Index · 313

Acknowledgments

Unlike other books of mine, this one did not grow out of an essay or shorter piece. Instead, it came from a sense that I could and wanted to contribute something to the conversations that were happening about relations between blackness and indigeneity. I am grateful to those whose scholarship in this area has helped inspire this project, including Yael Ben-Zvi, Jodi Byrd, Alyosha Goldstein, Sharon Holland, Shona Jackson, Tiffany King, Brian Klopotek, Malinda Maynor Lowery, Daniel Mandell, Kyle Mays, Tiya Miles, Jared Sexton, and Manu Karuka. I also would like to express my gratitude to the organizers of the Race and Sovereignty conference at the University of California, Los Angeles, in 2011, the Significance of the Frontier in the Age of Transnational History symposium at the Huntington Library in 2012, and the Settler Colonial Rearticulations symposium at the University of California, Berkeley, in 2016, since these were important moments in the emergence of the ideas that eventually would give shape to *Fictions of Land and Flesh*.

I am deeply appreciative of those who have offered feedback on this project. Thanks to Shanté Paradigm Smalls, Aimee Bahng, Shona Jackson, Grace Hong, and the anonymous reader for the press for their incredibly generous engagement and immensely helpful comments. Parts of the project were presented at the Native American and Indigenous Studies Association, National Women's Studies Association, and American Studies Association, as well as talks and symposia at the University of California, Riverside; the University of North Carolina at Chapel Hill; Amherst College; the University of North Texas; Johns Hopkins University; New York University; Duke University; Princeton University; the University of Würzburg; and Johannes-Guttenberg-Mainz University. Thanks so much to everyone who invited me and to all the people who attended for their wonderful questions, comments, and provocations. Huge thanks to the students in my Black and Indigenous Futures class for helping me in formulating the stakes of this work (and for wonderful engagements around the significance of speculation as a mode of thought and political imagination). Thanks to Sarah Cervenak and J. Kameron Carter for organizing the year-long symposium The Black Outdoors, which was immensely helpful in clarifying for me the work I sought to do in this project.

I also have benefited immeasurably from ongoing conversations with a range of scholars, including Aimee Bahng, Joanne Barker, Nancy Bentley, Kevin Bruyneel, Jodi Byrd, Jessica Cattelino, David Chang, Eric Cheyfitz, Glen Coulthard, Pete Coviello, Colin Dayan, Jennifer Denetdale, Jean Dennison, Ashley Falzetti, Beth Freeman, Mishuana Goeman, Alyosha Goldstein, Sandy Grande, Lisa Kahaleole Hall, Shona Jackson, J. Kameron Carter, Malinda Maynor Lowery, Scott Morgensen, Dana Nelson, Robert Nichols, Audra Simpson, Kyla Wazana Tompkins, and Priscilla Wald.

UNC Greensboro has been my home base for more than a decade, and my colleagues there continue to uplift, challenge, and support me in innumerable ways. In particular, I would like to thank Risa Applegarth, Danielle Bouchard, Sarah Cervenak, Daniel Coleman Chávez, Asa Eger, Jen Feather, Tara Green, Ellen Haskel, Gwen Hunnicutt, Karen Kilcup, Derek Krueger, Christian Moraru, Noelle Morrisette, Gene Rogers, Scott Romine, María Sánchez, Amy Vines, and Karen Weyler.

Thanks so much to my editor Courtney Berger for all her support and for making things so smooth.

When I look up from reading and writing, I remember there's a world beyond the dynamics of academic study—one not merely speculative. For reminding me of that fact, in addition to those mentioned above, I'm deeply grateful to Sheila and Alex Avelin, Zivia Avelin, Jon Dichter, Kevin and Justin Dichter, Mike Hardin, Lisa Dilorio Smith, Tiffany Eatman Allen and Will Allen, Alicia and Bobby Murray, Debbie and Andy Johnson, Craig Bruns, Keith Brand, J. J. McArdle, Jon Van Gieson, and Ali Cohen. I find it hard to imagine a world I would want to inhabit without Erika Lin. My parents, Neal and Sharon Rifkin, and sister, Gail Dichter, have been central to all the futures I might envision, and I owe them immeasurably.

Finally, my speculations about my own future changed utterly when I met Rich Murray. Potentials appeared I had not even imagined. I am deeply grateful for the ways he expands my felt understanding of the possible.

INTRODUCTION

In a statement of support for the protestors seeking to stop the construction of the Dakota Access Pipeline on land near the Standing Rock Sioux reservation, members of the Black Lives Matter network describe it as "a movement for all of us" by those "Indigenous peoples who are putting their bodies and lives on the line to protect our right to clean water."[1] The statement goes on to insist, "[T]his is not a fight that is specific only to Native peoples—this is a fight for all of us and we must stand with our family at Standing Rock," later adding, "We are in an ongoing struggle for our lives and this struggle is shaped by the shared history between Indigenous peoples and Black people in America, connecting that stolen land and stolen labor from Black and brown people built this country." Black and Indigenous struggles appear here to coincide as they emerge out of a "shared history" of white supremacist violence, exploitation, and expropriation.[2] From this perspective, Native actions and intentions in fighting the Dakota Access Pipeline (opposition to which coalesced and circulated under the hashtag #NoDAPL) take part in a united movement whose subjects form a "we" that exceeds the specificity of Native peoplehood, since the trajectory of such opposition is shaped by, in the statement's terms, "a critical fight against big oil for our collective human right to access water." Since Black people also are subject to environmental racism, which "is not limited to pipelines on Indigenous land," they, too, are represented within the efforts at Standing Rock; thus, Black Lives Matter's solidarity with Native activists emerges from a sense of mutual subjection as people of color to environmental degradation and abjection by the racist policies of the U.S. state.

However, to what extent does this framing reflect Indigenous understandings? As described by Nick Estes, an Indigenous studies scholar and citizen of the Lower Brule Sioux, the current conflict arises out of "the longer histories of Oceti Sakowin (The Great Sioux Nation) resistance against the trespass of settlers, dams, and pipelines" across the Missouri River, itself understood as unceded Oceti Sakowin territory—recognized as such under the treaty of 1851 with the U.S. government. Moreover, in the introduction to a series of articles on #NoDAPL, Estes and Jaskiran Dhillon present the pipeline as "a continuation of the nineteenth-century Indian wars of extermination" while also posing the question, "How do we situate Standing Rock within a social, political, cultural, and historical context of Indigenous anticolonial resistance against occupation and various forms of state violence inherent to settler colonialism?"[3] These articulations conceptualize the struggle at Standing Rock as an expression of Oceti Sakowin sovereignty and self-determination as Indigenous peoples, rightfully exercising jurisdiction and stewardship over their homelands while being assaulted in ways consistent with an ongoing history of settler colonial theft and refusal to acknowledge the political authority of Native nations. Although the Black Lives Matter statement notes that "there is no Black liberation without Indigenous sovereignty," such sovereignty does not feature as a meaningful part of the analysis offered, either in terms of what is at stake in Indigenous opposition or what might be at play in imagining and negotiating an "our" in which non-natives might participate. While the statement suggests a convergence around the kinds of materials used for the pipeline and the failed water pipes in "Black communities like Flint," as well as the fact that many of the same companies funding the pipeline also sponsor "factories that emit carcinogenic chemicals into Black communities," the political imaginary at play in Indigenous opposition gets translated and refigured within an alternative set of conceptual, political, and historical coordinates. That process allows the rhetorical emergence of a "we" who have a "shared" set of rights/claims to the space of "this country" in ways fairly disconnected from the question and practice of Indigenous sovereignties. If the actions at Standing Rock and in Flint might be brought into relation around access to water, does such a conjunction provide a basis on which to connect them? Or, perhaps more usefully, what kinds of relation does it engender, and what dangers lie in presuming that this apparently shared object or set of concerns bespeaks an underlying unity in the movements' frames and aims? As Dipesh Chakrabarty cautions in *Provincializing Europe*, "The Hindi *pani* may be translated into the English 'water' without having to go through the superior positivity of H$_2$O," and this movement across languages "appeal[s] to models of cross-cultural and cross-categorical translations that do not take a universal middle term for granted."[4] Similarly, while water may provide a basis for mutual engagement and solidarity, the significance of water—the political geographies, collective histories, and constellations of meaning in which it and sustainable access to it are enmeshed—cannot be presumed to be the same. How might water, as an example, provide a site for translation among disparate political imaginaries and trajectories in ways that do not seek to efface their difference in the process?

Rather than seeking to diminish the gesture of solidarity by members of the Black Lives Matter movement, then, I want to underline the ways that, even in good faith efforts toward meaningful engagement, the assumption of a shared set of terms, analyses, or horizons of political imagination between Black and Indigenous struggles may be premature or may obfuscate significant distinctions.[5] The question of how to understand the specificity of political movements appears as a central issue in the articulation of the aims of the Black Lives Matter network. The Black Lives Matter movement began as a response to the state-sanctioned murder of Black people (particularly by the police), with the hashtag arising specifically in 2013 in response to the failure to hold George Zimmerman legally accountable for his killing of Trayvon Martin. Since then, it has grown into a broader mass movement focused on challenging various institutionalized systems of antiblack oppression.[6] As part of "A HerStory of the #BlackLivesMatter Movement," the three creators of the hashtag—Alicia Garza, Opal Tometi, and Patrisse Cullors—observe, "Progressive movements in the United States have made some unfortunate errors when they push for unity at the expense of really understanding the concrete differences in context, experience, and oppression. In other words, some want unity without struggle." The aim here lies in challenging the appropriation of Black activist and intellectual work by others in ways that do not acknowledge the significance of antiblack oppression, how Black lives "are uniquely, systematically, and savagely targeted by the state." However, this emphasis on the particularity of the forms of domination to which Black people are subjected and their struggles against such domination—the push against, in the creators' terms, "the worn out and sloppy practice of drawing lazy parallels of unity between peoples with vastly different histories and experiences"—can also apply to the process of seeking to put Black and Indigenous movements into relation.[7] Garza, Tometi, and Cullors's cautions here apply not only to the imagination of an inherent "we" or "us" that unites these struggles but to the ways "concrete differences in context, experience, and oppression" can be displaced when positing a given analytical framework as necessarily providing the encompassing conceptual structure in which to situate Black and Indigenous histories, political imaginaries, and efforts to realize justice. What difficulties arise in trying to resolve these differences by incorporating them into a unifying, singular model, and what other possibilities might there be for movement between and among such differences other than merger or triangulation within a putatively supervening structure that supposedly can envelop and explain them?

From this perspective, we might understand Black and Indigenous struggles less as incommensurable than as simply nonidentical, as having distinct kinds of orientation shaped by the effects of histories of enslavement and settler colonial occupation.[8] To describe movements and the political imaginaries to which they give rise and that animate them as *oriented* suggests that they are given form, trajectory, and momentum by the particular histories of domination to which they respond, as well as the visions of liberation that emerge to contest the dominant terms of subjugation and subjection. As Sara Ahmed suggests, "[W]e do not have to consciously exclude those things that are not 'on line.' The direction we take excludes things for us, before we even get there." She further observes, "[A] background is what explains the conditions of emergence or an arrival of something as the thing that it appears to be in the present," adding, "Histories shape 'what' surfaces: they are behind the arrival of 'the what' that surfaces."[9] Characterizing movements as having disparate backgrounds indicates that they have distinct "conditions of emergence" that shape the "what" of the movements themselves: the kinds of subjects and subjectivities that they represent, the particular institutional conjunctures that they contest, and the aims toward which they move.

In this vein, we might quite roughly schematize the distinction between Black and Indigenous political imaginaries as that of flesh and of land, a contrast between a focus on the violence of dehumanization through fungibility and occupation through domestication.[10] In "Fugitive Justice," Stephen Best and Saidiya Hartman argue, "A 'plan' for the redress of slavery is what is urgently needed, but any plan, any legal remedy, would inevitably be too narrow, and as such it would also prove necessarily inadequate," and they further suggest, "We understand the particular character of slavery's violence to be ongoing and constitutive of the unfinished project of freedom," adding that "the kinds of political claims that can be mobilized on behalf of the slave (the stateless, the socially dead, and the disposable) in the political present" illustrate "the incomplete nature of abolition."[11] The legacies of enslavement continue to shape the possibilities for Black life in the present, an inheritance and contemporary force that exceeds the potential for formal legal redress through enactments of equality due to the ways that Black people continue to be made "socially dead" and "disposable" within structures of state racism—particularly in terms of criminalization and mass incarceration. Similarly, in "The Case of Blackness," Fred Moten argues that "[t]he cultural and political discourse on black pathology has been so pervasive that it could be said to constitute the background against which all representations of blacks, blackness, or (the color) black take place."[12] This widespread understanding of blackness in terms of aberrance and anomaly gives rise to "fugitive movement in and out of the frame, bar, or whatever externally imposed social logic—a movement of escape, the stealth of the stolen," a "fugitive movement [that] is stolen life" and that is the "special ontic-ontological fugitivity" of "the slave."[13] The continued remaking of bodies via blackness as malleable and disposable flesh extends the dynamics of chattel slavery, engendering a ubiquitous pathologization for which flight from the enclosures of the law—stolen modes of individual and collective subjectivity—provides the principal recourse.

By contrast, Native political imaginaries tend to turn on questions of collective territoriality and governance. Even while speaking in the critical idiom of flesh and of the violence done to Native women's bodies, Audra Simpson highlights in "The State Is a Man" how "[a]n Indian woman's body in settler regimes such as the US . . . is loaded with meaning—signifying other political orders, land itself, of the dangerous possibility of reproducing Indian life and most dangerously, other political orders."[14] As Jodi Byrd notes of efforts to cast Native self-determination as a project of contesting racist exclusion, "American Indian national assertions of sovereignty disappear into U.S. territoriality as indigenous identity becomes a racial identity and citizens of colonized indigenous nations become internal ethnic minorities within the colonizing nation-state."[15] Emphasizing the existence of Native peoples as landed polities who exercise their own modes of sovereignty functions as a central animating principle of Indigenous movements, in ways at odds with the foregrounding of statelessness, social death, and fugitivity in Black political and intellectual framings.

Approaching Black and Indigenous political struggles and imaginaries as oriented in different ways—as following their own lines of development and contestation that are not equivalent to each other—does not mean understanding them as utterly dissimilar or as having no points of intersection or mutual imbrication. Rather, foregrounding such orientations and how they militate against a priori incorporation into a singular account enables a more searching consideration of the processes by which they might be brought into meaningful and productive relation so as to avoid forcing them into alignment and, thereby, generating an illusory and misleading sense of "unity without struggle." In discussing her relation as a non-Indigenous person with Quechua intellectuals, Marisol de la Cadena observes, "Our ways of knowing, practicing, and making our distinct worlds—our worldings, or ways of making worlds— had been 'circuited' together and shared practices for centuries; however, they had not become one." Describing the movement between those "worlds" as a process of *equivocation*, she further argues, "Controlling the equivocation means probing the translation process itself to make its onto-epistemic terms explicit, inquiring into how the requirements of these terms may leave behind that which the terms cannot contain, that which does not meet those require- ments or exceeds them."[16] This approach highlights the potential for Black and Indigenous political imaginaries to be "circuited together" yet still distinct while aiming to trace processes of translation among them in ways that address the transformations of meaning that occur in such transits.[17]

Before describing the arc of the project in its turn to the speculative as a basis for approaching Black-Indigenous relations and translations, though, I should note my own positioning within these scholarly and political conversations. I enter into these processes of translation as a non-native, white scholar who has sought over many years to develop sustained, respectful, and accountable relations with Indigenous scholars and to generate intellectual work through ongoing dialogue with and critique by them. I approach the questions and con- cerns of this project, then, as a white ally whose own primary intellectual coor- dinates are those of Indigenous studies and who seeks to engage work in Black studies and Black social and political movements from this position, while also having long-term commitments to challenging forms of antiblackness (as well as white privilege) as a scholar, teacher, and activist. I neither seek to position myself as speaking for Indigenous people(s) nor as offering a neutral location from which to assess Black-Indigenous discussions, debates, tensions, and ne- gotiations. To do either would involve evading the significance of my whiteness by implicitly using it to present myself as transcending what would by contrast appear as the located particularities of blackness and indigeneity.[18] Rather, my aim, as a scholar of Indigenous studies, is to engage the prominent and pressing issues of how Black and Indigenous movements might engage each other by questioning the value of triangulation as the vehicle for doing so, including the ways that the attempt to bring Indigenous and Black movements into align- ment as part of a single struggle tends to center whiteness as the mediating principle. While foregrounding whiteness as a shared object of critique and a shared source of various modes of structural violence can create a basis for co-alition, whiteness then remains the medium for relation among people of color instead of attending to how their experiences of collectivity, analyses of past and present domination, and visions for a more just future may be meaningfully discrepant from each other. I therefore am not so much aiming to specify the precise forms that Black-Indigenous dialogue and relation should take as pointing to certain impasses that arise in seeking to think and enact such relation and suggesting the value of holding on to a sense of the differences between these movements (instead of seeking to resolve them into a single structural formula).

Fictions of Land and Flesh turns to futurist fiction as a means of exploring some of the central conceptual framings employed within Black and Indigenous political imaginaries in order to illustrate the often unrecognized forms of translation through which they encounter and engage each other. How might we understand the movement between Black and Indigenous political formations as something of a speculative leap in which the terms and dynamics of the one are disoriented in the encounter with the other? How can recognizing such translations between and among historical and political framings, orientations, and imaginaries help generate critical modes that can address those processes (rather than efface them through attempts at unification)? In this vein, futurist fiction provides a compelling site for exploring such potential disjunctions while refusing to resolve them into a singular, systemic account. If both Black and Indigenous political imaginaries make powerful claims on how to narrate and navigate the actual, turning to speculative writing enables those forms of narration and conceptual/perceptual approaches to be made more visible as such, highlighting how these ways of accounting for reality are shaped by particular modes of analysis and visions for liberation/decolonization/abolition. Not only does futurist fiction generate "what if" scenarios that enable forms of conceptual and representational experimentation; its constitutive break from concrete events and experiences, in the sense of a setting that is neither in ostensibly known historical reality or the contested dynamics of the present, allows its imaginative spaces and relations to be understood as something other than a referential account of reality. Instead, futurist narratives allow us to see divergent ways of conceiving and perceiving, variable frames of reference through which to understand how things work in the world. Seeing them as framings—as *possible* ways of describing what was, is, and could be—allows for the potential for there to be multiple modes of understanding that all may be true while also being nonidentical. Engagement with Afrofuturist and Indigenous futurist fiction provides a means of tracking disparate orientations and the kinds of mutual (mis)translations that they engender. Thus, the speculative is less a specific genre for me than a mode of relation (which I also refer to as the subjunctive, in ways discussed in chapter 1). It opens the potential for acknowledging a plurality of legitimate, nonidentical truth claims, none of which should be taken as the singular and foundational way that the real is structured. The speculative as a mode opens intellectual, political, and ethical possibilities for thinking and valuing the differences among Black and Indigenous political imaginaries, which is what motivates my turn to futurist fiction as the principal site of study.

Each of the main chapters (after the first, largely introductory one) takes up a widely employed set of tropes for mapping and contesting antiblackness— fungibility, carcerality/fugitivity, and marronage—in order to explore the ways they shape figurations of domination and freedom, moving from least to most engaged with questions of place and collective inhabitation. My choice to foreground Afrofuturist texts speaks to their greater prominence popularly and critically, bringing questions of indigeneity and settlement into a well-established conversation and aiming to speak to those scholars who are part of that conversation. My aim also, as an Indigenous studies scholar, is to engage in sustained ways with these texts, these conversations, and the framings they raise—tracing the contours and trajectories of Black sociopolitical imaginaries while exploring the ways indigeneity enters into their modes of worlding. In other words, I seek to understand and appreciate the texts' ways of analyzing and critiquing antiblackness and their ways of envisioning possibilities for freedom, and doing so enables an exploration of, in de la Cadena's words, "how the requirements of these terms may leave behind that which the terms cannot contain"—an exploration that is neither dismissive nor condemnatory. In studying the kinds of analytical and oppositional possibilities these tropes offer, I engage with the ways they affect how important elements of Indigenous peoplehood and self-determination (such as collective placemaking, enduring connections to particular lands and waters, and exertion of sovereignty as autonomous polities) emerge within Black imaginaries. For this reason, Indigenous futurist texts appear largely as a counterpoint to help highlight the impasses that can arise when trying to engage indigeneity through the main texts' governing tropes.

To clarify, though, rather than marking something like a failure to engage indigeneity or the need for a more expansive or integrated kind of sociopolitical imagination, I seek to illustrate how the framings or orientations at play in these fictions provide the context in which indigeneity gains meaning, or not. My aim is to explore the relational capacities and opacities of various framings, not to declare certain framings suspect or verboten in light of the ways they may orient away from other issues (such as place-based peoplehood and Indigenous dispossession). I am not advocating a zero-sum logic whereby Indigenous futurist texts are envisioned as getting it *right* at the expense of Afrofuturist ones. Such an approach would create a *damned if they do, damned if they don't* dynamic with respect to indigeneity. Instead, I want to address how legitimate and powerful modes of Black analysis *also* are oriented in ways that can create difficulties for engaging with Indigenous projects of self-determination. Moreover, the possibilities of the speculative as a mode do not mean that any given (set of) text(s) of speculative fiction can resolve the tensions between those movements or necessarily offer a way through/beyond such tensions. For this reason, for each of the main texts, I seek to trace both its own political investments and imagination and to address how its orientations affect how it engages with or translates Indigenous framings. The larger goal is to consider the implications of such engagements and translations for relations among Black and Indigenous political movements and imaginaries in their ongoing differences from each other. The readings in the chapters, then, can be understood less as critique on my part (an effort to indicate where texts have failed to do or to be what they should) than as an effort to consider what certain conceptual and political framings enable and what they frustrate. How do differences in background principles, historical experiences, and directionalities of collective struggle affect the ways indigeneity enters into Black imaginaries, helping shape the dynamics of Black-Indigenous relation? How do disparate political analyses and envisioned horizons of liberation arise out of varied historical trajectories? What is at stake in refusing to see those frameworks as inherently needing to be brought into unifying alignment, and what problems, then, arise in the necessary and inevitable translation that occurs among nonidentical movements?

The first chapter, "On the Impasse," takes up these questions, laying out the project's theoretical and methodological itineraries. It explores the difficulties generated by seeking to bring blackness and indigeneity into an overarching structural account(ing), including the ways doing so can situate disparate movements within a set of background principles that are at odds with the movements themselves or can privilege one movement's animating terms at the expense of the other's (or others') in implicitly exceptionalizing ways. As against the effort to resolve apparent contradictions in articulations of Black and Indigenous struggle by illustrating how they are expressive of differentiated strands of an encompassing system or logic, I turn to Black feminist theorizations of difference that see it less as a distinction to be sublated within an enveloping structural dialectic than as indicative of nonidentical formations. Such divergence is less a problem to be eliminated or superseded than a normative condition of nondominating relation between/among sociopolitical formations. Understanding these movements as oriented by nonequivalent kinds of collective identity, modes of oppression, and forms of political aspiration provides the condition for putting them into relation in ways that do not presume some version of false consciousness or invidious unknowing as the basis for the discrepancies in articulations and experiences of blackness and indigeneity. Through discussion of the largely incommensurate ways the concepts of *sovereignty* and *the settler* are understood within scholarly accounts of blackness and indigeneity, the chapter addresses how varied intellectual and political orientations contour what such concepts come to mean and do. Tracing the fields of significance at play in these scholarly accounts, I demonstrate how they frame questions of belonging, placemaking, governance, and futurity in ways that emerge out of particular histories, thereby also characterizing the contours and force of ongoing patterns of institutionalized violence differently. Rather than suggesting the need to adjudicate among these accounts, or to synthesize or triangulate them, I argue for the value of acknowledging them as having disparate frames of reference while also bringing them into accountable relation to each other. The speculative serves as a means of doing so by providing a way of suspending the exclusivity of claims to what is real. Addressing theorizations of the work of science fiction, I illustrate how the speculative can function as a mode of hesitation. It offers what might be termed an ethics of equivocation that enables something like an ontological humility—or ethos of ontological multiplicity—in the face of others' ways of explaining what was and is and envisioning what might be. In this way, the speculative as a mode or an ethics facilitates the project of imagining oneself into others' frames of reference without suspending the efficacy of the explanatory frameworks one has, allowing both to coexist while opening up room for the difficult and potentially fraught dynamics of equivocation that arise in moving among disparate worldings.

Chapter 2, "Fungible Becoming," engages with efforts to explore the stakes of racial embodiment, particularly the historical and ongoing pathologization of Black flesh—or constitution of blackness as a reduction to flesh. Blackness functions as a process of social inscription that converts human beings into fungible potentiality—not simply objects for ownership and sale as chattel but as the vehicle for manifesting economies, geographies, and modes of personhood for whom others will serve as the subject. However, what might it mean to turn toward a conception of embodiment as malleability, to forgo the claim to normative personhood in favor of embracing the possibilities of blackness as a means of moving beyond propertied, and inherently racializing, modes of selfhood? In the *Xenogenesis* trilogy, Octavia Butler opens potentials for thinking about modes of embodiment and interdependence that displace existing, institutionalized ways of defining and calculating racial being. The novels do so in two ways: by insisting on the significance of shared humanness; and by staging human-alien encounter in ways that suggest the possibility for a less reifying way of understanding bodily identity, relation, and becoming. Butler does not so much envision human-alien miscegenation, the emergence of a new mixed species-being, as speculatively envision possibilities for more capacious and less insulating and hierarchical forms of sociality—a process that can be characterized as amalgamation. These forms of fluidity challenge existing institutionalized ways of defining privatized, biologized racial identity. In figuring these potentials, though, Butler also explores how such a sense of malleability emerges out of histories of equating blackness with fungibility, particularly through the trilogy's portrayal of reproduction and motherhood through its first protagonist—an African American woman named Lilith. Even as the novels' account of protean enfleshment implicitly reflects on the social production of blackness, the forms of alien sociality that seem to offer a way beyond racializing conceptions of property are themselves described in ways that draw on longstanding (stereotypical and ethnological) conceptions of indigeneity in the Americas. While repeatedly gesturing toward the politics of sovereignty and self-determination when addressing the ethics of human resistance to alien-managed transformation, the novels tend to present such Indigenously inflected concepts in ways that cast expressions of collective identity as a reactionary investment in forms of racial identity (a dynamic that I explore through brief engagements with Native futurist short stories by Drew Hayden Taylor and Mari Kurisato). Liberation from racialized modes of embodiment, and the notions of the human that they instantiate, gets linked to the absence of place-based peoplehood. Doing so defers the potential for a robust engagement with Indigenous sovereignties and implicitly translates indigeneity as a reactionary investment in the preservation of a naturalized group identity, itself understood as inherently racialized/racializing.

Turning to speculative imaginings of captivity and flight, chapter 3, "Carceral Space and Fugitive Motion," addresses the vast proliferation of apparatuses of imprisonment over the past forty years and the growing experience of emplacement in terms of racialized carcerality for Black subjects in the United States. This expansive matrix of mass incarceration also entails surveilling and regulating Black neighborhoods, particularly in urban areas. That sustained intervention, however, is not justified in race-explicit terms, instead being legitimized as part of a broader need to maintain "law-and-order" in putatively high crime areas, and therefore it does not present itself as a mode of institutionalized racism. In *Futureland: Nine Stories of an Imminent World*, Walter Mosley offers a speculative theorization of the principles immanently at play in such modes of neoliberal apartheid while addressing the central function of processes of racialization in the kinds of datafication on which such social mappings increasingly rely. Mosley explores the proliferation of carceral mechanisms and technologies beyond the prison, including the reorganization of everyday geographies so as to facilitate state-sanctioned containment separate from punishment for criminal activity per se in ways that build on existing racial demarcations while also generating additional and compounding modes of racialization that arise out of the application of ostensibly race-neutral criteria. The text explores the racializing effects of intensifying population-making modes of calculation (massive data gathering, algorithmic formulas for sorting kinds of persons, construction of biometric categories) as they emerge within legally mandated modes of putative racial neutrality, and it investigates how such institutionalized and state-sanctioned determinations of risk and value shape everyday geographies. In response, Mosley offers a poetics of fugitivity that disowns an oppositional politics of collective inhabitance in favor of figuring freedom as flight, in which not being located anywhere in particular becomes the avenue to emancipation from omnipresent topographies and strategies of incarceration. By contrast, Daniel Wilson's *Robopocalypse* series figures situated relation to place and other beings as vital, offering what might be characterized as an ontology of emplacement. While not primarily focused on Indigenous peoples' struggles for self-determination as such (although featuring an account of Osage nationhood), Wilson's novels draw on what might be understood as Indigenous principles to highlight the existence and emergence of forms of collective territoriality that not only serve as the basis for human social organization and survival but appear as necessary for the continuance and flourishing of life itself. However, if Wilson's texts suggest the difficulty of engaging place-based collectivity from within the topos of fugitivity, they also themselves leave little room for thinking the dynamics of diaspora (both as a political formation and as an effect of dispossession). The chapter closes by turning to Mosley's later novel *The Wave* in order to explore the text's meditation on questions of Black placemaking in the United States and how that exploration of located belonging itself comes to be configured around flight. The novel imagines a kind of Black indigeneity in the Americas while also suggesting the problems of such a vision. In this way, the novel seeks to think the complexity of relations between blackness and indigeneity in the Americas, and the difficulties of that speculative process are brought into relief by the novel's framing of its narrative in terms of tropes of mobility and escape.

Chapter 4, "The Maroon Matrix," turns to ways of envisioning Black collective placemaking and explicit efforts to conceptualize such political formations in relation to Indigenous sovereignties and histories of settlement. More than perhaps any other trope within diasporic Black political discourses and movements, marronage has served over the past century as a principal way of signaling opposition to the violence of the slave system and the forms of antiblackness that have persisted and arisen in its wake—particularly in the Caribbean and Latin America. The previous chapter addresses tensions between flight and collective emplacement, but as a critical-political trope marronage contains them both within one figure—in what might be called *the maroon matrix*. Maroon communities arise out of literal fugitivity from enslavement and are maintained through an ongoing refusal to be subjected to the plantation system and its legacies of racial capitalism, private property, and criminalization/incarceration. That separateness, both metaphorical and literal, has been conceptualized by intellectuals as expressive of a process of *indigenization* and acknowledged under international law (and, by extension, as part of domestic law in parts of Latin America) through the terms developed to define and recognize Indigenous peoples. Marronage, then, provides a framework through which to think Black emplacement and self-determination in the Americas while, at the same time, the intimate role played by indigeneity in form(ul)ations of marronage also threatens to situate non-native people of African descent in a relation of substitution/replacement to Native peoples, rather than one of mutual engagement and negotiation within landscapes shaped by the dynamics of empire. Nalo Hopkinson's *Midnight Robber* and Andrea Hairston's *Mindscape* explore the possibilities for Black collective territoriality in the diaspora while situating it in relation to enduring Indigenous presence and Native peoples' pursuit of self-determination. These novels address, in different ways, how Black presence can participate in Indigenous dispossession while also suggesting that indigeneity can serve as a conceptual and political resource for challenging dominant equations of blackness with placelessness, or the absence of a proper space of collective inhabitance. Hopkinson's and Hairston's texts illustrate the difficulty of translating indigeneity into the terms of marronage without the former becoming something like setting—functioning as a background or vehicle for non-native modes of struggle for change. What, though, does it mean to acknowledge Indigenous specificity and (geopolitical) distinctness? Native futurist work, such as Melissa Tantaquidgeon Zobel's *Oracles* and Stephen Graham Jones's *The Bird Is Gone: A ~~Monograph~~ Manifesto*, investigates these problematics of acknowledgment, addressing the double-edged character of state-recognized Indigenous territorial boundaries while also tracing how historically shifting Native social formations are congealed into notions of static Indian difference (potentially appropriable by non-natives for their own purposes). Together, these two sets of texts highlight the difficulty of conceptualizing how Black projects of placemaking and of Native self-determination might articulate with each other in ways neither superintended by the state nor predicated on an indigenizing politics of analogy. The chapter closes by considering the appearance of representations of treatying within Hairston's novel and the possibilities such an invocation of diplomacy might offer for envisioning and enacting relations of reciprocity—the potential for sustained modes of Black-Indigenous collective negotiation that do not mandate that these modes of placemaking (and the political imaginations from which they emerge) be defined through or in contrast to each other.

The coda, "Diplomacy in the Undercommons," seeks to think Black-Indigenous relation from two nonidentical trajectories in order further to suggest ways political imaginaries can open onto and engage each other without becoming a single framework. Addressing how the kinds of negotiation discussed at the end of chapter 4 might provide one way of conceptualizing productive translation across political difference, I approach this dynamic through Stefano Harney and Fred Moten's figuration in *The Undercommons* of "bad debt," considering the ways such debt might open onto a conception of diplomacy. In this vein, I take up the work of the hashtag #nobanonstolenlands. Created by Melanie Yazzie in response to the prominence of forms of American exceptionalism in the resistance to the Trump administration's anti-Muslim travel ban, the hashtag offers a way of envisioning generative Native connections to and embrace of non-native presence that is neither dispossessive nor routed through forms of state recognition and belonging. Conversely, I also return to the discussion of Black Lives Matter, considering the choice by movement leaders to reference the contemporary presence of Indigenous peoples. These examples do not create a unified political imaginary, but they do suggest speculative engagements across difference that can facilitate modes of mutual accountability through ongoing projects of translation.

1

ON THE IMPASSE

How can Black and Indigenous struggles be put into relation with each other? Both have been crucial to the history of the United States and the Americas more broadly, and trying to address one without a sense of the importance of the other can produce deeply problematic historical and political blindnesses, as well as generate dismissive and demeaning forms of exceptionalism. However, a range of difficulties arise in trying to hold them both in the same conceptual or analytical frame. One prominent strategy for doing so has been to situate settler colonialism and enslavement within a single system, explaining antiblackness and anti-indigeneity as mutually participating within an overarching power structure. Doing so aims to think together the uneven distributions of power, resources, and life chances for a range of oppressed racialized populations while suggesting that these groups share a set of objectives in the dismantling and transformation of that larger matrix of ideologies, institutions, and coercions. While the goal may be to provide a basis for solidarity predicated on a common analysis of the forces that shape what seem like varied vectors of domination, that very theoretical unification can short-circuit the process of relation by relying on the analytical structure itself to resolve prominent differences and discrepancies among these movements. Doing so also de facto can privilege a particular political analysis (in terms of both the character of oppression and ways of envisioning desired change) and thereby subordinate or delegitimize other formulations. That process of unification further can entail presenting alternative forms of political imagination as merely reproducing dominant logics, discounting them by casting them as surrogating for the forms of state identification under critique. As against such totalizing or foundationalizing gestures, a critical praxis organized around translation starts from the premise that these movements are not so much inherently commensurable or incommensurable as simply nonidentical; that they are shaped and given momentum by nonequivalent sets of concerns, emphases, and self-understandings. Articulating them to each other, then, requires engaging the ways the terms and models generated within one (set of) movement(s) cannot simply encompass those of another, or be incorporated into a supposedly neutral supervening framework, without producing profound shifts in meaning and orientation.

Enchattelment and settlement operate as differentiable backgrounds in ways that engender varied trajectories for Black and Indigenous political and intellectual formations. Native peoples also were subject to enslavement, and Black people have been subject to territorial expropriation and dispossession,[1] but one might approach, in Sara Ahmed's terms, as discussed in the Introduction, the predominating "what" that "surfaces" in histories of Black and Indigenous struggles as divergent. My aim, then, lies less in suggesting that Black and Native people(s) have not been subject to similar or interdependent forms of state and popular violence than that those potentially cross-cutting parallels and intersections come to signify in relation to disparate historical and experiential trajectories. Those experiences that might be understood as shared or interwoven are contextualized and oriented differently depending on the political imaginary of which they become part, the background against which they gain meaning. Conversely, this nonequivalence between varied struggles and movements affects how they relate to each other, as each transposes events, dynamics, figurations, articulations in ways that align them within a given movement's own particular conceptual and historical orientations. As Ahmed suggests, "[a] 'we' emerges as an effect of a shared direction toward an object," and she adds, "Groups are formed through their shared orientation toward an object. Of course, a paradox is already evident here in that to have 'something' that can be recognized as 'the same object' is an effect of the repetition of the orientation toward 'it,' just as the orientation seems directed toward the object that exists 'before' us. In a way, 'what' is faced by a collective is also what brings it into existence."[2] Blackness and indigeneity as ongoing processes of group formation can be understood as differentiated by the objects by which they are oriented (such as the terms of law and policy, collective memories, shared social dynamics and frames of reference) and the "what" toward which they turn (horizons of futurity, possibility, freedom, liberation).

The process of moving among these formations, then, might be understood as one of translation. We can approach Black and Indigenous imaginaries as, in Marisol de la Cadena's terms, varied "ways of making worlds,"[3] ways of articulating and mapping present sociopolitical dynamics while connecting forces from the past to the emergence of future potentials. She suggests of her own relation to Indigenous Andean intellectuals, "Our worlds were not necessarily commensurable, *but* this did not mean we could not communicate. Indeed, we could, insofar as I accepted that I was going to leave something behind, as with any translation—or even better, that our mutual understanding was also going to be full of gaps that would be different for each of us, and would constantly show up, interrupting but not preventing our communication," adding, "[O]ur communication did not depend on sharing single, cleanly identical notions—theirs, mine, or a third new one. We shared conversations across onto-epistemic formations."[4] She later observes, "I learned to identify radical difference as a relation, . . . the condition between us that made us aware of our mutual misunderstandings but did not fully inform us about 'the stuff' that composed those misunderstandings."[5] When not conceptualized as a project of generating equivalence, of finding correlations ("cleanly identical notions"), translation draws attention to the existence of semiotic gaps—forms of relational *difference*—that "leave something behind" and that function less as obstructions to communication than as a crucial part of being-in-relation.[6]

The figure of translation, though, also suggests a methodological problem with respect to defining what constitute Black and Indigenous formations. Translation can imply a movement between different languages in ways that attribute an inherent coherence to the formations in question, but any given language itself is not a stable, easily delineated entity. Rather, all languages are internally multiple and heteroglossic while also having porous boundaries with other languages: the standardization of a particular version of a language as paradigmatic allows other versions to be cast as dialects, degraded improprieties, creolizations, and pidgins. Similarly, employing the trope of translation raises the question of what gets to count as "Black" and "Indigenous" within my own analytic framing. What versions of these identities, movements, political visionings provide the baseline through which to conceptualize horizons and thresholds of relation, difference, translation? As Grace Kyungwon Hong notes of conceptualizations of blackness within Audre Lorde's work, "Black communities are not homogenously unified but are themselves made up of diverse and heterogeneous entities," and as such, "they are themselves always already coalitional."[7] Reciprocally, the category of *Indigenous* itself emerges through a series of transnational movements over decades and has been taken up in uneven and shifting ways around the world.[8] Even if one were to use "Native American" or "American Indian" instead, those rubrics can perform a homogenizing agglomeration that displaces the very idea of distinct, self-determining peoples toward which such naming usually seeks to gesture. Moreover, I should underline that Black and Indigenous are not inherently separate categories, that there are many Black Native people in at least two different senses: people of African descent who can trace their lineage to non-Afro-descended Native people; and Black people who are citizens of Native nations, by adoption, treaty, or other means.[9] Efforts to speak about differences between "Black" and "Indigenous" formations or modes of "we"-ness, then, run the risk of occluding Black Native people. Conversely, though, I am wary of positioning Black Native people as the necessary bridge between what otherwise may function as nonidentical groups, even as I seek to formulate accounts of "we"-ness that would not exclude, delegitimize, or erase Black Native histories and experiences and the effects of those histories and experiences on understandings of what blackness and indigeneity were, are, and might be.[10]

As opposed to seeking to stabilize Black and Indigenous as categories in order clearly to delineate their separation, to map the frontier that constitutes their difference, my aim lies in sketching the processes through which these modes of groupness gain cohesion as identities and movements that tend not to follow the same intellectual and political trajectories. While neither blackness nor indigeneity is singular, they still might be understood as occupying discrepant problem-spaces. In *Conscripts of Modernity*, David Scott describes a problem-space as "an ensemble of questions and answers around which a horizon of identifiable stakes (conceptual as well as ideological-political stakes) hangs," adding that differences among problem-spaces can be registered in the variance in their "tropes, modes, and rhetoric" and the "horizon in relation to which [a given problem-space] is constructed."[11] Broadly stated, if the histories of enchattelment and settlement produce differently configured kinds of problem-spaces with their own horizons and stakes, then the framings, narrative strategies, governing tropes, and forms of analysis at play in Indigenous and Black struggles will unfold in ways that give rise to discrepant ensembles—in Ahmed's terms discussed earlier, varied formations of "we"-ness that take shape through repeated and ongoing dynamics of turning toward different objects/objectives. This chapter begins by critically engaging the effort to generate singularizing accounts that either foundationalize a particular framework (organized around blackness or indigeneity) or that seek to encompass varied frameworks into a kind of meta-structure treated as having greater explanatory power. After exploring the conceptual and political problems generated by this impulse toward unification, I turn to addressing two keywords—*sovereignty* and *settler*—that generate impasses in thinking about differences between Black and Indigenous formations/movements, thereby also illustrating the varied orientations of such movements. The chapter closes by turning to the concept of *speculation* to explore the possibilities it offers for understanding and negotiating those impasses, foregrounding the potential for an ethics of multiplicity that might guide movement among apparently mutually exclusive truth claims.

Structure

Systemic analysis can be used to model and explain the relation among a range of sociopolitical processes, highlighting the significance of the structural dynamic(s) in question across seemingly disparate phenomena while also situating disparate populations affected by those phenomena in a determinate set of relations to each other and, thereby, providing the basis for shared understanding and organizing. However, such system building also can have the effect of interpellating populations in ways that defer or disavow their own analyses of how they are situated with respect to other groups as well as the sociopolitical formations in and against which they struggle. Speaking about the insertion of human social formations into a developmental narrative in which they all can be understood as undergoing an inevitable "transition" to Euro-American political economy, Dipesh Chakrabarty suggests, "This transition is also a process of translation of diverse life-worlds and conceptual horizons about being human into the categories of Enlightenment thought." In the place of such a universal narrative of time's unfolding, he argues for the importance of "translations [among such diverse life worlds] that do not take a universal middle term for granted."[12] While contemporary analyses that seek to put Black and Indigenous histories and struggles into the same frame usually do not endorse the kinds of universalizing history Chakrabarty critiques, they do have a propensity for collating varied collective experiences into a singular account. The terms and categories of that account's intellectual structure appear as a neutral matrix in which all manner of events, oppressions, and movements can be securely situated and explained. Thus, the complicated and potentially fraught processes of translation through which various lifeworlds, political imaginations, problem-spaces, backgrounds, orientations, and conceptual horizons are brought into relation with each other can be displaced by the apparently immanent coherence and explanatory reach of the analytical structure itself. In contrast to this kind of framework, which can have exceptionalizing effects by presenting one group's experiences as paradigmatic of how the system works, I would like to draw on Black feminist conceptions of *difference* as a means of holding on to the conceptual, political, and ethical significance of not resolving forms of oppression and resistance into encompassing structural narratives.

In order to explore the dynamics and stakes of this kind of system modeling, I turn to two theorists whose work has been increasingly important in current scholarly conversations: Sylvia Wynter and Glen Coulthard. They each offer powerful accounts that explain broad patterns of structural violence; they have been quite influential; and they each illustrate some prominent tendencies within Black studies and Indigenous studies. In particular, both scholars generate differently configured kinds of what might characterized as "in the last instance" effects.[13] By this phrase, I mean that even as these models may posit the existence of varied kinds of institutional formations, modes of collective identification, and vectors of institutional power and oppression, they suggest that there is an underlying or overriding structure that has a particular character that ultimately shapes or overdetermines the terms, dynamics, and possibilities for change for what is understood as the system as a whole (call it coloniality, racial capitalism, modernity, the world-system, etc.).

Wynter argues that a specific Eurocentric way of envisioning what it means to be human, a "genre of the human" that she refers to as "Man," has come to dominate global political economy.[14] In "Unsettling the Coloniality of Being/ Power/Truth/Freedom," Wynter suggests that "the struggle of our new millennium will be one between the ongoing imperative of securing the well-being of our present ethnoclass (i.e., Western bourgeois) conception of the human, Man, which overrepresents itself as if it were the human itself."[15] In casting nonwestern populations as evolutionarily backward due to their racial impediments, this framework legitimizes "the large-scale accumulation of unpaid land, unpaid labor, and overall wealth expropriated by Western Europe from non-European peoples . . . from the fifteenth century onwards."[16] Globalizing discourses of race from the early-modern period onward, then, generate the conditions for a process of humanization/dehumanization that undergirds both the conquest of the New World and the African slave trade. European settlement in the Americas gave rise to "the modern phenomenon of race, as a new extrahumanly determined classificatory principle and mechanism of domination. . . . For the indigenous peoples of the New World, together with the mass-enslaved peoples of Africa, were now to be reclassified as 'irrational' because 'savage' Indians, and as 'subrational' Negroes"—"the new idea of order was now to be defined in terms of degrees of rational perfection/imperfection."[17] This notion of rationality enacts a process of *degodding* or secularization by which relations of rule are organized along physical rather than spiritual principles—later to be supplemented or perhaps superseded, Wynter suggests, by an evolutionary conception of those who are "selected" and those who are "deselected." In being consigned to the "space of Otherness," "Indians" and "Negroes" serve as examples of irrational/subrational backwardness against which to define "human" progress and, thereby, position Europe and its descendants as the pinnacle of human achievement to date, legitimizing enslavement and colonial dominance/expropriation.

Wynter's articulation of this global (set of) dynamic(s) and the role of a universalizing, racializing conception of the human within them arises out of her effort both to develop an analysis that extends beyond a project of inclusion and to envision alternative possibilities for social life that can arise out of existing practices and principles among the oppressed. As Katherine McKittrick suggests in *Demonic Grounds*, "Sylvia Wynter's work entails not only 'deconstructing' or denaturalizing categories such as 'race'; it also means envisioning what is beyond the hierarchical codes and partial human stories that have, for so long, organized our populations and the planet."[18] Wynter argues that antiracist and anticolonial movements from the mid-twentieth century often ended up seeking to contribute and be recognized within the very systems they had set out to dismantle, particularly in terms of the scholarly work conducted in these movements' name, and she positions her work in direct contrast to that implicit inclusionary impulse. For example, in "On How We Mistook the Map for the Territory," she says that in these movements' entry into the "academic mainstream" they often "find their original transgressive intentions defused, their energies rechanneled as they came to be defined (and in many cases, actively to define themselves so) in new 'multicultural terms' [such] as African-American Studies; as such, this field appeared as but one of the many diverse 'Ethnic Studies' that now served to re-verify the very thesis of Liberal universalism" against which Black study and critique "had been directed in the first place."[19] Her effort to think the global politics of racialization as a predicate for modernity, then, emerges out of a realization of the ways the "devalorization of racial blackness was in itself, *only* a function of another and more deeply rooted phenomenon—in effect, only the map of the real territory, the symptom of the real cause, the real issue."[20] Her work, then, seeks to enable what she elsewhere has characterized as "ontological sovereignty," a new way of understanding potentials for social life that arises when racially oppressed peoples "move completely outside our present conception of what it is to be human, and therefore outside the ground of the orthodox body of knowledge which institutes and reproduces such a conception."[21] This process entails, in Rinaldo Walcott's terms, "a cosmopolitanism from below," one in which forms of collective worldmaking among the oppressed serve as the basis for forms of self-fashioning that challenge the givenness of the current racialized world order.[22]

In articulating this analysis of racializing global structural transformation, though, Wynter takes blackness as paradigmatic of the dynamics of dehumanization through which Man is (re)constituted. She observes in "Unsettling the Coloniality of Being/Power/Truth/Freedom," "While 'indios' and 'negros,' Indians and Negroes, were to be both made into the Caliban-type referents of Human Otherness to the new rational self-conception of the West, there was also . . . a marked differential in the degrees of subrationality, and of not-quite-humannness, to which each group was to be relegated within the classificatory logic of the West," earlier suggesting, "it was to be the peoples of Black African descent who would be constructed as the ultimate referent of the 'racially inferior' Human Other, with the range of other colonized dark-skinned peoples, all classified as 'natives,' now being assimilated to its category."[23] In situating settler colonial occupation of the Americas and the transatlantic slave trade within a single framework, Wynter highlights their mutual participation within a modern world-system predicated on naturalized racial ideologies and attendant forms of institutionalized violence that work to secure the interests of the dominant "ethnoclass," which narrates its own particular identity as simply the character of "the human itself." Yet in producing a structural account of post-Columbian Euro-dominance ordered around the construction of modes of racial otherness, Wynter locates blackness as the "ultimate referent" for those processes, such that all other forms of racialization and oppression against non-European peoples can (and should?) be understood within a framework in which blackness and antiblackness provide the background.

Within such critical and political mapping, though, what place is there for engaging Indigenous geographies and modes of peoplehood? Wynter's earlier essay "1492: A New World View" suggests some of the implications for thinking Indigenous sovereignty that emerge within the overarching structural account she articulates. As in "Unsettling the Coloniality of Being/Power/Truth/Freedom," her interest lies in tracing how a particular "genre of the human" comes to function as the basis for creating and ranking modes of racialized being, in which white supremacist narratives of Euro-superiority circulate as if they merely index the natural dynamics of human evolution and development. In insisting on the need for a global vision that can move beyond this account of the human, and its oppressive distributions of privilege and immiseration, Wynter underlines the need for a shared sense of species identity as the primary way of redressing the structural violences about which she theorizes. That new account of the human, though, leaves little room for envisioning self-determination for Indigenous peoples. Addressing Native critiques of the quincentenary of Columbus's landing, she asks, "[C]an there be . . . a third perspective," beyond affirmation of Euro-conquest and denunciation of its genocidal effects, that offers "a new and ecumenical human view" of 1492 and its aftermath?[24] Characterizing "both celebrants and dissidents" of the quincentenary as offering "partial perspectives" that follow from "partial interests," Wynter suggests that Columbus's journey to the Americas and all that followed in its wake should be thought "from the perspective of the species," "taking as our point of departure both the ecosystemic and global sociosystemic 'interrelatedness' of our contemporary situation" in ways that move toward a globally shared sense of common humanness.[25] She suggests that the forms of global connection that proliferate in the wake of the Columbian encounter can enable a conceptual revolution allowing "knowledge of our specifically human level of reality," thereby enabling a thinking of "the *propter nos*" for the entire species.[26] This explicitly antiracist account seeks to displace the Euro-bourgeois subject as the metric through which to assess relative humanness.

However, what happens to Indigenous articulations of peoplehood and self-determination, in terms of both the critique of the ongoing history of settler occupation of their lands and the insistence on substantive acknowledgment of Native nations as crucial to any meaningful trajectory for decolonization? If Wynter understands her analysis as marking the *coloniality* of what she presents as the contemporary world-system, implicitly casting the dislodging of Man as a process of decolonization, Eve Tuck and K. Wayne Yang raise questions about what it means to envision decolonization in ways that do not address Indigenous projects of self-determination as landed peoples. In "Decolonization Is Not a Metaphor," they argue, "Decolonization brings about the repatriation of Indigenous land and life: it is not a metaphor for other things we want to do to improve our societies." They further suggest that not engaging in sustained ways with Indigenous projects of self-determination "turns decolonization into an empty signifier to be filled by any track towards liberation. In reality, the tracks walk all over land/people in settler contexts."[27] From within Wynter's analytical structure, to what extent do such Indigenous political geographies appear as merely "partial interests" that need to be transcended in favor of a vision of "humankind in general"? The existence of distinct peoples with their own complex (and potentially overlapping) modes of placemaking can come to appear either as a drag on the antiracist envisioning of a global "we" or as a regressive investment in forms of collective identity tied to particular lands and waters.[28] As Sandy Grande notes in *Red Pedagogy* with respect to leftist non-native political imaginaries, "[A] key question, then, is whether a revolutionary socialist politics also envisages the 'new' social order as unfolding upon occupied land," adding, "How does the 'egalitarian distribution' of colonized lands constitute greater justice for Indigenous peoples?"[29] Understanding forms of racialization as causally and systemically crucial to the oppressions, inequities, and violences of, in Wynter's terms, "our present single world order and single world history" generates a structural account in which the expropriation of Indigenous lands can be explained as a function of the institutionalized narration of Native peoples as irrational/subrational savages, a status for which blackness provides the model.[30] Incorporating Indigenous peoples into the kind of global structural formulation Wynter offers, then, raises questions about the possibilities for addressing the (geo)political imaginaries offered by Indigenous intellectuals and activists.[31]

In suggesting the existence of "genres of the human," though, Wynter does gesture toward the potential for pluralizing the possibilities for being and becoming in ways that might provide intellectual resources for engaging with Indigenous (and other modes of) peoplehood. In "On How We Mistook the Map for the Territory," she suggests that those populations who come to be classified under Euro-conquest and enslavement as "*Indians* and *Negroes*" were "forcibly uprooted from their own indigenous genres of being human and, therefore, from their once autocentric self-conception and classified instead as now subordinated groups."[32] She further argues that global forms of Western coloniality "had to repress the reality of the quite different self-conceptions and sociogenic codes of the multiple groups now subordinated and classified as *natives*, in order to enable their multiple societal orders to be studied by anthropologists, *not* as the institutions of alternative genres of the human that they were . . . but, rather, in Western classificatory terms, as 'cultures.'"[33] Even as the presence of "multiple societal orders" often appears in Wynter's work in the past tense, as what was assaulted and erased through the imposition of Western notions of the human, the existence of a range of "alternative genres of the human" opens the potential for thinking such modes of being, which have been effaced through Euro-dominance, as what lies beyond coloniality—or as contributing to the critique and dismantling of coloniality. Although, at other moments, Wynter seems to suggest that all extant genres of the human obey a "master code"—a "governing *sociogenic principle*"—that provides the shared framework for the current world-system,[34] but the prospect of the plurality of genres opens toward a conception of translation across nonidentical "societal orders," even as the diversity of such collective worldings is staged within a problem-space organized around racialized relations to the human rather than, say, negotiating relations to particular lands and waters.[35]

By contrast, in *Red Skin, White Masks*, Coulthard foregrounds the historical and continuing centrality of settler assertions of authority over Indigenous peoples and territories to existing political economies (particularly within and among settler-states). He argues for the importance of understanding "primitive accumulation" less as a completed stage in the process of capitalist development than as persistent and crucial in the operation of contemporary capitalism. He observes, "[I]n the Canadian context, colonial domination continues to be structurally committed to maintain . . . ongoing state access to the land and resources that contradictorily provide the material and spiritual sustenance of Indigenous societies on the one hand, and the foundation of colonial state-formation, settlement, and capitalist development on the other." In underlining this point, he cites Patrick Wolfe's formulation that "the primary motive [of settler colonialism] is not race (or religion, ethnicity, grade of civilization, etc.) but access to territory. Territoriality is settler colonialism's specific, irreducible element." Coulthard presents ongoing and intensifying forms of settler expropriation (often conducted through forms of state recognition) as structurally necessary—as *foundational*—to extant modes of state formation and capitalist development, later noting, "it is correct to view primitive accumulation as the condition of possibility for the developing and ongoing reproduction of the capitalist mode of production."[36]

This argument responds to calls for the recognition of Indigenous peoples by the settler-state and for forms of reconciliation between such peoples and the state. To the extent that Canada and other settler-states seek to engage Indigenous struggles for self-determination by legally acknowledging the existence and claims of Native nations, the pursuit of such acknowledgment, Coulthard indicates, eventuates in the translation of Indigenous geopolitical self-understandings and horizons of governance into terms compatible with the existence and jurisdiction of the state itself. He indicates the need "to challenge the increasingly commonplace idea that the colonial relationship between Indigenous peoples and the Canadian state can be adequately transformed via such a politics of recognition," especially inasmuch as "the politics of recognition in its contemporary liberal form promises to reproduce the very configurations of colonialist, racist, patriarchal state power that Indigenous peoples' demands for recognition have historically sought to transcend."[37] Moreover, Coulthard illustrates how discourses of recognition and political theories that draw on them tend to rest "on the problematic background assumption that the settler-state constitutes a legitimate framework within which Indigenous peoples might be more justly included,"[38] and within that framework, Indigenous sovereignty largely is cast as a set of "cultural" dynamics that can be severed from questions of political economy, with the juridical and capitalist infrastructure of the state remaining as the de facto formation into which Indigenous peoples can be incorporated. His insistence on "primitive accumulation" as ongoing, then, contests the notion that the state can engage indigeneity in substantive and sustained ways without fundamentally transforming the structure of the state and its relation to the lands it claims as part of its "domestic" space. Moreover, this line of analysis aims to contest leftist frameworks that posit the potential for shared landbases in ways that efface Indigenous peoples' territorialities. If the notion of restoring a "commons" circulates as a way of challenging and thinking beyond capitalist modes of extraction and privatization, Coulthard, like Grande, reminds readers that the so-called commons "belong[s] to somebody—*the First Peoples of this land*" and that the "place-based foundation of Indigenous decolonial thought and practice" lies in forms of "*grounded normativity*" that emerge from "modalities of Indigenous land-connected practices and longstanding experiential knowledge" that "inform and structure ethical engagements with the world [as well as] relationships with human and nonhuman others over time."[39] In a similar vein, Jodi Byrd argues that "the current multicultural settler colonialism that provides the foundation for U.S. participatory democracy [is not] understood as precisely that," later observing, "Because settler colonialism arises from the forced domination of indigenous lands that have been reconstellated as the metropole, indigeneity itself becomes the site of inclusive remediation for all settlers and arrivants."[40]

Yet Coulthard also qualifies his analysis by suggesting that "the colonial relation of dispossession" should be understood as *co-foundational* with more conventional Marxian accounts of the exploitation of labor in engaging with contemporary capitalism. He observes, "Although it is beyond question that the predatory nature of capitalism continues to play a vital role in facilitating the ongoing dispossession of Indigenous peoples in Canada, it is necessary to recognize that it only does *in relation to or in concert with* axes of exploitation and domination configured along racial, gender, and state lines": "I suggest that shifting our attention to the colonial frame is one way to facilitate . . . radical intersectional analysis. Seen from this light, the colonial relation should not be understood as a primary locus or 'base' from which these other forms of oppression flow, but rather as the inherited background field within which market, racist, patriarchal and state relations *converge* to facilitate a certain power effect."[41] In displacing the notion of a singular "base," he opens the potential for engaging with multiple modes of oppression in intersectional ways. By positioning the dispossession of Indigenous peoples as "the inherited background field," though, he implies that such processes of settlement function as the enframing condition of possibility for other relations of domination. Indigeneity, then, becomes paradigmatic within Coulthard's framework. Even if those other vectors of institutionalized violence cannot be understood simply as an extension of the imposition of settler *territoriality*, as superstructural or epiphenomenal effects of a "primary" settler colonialism, they gain meaning here through being situated within a conceptual and political field organized around Indigenous landedness and the challenge it poses to the legitimacy of the state and non-native modes of sociality and governance. As Ahmed suggests, "[A] background is what explains the conditions of emergence or an arrival of something as the thing that it appears to be in the present";[42] in this vein, taking what Coulthard terms the colonial relation as the background conditions how other struggles will emerge or arrive onto the scene of analysis, raising questions about what difference they ultimately can make in understanding settlement as the structural frame. Such an orientation certainly generates powerful conceptual and political possibilities, also providing an important counterpoint to the tendency to efface the continuing existence of Indigenous peoples and ongoing efficacy of settlement for Natives and non-natives alike. However, in seeking to model a particular sociopolitical formation (whether set at the scale of the nation-state, relations among states, or globally), this orientation can rearticulate other political imaginaries through the prism of Indigenous critique in ways not acknowledged as such, thereby generating impasses in establishing relations with non-Indigenous movements.

One prominent aspect of this difficulty lies in envisioning roles for non-native people of color within Indigenous projects of resurgence.[43] For non-Indigenous people on the lands claimed by settler-states such as Canada and the United States, people who presumably do not have the kinds of knowledges and grounded modes of being to which Coulthard refers, what does "ethical engagement" with Indigenous self-determination look like, especially a form not routed through the kinds of indigenizing "inclusive remediation" Byrd addresses? More pointedly, what kinds of decolonial relations to Indigenous processes of resurgence are possible for "arrivants"—nonwhite, non-native people—who have been subjected to, in Coulthard's words, "other forms of oppression"? As Zainab Amadahy and Bonita Lawrence note, a vision organized around Indigenous sovereignties and a nation-to-nation relation with the settler-state can leave Black people "completely disempowered in that process," placing them "in a kind of limbo, waiting for a colonial state and Indigenous nations to 'work out' a relationship." Amadahy and Lawrence further insist on the need for "Indigenous leadership" and, by extension, Indigenous intellectuals "to develop a vision of sovereignty and self-government that addresses the disempowered and dispossessed from other parts of the world who were forced and/or coerced into being here on Turtle Island."[44] Where and how do questions related to blackness and antiblackness come to matter when issues of Indigenous territoriality and peoplehood provide the background against which to envision political critique and transformation?

As suggested in the discussion thus far, large-scale structural modeling that seeks to provide an explanatory framework for a range of forms of institutionalized violence can end up transposing social dynamics into the terms of the model in ways that de facto foreclose other horizons of political experience, critique, and imagination.[45] Recognizing such implicit lacunae or disavowals could provide the impetus for new forms of model building that seek better to incorporate what previously has been left out or denigrated in the construction of a given (set of) analytical system(s). However, if extant structural accounts can tend toward forms of exceptionalism ("in the last instance" dynamics that make one kind of oppressed group's experiences paradigmatic of the system as a whole), it is not clear that seeking to generate more capacious or expansive accounts actually will address the disparities in intellectual/political backgrounds that engender exceptionalist inclinations in the first place. In "Black History in Occupied Territory," Justin Leroy asks "what intellectual pathways are foreclosed when slavery and settler colonialism vie for primacy as the violence most foundational to the modern social order," explaining with respect to "Indigenous and black critical theory" that

> [e]ach has supplanted facile notions of racial exclusion, but in doing so has proposed alternatives—colonialism and slavery—premised upon [an] exclusive claim to accounting for the violence of modernity. These claims are internally coherent and broadly useful, but are incompatible. Either colonialism or slavery must be subordinated to the other, forcing

them into aporetic tension. Each field reduces the other to a variation on the theme of liberal multiculturalism in order to maintain the integrity of its own exceptionalist claims.[46]

While both sets of intellectual projects have internal coherence, they seem to foreclose each other, especially to the extent that each portrays the other as a version of "liberal multiculturalism" complicit with the very forms of state violence under critique. Furthermore, Indigenous and Black political imaginaries can present themselves as offering *the* means of accounting for racializing and colonial domination, staking a claim to foundationality that excludes or subordinates other analytical frameworks. Doing so premises the integrity of the analytical-political formation in question on its capacity to displace, underlie, or encompass all others, thereby producing exceptionalist effects in which a particular way of framing ongoing histories of violence—a specific problem-space—is positioned as having a semi-transcendent supremacy over alternatives. Furthermore, as Iyko Day suggests in "Being or Nothingness," that process depends on employing dichotomies that a priori organize conceptual engagement with the events, movements, dynamics in question: "This is expressed either as an Indigenous/settler binary constituted in relation to land or a black/nonblack binary founded on racial slavery," generating "exceptionalisms" in which "the Native and the black body signify a genocidal limit concept."[47] In the place of such binaries, Day suggests the importance of viewing "race and colonialism" as mutually forming "the matrix of the settler colonial racial state." She argues that "[p]utting colonial land and enslaved labor at the center of a dialectical analysis" enables an understanding of "settler colonialism [as] abid[ing] by a dual logic that is originally driven to eliminate Native peoples from land and mix the land with enslaved black labor," and these two *logics* "work together to serve a unitary end in increasing white settler property in the form of land and an enslaved labor force."[48] The answer to exceptionalism, then, appears to be connecting these two modes or areas of analysis by treating them as interdependent aspects of a single phenomenon or formation that itself "serve[s] a unitary end." Dialectical movement resolves into a conceptual and political synthesis in which Black and Indigenous political imaginaries can be articulated in mutual relation to "white settler property."[49]

To what extent, though, does such apparent intellectual resolution end up deferring differences among movements in ways that can reiterate the problems generated by exceptionalism? For example, what principles will be used in undertaking the process of synthesis, and how will they shape the possibilities for change, remediation, or resurgence a given synthesis or framework offers?

Against what backgrounds do such principles emerge, and in what kinds of political imaginaries are they enmeshed? While attending to "slavery and settler colonialism" can enable exploration of how they influence and even co-constitute each other, triangulating them as part of a singular structure (call it "the modern social order" or "the settler colonial racial state") does not necessarily address the dynamics by which Black and Indigenous movements encounter and engage each other. Rather than exploring the *process* of relation among such movements in their varied paradigms and orientations, the kind of dialectical or synthetic mode of analysis Day and Leroy suggest posits a resolution of difference at the level of intellectual or analytical form—an overriding structural "logic" that itself is meant to serve as the basis for (potential) solidarity or political rapprochement among movements. In place of attending to the immanent perspectives, regularities, momentum, and trajectories that shape Black and Indigenous political formations and analyses, these accounts offer a somewhat static conception of a singular system (albeit one that may have differentiable parts) that provides the conceptual architecture for thinking Black-Indigenous engagement.

By contrast, I want to suggest that starting from the premise of irreducible difference might generate another set of intellectual and political possibilities, ones based on open-ended processes of relation, negotiation, and translation. By *irreducible difference*, though, I do not mean that Black and Indigenous formations are utterly incommensurable and must be understood as completely disjunct from each other. Rather, I want to highlight commensuration as an ongoing set of practices, reorientations, and shifting relationships that, in de la Cadena's terms discussed in the Introduction, involves continuing forms of "equivocation" in which mutual understanding can occur but neither necessarily in the same "onto-epistemic terms" nor in a way outside the frames of reference of those involved in the relation. Drawing on women-of-color feminisms, Hong characterizes difference as "a cultural and epistemological practice that holds in suspension (without requiring resolution) contradictory, mutually exclusive, and negating impulses." She further suggests that difference for Audre Lorde "inheres in her ability to both mark the uniqueness of anti-Black violence as well as insist that it is possible to connect this violence to those experienced by other racialized, gendered, devalued peoples," adding that "the self-consciously named 'women of color feminism' or 'Third World feminism' of the 1970s and 1980s, of which Lorde is an important contributor, emerged precisely to enable such a political analytic able to articulate coalitional practice based on, rather than in spite of, historical and material differences within and among racial groups."[50] To develop analytics that are rooted in "historical and material differences" requires not setting aside such discrepancies and forms of uniqueness, but instead foregrounding them as the basis on which sustained engagement becomes possible. As Lorde observes, "Difference must be not merely tolerated, but seen as a fund of necessary polarities between which our creativity can spark like a dialectic. Only then does the necessity for interdependency become unthreatening." She further argues, "[W]e have no patterns for relating across our human differences as equals. As a result, those differences have been misnamed and misused in the service of separation and confusion," suggesting, "It is a lifetime pursuit for each one of us to extract these distortions from our living at the same time as we recognize, reclaim, and define those differences upon which they are imposed."[51] Taking difference as a basis for relation, as opening the possibility for creative and sustaining engagement, involves tracking and contesting forms of *misnaming* and *misuse* that reify and distort distinctions in political formations and trajectories while still *recognizing* and *reclaiming* such distinctions as the medium through which to build connections.

Approached in this way, difference is not a clearly delineated set of positionings within an overarching systemic logic (or structurally integrated set of such logics). Audra Simpson, among others, has raised sustained questions about notions of "difference," especially when applied to Indigenous peoples. She suggests that there "is a historical attitude that supplants the ravages of settler colonialism with definitions of 'difference,'" in which Indigenous *political* orders are transposed as Native *cultural* difference in ways that get "defined by others" and that need to be performed to settler satisfaction in order legally to be recognized.[52] However, rather than understanding difference as a determinate distinction within an existing configuration, as implicit differentiation from a dominant standard that remains unmarked and is treated as the de facto norm, it can be approached as marking nonidenticality: that two (or more) movements, formations, and problem-spaces are not the same as each other and cannot be conceptualized through the same overriding terms and concepts without (disorienting) acts of translation. Recognizing difference, then, entails seeing it as an ongoing and dynamic potential for engaging with other persons and groups who cannot be reduced to the roles they play within the frameworks within which one operates. In "The Uses of Anger: Women Responding to Racism," Lorde observes, "The woman of Color who is not Black and who charges me with rendering her invisible by assuming that her struggles with racism are identical to my own has something to tell me that I had better learn from, lest we both waste ourselves fighting the truths between us."[53] "Struggles with racism" can take a range of forms whose configurations do not coincide with each other, and treating one as paradigmatic can end up rendering other such struggles invisible. However, the response to that problem of unknowing here lies less in seeking to create a broader, more encompassing analysis—one that could model all of the various modes of oppression and their interrelation, deriving connections among struggles from the dynamics of that model—than to take part in continuing interactions through which the differences among such struggles might be understood as illustrating multiple, nonidentical "truths."[54]

Various struggles each may offer their own perspectives on how oppression works and what justice might look like in ways that are neither reducible to each other nor sublatable within an overarching structural model. Lorde indicates that those discrepancies and the negotiations around them can serve as a source of *creativity* within social struggles, and she further suggests that the drive to make struggles identical, including by incorporating them within an account of the logic of the system that ostensibly encompasses them all, can foreclose the possibility of sustained communication and meaningful engagement among oppressed groups. Moreover, Lorde argues that the acknowledgment of not belonging to the same racialized group, and therefore not having the same experience of racism, is crucial to building a meaningful relation. Such relation is predicated on refusing to assume that an overarching account could capture their varied experiences precisely because the attempt to generate a systemic analysis so often ends up treating one mode of domination as if it were paradigmatic. Accepting that varied modes of domination are nonidentical is a denial neither of the specificity of Lorde's experiences of racism nor the truth of her analysis of those experiences. Instead, it is an opening to the possibility of relation across difference.

Such recognition provides the entrée to an ongoing negotiation in which the presence of multiple truths serves as an organizing ethical principle. Lorde suggests, "We have been taught either to ignore our differences, or to view them as causes for separation and suspicion, rather than as forces for change," adding that community across such distinctions involves "learning how to take our differences and make them strengths. *For the master's tools will never dismantle the master's house.*"[55] The acknowledgment of difference provides the impetus toward change because it refuses to replace a dominant frame of reference with a singularizing or implicitly foundationalizing alternative (whether that new framework is the overrepresentation of Man, the colonial relation of dispossession, the settler colonial racial state, or something else). This conception of difference envisions forms of coalition not predicated on resolving what may seem to be contradictory positions or inclinations, which appear as such when viewed from the perspective of attempted unification. Lorde's feminist ethics points toward relations among persons, oppressed groups, and movements for justice and liberation that do not presume an inherently shared frame of reference. This plurality of perspectives (of variable analyses, backgrounds, orientations, horizons of political imagination) can be seen as a source of *strength* instead of as a blockage or a form of false consciousness, provided that people are willing to engage with how they (and the struggles in which they're enmeshed) might be understood within the framings of other struggles—a willingness to be accountable to and changed by ongoing encounters with difference.[56]

Such an account of difference, however, can run against the grain of certain approaches to intersectionality. In particular, treating Black and Indigenous movements as if they have determinate boundaries that separate them from each other can end up reifying those boundaries in ways that not only rigidify both forms of identity/struggle but that make paradigmatic the experiences of more privileged members of both groups and that efface those who belong to both—namely, Black Native people. As Anna Carastathis argues, "Models of coalitions that presuppose the fixity of coalescing groups—and the homogeneity of collective identities—elide intragroup differences, a danger to which intersectionality as a critique of categories alerts us. But such models also naturalize politicized identities, constructing the boundaries between groups as pre-given and obscuring their genealogies," such as, in this case, the complex history of shifting modes of legal identification from which "Black" and "Indian" as categories emerge.[57] She further addresses the dangers of a vision of relation among political struggles organized around notions of "merging, compounding, adding, joining, or uniting discrete, mutually exclusive, and stable categories of identity (race and gender, paradigmatically) that (on this view) correspond to analytically and/or ontologically discrete—if intersecting— systems of power." To treat identities and associated forms of oppression as if they were "analytically and/or ontologically discrete" can end up producing visions of those identities organized around the most privileged members of those groups: "Intersectionality, in [Kimberlé] Crenshaw's account, reveals the inadequacy of categories of discrimination—as well as of struggle— constructed using the logics of mutual exclusion and prototypicality that abstract the experiences of relatively privileged members of oppressed groups and, falsely universalizing them, render them representative of all members of the group in question."[58] Approaching kinds of identity as separable and analytically discrete, then, can treat them as if they de facto operate in isolation from each other. Ange-Marie Hancock offers the notion of "ontological complexity" as a way of naming the refusal to treat identity categories as de facto mutually exclusive—"the idea that analytical categories like 'race,' 'gender,' 'class,' and the hegemonic practices associated with them (racism, sexism, classism, to which imperialism and homophobia certainly could be added) are mutually constitutive, not conceptually distinct."[59] Similarly, Patricia Hill Collins and Sirma Bilge suggest that within such an intersectional understanding, "The focus of relationality shifts from analyzing what distinguishes entities, for example, the differences between race and gender, to examining their interconnections."[60] From this perspective, foregrounding distinctions between "Black" and "Indigenous" groups can convey the impression that there is no crossover or shared oppressions between those inhabiting these two categories, offering the impression that they are inherently disjunctive. In "From Flint to Standing Rock," for example, Kyle T. Mays wonders, "[H]ow have blackness and indigeneity been conceived as inherently different?" and further observes that "Black and Indigenous struggles have been considered separately and falsely seen as mutually exclusive with different aspirations and different goals."[61]

However, must the process of relation proceed from the premise of the inherent imbrication of blackness and indigeneity? Must recognizing "different aspirations and different goals" be the same as the notion that groups are "mutually exclusive" or locked in an inherent antagonism? Can one talk about difference in ways that neither reify the boundaries between nor ignore potential overlap among experiences and struggles? Carastathis juxtaposes "essentialist, analytically discrete categories" with "a (more) unified theory of oppression," later observing that many "social movements . . . have failed to grasp the social totality and lived experiences of multiple oppressions in a nonfragmented way," and she quotes Sharon Parker's argument that "unity is not achieved through homogeneity, but by bringing heterogeneous elements into a whole."[62] Similarly, Collins and Bilge observe, "By using the terms 'interlocking,' 'manifold,' 'simultaneous,' and 'synthesis,' the analysis treats oppression as resulting from the joint operations of major systems of oppression that form a complex social structure of inequality."[63] As with the other kinds of structural modeling discussed earlier, do the kinds of unification toward which such intersectionality gestures create a "totality" or "whole" that can engage, in Sara Ahmed's terms, the ways various kinds of "we"s—forms of collective identity—may have disparate backgrounds and orientations? If any given "we" is cross-cut by varied kinds of experiences among its members (including of relative oppression and privilege) that affect the contours of that identity and that give rise to complicated and shifting negotiations about the terms and trajectories of belonging, does that mean there is no such "we" at all or that understanding it as substantively different from another "we" is just a result of analytical and political *fragmentation* or a failure to appreciate the larger "social structure" of which they both are a part? Hancock suggests that, with respect to many feminist approaches to intersectionality, "diversity within [identity categories] is a train stop on the way to a destination of political and/or coalitional unity. In contrast, for Audre Lorde and others, who are part of the intellectual history of intersectionality, difference is the home, the ontological reality from which all experiences and, more importantly, their aftermaths are dealt with in a way that does not rely on the eradication of categories."[64] She seeks here to affirm difference as a primary "ontological reality," which preserves potential distinctions among categories of identity, while at the same time not positing an a priori framework through which to bring forms of identity and struggle into meaningful political relation.[65] Starting from the premise of the difference between Black and Indigenous sociopolitical formations runs the risk of reifying them or treating them as discretely bounded in ways that efface overlapping forms of struggle and belonging between them, as well as distinctions and complexities within blackness and indigeneity. However, positing such difference works as a way of staving off the kinds of, in Lorde's terms, *misnaming* and *misuse* that come with efforts to treat varied struggles as if they either were identical or could all be characterized through the one set of terms/framings (call it coloniality, racial capitalism, the world-system, the settler colonial racial state, etc.)— which itself would constitute a denial of ontological complexity.

The notion of *opacity* offers a way of further clarifying the ethical content and dynamics of the emphasis on difference that emerges within Black feminisms. In *Poetics of Relation*, Édouard Glissant suggests, "The opaque is not the obscure, though it is possible for it to be so and be accepted as such. It is that which cannot be reduced, which is the most perennial guarantee of participation and confluence." He juxtaposes opacity with a vision of "difference" that "can still contrive to reduce things to the Transparent," characterizing *transparency* as "the perspective of Western thought" that "measure[s] your solidity with the ideal scale providing me with ground to make comparisons and, perhaps, judgments" in a process of "relat[ing] it to my norm." By contract, *opacity* indicates the refusal to reduce others to the terms of the same, to commensurate them with a pre-given and imposed set of measurements and norms. Instead, it marks the potential "solidity"—the being and becoming—of another person, group, political formation beyond the modes of understanding I bring to the encounter. Glissant further observes, "Opacities can coexist and converge, weaving fabrics," indicating the potential for undertaking and understanding forms of interaction that can create new possibilities without in the process *reducing* difference to transparency—recasting them and their relation in terms of an encompassing (set of) norm(s), such as positing participation in an inherently shared structure.[66] In this vein, Tuck and Yang argue that "opportunities for solidarity [between Natives and non-natives] lie in what is incommensurable rather than what is common across these efforts," "highlight[ing] opportunities for what can only ever be strategic and contingent collaborations." They later add, "The answers will not emerge from friendly understanding, and indeed require a dangerous understanding of uncommonality that uncoalesces coalition politics—moves that may feel very unfriendly," offering a similar caution to that of the Black Lives Matter founders on the dangers of an imagined "unity without struggle" (as discussed in the Introduction).[67] What is at stake in this kind of comparative method is not locating a determinate set of distinctions between Black and Indigenous movements and political imaginaries, but, instead, exploring the horizon of *uncommonality* as the basis for an opening toward solidarity or coalitional practice as a continuing process where frames of reference cannot be presumed to be shared, especially based on an analysis of the system that supposedly encompasses all positions and situates them relative to each other.[68] Mutual accountability among forms of struggle, then, does not necessitate being situated within a singular *social totality* or *social structure*. Instead, it can emerge through engagement with the potential truth value of others' descriptions offered from within their own framings and orientations.

Recognizing the existence of nonequivalent "we"s and the potential differences among them without seeking to resolve them into an integrated whole of one kind or another provides the basis for mutual learning, a process that structural modeling (including when intersectionality itself is understood as an *ontology* or a necessarily enframing set of epistemological procedures) can both shortcut and short-circuit.[69] For the negotiations engendered by recognizing difference truly to be open-ended—not already immanently organized by certain formulations, struggles, goals—some supervening set of terms cannot be treated as inherently providing the framework for negotiation, as a predetermined basis for "unity." Starting from the premise that Black and Indigenous movements might be nonidentical in their orientations suggests the possibility that multiple ways of explaining dynamics in the world might be true, even when they are not readily resolvable into each other. The reason to adopt such a premise is to obviate the need to subordinate one account to another or to seek to merge or sublate them into another account. Such moves not only necessarily reduce difference to differentiation but require positing some kind of epistemological failing on the part of one or both accounts (that they operate from false, merely interested, or inappropriately limited premises) that will be remedied through proper (putatively more rigorous or more expansive) analysis. This mode of intellectual and political proceeding casts other accounts of the world as misguided, partial, or wrong in ways that tend toward a lack of intellectual generosity as well as suggest a normative commitment to the value of singularity: one true account that serves as the basis for relation, struggle, change—where all the parts fit together in determinate ways following a given set of analytical principles or procedures. That approach cannot address difference—nonidenticality—as a positive principle, in the sense of both the legitimate variability among frames of reference and the potential for such nonequivalence to serve as an ethical source of strength, creativity, and respectful engagement.

The turn toward multiplicity, then, in some sense begins with the following question: what if these accounts, whose terms and trajectories differ significantly, are both right? That speculative gesture, which I explore in greater detail in the last section of this chapter, opens the potential for negotiated and open-ended processes and ethics of relation, rather than seeking logical resolution and unification. Acknowledging the potential for nontotalizable difference, then, suggests that the process of negotiating relationships among groups—variously constituted "we"s—need not occur through a presumed sameness or a predisposition toward commonality (including occupying the same metastructure of interlocking or intermeshing oppressions), which would allow for them to be triangulated and made transparent. Antiblackness and settler colonialism need not be understood either as the same or as integrated within an encompassing (set of) structure(s) in order to engage them as, in de la Cadena's terms, "circuited' together" in ways that still do not make them "one."[70] Instead, this approach highlights ongoing forms of negotiation and (mis)translation among groups whose *difference* from each other (which need not make them mutually discrete) is fundamentally not taken as a conceptual and political problem in need of structural, dialectical, methodological resolution.[71] Attending to the process of moving between Black and Indigenous formations, then, highlights the *potential* absence of shared terms and frames of reference (although, not always, as I explore in particular in chapter 4), and difference can be understood as characterizing the dynamics of engagement rather than serving as a blockage that needs to be overcome, sublated, or dissolved through mutual enmeshment within a supervening logic or set of foundationalist propositions or principles. Put another way, how can various orientations and modes of "we"-ness, and the problem-spaces in which they are formed and that they generate, be acknowledged while putting them into meaningful, nonexceptionalizing, and nonunifying relation?

Sovereignty

The concept of sovereignty usually serves to designate the exercise of exclusive political authority over a delimited landmass, as well as adjacent waters and airspace. While this notion emerges from ideas of undivided monarchical power (the will of the *sovereign*), the nation-state provides the contemporary template for this vision of governance, in which a centralized legal and administrative apparatus exerts jurisdiction over a clearly bounded space. In dominant post-Westphalian conceptions of political order, the undivided nature of such rule remains crucial to its character: spheres of sovereignty cannot overlap or they cease to constitute claims to sovereignty.[72] A single state will manage its own domestic territory without interference from any other state, and any ceding of control to other entities within those boundaries putatively will be determined by the state as part of enacting its sovereignty.[73] This way of approaching governance can be understood as predicated on casting persons and lands as a kind of national property, as belonging to the state.[74] Indigenous peoples face the problem of having themselves and their homelands claimed as part of settler-states that were established over top of them, through the seizure and jurisdictional incorporation of their territories, and without their consent to such domestication. Asserting that Indigenous peoples exert sovereignty over their lands and waters, then, operates as a way of challenging settler colonial assertions of dominance and dominion over those spaces while insisting that such peoples constitute polities whose right to self-determining governance must be acknowledged. However, even as citations of Indigenous sovereignty seek to disjoint colonial legal geographies, they can be overdetermined by settler modes of political structure and legitimation, creating a complicated counterpoint between articulations of sovereignty by Native nations and the very colonial processes and grids of intelligibility with which they are entangled.[75] Yet sovereignty remains a crucial topos within Indigenous political discourses and Indigenous studies approaches and often is used as a way of indexing non-statist forms of collective life and governance. To the extent that Black subjects remain marginal to the nation-state—in terms of not enjoying full belonging as citizens or, for majority Black postcolonial nations (such as Jamaica), full recognition internationally as equal sovereigns—sovereignty appears less useful as a form of collective political imagination and advocacy. Much recent work in Black studies not only challenges the desirability of sovereignty as a horizon of aspiration but suggests that the mobilization of sovereignty within struggles for social justice actually contributes in significant ways to the proliferation and normalization of antiblackness, particularly inasmuch as sovereignty is understood as itself an expression of the logics of property that produced enchattel-ment and within which Black people continue to appear as non-self-owning (and, thus, fungible and pathological) subjects. As an intellectual and political concept, then, sovereignty manifests the profound disjunctions that can arise between the problem-spaces formed by Black and Indigenous movements while also drawing attention to the kinds of (mis)translation (and resulting impasses) that can occur in efforts to understand them in relation to each other.

The politics and struggles of Indigenous peoples are partially oriented by the need to convey their existence as polities in the context of the settler-state's assertion of jurisdiction over them and their lands, and the topos of sover-eignty marks that problematic while also emphasizing the ways Native gover-nance remains irreducible to settler legal and administrative frameworks. In "For Whom Sovereignty Matters," Joanne Barker observes that "[f]ollowing World War II *sovereignty* emerged as a particularly valued term within indig-enous scholarship and social movements and through the media of cultural production. It was a term around which analyses of indigenous histories and cultures were organized and whereby indigenous activists articulated their agendas for social change." The reason for this proliferation lies in the fact that "[s]overeignty had come to represent a staunch political-juridical iden-tity refuting the dominant notion that indigenous peoples were merely one among many 'minority groups' under the administration of state social service and welfare programs. Instead, sovereignty defined indigenous peoples with concrete rights to self-government, territorial integrity, and cultural autonomy under international customary law."[76] Native intellectuals and activists seized on the notion of sovereignty in order to mark the ways that their peoples could not be treated merely as domestic subjects under the regular governance of the states that enclose them and their lands. Native communities insisted on their existence as *peoples* under international law, as rightfully exerting forms of po-litical autonomy and self-determination that exceed the parameters of settler rule and that challenge the legitimacy of settler governments' claims to exercise overriding authority within the borders of what they have mapped as national space. As Barker notes, "The blatant contradictions are between the recogni-tion of the sovereignty of indigenous peoples through the entire apparatus of treaty making and unmitigated negation of indigenous peoples' status and rights by national legislation, military action, and judicial decision."[77] While treaties provide prima facie evidence of histories of U.S. diplomatic negotia-tion with Native peoples in ways that indicate their political separateness and existence prior to and outside the sphere of domestic law, the dynamics of Indian policy point to a continuing (and in many ways intensifying) pattern of treating

Indigenous peoples as lacking any substantive political status other than as racial/cultural conglomerates at the mercy of U.S. largesse.[78] In this vein, insisting on the *sovereignty* of Native nations contests the validity of these forms of settler superintendence, intervention, and assault by foregrounding the ways that such actions operate as modes of colonial aggression.

Invoking sovereignty functions as both a form of conceptual space-clearing and a means of drawing attention to the existence and authority of Native nations in their enactment of governance over their own lands and populations. As Jean Dennison observes, "The nation-state model with its power dynamics and internal workings is anything but ideal, but it is currently the primary tool for exerting sovereignty." In this context, Native peoples need to figure themselves in relation to the state form in order to be able to assert the legitimacy of their own acts of governance: "Given these tensions, the nation is clearly a necessary entanglement. The key is making something out of this structure that does not mirror the oppression of the colonizer."[79] Challenging the violence of settler colonialism entails refusing the various ways that the state seeks to cast Native peoples as internal to the settler nation, as contributing to its multicultural diversity but in ways that do not disturb the framework of settler jurisdiction. Barker observes that the "*making ethnic* or *ethniciziation* of indigenous peoples has been a political strategy of the nation-state to erase the sovereign from the indigenous," and Dennison suggests, "Culture in this context becomes a burden: American Indian peoples are forced to overturn a destructive legacy of U.S. policies. . . . American Indian culture is made to stand for all that is fundamental, pure, and noncolonized."[80] Insisting on the acknowledgment of Native peoples' *sovereignty* displaces culturalizing or ethnicizing narratives that cast indigeneity as a bundle of traits, practices, beliefs, and so on, that can be adjudicated in relation to authentic Indianness by non-natives in ways implicitly contradistinguished from questions of governance, especially the right to exert control over seized and stolen lands. Citations of Indigenous sovereignty, then, arise and circulate within the particular problem-space generated by (Anglophone) settler colonialism.[81]

Moreover, Native nations have their own juridical formations, and even as they remain subjected to the colonial oversight and management of the settler-state, these governments enact processes of decision making, lawmaking, jurisdiction, and resource distribution that usually would be included under the rubric of sovereignty. In other words, to set aside Native peoples' sovereignty implies a colonial disregard for the actions and authority of such governments. As Dale Turner suggests of settler governance in Canada, "[T]he brutal reality is that the Canadian state's legal and political culture *does not* recognize the moral worth of Aboriginal legal practices—whatever they are—as legitimate alternatives to what is unproblematically recognized as the *only* legitimate legal system in Canada."[82] In the absence of an effort to wrench the notion of sovereignty free from its equation with the power and self-articulation of the settler-state, Indigenous practices of law and governance do not signify as such, instead appearing as cultural expressions that can be disregarded when they come into conflict with non-native legal and administrative imperatives. Efforts by non-Indigenous scholars to set aside the concept of sovereignty as merely a tool of domination, then, overlook the significance of its mobilization by Indigenous polities in their effort to be engaged as such. Dennison argues, "The academic compulsion to deconstruct sovereignty threatens to aid settler colonial efforts to discredit indigenous authority. These debates over sovereignty take place within larger colonial struggles over authority and power, where there is a lot at stake in claiming, denying, or even dissecting sovereignty. The academic debate over sovereign power too often limits sovereignty to an attribute of statehood and statehood to European styles of governance."[83] The effort to dismiss the notion of sovereignty as simply a vector of state control and violence can contribute to disregarding the authority of Indigenous peoples to govern themselves, overlooking how Native peoples mobilize figurations of sovereignty as part of current and ongoing strategies and struggles with respect to law, policy, placemaking, and belonging, among other matters. The employment of sovereignty to productive ends can be seen in work, such as Dennison's, on Native nations' redrafting of their constitutions.[84] Moreover, in his study of shifting aims and configurations of environmental policy in the Cherokee Nation, Clint Carroll explores expressions of an "ecological nationalism" that "employs indigenized state structures in order to converse with and contest those of the settler-state," foregrounding "the use and modification of state structures by indigenous nations" and the ways that process enacts a "dialectics of indigenous state transformation" by "filtering state structures through the matrix of people-hood." While addressing how certain bureaucratic approaches to governance inherited from (or imposed by) the settler-state hamper the implementation of relationship-based Cherokee environmental frameworks, Carroll illustrates how grassroots Cherokee initiatives have been pushing the Cherokee government to "reconfigur[e] state practices and acknowledge alternative sources of authority."[85] These dialectics of indigenization occur in and through expressions of Native nations' sovereignty, the assertion of a right to govern their lands and people in ways consistent with their own self-determined goals and principles. Even though the policies of settler-states can constrict Indigenous possibilities for political self-organization, state structures—and the dynamics of sovereignty on which they depend—can be filtered, or translated, through the prism of peoplehood in ways that make them more than simply an extension of settler governance.

The topos of sovereignty also works to mark the existence of non-statist forms of peoplehood, whether or not those *modes of life* (in Coulthard's terms) are recognized by the settler-state. As Barker observes, "Translating indigenous epistemologies about law, governance, and culture through the discursive rubric of sovereignty was and is problematic. Sovereignty as a discourse is unable to capture fully the indigenous meanings, perspectives, and identities about law, governance, and culture, and thus over time it impacts how those epistemologies and perspectives are represented and understood."[86] Although settler discourses of political authority and legitimacy can exert colonial pressure on Native structures of governance, Native formations of peoplehood and place-making extend beyond the institutions and principles acknowledged as such by the state, and the concept of sovereignty can function as a way of highlighting the political character of such Indigenous epistemologies. In *Dancing on Our Turtle's Back*, Leanne Simpson suggests of the process of enacting self-determination, "Building diverse, nation-culture-based resurgences means significantly re-investing in our own ways of being: regenerating our political and intellectual traditions; articulating and living our legal systems; language learning; ceremonial and spiritual pursuits; creating and using our artistic and performance-based traditions."[87] The process of *resurgence* of which Simpson speaks, then, itself builds on existing feelings of being part of a people, a potentially fluid matrix of relation but one shaped by past and continuing dynamics of governance and placemaking. As Simpson notes, "Nishnaabeg concepts of 'nation' and 'sovereignty' are much different than modern constructs, but they exist and were expressed."[88] *Sovereignty*, then, serves as a way of naming the autonomy of the nation/people with respect to not only the exercise of jurisdictional authority by particular settler governments but the character of what constitutes Indigenous governance and processes of being and becoming as place-based collectivities. Describing quotidian experiences of Kahnawà:ke Mohawk identity, Audra Simpson indicates that it is "drawn from their own traditions, their interpretations of that tradition, their shared archive of knowledge of each other, their genealogies, and their relationships with each other through time," later adding, "[T]hese *living, primary, feeling citizenships* may not be institutionally recognized, but are socially and politically recognized in the everyday life of the community."[89] Characterizing such feelings as expressions of sovereignty highlights their role in the ordinary renewal of Kahnawà:ke political existence, foregrounding how such affects, histories, and webs of relation provide the ongoing, in Ahmed's terms, conditions of emergence and direction for the polity. Thus, even as settler administrative and legal frameworks may seek to constrain the possibilities for Indigenous self-determination, Native peoples continue to have their own ways of formulating *nation* and *sovereignty* that operate in complex, sometimes amplifying and sometimes disjunctive, relation to the institutional structures recognized by the state.[90]

While the concept of sovereignty provides a way of indexing the presence and significance of Native peoples as *political* entities, its common association with state geographies of authority and belonging makes it far less useful as a means of outlining the aims of Black struggle. For people of African descent in the diaspora created by the transatlantic slave trade, the question of political belonging remains deeply vexed, neither at home in majority white nation-states nor having a site of identification that could provide a geopolitical frame for peoplehood. In *A Map to the Door of No Return*, Dionne Brand characterizes histories of enchattelment and fungibility as "a rupture in history, a rupture in the quality of being. It was also a physical rupture, a rupture of geography," noting of her own experience in Canada, "We were not from the place where we lived and we could not remember where we were from or who we were. My grandfather could not summon up a vision of landscape or a people which would add up to a name": "[H]aving no name to call on was having no past; having no past pointed to the fissure between the past and the present. That fissure is represented in the Door of No Return: that place where our ancestors departed one world for another; the Old World for the New."[91] The rupture of enslavement persists as an animating part of the present, an ongoing experience of placelessness that follows from the absence of an enduring connection to a "landscape or a people"—the very kinds of attachments signaled by the figure of sovereignty. Saidiya Hartman suggests of diasporic identification with Africa in *Lose Your Mother*, "We may have forgotten our country, but we haven't forgotten our dispossession. It's why we never tire of dreaming of a place that we can call home, a place better than here, wherever here might be. It's why one hundred square blocks of Los Angeles can be destroyed in an evening. We stay there, but we don't live there." She later suggests, "You're tired of being a problem; you're tired of loving a country that doesn't love you or hating the place you call home," also at several points describing African Americans as "stateless."[92]

Even as the state of one's formal citizenship may function nominally as *home*, the continual production of blackness as "a problem" regenerates dispossession by making Blacks outsiders to the nation, an alienation that forms the background to quotidian engagements with place and that consistently unsettles one's relation to the state of which one putatively is a subject. Brand observes, "The body is the place of captivity. The Black body is situated as a sign of particular cultural and political meanings in the Diaspora. All of these meanings return to the Door of No Return," or in Hartman's framing, "The most universal definition of the slave is a stranger. Torn from kin and community, exiled from one's country, dishonored and violated, the slave defines the position of the outsider," adding, "I am a reminder that twelve million crossed the Atlantic Ocean and the past is not yet over."[93] The process of enchattelment and the history of captivity—the meanings attached to the immutable fact of blackness—live on, borne in the bodies of those who in the current moment remain estranged from the space of their inhabitance.[94] As Samantha Pinto suggests in her discussion of Adrienne Kennedy's plays, "[A]n inquiry into that alienation is all that we are left with as a collective project of history making, one that centers the difficult and divergent paths of black women across the diaspora," what Pinto earlier describes as "the transgressive and often unexpected loops of circulation that cannot easily be traced to fixed points of origin and return."[95] Such experiences shape Black struggle in ways that generate a different kind of problem-space than that of Indigenous collective landedness. It is oriented by a kind of dispossession other than that lived by Native peoples in that there is not a clear landscape or country to which return is possible (a situation different than in expressions of Black majority governance in postcolonial nations, such as Jamaica and Haiti, which are discussed in chapter 4). Moreover, the question remains as to how Black people fit within Native geographies of sovereignty and self-determination, placing them, as Amadahy and Lawrence suggest, in "a kind of limbo" in the relation between the settler-state and Native national governments.[96]

This wariness with respect to narratives of Black locatedness, in the United States and Canada in particular, also needs to be understood in relation to the decades-long pattern of concentrating Black people in structurally impoverished urban centers, through which such spaces come to be represented as hopeless and wretched zones of blackness. Habiba Ibrahim argues, "[T]he city had to gain its character of deviance from a naturalized affinity with black people, who are not coincidentally determined by black families. If the ghetto was a place for sequestering, criminalizing, and regulating blackness, the new national goal tautologically suggested that blackness transformed the city into a dangerous, dysfunctional ghetto, and blackness was dysfunctional, which then justifies the growth of the carceral apparatus," adding, "[T]he city was an increasingly potent symbol of a particularly black form of difference."[97] The

Great Migration from the 1870s to the 1930s in which millions of African Americans moved primarily from the rural South to cities in the Northeast and Midwest created large urban Black populations, and, in the decades after World War II, various federally funded measures (including federally backed mortgages in which Black neighborhoods were redlined and denied loans, as well as massive investments in building the highway system) produced and subsidized white flight from cities to suburbs while disabling African Americans from moving. As Douglas S. Massey and Nancy A. Denton argue, from 1940 to 1970 "racial segregation became a permanent structural feature of the spatial organization of American cities."[98] In the 1960s through the 1980s, many urban nonwhite neighborhoods were razed in order to build freeways that would allow those suburbanites to commute into cities (thereby creating greater concentrations of urban poverty), manufacturing positions largely evaporated due to postindustrial shifts of production overseas, and federal funding for cities steadily decreased.[99] Together these dynamics resulted in the increasing immiseration, immobility, and criminalization of people of color in urban areas, particularly Black people.[100] In this way, blackness appears in governmental and popular discourses as a particular mode of territoriality, a generationally iterated embeddedness in place that expresses a tendency toward destitution, violence, and degeneration (often characterized as the "culture" of the "underclass").

Hartman and Brand both raise questions about the ultimate desirability of the kind of belonging that can be narrated as "sovereignty," particularly given the ways it can redeploy and naturalize racializing notions of origin that present Black people as "ungeographic" and belonging elsewhere.[101] Brand observes that "[s]ome of us in the Diaspora long so for nation—some continuous thread of biological or communal association, some bloodline or legacy which will cement our rights in the place we live," insisting, though, that "[w]hat we have to ask ourselves is, as everyone else in the nation should ask themselves also, nation predicated on what?"[102] Similarly, as against the notion that triangulation through Africa enables Black people globally to envision they have an inherent connection to one another that serves as the basis for political solidarity, Hartman argues, "Africans did not sell their brothers and sisters into slavery. They sold strangers: those outside the web of kin and clan relationships, nonmembers of the polity.... In order to betray your race, you had first to imagine yourself as one." In the place of what she presents as the re-racializing presumption of immanent Black connection generated by the figuration of Africa-as-motherland, Hartman instead foregrounds shared processes of refusal in response to varied contemporary forms of unfreedom:

[M]y Africa had its source in the commons created by fugitives and rebels. . . . The legacy I chose to claim was articulated in the ongoing struggle to escape, stand down, and defeat slavery in all of its myriad forms. It was the fugitive's legacy. It didn't require me to wait on bended knee for a great emancipator. It wasn't the dream of a White House, even if it was in Harlem, but of a free territory. It was a dream of autonomy rather than nationhood. It was the dream of an elsewhere, with all its promises and dangers, where the stateless might, at last, thrive.[103]

Fugitivity offers a way of envisioning political relation with respect to histories and legacies of slavery without routing it through a notion of blackness as belonging to a determinate collective for whom "nationhood" could serve as a horizon (a dynamic that is addressed further in chapter 3). The absence of such a "polity" means the absence of a sense of immanent unity, but it also defers the creation of boundaries through which some will end up as "nonmembers" who can then legitimately be subjected to extraordinary violence. In these formulations, having a "nation" entails *predicating* it on something, and that something simultaneously opens the potential for others to be made "stateless"— strangers whose alienation secures the bounds of the nation. The longing for a "free territory"—what Nadia Ellis characterizes as a diasporic "pull from elsewhere"—suggests less a kind of collective placemaking that might be signified through/as sovereignty than the continual making and remaking of forms of alliance that arise out of the repudiation of conditions of subjection and flight from them.[104]

Furthermore, if decolonization conventionally has been conceived as struggle toward autonomous governance over a particular land base, including with respect to Indigenous peoples' insistence on rightful sovereignty over their homelands, Black thinkers and activists also have been recasting the concept in terms of modes of post-sovereign transnational affiliation, association, and accountability, including in response to forms of postcolonial statehood in the Caribbean. These intellectuals argue that conflating the end of colonial rule with the emergence of a sovereignty-bearing political entity whose territorial self-governance is modeled on the form of the nation-state effaces other possibilities for contesting the legacies of colonialism. As Gary Wilder suggests of United Nations–orchestrated discourses of decolonization in the mid-twentieth century, "[A] procedural understanding of self-determination as a people's free choice about its future political status, about a specific framework for self-government, was conflated with a limited understanding of self-determination as state sovereignty for a national people."[105] Similarly, Yarimar

Bonilla observes that frameworks for decolonization within international law "operated as part of a larger project that sought to naturalize the idea of nation-states as discrete and necessary units of political and economic organization, while silencing and foreclosing other forms and alignments."[106] Both scholars also point to the ways that formal independence, and thus ostensible national sovereignty, for nations in the Caribbean has not yielded substantive self-determination.[107] Bonilla argues, "[T]he *majority* of Caribbean polities are non-sovereign societies; even those that have achieved 'flag independence' still struggle with how to forge a more robust project of self-determination, how to reconcile the unresolved legacies of colonialism and slavery; how to assert control over their entanglements with foreign powers, and how to stem their disappointment with the unfulfilled promises of political and economic modernity," and Wilder notes that Haitian independence from the early nineteenth century onward "underscored the fact that national independence and state sovereignty would not necessarily protect a 'free' people from economic impoverishment, political instability, territorial insecurity, and international isolation, let alone financial and military interference by foreign powers."[108] Similarly, Michelle Ann Stephens traces processes of Caribbean diasporic political visioning in the early twentieth century, which offered conceptions of Black transnational collectivity that exceeded the notion of sovereign statehood that became dominant in the 1960s. She argues with respect to the 1910s and 1920s, "Revolutionary internationalism . . . provided new ways of imagining and articulating black identity and ethnicity outside the bounds of the national," later adding that "the benefit of not having a Caribbean national identity was the ability to imagine a transnational Black identity uniting Black subjectivities across the Americas and beyond. In place of nations and nationality, the race would represent itself as and through global movement."[109] From this perspective, sovereignty can look like a kind of captivity, a form of territorialization that not only disables discussion of the broader imperial dynamics of antiblackness and the *longue durée* of the slave trade but that confines Black people within states either to which they cannot fully belong or that remain subject to neocolonial management and extraction. Refusing to treat sovereignty as the background or horizon for political struggle, then, can open possibilities for Black organizing, movement, and relation that exceed the terms of place-based nationalism.

However, what happens when Native assertions of sovereignty are transposed into the problem-space of these Black political geographies? One can see within some contemporary scholarship a tendency to interpret modes of place-based peoplehood (including indigeneity) as merely a reactionary attachment to Euro-American ideologies of propertied selfhood. In "The *Vel* of Slavery," Jared Sexton rightfully critiques the tendency within Indigenous studies of reading blackness in terms of an investment in belonging to the nation-state or as the failure to possess a conception/practice of place-based political collectivity (which I address further in the next section), but he goes on to suggest that the "preoccupation with sovereignty" that accompanies attention to Indigenous peoplehood(s) leads to "an elision of the permanent seizure of the body essential to enslavement" and an erasure of the fields of force to which the "captive body" is subjected. Instead, he advocates, quoting Nahum Dimitri Chandler, "tracking the figure of the *un*sovereign," further indicating that the political project of "abolition" lies "beyond (the restoration of) sovereignty" since "the slave's inhabitation of the earth precedes and exceeds any prior relation to land."[110] Indigenous sovereignty appears here as a commitment to the forms of propertied autonomy that characterize Euro-American systems of enslavement and their continuing effects in the wake of formal emancipation, and abolition involves a liberation of "the body" from its enthrallment to notions of possession, of which landownership is a key index. In a related vein, Alexander Weheliye argues, "[P]eoplehood represents the foremost mode of imagining, (re)producing, and legislating community, and thus managing inequality in the intertwined histories of capitalism and the nation-state."[111] To identify as landed means to identify with ideologies of property and self-ownership, and, thus, to defend a collective claim to place reinvests, in Sexton's terms, in *natality* and *nationality* in ways that cannot but fail to liberate "the body" from the force of enslavement.[112] Sexton takes sovereign selfhood as the foil for his vision of "uprooting," characterizing abolition as "the perverse affirmation of deracination," and, as Weheliye suggests, "Partaking of the flesh . . . tenders flavors and textures found in lives of imprisoned freedom, desires for survival, and viscous dreams of life that awaken future anterior humanities."[113] These formulations articulate the need to escape from "the human" through a *deracinating* opening to *fleshly* "flavors and textures" that enable forms of becoming that exceed existing social formations but that do not themselves constitute forms of "peoplehood" or collective placemaking (echoing the work of Sylvia Wynter, discussed earlier).

From within this conceptual and political (set of) orientation(s), collective potentials based in experiences of territoriality indicate a retrograde investment in propertied modes of being. This dynamic can be seen in *Red, White, and Black*, in which Frank Wilderson distinguishes (Black) "fungibility" from (Native) "sovereignty." In his interpretation of the film *Skins*, he suggests that "[the] subordination of genocide to sovereignty enables the dream of a cultural alliance between the 'Savage' and the Settler . . . , while it simultaneously crowds out the dream of a political alliance between the 'Savage' and the Slave." He later adds that Natives and settlers (by which he means whites) "can both practice cartography, and although at every scale their maps are radically incompatible, their respective 'mapness' is never in question," a territoriality that works to defer "the horrifying possibility that Black fungibility might somehow rub off of the Slave and stick to the 'Savage'" in ways that would bring Natives "perilously close to their own object status, that is, to the genocide modality of their ontology."[114] Following this logic, Native sovereignties reinstitute dominant notions because they invest in political cartography rather than attending to the violence done to (Native and Black) bodies via their being made fungible and murderable objects.[115] "Mapness" per se appears as a deferral or denial of the (genocidal) violence of racialized corporeality, because it presumptively depends on becoming a subject through/of property, and reciprocally, to assert a collective claim to place is to desire to gain entry to the privileges of dominant personhood.[116] In *Poetics of Relation*, Glissant offers a distinction between "Root" and "Relation" that resonates with this critique of collective locatedness. He defines the former in terms of "a claim to legitimacy that allows a community to proclaim its entitlement to the possession of a land, which thus becomes a territory," whereas the latter "does not devise any legitimacy as its guarantee," and he earlier locates the force of "Relation" in the experiences and legacies of the "abyss" of the Middle Passage ("They live Relation and clear the way for it, to the extent that the oblivion of the abyss comes to them").[117] Moreover, the possibility of Relation, of means of being and becoming that exceed "entitlement" and "possession," emerges out of the elimination of Indigenous peoples from the Caribbean: "According to the mysterious laws of rootedness (of filiation), the only 'possessors' of the Archipelago [of the Caribbean] would be the Caribs or their predecessors, who have been exterminated"; "the consequences of European expansion (extermination of the Pre-Columbians, importation of a new population) is precisely what forms the basis for a new relationship with the land: not the absolute ontological possession regarded as sacred but the complicity of relation."[118] An antiracist account of "Relation" as such appears to depend on repudiating *rootedness*, including Indigenous geographies of peoplehood and placemaking.

The kinds of fungibility that continue to orient blackness defer the potential for national belonging and territorial self-determination, producing Black people as, in Best and Hartman's terms, "the stateless, the socially dead, and the disposable."[119] This dynamic of statelessness gives rise to a theorization of fleshly relation that moves toward a vision of abolition, a post-sovereign or unsovereign transnational imaginary in which other modes of being human emerge beyond the logics of property. When engaging articulations of Indigenous peoplehood, though, such formulations often translate the topos of sovereignty as if it necessarily is indicative of a reactionary attachment to the state form (or forms of possession that proliferate through liberal governance).

Indigenous intellectuals, however, also have mounted various critiques of the concept of sovereignty and the ways it is enacted in Native governance, but these analyses do not contest Native peoplehood and placemaking as such. For example, Taiaiake Alfred has argued that articulations of "sovereignty" by Native peoples position them within the terms of settler governance in ways that disable the potential for more robust performances of self-determination. He suggests that "[s]overeignty itself implies a set of values and objectives that put it in direct opposition to the values and objectives found in most traditional indigenous philosophies," requiring that Indigenous peoples "conform to state-derived criteria and represent ascribed or negotiated identities in order to access these legal rights."[120] In a related vein, Mishuana Goeman contests the tendency to take U.S. legal and administrative mappings of Native space as the frame for Indigenous placemaking. She argues, "We also have a tendency to abstract space—that is to decorporealize, commodify, or bureaucratize—when the legal ramifications of land or the political landscape are addressed." But Goeman also insists, "Unlike the maps that designate Indian land as existing only in certain places, wherever we went there were Natives and Native spaces, and if there weren't, we carved them out."[121] If sovereignty names officially recognized geographies of Native governance, Goeman's analysis suggests the danger of using it as the definitional matrix through which to understand Native people's and peoples' relationships to land and each other. Moreover, a number of scholars have addressed the exclusions and oppressions enacted by certain Native governments in the ways they cite and institutionalize sovereignty, including sexist definitions of membership, heteropatriarchal notions of marriage and patriotism, and various kinds of disenrollment.[122]

Indigenous studies scholars also have addressed the roles that antiblackness can play in contemporary assertions and affirmations of Native sovereignty.[123] One of the most prominent examples has been the challenge to the citizenship of persons of African descent among the Five Tribes (Cherokees, Creeks, Choctaws, Chickasaws, and Seminoles), the peoples removed from what is now the U.S. Southeast in the 1830s. Treaties negotiated and ratified in the wake of the Civil War provide for the end of slavery among these peoples and for the inclusion of Black persons as full citizens of the Native nation with whom they had resided or by whose citizens they were held as slaves. While people of African descent were incorporated into the voting citizenry, although not without controversy and contention, the censuses of tribal citizens generated as part of the allotment process—the Dawes Rolls—listed all persons suspected as being of African descent on separate "freedmen" rolls, even when genealogically they were also "Indian." The governments of the Five Tribes over the course of the twentieth century and twenty-first century have sought at various points to repudiate the citizenship of the "freedmen," usually on some version of the claim that they are not "Indian" and, therefore, cannot truly belong to an "Indian" nation. Such claims come despite the fact that the majority of the citizens of these nations also have various forms of non-"Indian" descent, which is not seen as a bar to their status as political subjects (even leaving aside the question of what genealogies have historically been recorded based on extant practices of racial documentation). As others have noted, the concerns about the boundaries of racial *Indianness* seem to be activated most forcefully in relation to blackness, which de facto gets understood as beyond the bounds of indigeneity even when other genealogical combinations are not seen as preventing identification as Native. In this vein, attempts to pursue federal recognition as a tribe can be stymied by perceptions that a group is *really* Black rather than Indian. When peoples who are not currently acknowledged as an "Indian tribe" by the federal government pursue that status under the regulations of what is now called the Office of Federal Acknowledgment (regulations first issued in 1978 and periodically revised since then), they need to demonstrate, among other things, that "the petitioning entity have been identified by reliable external sources on a substantially continuous basis as an Indian entity since 1900."[124] Ostensibly, this requirement has nothing to do with race per se, but what has constituted evidence of *Indianness* for non-native observers—such as government officials, scholars, and journalists—such that a group would be identified as "an Indian entity" has never been free from stereotypical, racialized notions of who Native people(s) are. In particular, given the hypodescent logic that tends to guide understandings of who counts as Black in the United States (regardless of actual legal definitions at various points and in different locations), evidence that a group's members are of African descent often is treated as a de facto indication that they are not *really* Indian, including also at times by the governments of federally acknowledged tribes.

Native critiques of sovereignty and the way it is institutionalized, though, do not suggest that emplaced political collectivity itself is the problem. Thus, while raising questions about what citations and enactments of Native sovereignty mean in the context of ongoing racializing modes of settler colonial occupation, the intellectual and political trajectories of this work remain disjunct from those at play in much Black political theorizing. In such work, indigeneity can appear to reinforce a vision of *rootedness* that is understood as itself a racializing attachment of persons and peoples to place by which Black subjects continue to be made alien, fungible, and subject to the will of another. However, there also are modes of Black collective placemaking that could be understood as tending toward sovereignty. Beyond the postcolonial state as such, various projects of Black communal landedness across the Caribbean and Latin America (usually connected in some fashion to histories of marronage, addressed in chapter 4) seek acknowledgment for those territorialities as self-governing political entities. In doing so, they raise further questions about the place of place in Black political imaginaries (such as in the critique of sovereignty), the potential for horizontal relation among Black and Indigenous political framings (even amid the ways they are oriented differently due to nonidentical histories of racial and colonial violence), and the difficulties posed by Black assertions of legitimate presence in the Americas in the context of Indigenous emphasis on ongoing dispossession by non-natives.

Settler

What does it mean to conceive of the Americas as Native space, and where does doing so leave non-native people of color, particularly the descendants of those stolen and transported across the Atlantic in the African slave trade? If the latter are not Indigenous, does that make them *settlers*? What's at stake in the mobilization and refusal of this term to refer to non-natives of African descent? More specifically, what happens when the coerced diasporas of blackness created by the transatlantic slave trade are transposed into a conceptual structure oriented around Indigenous self-determination and the repudiation of a presumptive non-native right to occupy Native lands? The tensions generated by the use of the term *settler* in characterizing Black people's presence in the Americas can be understood as resulting from a clash between articulations of ongoing collective injury. How can people of African descent be settlers when blackness continues to operate as a site of fungibility for projects of possession, accumulation, and property making? Conversely, how can a group of non-natives not be understood as settlers when they participate, often in unacknowledged ways, in the colonial occupation of Native lands and for which full inclusion in the settler-state sometimes serves as a horizon of political aspiration? These framings are incommensurate, and each implicitly seeks to render the other *transparent*, to incorporate it without remainder or difference into its own account of the real. Instead, we might highlight the ways these narrations remain opaque to each other, the ways that their nonequivalent normative orientations produce disjunction and contradiction when they are brought into relation. From this perspective, *settler* might be envisioned as marking less an identity than a process of translation in which various groups are brought into relation with Indigenous formations, a process that may run athwart of other trajectories of political struggle and imagination.

To understand Black people as settlers may entail positing forms of belonging to the nation-state, and participation in legally sanctioned modes of ownership, that do not reflect the ongoing forms and force of antiblackness. If one defines settlement as the exertion of possession by non-Indigenous persons and groups over the space of the Americas, then Black people's continuing subjection to white-dominated property regimes would trouble their classification as agents of settler colonialism. In "In the Clearing," Tiffany King offers an extended analysis of the problems at play in the "curious conjunction, 'Black Settler.'"[125] She argues,

> Settler colonial relations [have] made it imperative for people to own land or establish a relation to land as property in order to survive. In this way, they are certainly implicated in relationships to land that maintain a genocidal project against Native peoples. However, Black people's relationship to both land ownership and Native people remains different than white/settlers' relationships to land and Native peoples. Ongoing struggles against gentrification and disasters like Hurricane Katrina, which displaced thousands of Black people from New Orleans, continue to reveal the tenuous relationship that Blacks have to land tenure.[126]

To fold Blacks into a category formed around whites' relationships to land and ownership effaces how blackness enacts denials of belonging in ways that also are dispossessive. Although non-native Black forms of placemaking in the Americas are not expressive of indigeneity, they remain the object of white aggression and projects of displacement through direct violence, state-sanctioned modes of ostensibly race-neutral foreclosure and eviction, and the institutionalized withholding and retraction of resources of all sorts (making inhabitance precarious in spaces deemed Black).[127] King observes, "Blackness is a very specific structural and world ordering position made possible through Conquest that cannot inhabit a Settler ontology," and as a result, "The term 'Black Settler' represent[s] discursive evidence of a conceptual block."[128] Part of the specificity of blackness as a racial formation, and of antiblackness as a mode of domination, lies in its rendering of Black people as ungeographic, refusing to engage with Black forms of placemaking or treating Black people as fundamentally unplaced.[129] In this way blackness cannot provide a subjectivity consistent with a "Settler ontology" organized around (legally sanctioned) possession.

Moreover, articulations of Indigenous sovereignty can raise questions about how Black people fit within Native geographies. As King recounts with respect to her time in INCITE Toronto, "We had agreed Native sovereignty must be achieved to end Native genocide. However, we had just begun to conceive of and envision what Native sovereignty would look like. Right now, it was being loosely defined as Native governance or a time when Native peoples would be in charge. This created anxiety for the Black women in the room. Black people in settler colonial states often imagine themselves as facing a no win situation under the current order or under Native sovereignty."[130] Although one might raise questions about equating Native and settler modes of sovereignty, as discussed in the previous section, the issue of Black place within either form(ul)ation remains. How do the violences of antiblackness register within conceptualizations and narrations of Indigenous peoples' self-determination? If the term *settler* marks the ways Black people are translated into Indigenous political imaginaries, what room is there for negotiating modes of recognition and relation that do not reiterate the normalization of blackness as nonbelonging? One might understand such questions as animating the equation of Indigenous sovereignty with antiblackness at play in some scholarship, such as Sexton's and Wilderson's arguments discussed earlier.

While the concept of settler may bracket the ways enfleshment and fungibility contour blackness, including the ways they defer or outright deny access to ownership and landedness, viewed from the perspective of Indigenous struggles the question remains as to how to understand non-native Black people's relationship to processes of settlement and ongoing Indigenous dispossession. Positing the potential for Blacks to be settlers functions as a way of holding open this question, forestalling the translation of Indigenous self-determination into another political framing in which it becomes marginal. In this vein, Amadahy and Lawrence articulate their aim as "break[ing] through and deconstruct[ing] postures of innocence—the ways in which both Black and Indigenous people may insist that the primacy of their own suffering and powerlessness is so unique and all-encompassing that it erases even the possibility of their maintaining relationships of oppression relative to another group."[131] Such postures entail presenting non-native Black people as, "in fact, not colonizers, but victims, of slave-owning Native people" while "normaliz[ing] relations of colonialism," including by displacing the politics of Indigenous sovereignty: "[B]oth the theoretical and literary writing coming out of Black America positions Black people as being at the core of racial oppression and marginality in the United States in ways that exclude the possibility of an Indigenous presence fundamentally *mattering.*"[132] To the extent that elaborating the continuing structural violence of antiblackness works to forestall discussion of how Indigenous sovereignty might *matter* in relation to Black struggles, such analysis of Black oppression can operate in exceptionalizing ways that repudiate the possibility of addressing how Black people as non-natives might participate in the dynamics of settler colonialism.[133] Put another way, postures of innocence—or in Tuck and Yang's phrasing "moves to innocence"[134]—do more than deny a role for Black people in the oppression of Indigenous peoples; they orient discussion such that antiblack racialization provides the framework through which to figure (or not) the existence and significance of Indigenous peoplehood. In that process, indigeneity tends to be relegated to "the 'position of the unthought,'"[135] and centering blackness in ways that present it as paradigmatic of extant systems of oppression disables discussion of how settlement might shape Black life in the settler-state.[136]

Using the term *settler* as a way of marking Black people as non-Indigenous can be understood as a means of insisting on the importance of engaging with Native struggles and political framings, on taking settler colonialism and Indigenous self-determination as a meaningful background—as a particular kind of problem-space—through which to figure Black-Native relations. Thus, even as Amadahy and Lawrence observe that "Black peoples have not been quintessential 'settlers' in the White supremacist usage of the word," they note that people of African descent "have, as free people, been involved in some form of settlement process. What seems more important than the semantics about whether or not individuals should be called settlers is the question of the relationships that Black 'settlers' have, by virtue of their marginality, with those whose lands have been taken, and what relationships they wish to develop, *at present*, with Indigenous peoples."[137] While characterizing non-native Black people as settlers may overlook the ongoing (re)production of blackness as fungibility, including the ways that dynamic helps consolidate whiteness as a mode of possession,[138] this political semantics highlights *relation to* Native peoples as the central focus of analysis, shifting the frame of reference through which one maps the sociopolitical landscape.[139] In *Settler: Identity and Colonialism in 21st Century Canada*, Emma Battell Lowman and Adam J. Barker suggest, "[I]t is important to understand that being Settler Canadian is not necessarily predicated on experiencing the benefits or the oppressions of white supremacy, nor is it necessary to be accepted by all other Settler people," adding, "It is entirely possible—and in fact quite common—for communities of marginalized peoples to buy in to the structures of invasion, to identify strongly with Settler

Canadian myths and narratives, and to participate in systemic dispossession of Indigenous peoples, all the while struggling against their own marginalization or oppression."[140] Although one might object to the notion that Blacks "buy in" to or "identify strongly" with the dynamics of settlement, their characterization as settlers underlines the existence and efficacy of "structures of invasion" and the "systemic dispossession of Indigenous peoples," approaching Black political goals and strategies *in terms of* their relation to Native polities.[141]

Participation within processes of settlement as a non-Indigenous person gets shorthanded as *being a settler*, casting large-scale patterns as a kind of (singular) subjectivity, but suspending for a moment the justifiable critique of that condensation (or, perhaps, reification), one could see the term *settler* as projecting an analytical trajectory, as pointing toward the question, in Tuck and Yang's terms, "[H]ow can we belong in a way that doesn't reproduce colonial dispossession and harm?"[142] If the effort to engage both blackness and indigeneity generates friction, that dissonance, and the associated intersectional shuttling between disparate frames, foregrounds understanding as an open-ended, difficult, and potentially conflictive process in which translation is enacted through terms, tropes, and modes of narration that may not be flagged as such. If, as Byrd suggests, "imperialism has forced settlers and arrivants to cathect the space of the native as their home," engagements with the term *settler* might focus less on the accuracy of its referential scope—such as its capacity to engage ongoing histories of Black abjection—than its role in making "colonial dispossession" and "the space of the native" paradigmatic as a political frame, indicating a particular direction for analysis and struggle. Attending to how colonial dispossession is reproduced foregrounds how forms of Indigenous sovereignty and self-determination are deferred, contained, denied, and erased through non-native action (governmental and otherwise, intentional and not). Byrd argues that "[i]dentifying the competing interpretations of geographical spatialities and historicities that inform racial and decolonial identities depends upon an act of interpretation that decenters the vertical interactions of colonizer and colonized and recenters the horizontal struggles among peoples with competing claims to historical oppressions," and she later asks, "How do arrivants and other peoples forced to move through empire use indigeneity as a transit to redress, grieve, and fill the fractures and ruptures created through diaspora and exclusion?"[143] Refusing the singularity (and verticality) of *settler* as a way of characterizing all non-natives does not displace horizontal exploration of how political struggles by non-natives of color may be oriented in ways that do not engage with Indigenous collective formations and self-articulations.

Centering the dynamics of settlement brings into relief how people of color, in mobilizing against their own "historical oppressions," may participate in settler colonial processes. Byrd here addresses what might be characterized as indigenization, the ways that non-natives explicitly or implicitly claim some version of indigeneity as a way of negotiating the particular modes of violence that they face. In *Creole Indigeneity*, Shona Jackson explores how Black articulations of belonging can take part in processes of Indigenous dispossession. Particularly, she examines the ways that figuring people of African descent as, in Sylvia Wynter's terms, "new natives" in the New World—whose relationship to place is forged through enslaved and emancipated forms of labor—creates a sense of anticolonial "indigeneity." In the context of Caribbean decolonization, "Creole social and political subjectivity reflects a dual difference and deferring: a difference from the colonizer and a deferring of the existence of Indigenous Peoples."[144] While addressing Caribbean modes of postcolonial nationhood, Guyana in particular, Jackson's discussion of the relation between Black experiences of collective placemaking and Indigenous dispossession point toward the difficulties of trying to think Black and Indigenous struggles simultaneously. She points to the way figurations of Black belonging and emplacement in the face of institutionalized racisms may erase Indigenous peoples or may actively mobilize assertions of nativeness as a rejoinder to antiblackness in ways that erase Native geographies and sovereignties (as well as the political question of how Black people relate to such geographies and sovereignties).[145]

Conversely, critiques of Black participation in forms of non-native indigenization can implicitly align Black people with the state, seeing them simply as stand-ins for the state or as inherently aligned with its interests in ways that are particularly problematic in the context of white-dominated nations (such as the United States and Canada). Leroy observes, "Native studies understands slavery and emancipation in a liberal, progressive narrative, relegating slavery to the past so that Black people can more seamlessly be cast in the role of settler (or arrivant, or appellant). Second, Black politics are subsequently subsumed into this narrative, leaving no room to think about how politics which fall outside of it—such as Black internationalism and anti-colonialism—relate to indigenous struggles."[146] The translation of Black people as settlers, then, can present Black movements as if inclusion in the state were their principal (or perhaps only) orienting objective, thereby rendering blackness transparent as simply an extension of settler nationalisms.

In the U.S. context, accounts that figure Black political aspirations as principally toward civil rights, particularly understanding them as a mechanism for inclusion in citizenship, overlook the scope and significance of various modes of Black internationalism and transnationalism. In *Black Is a Country*, Nikhil Pal Singh argues that "black freedom struggles have not only been about obtaining market access, equal citizenship, or integrating black people into common national subjectivity. Rather, they represent the counter-statements of political subjects who have struggled to widen the circle of common humanity" and to construct "new universals from the forcible enclosures of racial stigma." He further suggests the importance of "recognizing that perhaps the most consistent and enduring strand of modern black activism has been opposition to imperialism and colonialism": "By refusing to accept the limitations of liberal reform at home, and by challenging the depredations of U.S. imperial politics abroad, black movements consistently advanced more worldly and expansive political conceptions—toward democratic anticapitalism and anti-imperialism—that were regularly disparaged and rejected as un-American."[147] Beyond seeking to increase participation within the U.S. nation-state, Black movements have understood themselves as participating within a broader challenge to a racialized and racializing international system in which whiteness de facto serves as the site of universal value.[148] In situating critiques of U.S. policy and society within an analysis of global imperialisms, Black intellectuals have cast criticism of the U.S. state less as an expression of desired belonging than as a challenge to the state's legitimacy (and potentially that of the nation-state form itself).[149] As Cynthia Young observes with respect to Angela Davis's work as a scholar and activist, "If integration's political appeal required an affirmation that Black people were indeed citizens faithful to the ideals of the nation-state, Davis implicitly reframed civil rights disobedience as an act of resistance to the nation-state that went beyond challenging Jim Crow segregation."[150] Moreover, there is a long history of African American participation within Black diasporic networks that indicate horizons of imagination and organizing that far exceed the boundaries of any given nation-state. In his discussion of the dynamics of such networks between World War I and World War II, Brent Edwards notes that "in these transnational circuits, Black modern expression takes form not as a single thread, but through the often uneasy encounters of peoples of African descent with each other," later suggesting that these networks generate and circulate "a common 'elsewhere,' a shared logic of collaboration and coordination at a level beyond particular nation-states."[151] Axiomatically differentiating Native Americans and African Americans on the basis of the latter's supposed investment in naturalizing the nation-state's claims to "domestic" space, then, edits out significant swaths of Black political theorizing and collective self-articulation, and to the extent that naming African Americans as "settlers" requires such a presumption, doing so can offer a homogenizing misrepresentation of the character of Black movements.

However, even when connecting struggles on lands claimed by the United States to broader anti-imperial formations, Black movements still can engage in political mappings that efface Indigenous sovereignty and self-determination—the kinds of dynamics that the concept of the settler can bring to the fore. Such difficulties particularly arise around understanding the ways that non-native racial minorities participate within a broader Third World Left, especially the extent to which forms of U.S. state-sanctioned violence, exploitation, and extraction are understood as making such groups into internal colonies. In addressing how movements within the United States were connected to struggles for decolonization elsewhere, Young indicates, "The translation of this theory to the United States, of course, meant several substitutions. For 'national,' U.S. Third World Leftists had to make do with local communities of color. 'Underdeveloped countries' became U.S. national minorities, and specific incidents had to be read as events in a national liberation struggle," and after sketching the history of understandings of African Americans as an "oppressed nation" within early-twentieth-century communist discourses, she notes, "If the theory itself is incoherent in places, it nonetheless constitutes an attempt to resolve at the ideological level the situation of U.S. national minorities that are at once residents of the United States without being fully enfranchised citizens of the nation."[152] The project of seeking to connect the dynamics of institutionalized racism domestically to various extant racializing modes of imperial management, aggression, and extraction enacted by the United States and other Western powers contests U.S. claims to democratic legitimacy while also refusing the clear distinction between the inside and outside of the nation-state through which the United States often justified its acts abroad (policy supposedly undertaken in the national interest to promote the welfare of the American people).

In addition, these forms of collective identity among the oppressed were not routed through membership in the U.S. state. Even as many Black intellectuals have questioned the value of the concept of *nation* as a way of framing possibilities for freedom in the wake of the history of enchattelment and the incomplete work of emancipation (such as in Hartman's, Brand's, and Sexton's work discussed earlier), others have drawn on the notion of nationhood as a means of formulating the significance of blackness in the United States. Singh suggests of W. E. B. DuBois's account of African Americans as a "nation within a nation" that "Du Bois did not defend black nationhood in conventional terms—it did not depend on capturing state power or achieving territorial sovereignty. Rather, he used 'nation' to signify the moral and intellectual coherence shared by black people as [a] result of their common exclusion within the United States."[153] Similarly, Cheryl Higashida traces a genealogy of what she describes as "Black internationalist feminism," including the work of Audre Lorde, that "challenged heteronormative and masculinist articulations of nationalism while maintaining the importance, even centrality, of national liberation movements for achieving Black women's social, political, and economic rights," and this perspective from "the Black anticolonial Left" "championed self-determination for all oppressed nations, including African Americans, to bring about worldwide socialism."[154] In these movements, being part of an oppressed nation provides an orienting framework through which to conceptualize Black collective identity—a "we" that has been produced through slavery and its aftermaths. Nationality suggests situated coherence, a sense of belonging in displacement. If Hartman and Brand suggest the ways ongoing histories of antiblackness frustrate a sense of home, articulations of Black nationality make that unhomeliness into a political project of placemaking within empire. Insisting on located Black presence functions as a way of tracking the force of antiblack unmapping, of making Black people disposable, fungible, a tool of placemaking for others (of which the plantation is paradigmatic) but not for themselves. In *Demonic Grounds*, McKittrick argues, "[T]he landless black subject is, importantly, anchored to a new world grid that is economically, racially, and sexually normative, or, seemingly nonblack; this grid suppresses the possibility of black geographies by invalidating the subject's cartographic needs, expressions, and knowledges."[155] Figurations of Black nationhood in the United States, then, can both expose institutionalized patterns that work to foreclose Black geographies while also tracing the geographic relevancy of the specific understandings of Black collectivity that arise in white-dominated states (as they interface with a white-dominated international system).

To the extent that the figures of nationhood and the internal colony do not solely diagnose the imperial dynamics of white supremacy and antiblackness, though, what lies beyond state-sanctioned and state-legitimating geographies, and where do Indigenous people fit within such alternative political visions and mappings?[156] If the designation of Black people as settlers cannot register—and may actively erase—crucial dimensions of Black experience, critique, and radical imagination, the use of the term *settler* does potentially (re)focus on the following: the question of Indigenous sovereignty and self-determination; the differences between the problem-spaces in and through which Black and Indigenous movements emerge; and the difficulties in trying to fold Native peoples into struggles not oriented around their autonomous self-governance and landed resurgence. In this way, the concept of the settler marks the problems of (mis)translation at play in moving between sociopolitical formations—ones whose histories, phenomenologies, and trajectories remain distinctive in ways that potentially also make them disjunctive. Or, recognizing that movements arising from the situated circumstances of Black and Indigenous lives may be irreducibly *different* from each other opens the potential for nonappropriative, nonassimilatory, and nonantagonistic modes of negotiation, thereby giving rise to, in Hong's terms quoted earlier, "coalitional practice based on, rather than in spite of, historical and material differences." What enables such work? As a form of discourse and imagination, the speculative, I will suggest, opens toward an ethics of difference that can provide a basis for mutual engagement. Or, more precisely, the speculative opens avenues for seeing and acknowledging the processes that block or defer such engagement. It offers a medium for recognizing the dynamics of (mis)translation and, thus, for generating productive understandings of uncommonality—the equivocations that arise in moving among Black and Indigenous imaginings.

Speculation

If Black and Indigenous struggles may be oriented differently in ways that can make them opaque to each other, and if such opacity might be understood as immanently generated by the trajectories of the struggles themselves (rather than as a conceptual error to be corrected by better and more encompassing structural modelling), why turn to futurist fiction as a way of exploring these dynamics and their implications for Black-Indigenous relation? Indigenous futurisms and Afrofuturisms draw attention to the power of the speculative to challenge the transparency of the real. Futurist narratives explicitly address that which has not yet happened, what is beyond the present but what might be. They envision what's to come, and that process of visioning employs the backgrounds, principles, experiences of the present as a way of imagining a potential reality. Yet, when staged as an account of the future (albeit fictional), the narrative's organizing tropes, strategies, and framings cannot be understood as themselves simply reflecting the facticity of the present or the past. That very disjunction from the actual, from casting its vision in directly referential relation to what is or was, though, helps promote reflection on how those same kinds of framings (in Scott's terms quoted earlier, the "tropes, modes, and rhetoric" of the problem-space and the "horizon in relation to which it is constructed") play a vital role in producing a sense of the real in other circumstances.[157] Rather than solely pointing toward the future, then, speculation broadly considered points toward questions about what counts as real in the present, highlighting how varied ways of envisioning what *might be* grow out of varied ways of living and perceiving *now*. We might conceptualize speculation as an engagement with the not-known in which the tools of knowing and making become visible. In this way, the speculative opens a conceptual and narrative gap that allows framings to come into view as such, as forms of orientation, and doing so dislodges them from the epistemological and phenomenological tendency to normalize their perspective as simply expressive of the singular facticity of *the real*.[158] Futurisms, then, can serve as a tool for doing the following: pluralizing conceptions of what is; recognizing the existence of such differences; and tracking the ways frames of reference shape understandings of what is, was, and could be.[159]

Futurism confronts the difficulties in envisioning Black and Indigenous futures created by antiblackness and settler colonialism. Black people continually are cast as backward, technophobic, and incapable of advancement, and in this way, blackness is juxtaposed with progress and is cast as civilizationally regressive rather than as contributing to humanity's development. As Anna Everett argues, "[T]he overwhelming characterization of the brave new world of cyberspace as primarily a racialized sphere of whiteness inheres in popular constructions of high-tech and low-to-no-tech spheres that often consign black bodies to the latter, with the latter being insignificant if not absent altogether," and Alonda Nelson observes, "Racial identity, and blackness in particular, is the anti-avatar of digital life. Blackness gets constructed as always oppositional to technologically driven chronicles of progress."[160] To the extent that the future entails ever expanding modes of technological mastery and the creation and exploration of new worlds through electronic and virtual means, narratives of Black incapacity on this front suggest not just the absence of meaningful contributions to the advancement of society but a permanent belatedness in which people of African descent perpetually lag behind. The possibility of envisioning a future for Black people, then, becomes ironic, as blackness gets cast as a drag on the possibility of development. Conversely, the obliteration of the past enacted by the Middle Passage creates problems for conceiving of Black futurities. In the article in which he coins the term *Afrofuturism*, Mark Dery asks, "Can a community whose past has been deliberately rubbed out, and whose energies have subsequently been consumed by the search for legible traces of its history, imagine possible futures?" In that same piece, Samuel Delany asserts, "The historical reason that we've been so impoverished in terms of future images is because, until fairly recently, as a people we were systematically forbidden any images of our past. I have no idea where, in Africa, my black ancestors came from because, when they reached the slave markets of New Orleans, records of such things were systematically destroyed."[161] The erasure of the past for Blacks in the diaspora as a result of the transatlantic slave trade produces something like a temporal vacuum, in which the attempt to construct usable histories in and for the present can direct attention away from the project of imagining potential futures. On what or out of what could such futures be built? Moreover, what's the value of such an effort to conceptualize what's to come in the face of known genealogies of racism that continue to (de)form the current moment? As Sandra Jackson and Julie Moody-Freeman note, "Exploration of future possibilities and the fantastic, and speculation about alternative possibilities to the world we inhabit now, . . . have been viewed as iconoclastic, trivial pursuits in the face of the harsh realities of the here and now, shaped by colonialism, slavery, servitude, underdevelopment, Jim Crow terror, segregation, violence and repression."[162] Seen in this way, speculative imaginings less offer possibility than provide distraction, deferring engagement with the current conditions of antiblack domination.

Indigenous peoples face their own set of challenges in being seen as having futures. If people of African descent are cast as retrograde and techno-incompetent, Natives often are envisioned as, in fact, already gone, or as imminently so. In this way, Indigenous futurity becomes not simply an oddity but a full-on paradox. As Jean O'Brien argues, non-natives employ "temporalities of race" such that "Indians reside in an ahistorical temporality in which they can only be the victims of change, not active subjects in the making of change," earlier suggesting that in this framework "Indians could only be ancients, and refusal to behave as such rendered Indians inauthentic in their minds. Indians, then, can never be modern."[163] When Native peoples are conceptualized as inherently vestigial, as necessarily belonging to the past, any movement away from static, stereotypical non-native images of Indianness will be understood as a loss of Native identity.[164] Change correlates with inauthenticity and the abandonment of Indianness as such, including with respect to the ways Native identity gets reduced to questions of supposed (and always diminishing) Indian bloodedness. As O'Brien notes, "[T]he requirements of blood purity and change as criteria of Indianness narrate Indian degeneracy, whereas for non-Indians, mixture invigorates the race and change is inextricable from the progress narrative that signals their difference and superiority."[165] Thus, in addition to also being presumed to be primitive and technologically inept, Native peoples often are presented definitionally as extinct or as soon to be such, thus rendering the future a nonissue.[166] As Lou Cornum observes, "In the colonial imaginary, indigenous life is not only separate from the present time but also

out of place in the future, a time defined by the progress of distinctly western technology," or, as Darcie Little Badger puts it, "It's hard to enjoy a future
where you no longer exist."[167] The site of Indigenous authenticity, then, always
lies in the past—in the recuperation of a tradition understood as ever in danger, as always in decline. In the introduction to his collection of science fiction
stories, Drew Hayden Taylor observes, "[A] lot of Indigenous novels and plays
tend to walk a narrow path specifically restricted to stories of bygone days. Or
angry/dysfunctional aspects of contemporary First Nations life. Or the hang-
over problems resulting from centuries of colonization. All worthwhile and
necessary reflections of Aboriginal life for sure. But I wonder why it can't be
more."[168]

In addition to the difficulties in envisioning Black and Indigenous futures
generated both by extant forms of racialization and the demands to respond
to histories of oppression as they manifest in the present, speculation itself
can be understood as intimately part of antiblack and settler colonial modes
of domination. The attempt to secure the future for white supremacy, settlement, and capital involves a range of speculative technologies that project
forward current conditions of subjection as the basis for what's to come. As
Aimee Bahng observes in *Migrant Futures*, "As of December 2014, approximately $710 trillion of the world's capital was circulating in the global financial
derivatives market, a metamarket of trading in commodity futures, options,
and swaps" that "render[s] value out of the not yet," later adding, "Financial
speculation, extrapolation, and prediction rely on mathematical models and
probabilistic logics to transform quantitative data into a narrative arc" in ways
that can be understood as a "colonization of the future."[169] Datafying modes
of financial futurism, what Kodwo Eshun refers to as the "futures industry,"
function alongside efforts to mobilize surveillance information and biometric data toward forms of predictive profiling that work to define (racializing)
kinds of personhood understood as inherently posing an imminent threat.[170]
These forms of investment and securitization build on long histories of seeking
to capture and control the future in order to stabilize regimes of violence in
the present. For example, the rise of the insurance industry in England made
possible the economies of the slave trade, and trade in the probable value of territories prospectively or recently appropriated from Indigenous peoples drove
massive expansions in the political economies of settler occupation.[171] One
might understand policing practices and technologies, mass incarceration, and
the expanding seizure of Native lands and waters as themselves predicated on
forms of speculation, extending carceral control supposedly to protect the general public from danger and accessing natural resources as the basis for energy

and development futures.[172] Moreover, science fiction itself has participated in such racializing and imperial projects and projections. Eshun refers to "the positive feedback between future-oriented media and capital" as "SF capital," adding, "[I]t would be naïve to understand science fiction, located within the expanded field of the futures industry, as merely prediction into the far future, or as a utopian project for imagining alternative social realities."[173] Characterizing popular mid- to late-twentieth-century fictionalizations of the future as "astrofuturism," De Witt Douglas Kilgore observes, "Within astrofuturism's discursive field, they have no alternative but to follow the course of empire and to prove that they can repeat its history without its flaws," including deploying settler tropologies of space as terra nullius or a New World awaiting discovery, and andré m. carrington contests the presumption that "doing cultural work in a marginal genre is tantamount to identifying within an oppressed social formation."[174]

Responding to these challenges in imagining futures of decolonization and freedom, Indigenous futurisms and Afrofuturisms contest racialized temporalities but also offer a powerful medium for representing present possibilities beyond those available within dominant narratives and formations. Lisa Yaszek suggests, "Afrofuturism is not just about reclaiming the history of the past, but about reclaiming the history of the future."[175] In this sense, it is less about the future per se—what actually lies beyond the present—than the patterns by which people conceptualize what is possible.[176] In the introduction to *Walking the Clouds*, her collection of Indigenous futurist writing, Grace L. Dillon suggests, "It is almost commonplace to think that the Native Apocalypse, if contemplated seriously, has already taken place. Many forms of Indigenous futurisms posit the possibility of an optimistic future by imagining a reversal of circumstances, where Natives win or at least are centered in the narrative," but that future itself arises out of a reconceptualization of the trajectories flowing from the past: "It might go without saying that all forms of Indigenous futurisms are narratives of *biskaabiiyang*, an Anishnaabemowin word connoting the process of 'returning to ourselves,' which involves discovering how personally one is affected by colonization, discarding the emotional and psychological baggage carried from its impact, and recovering ancestral traditions in order to adapt in our post-Native Apocalypse world."[177] To turn toward the future in this case entails "returning" to possibilities for being and becoming that have been disowned, disparaged, deferred, or dismissed in the present due to the imperatives and impositions of colonization. Thus, rather than approaching such speculative imaginaries as inherently pointed toward what's yet-to-be, we might understand them as disrupting processes of reification through which trajectories of racial and colonial violence continue to be materialized. In *Freedom Dreams*, Robin D. G. Kelley notes, "[T]oo often our standards for evaluating social movements pivot around whether or not they 'succeeded' in realizing their visions rather than on the merits or power of the visions themselves," adding, "[I]t is precisely these alternative visions and dreams that inspire new generations to continue to struggle for change."[178] As with Dillon's discussion of *biskaabiiyang*, the kind of vision Kelley addresses is not so much *of the future* as one that does not conform to dominant orientations in the present. The speculative power of such visioning lies less in reaching beyond the current moment than in harnessing intellectual and imaginative resources that provide an *alternative* to the normalization of antiblack and settler colonial formations as the self-evident structure of the present out of which the future inevitably will flow.

This refusal of forms of institutionalized continuity—the mechanisms of stabilization through which current modes of social order and oppression are projected as the inevitable basis for future life—has been theorized as the eruption of utopian thought and energies. José Esteban Muñoz suggests that "hope is spawned of a critical investment in utopia." He juxtaposes the advent and articulation of such possibilities with "straight time," which "tells us there is no future but the here and now of our everyday life" extending endlessly forward, but the force of the utopian does not arise from something other than ordinary experience, instead it "is an impulse that we see in everyday life."[179] Furthermore, in *Archaeologies of the Future*, Frederic Jameson describes the utopian impulse as the form taken by "disruption" of the notion "that there is no alternative to the system." Characterizing that disjunction with existing institutional and ideological structures as a "break" that creates an "ability to imagine a different future,"[180] Jameson presents it as a negation, one that offers a "representational meditation on radical difference," and Muñoz describes utopian potentials as arising from and bearing within themselves a "radical negativity" that "becomes the resource" for alternative conceptions of what is and could be.[181] Although these accounts might be taken as describing the utopian as a break *with* the present, they perhaps more fruitfully could be read as pointing toward a break *in* the present, opening onto the radical difference of minoritized and subjugated knowledges. In negating the dynamics of dominant accounts of reality (how the world supposedly is and how it, inevitably, must continue to be), those forms of feeling and narration that Jameson and Muñoz name as utopian, and that also might be seen as a kind of speculation, emerge from quotidian principles and practices. Understanding them as part of an alternative "history of the future" or a process of "returning to ourselves" approaches the disruption they generate as an expression of existing oppositional orientations (or, in Raymond Williams's terms, structures of feeling) that are affected by dominant frameworks but irreducible to them, creating the sense of a break when viewed from the perspective of the tendencies and momentum of *straight time*. The negative force of the utopian bears within it an implicit insistence on the ongoing existence as well as legitimacy of other ways of being and becoming than those materialized as the self-evident basis for everyday modes of oppression.

If Afrofuturist and Indigenous futurist narratives can be interpreted as enacting forms of utopian negation in and for the present, how do we conceptualize the function of the future setting in them? If speculation ultimately is about what gets to count as real, how does turning to what *might be* facilitate and frame the struggle over what *is* and *was*, and more specifically, how could narratives of the not-yet enable negotiation between Black and Native articulations of the past and present? Perhaps more than any other author of futurist fiction, Samuel Delany has produced a rich body of criticism in which he theorizes such fiction's character and aims. In *The Jewel-Hinged Jaw*, he suggests that science fiction is marked by "a distinct level of subjunctivity," noting, "*Events that have not happened* are very different from the fictional events that *could have happened*."[182] As a grammatical mood, the subjunctive speaks of actions, feelings, desires that have a qualified relation to the indicative. If the latter refers to what is, the subjunctive comprises what might be, what should be, what one wishes were the case, and in this way, it marks a mediated and complex relation to the real. Or, put another way, levels of subjunctivity convey less a sense of unreality than the various ways what's described does not conform to existing grammars of facticity, norms of *being*. In this vein, the futuristic as a mode stretches the sense of the real. We can think about the futuristic orientation of science fiction as enacting and emphasizing an intentionally disjunctive relationship with dominant understandings of the world as it is. As Delany argues in *Starboard Wine*, "Science fiction poises in a tense, dialogic, agonistic relation to the given."[183] Here, *the given* refers not simply to present circumstances but also to social arrangements that are treated as self-evident (including attributions of Black backwardness and Indigenous disappearance). The power of the narrative move to the future, then, lies in leveraging accepted notions of what is actual and highlighting the processes through which such notions are (re)materialized in the world. Delany observes, "Science fiction is not 'about the future.' Science fiction *is in dialogue with the present*. We SF writers often say that science fiction prepares people to think about the real future—but that's because it relates to the real present in the particular way it does." Earlier, he stresses the need to distinguish "between the science-fictional world and the real world: for those differences are precisely what constitutes the tales' science-fictional aspect."[184] The fact that the setting is in the future marks the narrative as decidedly not determined by the practices and principles that govern conventional ideas of what exists now or is immediately possible (to the extent the latter is thought simply to unfold from the present), and its futuristic orientation enables the story to inhabit a tense and agonistic relation to what is taken to be "the real world" of the present.

While at times Delany speaks about science fiction as if its primary goal is to offer alternative horizons toward which people might move, "an image of tomorrow" or an "impetus for . . . human progress," he most forcefully theorizes the work of futurist narrative as a vehicle through which to pluralize the potentials of the present. He suggests that science fiction "uses the future as a narrative convention to present significant distortions of the present."[185] However, those distortions are less articulations of something utterly new that breaks with things as they are than a means of raising questions about the ability of particular ways of knowing to grasp extant forms of being and becoming in the world. Describing his own writerly practice, Delany notes, "What I, as an SF writer, do continually is to take *a real relationship* I have known or seen *that I also know is, collectively, unbelievable* and try to present it believably," "relight[ing] the relationship so that it becomes visible to those to whom it would have been 'unbelievable.'"[186] Narrative invocations of the future serve as a means of dislocating readers from their habituated frames of reference—within which certain formations and relations in the present would appear to be *unbelievable*—in order to turn their attention toward possibilities for being and becoming that otherwise would not be granted recognition as real (that do not appear as *given*). However, the goal is not to provide a more representationally adequate account of the world, one that would seek to capture what has not been properly acknowledged in dominant accounts. Delany insists that "science fiction does not try to represent the world"; rather, it engages in a process of "redescription"—altering the background against which one understands things and relations in the world.[187] The "science-fictional aspect" of such narratives lies in the ways they distort readers' sense of the real.

Drawing on the subjunctivity of the future enables these texts to challenge the principles and perceptions through which readers usually would engage in everyday sense making, but rather than trying to institute a new, more expansive sense of "the real world," such futurisms proliferate potentials for seeing differently, for having one's orientation shifted.[188] As Delany notes, "In science fiction the world of the story is not a given, but rather a construct that changes from story to story." Science fiction, therefore, draws attention to the process of such construction, the multiplicity of ways in which both *a* world and *the* world can be and are (re)made. This kind of speculation contests the notion of *the given* by holding open what Delany describes as "the concept of value plurality."[189] Routing redescription through the future draws on its sense as the not-already-known to open possibilities for engaging other accounts of the real, while simultaneously refusing to generate a supposedly more encompassing and putatively accurate picture of the present. The goal of valuing multiplicity is aided by futurism's refusal to try to stabilize the speculative/the subjunctive into a singular explanation of what is.

Interpreted in this way, Afrofuturisms and Indigenous futurisms work to destabilize the normalization of racializing and colonial frameworks by offering alternative accounts of how the world is and could be constructed. Among the ways they do so include contesting the logics of racial typology (chapter 2), mapping the carceral dynamics immanent in modes of data aggregation (chapter 3), suggesting the situatedness of all life and the necessary relation between humans and the nonhuman world (chapter 3), and displacing the nation-state in favor of other historical and ongoing forms of collective territoriality (chapter 4). These futurist texts forgo their claim to "the real world" in order to open rhetorical and imaginative space in which to challenge the obviousness of the given. In doing so, they illustrate and enact processes of (re)orientation without presenting them as simply a description of what is/was. The speculative form of Afrofuturist and Indigenous futurist fiction stages minoritarian and subjugated knowledges by disorienting readers from habituated perspectives, and that process of disorientation also enacts an ethos of multiplicity and openness to alternative framings (or constructions). Ahmed suggests, "When we are orientated, we might not even notice that we are orientated: we might not even think 'to think' about this point. When we experience disorientation, we might notice orientation as something we do not have," further noting that "[b]ecoming reoriented . . ." involves the disorientation of encountering the world differently."[190] The forms of futurist redescription, distortion, and antagonism Delany describes draw on that which is not (yet) real—such as extraterrestrial contact/invasion (chapter 2), genocidal robot uprisings (chapter 3), or human emigration to other planets (chapter 4)—to challenge normative orientations and to offer ways of encountering the world differently. The disorientation created by these narrative devices opens the potential for a reorientation that brings into the foreground past and current forms of institutionalized violence (pathologization of blackness, mass incarceration, de facto urban apartheid, expropriation of Indigenous lands, commodification of Native lifeways), as well as possibilities for alternative sociopolitical arrangements (transnational Black mobilities, collective Black landedness, expanded conceptions of human and nonhuman relations, Indigenous self-determination beyond settler legal regimes). In this vein, Greg Tate observes that science fiction narrative "devices reiterate the condition of being black in American culture. Black people live the estrangement that science fiction writers imagine," and Grace Dillon suggests that science fiction narratives about Native survivance "are about persistence, adaptation, and flourishing" in contrast to "creeds of isolation and victimhood, the apprehension of hopeless, helpless entitlement to an extirpated past."[191] Futurist fiction's ability to offer an alternative vision of the believable—including attending to the analyses offered by oppositional movements—depends, though, on taking part in a narrative mode that is explicitly not "the real world."

While speculative redescription might be said to aim for a new real (one that engages with minoritarian knowledges and critique), it relies on a medium that necessarily defers the referential realness of the representations generated through it. In this way, the subjunctivity of speculative fiction helps us see the conceptual and political frames it employs *as frames* while it also enacts an ethics of equivocation at the level of form. In the previous sections, I've addressed how varied understandings of the concepts of *sovereignty* and *settler* can foreclose or displace each other and how efforts to avoid or sublate such tensions through encompassing structural modeling often end up recreating the same problems. Entering into science fiction's subjunctivity creates a conditional connection to the real that suspends the exclusivity so often claimed in critical and political accounts. Instead of insisting on a particular vision of what *is*—recalling de la Cadena, a specific set of "onto-epistemic terms"—speculation as a mode opens the potential for there to be multiple "ways of making worlds," all of which are real but not all of which can be engaged when each presents itself as *the real*.[192] Such speculative imaginings hold open a space for the kinds of difference that Lorde addresses: that varied struggles may have disparate ways of interpreting and perceiving the world that can render each other invisible. The speculative, then, appears here less as a genre than a mode of relation, one that opens the potential for acknowledging a plurality of legitimate yet nonidentical truth claims—none of which should be taken as singularly foundational. Conversely, attending to the ways Afrofuturist and Indigenous futurist narratives redescribe the world foregrounds, in de la Cadena's terms, the kinds of *worldings* they perform—the backgrounds, principles, and forms of "we"-ness from which they emerge and that they then employ. Tracing the contours and dynamics of such Black and Indigenous worldings enables one to see how they open onto each other and (mis)translate each other, thereby also suggesting the ways they remain opaque to each other.[193] In other words, Black and Indigenous futurisms both engage in a project of challenging dominant conceptions of the real, offering their own accounts and analyses of what *is* through narrative stagings of what *might be*, but such futurisms employ existing frames of reference that are oriented by divergent histories of struggle and collective political aspiration.

Rather than presenting speculative fiction as a site for reconciling Black and Indigenous imaginaries, I am suggesting that the speculative *as a mode* allows us to see such frames of reference at work while simultaneously seeing them as nonidentical ways of worlding that do not need to be resolved in a single, structural sense of *the given*. Freed from the imperative to declare one political imaginary or structural framework as expressive of the singular truth of "the real world," speculative fiction offers conceptual resources for marking tensions and the dynamics of translation among movements.[194] The speculative, then, suggests an ethos, or an ethics, of hesitation in the drive to analytical and explanatory closure, an openness to others' potential *redescriptions* and the disorientations they enact but without the need for it all to be combined in a single story or structure. More than merely suggesting that there are other possible ways of understanding past and present circumstances, speculation can engender a critical reflexivity that attends to how operating within a particular frame of reference may shape ways of mapping extant forms of domination and of envisioning what a more just future entails. Investigating how futurist narratives seek to (re)orient readers within Black and Native histories and political imaginaries allows for charting the different problem-spaces out of which they emerge and to which they respond. Such analysis can also attend to the equivocations that occur when issues and formations related to one movement/struggle are engaged within the problem-space of the other. Thus, while I am suggesting that the speculative as a mode opens intellectual, political, and ethical possibilities for thinking and valuing the differences among Black and Indigenous political imaginaries, the possibilities of the speculative as a mode do not mean that any given (set of) text(s) of speculative fiction can resolve the tensions between those movements or necessarily offer a way through or beyond such tensions. Instead, futurist texts when engaged as forms of speculation in this way help reveal the existence and contours of such tensions, and in doing so, they open possibilities for exploring forms of mutual engagement, translation, and accountability that do not require a shared set of terms or horizons.

In turning to futurist fiction, and more broadly to speculation as an intellectual and political modality, my aim is to increase the potential for thinking how Black and Indigenous movements may be oriented differently in ways that cannot and should not be reduced to each other or imagined as inherently triangulable into some third model. If it were even possible to do so, does seeking to merge all frames of reference into a systemic account actually address the significant differences among social movements and struggles—their varied tendencies and horizons? If, in Lorde's terms quoted earlier, "difference must be not merely tolerated," how might embracing the nonequivalence between Indigenous and Black political imaginaries (as well as among them) open up possibilities for relation not predicated on an implicitly assimilatory impulse to unify varied perspectives into a single structural account(ing)? Rather than trying to resolve disjunctions (such as over the meanings and implications of sovereignty, nationhood, and belonging) by articulating an encompassing structural framework, this approach works to trace how disparate backgrounds, framings, and trajectories give rise to accounts that are potentially equally real although nonidentical. Speculative hesitation facilitates attention to the ways forms of conceptual and perceptual orientation affect processes of understanding and engagement—shaping how persons, peoples, historical patterns, and social formations emerge into view and become meaningful from within nonidentical frames of reference. Foregrounding the dynamics of such relation across difference less defers "the real world" (or the prospects of our knowing it) than seeks to pluralize it, pointing to possibilities for being disoriented in encounters with others' articulations, experiences, and phenomenologies. Such disorientation also would entail coming to understand how the oppressed within one frame can be the oppressor within another, without those frames needing to be fused. Solidarity, then, involves being accountable to how one's own position and actions might be understood within another movement's (re)description of what is, was, and might be. If there is no view except from within a particular frame of reference, increasing the capacity for disorientation—for acknowledging the potential disparity among such frames—opens possibilities for intersectional analysis, solidarity, and engagement that do not a priori require the production of unity. Recognizing that political struggles will vary from each other, including in their assessments of domination and projections of desirable futurity, can validate them in their mutual opacity, facilitating forms of negotiation and transformation predicated on complex, uneven, open-ended, and necessarily unresolved efforts to listen for difference.

2

FUNGIBLE BECOMING

Black bodies have functioned within dominant U.S. imaginaries as a medium of alchemical transfiguration and an object of phobic terror. This double valence has to do with the ways blackness as a process of social inscription converts human beings into fungible potentiality—not simply objects for ownership and sale as chattel but as the vehicle for manifesting economies, geographies, and modes of personhood for whom others will serve as the subject. As Tiffany King suggests, "[T]he concept of fungibility denotes and connotes pure flux, process, and potential," adding, "Blackness is a form of malleable potential and a state of change in the 'socio-political order' of the New World" in that "Black fungible bodies have unlimited figurative and metaphoric value."[1] To be understood as fungible means being seen as an instrument in the service of someone else's worlding, in which Black bodies appear as tools through which, for example, to enact desired transformations of raw materials and the environment (via Black labor), to test corporeal capacities (as in various kinds of medical experimentation), and to figure normative conceptions of the human (with blackness as a contrasting expression of degeneration, deviance, pathology, nonbeing). In order for blackness to serve as a nexus through which to generate such potentials for non-black (largely white) being and becoming, it also needs to be understood as discrete, as a quality, identity, genealogy whose limits can be mapped such that those who belong to the category can be known and distinguished from those who do not. The boundless latency of fungibility, then, is made possible by the policing of racial order through the management of mixture, including long-standing criminalization of what in the wake of the Civil War comes to be called *miscegenation*. The Black body historically has been constructed as a locus of generative plasticity and degraded immanence, as a technology employable by those who fully occupy personhood—itself envisioned as needing to be insulated from blackness as a kind of contagion. In this way, one might understand blackness less as a determinate racial identity, something like a bloodline of uninterrupted lineage directly traceable to some continental landmass (as in "of African descent"), than as an ongoing process in which persons not deemed persons either are put at the service of those positioned as full social subjects or cast as dangerous surplus to be contained, captured, and held.

Racial mixture, then, does not undo this dynamic. If guarding against miscegenation operates as a way of maintaining the color line, the corollary—that crossing that line eliminates it—does not necessarily follow. In the wake of the dismantling in the 1950s and 1960s of the legalized apartheid of segregation, the image of the interracial couple emerges as an avatar of the potential for erasing the legacy of prior official commitments to racial separation and subordination. Since Reconstruction, much of the resistance to Black integration, access, and enfranchisement at all levels had been presented and justified in terms of the dangers of cross-racial intimacy.[2] In 1967, the Supreme Court decision in *Loving v. Virginia* struck down states' efforts to criminalize interracial marriage, eliminating one of the last explicit legal mechanisms for policing and regulating racial difference.[3] However, a vision of mixture does not mean the absence of racial difference, instead actually depending on the ongoing production of such difference in order to register the supposedly transcendent, liberatory crossing of the color line in interracial union. As Jared Sexton argues, "[F]reedom from the one-drop rule is construed artfully . . . as freedom from the exigencies of being identified, or identifying oneself, with racial blackness," and he later observes, "There can be no claim to 'the multiracial experience' without the attendant affirmation of racial purity," such that "there is no *interracial* sexual relationship that does not resurrect the same racial frontier it purports to transgress or transcend."[4] Thus, challenging antiblackness less entails creating hybrid genealogies than undoing extant racializing conceptions of the human. As Tavia Nyong'o suggests, "American national fantasy . . . does not so much dismiss as *defer* racial hybridity, endowing it with the peculiar privilege and power of a horizon, one at which we never quite arrive," further wondering whether "the event of miscegenation" continually serves as little more than "a prelude to a recursive and renascent racialization."[5] Such racialization redraws the frontier between those who are autonomous persons and those who are fungible objects. The Black body, then, continues to signify in terms of its excess(iveness), its supplementarity, its indexing of a potential to be harnessed by others (and, thus, also a threat to be contained or disposed of)—what might be termed its *fleshliness*.[6]

However, what might it mean to turn toward a conception of embodiment as malleability, to forgo the claim to normative personhood in favor of embracing the possibilities of blackness as a means of moving beyond propertied, and inherently racializing, modes of selfhood? As Alexander Weheliye observes, "[T]he benefits accrued through the juridical acknowledgment of racialized subjects as fully human often exacts a steep entry price, because inclusion hinges on accepting the codification of personhood as property, which is, in turn, based on the comparative distinction between groups."[7] In displacing such distinction, refusing the drive to be(come) Man (in Sylvia Wynter's terms, discussed in chapter 1), what other kinds of being and becoming emerge in the wake of slavery's afterlives?[8]

Octavia Butler's *Xenogenesis* trilogy explores such possibilities for what it terms "difference."[9] The novels envision the introduction of humanity to alien presence and governance, including profound reorganizations of social life. The extraterrestrials, called Oankali, arrive on Earth after a nuclear holocaust that results from the explosion of Cold War tensions. They preserve the surviving humans in suspended animation, and after 250 years, they decide that one of the people they've awakened—an African American woman named Lilith—will guide and train other humans to become the nucleus of new human-Oankali settlements on an Earth restored/remade through Oankali intervention. However, humans will not be allowed to have children on their own and are physically altered so that they cannot do so. Instead, they will procreate through Oankali modes of kinship and reproduction, which involve gene-mixing by a third-sex entity known as an ooloi who combines genes from a human male and female and an Oankali male and female to produce a new kind of being—called a "construct."[10] While the possibilities and terrors of miscegenation can be understood as providing, in Isiah Lavender's terms, the "blackground" for scenes of human-extraterrestrial sexual encounter, *Xenogenesis*'s depiction of human-Oankali relation does not so much envision the possibility of transcending racial identity in the emergence of a new mixed species-being as open possibilities for thinking about modes of embodiment and interdependence that displace existing, institutionalized ways of defining and calculating privatized, biologized racial being.

The scenes and drama of interspecies eroticism and reproduction around which the novels are organized, then, might be approached as opening onto *amalgamation* rather than hybridity. Nyong'o highlights the ways the concept of amalgamation encompasses forms of "anomaly that cannot be accurately reproduced in terms of mixedness or halfness," engendering itineraries of transformation that cannot easily be collected into the retrospectively linear unfolding of "heritage." Nyong'o traces the ways that the concept of "amalgamation" precedes and exceeds that of miscegenation, including the implicit "dream of a transracial future" that inhabits the latter, illustrating that "amalgamation was not one but an ensemble of metaphors. Amalgamation can describe a process of *mixing*, one of *extracting*, or one of *transforming*. The idea of mixture or blend is the most familiar to us."[11] The concept marks a transgression of racial boundaries but not a crossing that transcends such boundaries on the way to inclusion in the human—a move that would just resituate lines of racial demarcation without eliminating them. Rather, the novels inhabit the transformative powers attributed to blackness by removing the exploitative and expropriative distinction between Black being and proper personhood (even as Butler continues to raise questions about the politics of Oankali intervention). As against the ideal of propertied selfhood, Butler imagines potentials for socioenvironmental plasticity that displace the normative ideal of self-possession and bodily autonomy, highlighting modes of fleshliness that are anomalous with respect to dominant Euro-American notions of the human.[12] With respect to the violence of slavery and its aftermath, Weheliye observes that "the flesh is not an abject zone of exclusion that culminates in death but an alternate instantiation of humanity that does not rest on the mirage of western Man as the mirror image of human life as such," and while such potentials arise out of "systemic political violence moored in the law and beyond," they also "produce a surplus, a line of flight."[13] In depicting Oankali "difference," the trilogy implicitly invokes the fungibility attributed to blackness as part of ongoing histories of antiblack subjection—especially in terms of Black reproduction and motherhood—in ways that refigure such malleability as a way beyond dominant conceptions of the human. If, as Sexton argues, contemporary figurations of racialized being must engage with "the permanent seizure of the body essential to enslavement," attending to the fields of force to which the "captive body" is subjected,[14] Butler's trilogy can be understood as oriented around past and present dynamics of racial embodiment and what might be entailed in envisioning humanness in other terms. *Xenogenesis*, then, operates in "a tense, dialogic, agonistic relation to the given" with respect to the dynamics of antiblackness.[15] In its speculative redescription of extant political economies of racialization, the novels offer an antiracist account that highlights humanness-in-common across racial lines (in the face of relation with extraterrestrials), as well as suggesting forms of being, becoming, and relation that exceed the terms of existing modes of racialized personhood.

However, due to its speculative mode—the fact that it does not present itself as offering a credible account of what is or was—the trilogy also offers insight into the character and limits of amalgamation or enfleshment as a conceptual framework.[16] From within this framing, placemaking and forms of collective identity come to appear as reactionary investments in forms of propertied being and the violence it engenders. Nyong'o observes, "A critical approach to race should encompass both the history of racial ideas and the forms of historicity and temporality embedded in those ideas and practices."[17] Yet, what about the forms of *territoriality* at play in racializing and antiracist imaginings? Butler's amalgamationist vision of alternative possibilities for selfhood and social relation consistently casts mobility as a means of evading the kinds of endemic violence that attend modes of racialization. If humans in the trilogy remain bound by a genetic "contradiction" that fuses intelligence to a drive toward (racial) hierarchy, one of the principal expressions of such ingrained tendencies is the creation of closed geopolitical units, largely villages in the novel, whose boundaries are jealously defended and that serve as fortified spaces from which assaults on other villages can be launched. By contrast, Oankalis continually move from planet to planet, settling only long enough to cultivate relations with new species before returning to journeying among the stars. The undoing of long-standing geographies of inhabitance and of collective attachments to place seems to open the possibility for modes of sociality that do not depend on the violent inscription of identity boundaries—interpersonal, political, or environmental. However, when seeking to provide a social content for possibilities of protean enfleshment, Butler invokes qualities and modes of familial and environmental relation that conventionally and ethnologically have been used to characterize Indigenous peoples in the Americas, even as those qualities are dissociated from those peoples and indigeneity as such. In the process, the signs of indigeneity are translated as the potential for altered ways of experiencing and enacting embodiment.

Conversely, amid the novels' embrace of Oankali "difference," they also explore human resistance to Oankali-managed transformation. The promise of a kind of aracial plasticity (in terms of corporeal form, relations with others, and inhabitance of one's environment) arrives, but without human consent, and while the texts convey a deep suspicion of the desire to preserve human collective identity, they do suggest a human right to territorial sovereignty and self-determination in the face of an invasion by alien settlers. The engagement with such Indigenously inflected concepts and struggles marks a process of equivocation, in which the trilogy encounters, in Marisol de la Cadena's words, a discrepant set of "onto-epistemic formations."[18] Yet even while Butler offers a robust discussion of peoplehood, territoriality, and self-governance, they gain meaning against the background of the politics of (Black) racial embodiment. In being transposed into a discrepant problem-space, commitments to collective landedness and political autonomy appear as if they were attachments to forms of racial corporeality and associated regimes of property. By highlighting alternative means of conceptualizing embodiment and relations with other beings and one's environment, Butler foregrounds Oankali *difference* from dominant notions of personhood in ways that emphasize a shared humanity but that also tend to bracket investigation of differences among *peoples*, their lifeworlds, and their visions for themselves. In this way, the trilogy illustrates how, from within a conceptual and political framework centered on questions of fleshliness, geographies of Indigenous peoplehood seem like an intransigent identification with dominant Euro-American notions of the human.

Enfleshment and Indigenous Potentials

Oankali-human interactions diverge from the dominant notions of personhood based on self-possession that animate the dynamics of racialization in the United States. As many scholars have observed, the (re)production of racial difference often operates through charges that nonwhites have failed to be properly delineated and autonomous subjects, while dominant institutions and practices simultaneously make such bodies more vulnerable by exposing them to routine, repeated, extensive, and invasive violence. As Rosi Braidotti suggests, "The human is a normative convention, which does not make it inherently negative, just highly regulatory and hence instrumental to practices of exclusion and discrimination. . . . It functions by transposing a specific mode of being human into a generalized standard."[19] Within this frame, arguing for inclusion within the human, much like the hybrid imaginary of miscegenation, simply regenerates the invidious modes of racial designation and denigration one would seek to challenge.[20] Not only does personhood gain meaning through its distinction from the non-owning, violable state of (possessable) flesh, but this way of envisioning personhood effaces the relational dynamics of violence through which such selfhood continually is (re)constituted. In *Xenogenesis*, though, the difference between the body and the flesh takes the form of the distinction between human and aliens, with Oankalis seeking to inculcate humans into more capacious and less proprietary and insulating modes of relation. Yet while the novels clearly invoke the history of enslavement in an amalgamationist vein, qualities associated with Indigenous peoples appear as the means of giving content to this nonhierarchical vision of fleshly potential.

The process of capturing humans, holding them under conditions dictated by the Oankali, seeking to foreclose the futurity of autonomous human communities by incorporating them into Oankali sociality, and conscripting humans in literally reproducing that sociality all evoke histories of New World slavery, particularly given Lilith's blackness.[21] Human characters continually refer to relations with the Oankali in terms of bondage and servitude. One of Lilith's earliest thoughts in *Dawn*, in response to finding a "long scar on her abdomen," is, "She did not own herself any longer. Even her flesh could be cut and stitched without her consent or knowledge."[22] While this laceration turns out to be due to Oankali surgery to treat emergent cancer of which Lilith was unaware, when assessing the veracity of what she's been told, she later thinks, "Why should they bother to lie? They owned the Earth and all that was left of the human species" (59). This sentiment is repeated at various points throughout the trilogy. In the next book, *Adulthood Rites*, readers learn that "resisters," those humans who have been returned to the Earth but have fled from Oankali villages to create their own nonreproducing settlements, say of Nikanj, the ooloi to whom Lilith becomes mated, that it "sold" humanity to the Oankali (298).[23] Toward the beginning of the final novel, *Imago*, fifty years after Lilith's son Akin (the first male construct child born on Earth) has secured the right of those humans who desire separation from the Oankali to be given back their full reproductive capacities and settled in their own colony on Mars (a development that occupies much of the plot of *Adulthood Rites* and that I discuss further later in the chapter), one of the women seeking emigration to Mars summarizes the promise of such separation as, "We'll be free—us, our children, their children" (531). In describing an isolated human community that somehow retains the potential for non–Oankali-assisted reproduction, one of its members, Jesusa, encounters Lilith's child Jodahs (the first-person protagonist of *Imago* and the first construct ooloi) and says of the village, "They own themselves. They don't belong to you" (637). These moments all suggest an understanding of Oankali-human relation as one of enchattelment, in which control over human habitats, bodily dispositions, and interpersonal attachments (including familial connections) constitutes a generationally iterative form of *ownership* and in which humans, therefore, function as Oankali property.

Moreover, the fact that Lilith will be the first to give birth to a "construct" child is represented as something of a monstrous act, in ways that resonate with long-standing ways of portraying Black maternity in the United States.[24] Éva Federmayer suggests that the "trade" with the Oankali "breeds Oankali-Human mutants," adding that the process of Oankali-controlled reproduction cannot help but "invoke nightmarish associations of slavery for the black protagonist."[25] While not serving as exploited labor, humanity within these formulations appears as an extension of Oankali will in ways that resonate with the centrality of Black fungibility in defining the dynamics and legacies of enslavement. As King argues, "[T]he Black female body as a bodily formation comes into existence in order to make plantation space, populate the plantation space with workers and commodities and order the plantation as a non-Native realm of existence. Black female slave bodies are the embodiment, both discursively and materially, of settler colonial space making units."[26] In this vein, Lilith's blackness speaks directly to her role in enabling Oankali conquest of the Earth, reiterating the capacitating role of blackness in the historical process of transforming the Americas into expropriable terra nullius through the remaking of the land in ways that facilitate settler occupation.

The assessment of Oankali rule as enslavement, though, does not quite capture the ways the novels portray the character and implications of the extraterrestrials' relations with humans. In response to charges that humans are being held as slaves, the Oankali insist that not only do they not aim to do so but that they never have done so, to any species. When the Oankali with whom Lilith initially engages (Jdahya) starts to discuss the fact that Oankali means "Traders," Lilith asks,

> "What do you trade?"
> "Ourselves."
> "You mean . . . each other? Slaves?"
> "No. We've never done that." (24, ellipsis in original)

Later, Lilith insists to Nikanj's ooloi parent (Kahguyaht), "You could kill us. You could make mules of our children," and it replies, "There was no life at all on your Earth when our ancestors left our original homeworld, and in all that time, we've never done such a thing" (55). Butler offers no reason to suspect that the Oankali are lying, and their utter disavowal of slavery suggests that they do not conceptualize humans as chattel. As readers see in the second and third books, once they have returned to Earth many humans become resisters, fleeing from direct Oankali oversight in order to set up communities of their own that are left undisturbed except in cases where violence has been committed against Oankalis or their construct children.[27]

Rather than making alien species (including humans) into commodities, servants, or vehicles for enacting conquest-enabling transformation, Oankali seek relations with other species so as to stimulate and further catalyze an ongoing process of transition through which Oankalis themselves continually are remade. In addition to indicating that they embarked on this interstellar "trade" billions of years ago, Jdahya explains that trading themselves means that the Oankali seek to reorder their own genetic makeup through contact with new life-forms: "We do what you would call genetic engineering. . . . We do it naturally. We *must* do it. It renews us, enables us to survive as an evolving species instead of specializing ourselves into extinction or stagnation," adding, "We acquire new life—seek it, investigate it, manipulate it, sort it, use it. We carry the drive to do this in a minuscule cell within a cell—a tiny organelle within every cell of our bodies" (40–41). Moreover, in each encounter with a new planet/species, Oankali split into three groups: one that moves onto the planet in question and will eventually return to traveling through space (in search of new species), one that combines with life from that new world but remains on an Oankali ship, and one that removes to its own ship without genetically interacting with the species from that planet. In the case of Earth, these three, respectively, are Dinso, Toaht, and Akjai (35). Such divisions indicate that the Oankali less seek unity, even a hybridized one, than a proliferation of potentials. As Naomi Jacobs suggests, Butler "posits an alien race whose very nature is premised upon metamorphosis and boundary-crossing by way of its practice of gene-trading. The Oankali's goal is not to preserve an essential species identity, but always to be transforming themselves into something else," later adding, "It is in their nature to be eternally changing their nature. Their hunger for the new is one characteristic that persists through each trade." As opposed to something like the teleology of miscegenation, a putative crossing that retrospectively posits and reinvests in the coherence of the discrete racial types undergoing mixture, Oankali-initiated modes of amalgamation engender ongoing processes for producing anomaly, through which the notion of a stable (racial) norm itself is travestied and displaced.[28]

In the *Xenogenesis* trilogy, Oankali trade does not so much subordinate humans by distinguishing them from a privileged Oankali bodily norm as enfold humanity within their own open-ended itineraries of becoming, which might be characterized as an effort to open human embodiment to alien fleshliness. Saidiya Hartman argues that "the self-possessed subject with his inalienable attributes is quite unthinkable or unimaginable in th[e] case" of chattel slavery and its aftermaths for persons of African descent. She further observes, "The longstanding and intimate affiliation of liberty and bondage made it impossible to envision freedom independent of constraint or personhood and autonomy separate from the sanctity of property and proprietorial notions of the self. Moreover, since the dominion and domination of slavery were fundamentally defined by black subjection, race appositely framed questions of sovereignty, right, and power."[29] To be Black, then, is to occupy a conditional relation to the human as such, to be admitted only ever in ways that are curtailed, surveilled, disciplined, and constantly subject to shifting and expansive spheres of white discretion. Reciprocally, the privileges of personhood that accrue to whiteness, of insulated and agential self-ownership, depend on contradistinction from ongoing processes of enfleshment by which fully independent selfhood perpetually is deferred for Black populations. The putative equality promised by the law through and in the wake of emancipation, then, functions less as a horizon of remediation for enchattelment than a racialized reduplication of differential access to the modes of self-making and self-fortification (through the legal alchemies of property) at play in slavery itself.[30] However, the Oankalis neither seek to "free" humans into self-possession nor to claim it for themselves, instead emphasizing the possibilities for troubling lines of distinction among bodies, species, and environments.

When they first confront the Oankali, Lilith and other humans are appalled. In her first fully conscious interaction with Jdahya, Lilith "did not want to be any closer to him . . . [S]he was certain it was his alienness, his difference, his literal unearthliness" (13), and she later describes her sensations as "a true xenophobia" (23). The novels repeatedly portray this terror as a human fear of "difference." In this vein, Jeffrey Tucker makes note of "the resisters' racist attitudes towards the Oankali," and Gabrielle Schwab suggests that the resisters "simply transfer the racism that generated their histories of colonialism, slavery, war, and genocide onto the Oankali."[31] However, rather than affirming this *xenophobic* impulse, Butler shows Lilith reaching an alternative set of conclusions about the character and meaning of Oankali modes of relation. Toward the beginning of *Adulthood Rites*, Tino, a human who has left one of the larger resister villages and ends up choosing to mate with Lilith and Nikanj and to join their family, insists that the people who mate with Oankalis are no more than "their clay," being molded and *built* to fit Oankali molds. In response, Lilith notes, "They change us and we change them. . . . I don't like what they're doing, and I've never made any secret of it. But they're in this with us. When the ships leave, they're stuck here. And with their own biology driving them, they can't not blend with us. But some of what makes us Human will survive, just as some of what makes them Oankali will survive" (282). Later in the novel, in a passage often cited by critics, Akin recalls Lilith telling him, "Human beings fear difference. . . . Oankali crave difference. Humans persecute their different ones, yet they need them to give themselves definition and status. Oankali seek difference and collect it. They need it to keep themselves from stagnation and overspecialization. . . . When you feel a conflict, try to go to the Oankali way. Embrace difference" (329).[32] In these moments, the novels describe human self-understanding as a *persecution* and policing of "difference" in order to establish "definition and status." Conversely, the novels describe Oankalis in ways that present them as "radical subjects-in-process," portraying the Oankali as "propagators of diversity."[33] The very malleability of their bodies—both in preparing for trade (at several points, Oankali characters note that in being Dinso they have been "bred" to interact with humans) and in its conduct—implies the absence of the kinds of strict corporeal boundaries usually taken as delimiting dominant Euro-American conceptions of personhood. Furthermore, as Lilith suggests, Oankalis are "in this with" humans, both changing and changed by the encounter in ways that not only are acknowledged by the Oankalis but actively desired.

However, the novels' account of the malleability of Oankali corporeality, its open-ended potentials for relation and transformation, cannot be separated from histories of blackness, especially given that Lilith serves as the vehicle for extraterrestrial-human trade and is the first person impregnated through Oankali processes of reproduction. As noted earlier, such procreation requires a human male and female and an Oankali male and female whose genes are mixed by an ooloi, a third-sex being, and then gestated by the human woman. To the extent that the socio-genetic mutations and crossings enacted through interspecies amalgamation displace the isolating autonomy through which propertied selfhood achieves definition, Oankali trade, including reproduction with humans, explores what Weheliye terms the "political facets of enfleshment"[34]—collective modes of life not constrained by dominant (racialized) forms of humanness and ownership. As King suggests of conceptions of Black fungibility, "Existing outside the borders of liberal humanism's stable individual, the fungible bodyflesh is an always-unfolding space of possibility."[35] The possibilities engendered by Oankali difference and amalgamation not only resonate with extant notions of blackness, but participation in this process is unchosen. When Lilith is first informed that the "ooloi will make changes in your reproductive cells before conception and they'll control conception," so as to breed out what are characterized as humans' inborn tendencies toward hierarchy and violence, Lilith responds, "No! You'll finish what the war began," in terms of the death of the human race as such (42).[36] Even as the novels suggest the value of Oankali modes of life and challenge the comparison of the trade to enchattelment, Oankali corporeal malleabilities and porosities gain meaning within the trilogy against the background of Black subjection, particularly the role of Black motherhood. As opposed to providing the basis for normative arrangements of gender difference, family formation, and homemaking, Black motherhood has been cast as generating anomalies, deviance, and pathology while also birthing blackness as a mutable resource. Christina Sharpe argues,

> Reading together the Middle Passage, the coffle, and, I add to the argument, the birth canal, we can see how each has functioned separately and collectively over time to dis/figure Black maternity, to turn the womb into a factory producing blackness as abjection much like the slave ship's hold and the prison, and turning the birth canal into another domestic Middle Passage with Black mothers, after the end of legal hypodescent, still ushering their children into their condition; their non/status, their non/being-ness.[37]

This process of presenting Black motherhood as something constitutively beyond (hetero)normative reproduction, as C. Riley Snorton argues, positions blackness as a principal vehicle of transness, in which "captive and divided flesh functions as malleable matter for mediating and remaking sex and gender as matters of human categorization and personal definition"—"To feel black in the diaspora, then, might be a trans experience."[38] The corporeal capacities of Oankali relation and their non-heteronormative modes of social reproduction draw on, and become a way of further theorizing, Black fleshliness. In the wake of the holocaust of nuclear war, Black reproduction becomes a means of remaking the character of the human, and reciprocally, Oankali deviance from dominant understandings of humanness serve as a way of reflecting on the parahuman potentialities that circulate around and through blackness.[39]

Oankali forms of anomaly invoke these dynamics of racialization, but when the texts seek to portray Oankali sociality and forms of relation in more concrete terms, they turn to conventional ways of figuring Amerindian indigeneity.[40] The trilogy's portrayal of various aspects of Oankali life shows how their privileging of networking and permeability undoes property-based understandings of identity (individual and collective). In particular, their reciprocal relations with their environment, kinship dynamics, and processes of decision making evidence the absence of bourgeois kinds of selfhood, providing an alternative model of personhood to racialized ideals of bodily enclosure. J. Adam Johns characterizes this vision as one of "a posthuman future," and Jacobs argues that "Butler's critical dystopia suggests a resource for hope . . . in the evolution of the human toward a posthuman body, posthuman subjectivity, and posthuman form of agency."[41] However, the very qualities that for many signify *posthuman* potential—ways of getting beyond dominant Euro-American paradigms of humanness—can be seen as less a move beyond humanity than as a citation of longstanding characterizations of Indigenous peoples of the Americas.[42]

The intimacy of Oankali connections to their space of inhabitance offers perhaps the most easily recognizable allusion to indigeneity in the texts' imaginary.[43] While cast as technologically superior, such as being able to cross interstellar space and engage in extensive terraforming to make planets habitable for them, Oankalis do not rely on nonorganic materials in doing so. Rather, their ships and the various tools that they employ are themselves alive, and Oankalis develop extensive and ongoing relationships with them. At one point, Lilith asks Nikanj whether Oankalis "ever build machinery," "using metal and plastic instead of living things," to which it responds, "We do that when we have to. We . . . don't like it. There's no trade" (85), and Jdahya observes of the relationship with their ships, "There is an affinity, but it's biological—a strong, symbiotic relationship. We serve the ship's needs and it serves ours. It would die without us and we would be planetbound without it. For us, that would eventually mean death" (35). A fundamental and readily acknowledged interdependence ties Oankalis and their ships to each other, making possible intertwined processes of becoming through which various species' "needs" are satisfied *symbiotically*. Moreover, the ships also refuse to relate to beings with whom they can have no continuing "biological" relation: "You either joined with them, shared their experiences, and let them share yours, or there was no trade. And without trade, the ships ignored your existence" (435).[44] In these moments, Butler suggests the absence of a clear dividing line between Oankalis and the environments they occupy, instead suggesting an organizing reciprocity in which these various kinds of entities participate within a complex, if shifting, matrix that provides the shared and indivisible context for their continuing development and well-being.

Indigenous peoples often are expected to perform just this sort of ideal of seamless connection to "natural" surroundings in order to be intelligible as Indigenous and to argue for recognition of the legitimacy of their status and emplacements as polities. As Ronald Niezen observes, despite "how readily indigenous peoples have tended to borrow and adapt useful features of majority societies with little or no apparent disruption," non-natives "tend to perceive indigenous societies as living in perfect harmony with the natural world," and "to satisfy the public that can help them . . . [Indigenous peoples] must also be noble, strong, spiritually wise, and, above all, environmentally discreet."[45] Attributions of environmental consciousness, then, regularly substitute for engagement with the politics of Indigenous self-determination. Karen Engle notes that "states even prohibit indigenous groups from using land in a manner that goes against what the state sees as the group's purported attachment to it": "When they do not behave toward the land in the idealized manner that has come to be expected of them, these groups might cease to be considered real Indians."[46] Contemporary Indigenous identities are adjudicated against this biopolitical standard of perfect stewardship and often found wanting, leading non-Indigenous authorities and publics to deem them inauthentic or fallen; thus, "this inspection always already constitutes indigenous persons as failures of indigeneity as such."[47] Given the ways that such complete symbiosis with other beings and with one's surroundings is cast as completely incommensurable with dominant Euro-American norms, it seems somewhat unsurprising that in the trilogy these kinds of connections would be attributed to those who are utterly alien—literally extraterrestrials—as an expression and signal feature of their nonhuman fleshliness.[48]

Oankali genders and kinships further illustrate their ability to traverse the conventional boundaries of selfhood, indicating a capacity for collective belonging that exceeds bourgeois norms and that implicitly points toward conceptions of indigeneity. The forms of individuality treated as given within liberal models of governance and social life gain meaning through their differentiation from the kinds of communal being attributed to Indigenous peoples. In *The Empire of Love*, Elizabeth Povinelli seeks to capture that disjunction between the "autological subject" and "the genealogical society." The former refers "to discourses, practices, and fantasies about self-making, self-sovereignty, and the value of individual freedom associated with the Enlightenment project of contractual constitutional democracy and capitalism," engendering forms of union only through the "intimate event" of heterocouplehood, and this vision of autonomous existence depends for its coherence on being distinguished from "the genealogically determined collective," defined by its racialized image as "illiberal, tribal, customary, and ancestral[ly determined]."[49] If the novels implicitly connect Oankalis' non-heteronormative reproduction to the deviances attributed to Black motherhood, what results from Oankali procreation is not the kind of protean kinlessness that historically has attached to blackness but, instead, enduring modes of extended genealogical relation that resemble the tradition of ethnological accounts of Indigenous peoples, particularly American Indians.[50] The sense of Oankali sociality conveyed to readers emphasizes belonging to non-nuclear *families*. In fact, all Oankali names are a complex aggregation of one's parents, mates, a "kinship group name," and the division to which you belong (Dinso, Toaht, or Akjai).[51] Enmeshment within these various nested units defines one's personal identity, and in order for humans to engage with Oankalis in any sustained way, they must be incorporated into these networks. When discussing Paul Titus, a human man who has lived most of his life among the Oankali, Nikanj says of the Oankali with whom he resides, "[T]hey are his family.... They have accepted him and he has accepted them. He has no other family, but he has them," and Lilith then wonders, "What did Nikanj tell others about her? Did it talk about her family? According to her new name, she had been adopted, after all" (101).[52] Moreover, the pairing of a "brother and sister" with an ooloi is "usual in Oankali matings" (106), suggesting an even tighter weave between the family into which one is born and the family generated in adulthood. The extensive and intensive genealogical orientations of Oankali life provide a contrast to the kinds of atomization attributed to humans in the novels, helping to contour and animate the trilogy's vision of human-Oankali "difference" and the possibilities offered by amalgamation.

There is nothing like citizenship in an Oankali polity that exists separately from immersion within complex arrangements of what can only be characterized as kinship, and in this way the *Xenogenesis* trilogy draws on the legacy of ethnology, in which Indigenous modes of social organization and governance have been characterized as familial rather than properly political. Dating from at least the mid-nineteenth century, most famously in the work of Lewis Henry Morgan, this comparative framework casts non-western peoples as transgressing the categorical distinctions (specifically, those delineating monogamous union, private property, and bureaucratic administration) that are taken as defining the terms of Euro-American modernity.[53] In *Ancient Society*, perhaps Morgan's most famous and influential book, he distinguishes between a "social organization" structured around "relations [that] were purely personal" (especially in the form of clans, or "gens") and a "political organization" in which "relations were purely territorial,"[54] and he offers elaborate discussions of several kinds of deviation from the "descriptive" dynamics of the nuclear family unit into "classificatory" systems in which the natural unit of reproductive homemaking and family formation veers into somewhat otiose and extravagant configurations of relation that, from his perspective, blur and distort the terms of family as such (or, rather, evolution itself moves from such confusions and conflations toward the slimmed-down elegance of heteromarital couplehood). However, the novels displace the division between descriptive and classificatory kinship, instead partially locating Oankali alienness in the ways their more expansive genealogical formations *are* reproductive units. In addition to the tendency among Oankali to have brother-sister relationships in adult matings (although mediated by a non-related ooloi in ways that bracket the potential for incestuous impressions of erotic contact among siblings), the standard procreative unit for human-Oankali constructs, as noted earlier, consists of a human male, a human female, an Oankali male, an Oankali female, and an ooloi.

Furthermore, Butler literalizes the conception of a "third sex" often attributed to non-western peoples as its own kind of body that functions as central in the process of propagation. As Jdahya cautions Lilith in their initial conversation, "It's wrong to assume that I must be a sex you're familiar with" (13). Through the ooloi, the novels allude to the ways gender roles may exceed the dimorphic binary instantiated by heteronormative models of personhood,[55] drawing on the tradition of European and Euro-American observations of alternative social configurations among Indigenous peoples largely, but not exclusively, from the Americas.[56] In doing so, *Xenogenesis* gestures toward the potential for variable assemblages of social functions, self-presentation, and eroticism that exceed the bodily binary of procreative union. While Butler avoids the tendency to use citations of thirdness merely as a way of destabilizing or deconstructing dominant Euro-American sex-gender systems,[57] instead depicting Oankali sexual and reproductive practices as constituting their own system with its particular rules and prohibitions, her portrayal of such gendered dynamics, particularly in the figure of the ooloi, somatizes them, thereby linking them to the reproductive matrix of Oankali families into which humans are adopted as active participants. Thus, the texts distend and deform the enclosures of "the human" by merging alternative (Indigenous) social structures and social roles with biology, providing a basis for imagining fleshly perversions of dominant social formations. One might understand this speculative gesture as translating the kinds of Indigenous sociopolitical formations often collated as "kinship" into a corporeal idiom in ways that seek to challenge the self-evidence of privatized notions of personhood—to draw on science fiction's subjunctivity to disjoint the obviousness of Man. To the extent that the trilogy can be conceptualized as mobilizing its account of the Oankali to denaturalize heteronormative arrangements by suggesting the potential for other configurations of pleasure, desire, homemaking, child making, and childrearing, it also contests the racialized politics of respectability, whereby the answer to racism is to assert the normality of people of color—to prove an ability to be fully human by performing proper gender identities, forms of erotic containment within monogamous heteromarriage, and nuclear-family housekeeping.[58] Instead, Oankali genealogies engender anomalies that do not conform to heteropatriarchal notions of lineage.

Yet while this corporealization of "difference" may travesty existing modes of racial classification, the focus on experiences of embodiment can defer engagement with Indigenous peoples as place-based polities. Transposing Indigenous social formations into a framework centered on the body can implicitly cast them in racializing terms that displace questions of Native political self-determination. To belong to a genealogically determined entity is to be imagined as the inheritor of a kind of physical substance that can provide the basis for conceptualizing the kinds of *difference* often characterized, and subordinated, as "culture." As Joanne Barker argues, "[I]f Native peoples are to secure the recognition and protection of their legal status and rights as defined therein, they must be able to demonstrate their *aboriginality*—as pursuit, as essence, as a truth that transcends," earlier observing, "Keeping the threats posed by Native governance and territorial rights at bay demands a reinforcement of racist ideologies and identificatory practices of Native authenticity."[59] The ways Native governance and territorialities precede and exceed the jurisdictional geography of the settler-state are translated as indexing an "essence" whose purity is rendered in terms of a racial-cultural unity that "transcends" the terms of politics even as it is subject to legal determinations made by the state, including about the terms and legitimacy of Indigenous identities. With respect to non-native appraisals of indigeneity, as Povinelli notes, "a status of common descent stands in the background. And this difference provides social traction for people like the land commissioner who need some distinction to operate the legal machinery of the politics of cultural difference," and "the lack of choice in the domain of genealogical classification effectively mirrors thick public presumptions about culture as determination."[60] From within this settler prismatics, Indigenous practices of collective placemaking appear to refer back to (and to be constituted through) modes of genealogical transmission that—in their duration, unchosenness, and generational iterability—seem almost interchangeable with conceptions of racial identity. Genealogy grounds Indigenous "difference" by casting it as emanating from a biological substrate, which itself can be distinguished from anything that could count as politics, nationhood, or sovereignty.[61] The trilogy's amalgamationist embrace of anomaly pushes beyond notions of racial lineage, but Butler's allusions to (extant accounts of) indigeneity emerge through the lens of (alien) fleshliness in ways that can resonate with ongoing settler processes of translating Indigenous political orders as an aggregation of bodies who bear a "culture"-capacitating bloodline. In this vein, technologies of Oankali historical recollection and social reproduction are fundamentally genetic in character. Lilith observes, "In all her time with the Oankali, . . . she had never seen any of them read or write anything" (61), but readers also are told that "she like[d to hear] the stories of the long, multispecies Oankali history" (63). This absence of writing and the presence of storytelling as a vehicle for communicating Oankali histories echo the convention of referring to the accumulation and transmission of Native knowledges as "oral tradition."[62] However, Jdahya indicates to Lilith that "memory of a division is passed on biologically" (36), such that all of the Oankalis' previous movements and encounters are preserved as information physically encoded in/as flesh, following patterns of genealogical inheritance and diffusion.

Signs of indigeneity serve as the means for marking Oankalis' deviance, for signaling the ways they represent an alternative to atomized and propertied modes of being, but that very linkage transposes these qualities and dynamics into physicalized tendencies rather than presenting them as modes of political relation that emerge and are sustained through connections to a shared land base. In this way, the trilogy can be understood as reorienting Indigenous social forms (or, at least, conventional accounts of them) by situating them within a problem-space organized around the question of fungibility—the kinds of transness through which blackness is (re)constituted—in ways that tend to divorce the trilogy's exploration of fleshliness from the potential for a sense of collective territoriality. Oankalis have no determinate relationship to place. In fact, they are defined not simply by the absence of such a connection but by an innate imperative toward self-dislocation. The "drive" toward movement and contact with new planets and species is contained within the "organelle" that all Oankalis share and that serves as a referent for the term "Oankali" itself (40)—to be "planetbound . . . would eventually mean death" (35). For billions of years, that cycle of contact, trade, and emigration has persisted (36), and without any sense of a continuing connection to the world from which they came or to any subsequent one, their connection to the place they occupy at any given moment is merely anticipatory of the time when they will journey again, never to return to any of the worlds they have inhabited. When Lilith asks Jdahya, "Do you remember your homeworld itself? I mean, could you get back to it if you wanted to?" he responds with evident amusement, "No, Lilith, that's the one direction that's closed to us. This is our homeworld now," adding, "We left it so long ago . . . I doubt that it does still exist. . . . It was a womb. The time had come for us to be born" (36–37, ellipses in original). Within Oankali understandings, to be intimately connected to a (set of) place(s) is not yet to be born, to be so undeveloped as to be fetal. In addition, the designation of Earth as a "homeworld" is not indicative of a futurity of occupancy, as the plan for Earth as revealed later in the trilogy is to inhabit it for another few centuries and then to leave "an uninhabitable rock behind" when they go (628), one that will be "as lifeless as the moon" (365).[63] Except for the ships themselves, which also provide their dwellings and village sites when on-planet, the spaces Oankalis occupy are nothing but collections of extractable resources that enable their further travel.[64]

Beyond the disjunctive figuration of Oankalis as quasi-Indigenous while categorically foreclosing any enduring collective relations to land, Butler actively disqualifies the place-based knowledges of Indigenous peoples. The parts of the novels set on Earth occur in South American rainforests, and Lilith is informed that the plan for humans entails taking "people [who] will all be from what you would call civilized societies" and setting them in locations where "they'll have to learn to live in forests, build their own shelters, and raise their own food all without machines or outside help" (32). Lilith observes, "I'm willing to learn what you have to teach me . . . but I don't think I'm the right teacher for others. There were so many humans who already knew how to live in the wilderness. . . . Those are the ones you ought to be talking to," and Jdahya replies, "We have talked to them. They will have to be especially careful because some of the things they 'know' aren't true anymore. . . . Your Earth is still your Earth, but between the efforts of your people to destroy it and ours to restore it, it has changed" (33–34). More than simply needing to adapt to changed conditions, Indigenous peoples' relations with place are imagined as actively misleading and in need of suppression or outright disavowal. They need to "be especially careful" due to their supposed inability to alter their sense of everyday cartographies of use and possibility, to respond to "change."[65] Instead, people from "civilized societies" who have no awareness at all of how to live in "forests," or presumably anywhere other than cities and suburbs, seem better candidates for Oankali training.

What I want to highlight here is less Indigenous peoples' greater knowledge of spaces deemed rural or the value of particular kinds of Indigenous placemaking (for example, those that can be characterized as non-statist and conforming more to environmental narratives of stewardship) than the novels' consistent dissociation of the possibilities it aligns with amalgamation (Oankali fleshliness and trade) from collective placemaking. As Mishuana Goeman notes with respect to contemporary understandings of Native territories and homelands, the aim is not a "utopian recovery of land through mapping pure ideas of indigeneity" but acknowledging and engaging the "ever-changing Native epistemologies that frame our understanding of land and our relationships to it and other peoples," also emphasizing the need to "uproot settler-colonial social and material maps that inform our everyday experiences."[66] Even as the particular configuration and character of Native landedness may be part of active processes of negotiation within and among Indigenous peoples, Indigenous sovereignty, as Leanne Simpson observes of Nishnaabeg peoples, was "territorial": "While the boundaries around that land were much more fluid than that of modern states, there was a territory that was defined by Nishnaabeg language, philosophy, way of life, and political culture. Nishnaabeg concepts of 'nation' and 'sovereignty' are much different than modern constructs, but they exist and were expressed."[67] From this perspective, the striking feature of the novels' translation of characteristics associated with indigeneity is the ways Butler utterly dislocates such features from Native peoples' connection to particular lands and waters, such that Indigenous peoples are disqualified from partaking in processes of becoming precisely for this reason.

The novels largely concretize the fleshly potentials of Oankali-steered amalgamation through figurations of indigeneity, but those qualities are corporealized—as expressive of genealogically inherited tendencies and genetic capabilities—and divorced from place-based modes of collectivity, as well as from actual Indigenous peoples. Notably, the resisters come to deride Oankali and human villages for the extent to which their forms of inhabitance fail to appear as "civilized." In a conversation with Lilith when Tino first comes to her village, having left the resister settlement of Phoenix, he asks her, "Why do you live this way?. . . . It's primitive! You live like savages!. . . . Hell, you have spaceships. *How can you live this way!*" (280). Although Lilith later notes that "Lo"—the organic substance out of which virtually everything in the village is constructed—is the same kind of entity as the Oankali ship in orbit on the other side of the moon, the force of this statement lies in the attribution of indigeneity to Oankali-led lifeways, such that (in addition to the look of Oankali bodies) charges of savagery and primitivity provide much of the content for the "human" experience of Oankali alienness. However, such Indigenously-inflected forms of inhabitance do not signal something like the potential for sovereignty or emplaced modes of governance, instead indexing the ways human socialities might be disjointed from their current formations through proliferations of anomalous relation that challenge the (racializing) circumscriptions of dominant Euro-American forms of selfhood and embodiment.

Capacity, Disability, and the Space of Refusal

The novels remain ambivalent about whether Oankali presence can be understood as fundamentally invasive. The trilogy both offers accounts of Oankali relations with humans as enslavement and significantly qualifies that claim, suggesting the operation of processes of amalgamation whereby both are transformed through their interaction in ways that are not regulated by systems of property but that do draw on blackness's role as, in King's terms, "flux, process, and potential"—as a mode of transness and excess through which (other) identities are (re)made. Even as Butler illustrates such Oankali fleshliness/ fungibility, she highlights the fact that humans are not able to refuse this process of transformation and continue to exist as human. Oankalis conceive of humans as inherently destructive due to their genetic "contradiction" (intelligence in the service of hierarchy), and from within this framing, the insistence that humans need to be altered appears as part of an effort to promote the potential for life, as against in-born tendencies toward self-destruction. The bodily identity of the human race, then, poses a double problem for the Oankali: humans need to be opened to transformation in order to escape the (racist) modes of (self-)possession and dominance that helped lead to the nuclear holocaust; and humans need to be directed away from their biologically immanent being-for-death.[68] In this way, Oankali interventions into human social systems and reproductive processes can be narrated not as annexation, enslavement, or violence but as a means of enabling survival and flourishing.

Through the Oankali insistence that humanity become otherwise (or cease to exist), the novels explore racializing dynamics that do not so much privilege an unmarked normative body as posit a deficient, disabled, dangerous kind of body that must be contained or altered due to its recalcitrance with respect to the project of enhancing life. In critiquing this Oankali biopolitics, the texts invoke humans' right to exist as a distinct, place-based "people." Yet, despite Butler's use of terminology associated with collective self-determination and self-governance, such "people"-hood consistently is cast in the trilogy as more or less expressive of the desire to maintain humanness as a particular discrete kind of embodiment. Thus, even when the trilogy seems to endorse place-based collectivity (as against Oankali presentation of it as merely a form of destructive and savage backwardness), Butler continues to portray the (geo)politics of refusing alien occupation and intrusion as if it were a struggle to retain the integrity of a kind of corporeality. Against this background, the resisters seem to reject an ethics of relation in favor of a reinvestment in the atomized, self-possessed body. This dynamic can be understood as symptomatic of a process whereby one set of political concerns/horizons is transposed into the "onto-epistemic terms," in de la Cadena's words, of a different frame of reference. The understanding of resistance to the Oankali as aiming to preserve a certain mode of embodiment, the preservation of which the novels associate with endemic and intensive patterns of violence, orients Butler's portrayal of the desire for territorial peoplehood. The struggle for what could be narrated as (Indigenous) sovereignty, then, appears as a reactionary investment in bodily(/racial) purity.

Oankali accounts of the contradiction present humans as immanently oriented toward violence in ways that constitute them as a racial type in need of management and aid. In Lilith's initial set of conversations with Jdahya, he indicates, "Your bodies are fatally flawed," further comparing the human race to Lilith's previously undiagnosed cancer by noting, "If ['your people'] had been able to perceive and solve their problem, they might have been able to avoid destruction": "You are hierarchical. That's the older and more entrenched characteristic [compared to intelligence]. We saw it in your closest animal relatives and in your most distant ones. . . . When human intelligence served it instead of guiding it, when human intelligence did not even acknowledge it as a problem but took pride in it or did not notice it at all . . . [, t]hat was like ignoring cancer" (38–39). The Oankali—and, to some extent, the novels themselves—offer this set of genetic tendencies as the explanation for the nuclear war that nearly ended the human race and the possibility for life on the planet.[69] Although humans share a hardwired propensity for hierarchy with other beings on Earth, the evolution of intelligence seems to have honed the capacity for materializing ever more destructive forms of hierarchy while also heightening the ability to ignore that process—the failure to attend to the "cancer" that will kill them. The solution to this problem seems to lie in forms of biological modification available through Oankali amalgamation. Jdahya notes, "The ooloi will make changes in your reproductive cells before conception and they'll control conception" (42), and Nikanj indicates that humans "won't have children without us. Human sperm and egg will not unite without us" (245). The goal of such intervention lies in breeding out humans' devastating propensity for violence, since allowing humans to continue in their current form after reviving them would have proved catastrophic.[70] As Nikanj explains, "[W]e couldn't carry on a normal trade. We couldn't let you breed alongside us, coming to us only when you saw the value of what we offered. . . . [W]e couldn't let your numbers grow. We couldn't let you begin to become what you were" (290–91). If relations with Oankalis generate open-ended potentials for becoming, especially in terms of movements away from possessive modes of privatized selfhood, the "human" as such must be denied futurity, since "to become" it through the return to prior forms of reproduction would decimate all other possibilities.

Humans exist as a biological type, defined by their contradiction, and that (racial) type innately moves toward self-annihilation. Oankalis know this dynamic to be an unquestionable fact due to their ability to interpret biological codes. As Lilith's son Akin asserts to a doctor in one of the resister villages,

"Human purpose isn't what you say it is or what I say it is. It's what your biology says it is—what your genes say it is" (501), and earlier he characterizes this sureness as "an Oankali certainty," "A certainty of the flesh" (476). Moreover, during the deliberations among the Oankali about Akin's plan to create a colony on Mars (in which humans could live and reproduce without Oankali intervention), one participant characterizes the proposal as "allow[ing humans] to ride their Contradiction to their deaths," adding, "To give them back their independent existence, their fertility, their own territory was to help them breed a new population only to destroy it a second time" (470). Decades after the colony is established, Akin's sibling Jodahs thinks of the project, "in the end it would all be for nothing. Their own genetic conflict had betrayed and destroyed them once. It would do so again" (530). There is no escaping this conclusion in the sense that Oankali knowledge does not posit the problem as one of behavior or learned responses. Rather, it lies in the "genes" that proliferate through the *breeding* of a "population." There is no sense that human social formations and (collective) desires might be opaque (in Édouard Glissant's terms discussed in chapter 1); instead, they are understood as completely intelligible within and transparent to Oankali modes of knowledge and perception, which supposedly grasp the inherent inclinations of humanity as a genetically preprogrammed species form. The biological identity of humans as a species inherently commits them to trajectories of obliteration, and the fleshliness of Oankali semiotics and technologies means that they are capable of diagnosing such pathological predispositions. The status of humans as such makes them inherently guilty of the potential violence unleashed by their immutable contradiction, and this attribution of antisociality is itself a function of their *race*, the unchosen and uncontrollable reproductive transmission of a particular kind of bodily identity or propensity.

Although the dangers humans pose to Oankalis receive some notice in the novels,[71] the greatest threat that human beings pose is to their own capacity for continued existence, and that danger must be countered due to the Oankalis' understanding of themselves as guided by a fundamental orientation toward enabling and enhancing life. During the deliberation on the prospective Mars colony, an Akjai highlights "the Oankali understanding of life itself as a thing of inexpressible value. A thing beyond trade. Life could be changed, changed utterly. But not destroyed" (470). The notion of restoring humans' independent reproductivity and allowing them to live on their own again appears as a "profoundly immoral, antilife thing" that, even when the Oankali come to accept the need for it, can be characterized only as "a cruelty" (475). "Life" functions here as a figure of mutability, as what may be "changed utterly" while still holding its "value." The form of life matters little, simply that it not be "destroyed." Given that Oankali collective thinking, action, and morality is animated by the promotion of the potential for life, it enacts a biopolitical mode of governance.[72] In *The History of Sexuality*, Michel Foucault defines biopolitics by sketching a shift from the prior location of (European) authority in the monarch's power to kill to a justification of the exertion of power based on "the right of the social body to ensure, maintain, or develop its life." The regularization of what constitutes viable/desirable "life" occurs "not by law but by normalization," assessing "effects and distributions around the norm" that itself constitutes the biosocial baseline for health, welfare, and future well-being.[73] As he suggests in *"Society Must Be Defended,"* the norm functions as part of generating "regulatory mechanisms [that] must be established to establish an equilibrium, maintain an average, establish a sort of homeostasis, and compensate for variations," and "security mechanisms have to be installed . . . so as to optimize a state of life" for what comes to be understood as the "population" to be governed. On the flip side of the positing and defense of this norm in the name of "life" lies "the internal racism of permanent purification," such that racialization operates as a necessary part of producing ostensibly life-enhancing modes of normalization—as the means of justifying a targeting for containment/destruction of those who deviate from the "norm" by understanding them as bearing biological incapacity/danger.[74] In this vein, a wide range of scholars have explored the ways that whiteness serves as a biopolitical norm, "an insidious liberal one proffering an innocuous inclusion into life" for those who can conform to its normative priorities, in terms of sexuality, family and household formation, and patriotic affects.[75]

Rather than defending a normative ideal, though, Oankali accounts of human biology present it, in its unaltered form, as antithetical to "life" per se, and the racialization of humans' biological tendencies as threats to the promotion of (Oankali-overseen) "life," then, does not operate as a form of *purification*. In addition to indicating that Dinso Oankalis have been "bred" to look more humanoid in order better to "trade" with the people of Earth, Butler introduces readers to Akjai Oankalis, who are "caterpillarlike" ("It was what the Oankali had been, one trade before they found Earth, one trade before they used . . . their vast store of genetic material to construct speaking, hearing, bipedal children" [453]), and readers earlier learn that "six divisions ago," Oankali "were many-bodied and spoke with body lights and color patterns" (63).[76] The absence of an ideal Oankali "body" complements the other aspects of their fleshliness, discussed in the previous section, but complicates an understanding of the dynamics of racialization at play in the trilogy's speculative imaginary.

What portrait does Butler offer of biopolitical rule, of racialized governmentality,[77] in the absence of a norm against which fleshly, affectable others can be understood as deviant? How do the novels envision, engage, and critique a mode of racialization that posits a failed or dangerous kind of body?

In the absence of a privileged model of embodiment (something like the Euro-American norm Wynter refers to as "Man"), processes of racialization can define a population as biologically deficient with respect to its ability to engender "life" itself. In talking about contemporary racial politics in the United States that "fold" otherwise racialized subjects back into "life," Jasbir Puar asks, "[W]hat kinds of subjects are formed through population construction, the subjects of regenerative capacity?"[78] With respect to humans in the trilogy, one might instead address how Oankali conceptions of humans as a population depend on constructing them as subjects of *incapacity*, as disabled. When initially explaining the human contradiction to Lilith, Jdahya says of it, "A complex combination of genes that work together to make you intelligent as well as hierarchical will still handicap you whether you acknowledge it or not" (39), and with respect to the Mars colony, Jodahs observes, "[T]he Oankali *know to the bone* that it's wrong to help the Human species regenerate unchanged because it *will* destroy itself again," adding by way of further explanation, "To them it's like deliberately causing the conception of a child who is so defective that it must die in infancy" (532). Humans are genetically "handicap[ped]" and "defective" with respect to the promotion of life, which is what makes the notion of the Mars colony so "immoral" and "antilife" (475). Megan Obourn argues with respect to Oankali aims that "the bodily and environmental changes needed to create a more interdependent and accessible future rely on practices of genetic engineering designed to eliminate humanity as a disabled species."[79] Oankali perceptions of "life" less involve calibrations around a model of health per se than the pathologization of opposition to their ways of envisioning the "value" of life.[80] Oankali capabilities with respect to optimizing humans' lifespan and bodily function, as well as curbing the ostensibly innate human drive toward dominance, work to justify modes of intervention as an inherent good. In addition to extending human lives by hundreds of years, the Oankali convert Lilith's cancer into ooloi abilities (such as radically reshaping ooloi morphology and regrowing limbs for themselves and others);[81] Akin cures a human resister of Huntington's disease; and Jodahs rids two resisters of their "genetic disorder" (asking "Why should you become more and more disabled?").[82]

In these ways, humans appear as the objects of Oankali pastoral care, and, thus, any effort to refuse such attentions itself serves as evidence of mental or emotional deficiency—as an expression of humans' genetic predisposition toward hierarchy and an attendant unwillingness to allow themselves to be aided and protected. This orientation can be characterized, in Alison Kafer's terms, as "a *curative imaginary*, an understanding of disability that not only *expects* and *assumes* intervention but also cannot imagine or comprehend anything other than intervention." Within this imaginary, "the political nature of disability, namely its position as a category to be contested and debated, goes unacknowledged," since disability "resides in the minds or bodies of individuals" rather than "in built environments and social patterns that exclude or stigmatize particular kinds of bodies, minds, and ways of being."[83] The various ways that humans are disabled in the novels (their contradiction, cancer and other diseases, wounding and maiming of various sorts) all appear as an aggregation of deficits in individual bodies, as diminished capacities that can be adjusted so as putatively to increase one's ability to participate in the various forms of amalgamation, biological relation, and engagement with "difference" that Oankalis offer. However, even in the absence of a specific biopolitical norm against which humans are found wanting, this atomizing somatization of them as disabled bodies in need of care thwarts the possibility of engaging with *the political nature* of Oankali rule, the ways it defers and dismantles the potential for human collective organization as such. As Sharene Razack argues with respect to the settler-state's representation of Native "vulnerability," "It goes without saying that a people seen as damaged and dying cannot be entrusted with self-governance and stewardship over the land."[84] To refuse Oankali governance means choosing to be disabled; such collective repudiation signifies a will-to-"antilife" that is explicable only in corporealizing terms (as an expression of a genetic defect), rather than a commitment to alternative *lifeways* and forms of (geo)political order other than those instituted by Oankalis. If "life" is "of inexpressible value" *because* it can be "changed, changed utterly" (470), then resistance to "becom[ing] something other" and to seeking "difference" through "change" indexes not opposition but recalcitrance borne from infirmity (34, 329).

The novels register the *politics* of the attribution of disability and the human desire for modes of sociality not superintended by the Oankali, and in this process, Butler begins to sketch an analysis of place-based political collectivity, one that resonates with the history of settler colonial efforts to present Native territoriality and self-governance as a kind of *antilife*—a savage and uncontrolled violence and the irrationality of turning away from the supposedly saving care of civilization.[85] Discussing non-native approaches to what often is cast as an epidemic of suicides among Inuit youth, Lisa Stevenson characterizes such efforts at intervention as a "biopolitical" "form of care and governance that is primarily concerned with the maintenance of life itself." She further notes that it treats Inuit personhood and peoplehood as "so many serialized bodies that needed to be brought back to health" and that the "desire to 'make live' at the level of a population can sometimes be experienced as murderous."[86] The elements of the trilogy that engage questions of sovereignty and collective self-determination suggest an equivocation in which Butler engages a different set of a principles from those at play in figurations of the violence and potentials of fungibility and fleshliness. This line of thought appears most powerfully in Akin's project of creating a Mars colony in which the resisters can live and reproduce free from Oankali intervention. The argument that he develops for a human Akjai (replicating the terminology used for the Oankali division that will not mix with humans) turns on the ways being human exceeds having a specific kind of biogenetic profile. Early in *Dawn*, Lilith refers to humans as "my people" (40), and in *Adulthood Rites*, Tate, the first person awakened by Lilith who becomes a resister and cares for Akin after he has been kidnapped by marauding resisters from another village, admits, "My own people disgust me sometimes, but they're still my people" (507). Moreover, long after having mated with Oankalis, Tino offers a sentiment with which Lilith expresses her agreement: "I'm a traitor to my people. Everything I do here is an act of betrayal. Someday my people won't exist at all, and I will have helped their destroyers" (424). These moments illustrate that no matter how they are positioned with respect to the Oankali, the human characters conceptualize humanity as a "people," not simply an aggregation of persons but a collective whose existence is threatened by Oankali modes of becoming.

Such peoplehood serves as the basis of Akin's argument for humans' right to self-determination, which appears to negate Oankali conceptions of change, value, and life. When living with resisters from the village Phoenix, Akin encounters two other constructs who had been kidnapped, and in discussing the future of the humans, Akin observes of the work of Oankali mating, "There won't be any more of them," to which the other constructs respond, "We are them! And we are the Oankali" (377). They also rehearse the story of humans as having been "flawed and overspecialized" due to their "ancient hierarchical tendencies," but Akin thinks that he has "been among resister Humans long enough to begin to see them as a truly separate people": "There should be Humans who don't change or die—Humans to go on if the Dinso and Toaht unions fail" (378). Claims by others of this "people"'s incapacity cannot diminish the legitimacy of *separateness* for them. In this vein, the resisters' territoriality bespeaks a political will to remain distinct, to champion their own peoplehood in the face of Oankali efforts to narrate that desire as symptomatic of their disablement. To the extent that resisters are "using their territory in a manner that is historically and philosophically consistent with what [they] know, then, it is an incident of a failed consent and *positive refusal*."[87] The active, organized, and ongoing nonconsent of the resisters to Oankali overtures can be understood as refusing to live a "life" acknowledged as such by the Oankali, and as Audra Simpson suggests of settler modes of engaging with Indigenous sovereignties, such terms of recognition are "politically untenable and thus normatively should be refused," earlier noting, "Refusal comes with the requirement of having one's *political* sovereignty acknowledged and upheld, and raises the question of legitimacy for those who are usually in the position of recognizing."[88] Akin raises such a question with respect to Oankali processes of amalgamation, describing them as "wrong and unnecessary" and indicating that humans should be able to "live in themselves": "What are we that we can do this to whole peoples?" (443). Particularly in using the plural "peoples," Butler here makes clear that Akin is referring to polities, not accumulations of persons. The individual body and its status is not the issue. Rather, what's at stake is political sovereignty, in terms of the ability of a collective entity to remain territorially distinct (to refuse incorporation into the encompassing jurisdiction of another political entity) and to continue to govern itself.

In these moments, the novel offers a speculative engagement with the dynamics of settler colonialism. Several international covenants available at the time that *Xenogenesis* was written (including the United Nations Draft Declaration on the Rights of Indigenous Peoples) include language to the effect that under international law, "peoples" have the "right to self-determination," and "by virtue of that right they freely determine their political status and freely pursue their economic, social and cultural development."[89] Whether or not Butler was aware of such documents, Akin's challenge to the legitimacy of Oankali-led development certainly resonates with the principles they articulate. For humans to function as a "people" (or a collection of "peoples") means having their relative autonomy acknowledged—their right to refuse absorption into the apparatus of Oankali biopolitics. At one point, an Oankali Akjai says to Akin, "If I were Human, little construct, I would be a resister myself. All people who know what it is to end should be allowed to continue if they can continue" (471). In this instance, the novel explicitly displaces the equation of "life" with the potentialities of a particular genetic profile or morphology, instead aligning the idea of an "end" with collective modes of belonging and becoming. The quote highlights a shared resister desire to "continue" in ways not shaped by Oankali-endorsed notions of relation and betterment. As Wallace argues, "[S]eeing violence embedded in [Oankali] 'trade' is precisely what is needed." She further observes that "the blurring of human and nonhuman" championed by many critics is, in fact, "characteristic of biodiversity discourse more generally": "It has been precisely by refusing to see prior labor or art involved in the development and use of medicinal herbs or conventionally cultivated crops—in seeing these as 'the common heritage of mankind'—that corporations have also seen them as available for patent."[90] Such "development and use" very often come out of ongoing Indigenous knowledges and practices, which are then extracted for putatively "life"-amplifying application by others.[91] The amalgamating imaginary of Oankali-overseen "change" depends on a colonial disavowal of humans' right to autonomous development, including an effort to sever their relationship with the place of the Earth. That project resonates with the program of allotment through which the U.S. government sought to *detribalize* Native peoples, divorcing them from their land bases through their incorporation into Euro-American modes of home and family (as humans are through forced incorporation into Oankali kinship formations).[92] Reciprocally, Oankali perspectives on the human contradiction reiterate in a different key persistent imaginings of Indianness as itself a kind of drive toward death, as inevitably tending toward disappearance and extinction.[93]

The collective identity as human championed by the resisters, then, emerges from and marks a particular relation to place. The profoundness of humans' sense of loss in their separation from the Earth appears in various resisters' opposition to the Mars plan. When Akin returns to Phoenix after having secured Oankali support for a human Akjai to be founded on Mars, Gabe (Tate's partner, who also had been woken by Lilith in the first book) objects, "We've lost almost everything already. . . . Now we lose our world and everything on it" (488). Another resister asserts, "*This* is my world. . . . I was born here, and I'll die here," to which Akin responds, Mars "will be a Human world someday. But it will never be Earth. You need Earth" (513). This dynamic resonates with the statement of one of the characters in Drew Hayden Taylor's "Lost in Space," in which an Anishinaabe astronaut's grandfather remarks, "[B]eing Native in space. . . . Now that's a head-scratcher. Think about it. We sprang from Turtle Island. The earth and water are so tied to who we are. . . . I know that everything we are we carry inside us, but I can't help wondering if it's possible to be a good, proper Native astronaut."[94] While Butler sets aside contemporary Indigenous peoples in ways I discussed earlier and address further in the next section, the novels link resister opposition—refusal of Oankali relation or enhancement—to indigeneity, implicitly recalling the violence of various projects of removal and allotment to which Indigenous peoples have been subjected. In this way, the trilogy—*Adulthood Rites*, in particular—gestures toward the significance of self-determination for peoples as polities whose identity as such cannot be divorced from complex histories of connection to place, specifically as against efforts to portray nonconsensual intervention as aid for an otherwise disabled population.

Butler seems to endorse collective self-determination as a form of political imagination and struggle that cannot be transposed into an idiom of embodiment without seriously misconstruing its character, aims, and ethical import. However, many critics have characterized resister assertions of their right to collective autonomy as merely replaying racializing visions of purity (not unlike the denunciations of Native peoples' supposedly backward investments in retaining tribal identity/Indianness). Scholars have described the resisters as desiring to maintain a biologically imagined sameness that seeks to thwart Oankali attempts to institute a sense of relationality, the potential for adaptability, and an embrace of newness. As Wallace suggests, "The human characters, in this reading, interested in preserving the 'purity' of their gene pool, represent precisely [the] 'essentialist identities'" the novels are taken as critiquing.[95] Obourn suggests that the trilogy illustrates a "human investment in maintaining a sense of cultural and racial identity by fighting their oppressors rather than submitting to change," and such opposition to "change" expresses an investment in particular "sacred images of . . . bodily purity."[96] The refusal of Oankali-ordered change stands as evidence of a deep investment in essentialist conceptions of identity, suggesting that the only way of construing such expressions of refusal in the name of "people"-hood is as a reactionary investment in "purity." Resistance to invasion necessarily signifies as a rearguard effort to preserve the coherence of bodily and racial boundaries.[97] Tucker suggests that "the Oankali represent an anti-teleological interrogation of origins," and from this perspective, human desires to preserve humanness as a collective relation to place must signal a reactionary identification with "origins" that seeks to thwart the forms of becoming represented by the Oankali.[98]

While such readings efface the novels' endorsement of some version of human self-determination, these interpretations also reflect Butler's tendency to cast the desire for a version of human autonomy as the preservation of a kind of body. The texts consistently translate the *geopolitical* refusal of Oankali interventions and narratives of disablement (in favor of a human agenda set for themselves) into the *biopolitical* reproduction of the genetic coherence of species distinction. In this way, a movement that might be understood as oriented around sovereignty is presented as about (racial) embodiment. Even while raising questions about the citation of "life itself" as a justification for large-scale sustained intervention and social engineering, Butler largely endorses Oankali assessments of human recalcitrance. The trilogy suggests less that the aliens have (mis)translated human peoplehood than that the defense of such peoplehood *is* an expression of a regressive investment in a kind of bodily norm.

"Humanity" appears in the novels less as a collective entity than as a sort of physicality or physiology. The objection to Oankali tampering with humans' reproductive systems, such that an ooloi becomes necessary for procreation, appears as a primary complaint lodged by the resisters. Their opposition to Oankali-led becoming appears less as a matter of resisting Oankali interference with human sociopolitical processes than as an objection to the disruption of the discreteness of human species-being as such. Lilith wonders in *Dawn*, "How could she Awaken people and tell them they were to be part of the genetic engineering scheme of a species so alien[?] . . . How would she Awaken these people, these survivors of war, and tell them that unless they could escape the Oankali, their children would not be human?" (117). After a brutal assault by other humans on the Oankalis that are holding them captive aboard the ship, Lilith responds to Nikanj's surprise at the ferocity of humans' feelings by asking, "What did you think would happen when you told us you were going to extinguish us as a species by tampering genetically with our children?" (231). The "human" becomes a function of a particular genetic profile, such that "tampering" with it induces an almost unbridled rage to maintain the intergenerational continuity of this biological typology. In *Adulthood Rites*, Tate expresses her anger about the effects of the Oankali management of human procreation, asserting, "Oankali drove us to become what we are. If they hadn't tampered with us, we'd have children of our own. We could live in our own ways, and they could live in theirs" (399). Soon thereafter, she states, "We don't get old. We don't have kids, and nothing we do means shit" (402). These comments point to the significance of children "of their own" (genetically patterned as exclusively homo sapien) in the continuation of human "ways."

The existential crisis marked here indicates an ongoing anxiety about the biological coherence of the human race, such that to want to "live in our own ways" or to contest Oankali interventions cannot but bespeak a concern about retaining the physiological identity of humanness per se. To get at the stakes of this series of linkages in Butler's texts, one might turn to an Indigenous futurist account of adoption such as Mari Kurisato's "Impostor Syndrome." In the story, an android seeks to escape from the kinds of labor enforced on those deemed machines by passing as human, and she draws on the DNA profile (and a literal transfusion) from a dying and then deceased Turtle Mountain Chippewa woman named Aanji Iron Woman, whom the android had met previously and who had agreed to aid in the android's transformation. By creating an impression of humanness through Aanji's blood, the android takes over her identity in order to leave on one of the Seed ships transporting humans to other worlds. The story concludes by noting,

> A few of the people on Seed ship knew that wasn't really Aanji Iron Woman in the jingle dress, dancing with the others around the bonfire. They also knew there was earth from old Terra in the soil here, but it was not the Turtle Island of old. They were Heaven Walkers now, and they adapted, to preserve the old ways.... So, even if Aanji Iron Woman was not the daughter they remembered, she kept to the old ways, and that was good enough ... She might never pass as human the way she wanted to, but to the Star River tribe, she was family.[99]

While playing on the figurations of blood as the marker of Indian authenticity, as well as histories of non-natives playing Indian for their own purposes (here, in an interesting twist on slave fugitivity), Kurisato suggests that the "ways" of the people to whom the android Aanji comes to belong remain irreducible to the blood she has acquired. Or, rather, the borrowed blood ultimately comes to signify in terms of a commitment to those collective ways and the process of adaptation in order to survive as a people, even amid removal. By contrast, Butler's novels raise the specter of a kind of human self-determination that highlights the political nature of Oankali knowledge claims and that exceeds the terms of Oankali care, but the texts simultaneously corporealize that possibility: it appears as an investment in the identity of the human body as against efforts to open it to genetic *difference*, trying to preserve what amounts to a kind of bloodedness. Within this imagination, resistance to allotment and removal can only involve a regressive investment in a version of racial identity (Indianness?).

The novels imply that the repudiation of a racializing narrative of human disablement is of a piece with a racializing insistence on human biological integrity. The question of the Mars colony, and of humans' right to live separately as a "people," arises in *Adulthood Rites* but then is dislocated from the narrative frame of *Imago*, which focuses on the emergence of construct ooloi, their relations with humans, and the amalgamative potentialities of this encounter.[100] In *Imago*, the community of resisters who can reproduce on their own are portrayed as Christian religious fundamentalists whose desire to remain human arises from dogmatism and who also are "becom[ing] more and more disabled" through inbreeding (618–19). In response to her brother's willingness to mate with Lilith's ooloi child Jodahs, Jesusa exclaims, "This is an alien thing Jodahs wants of us. Certainly it's an un-Christian thing, an un-Human thing. *It's the thing we've been taught against all our lives*" (648). Later, the text emphasizes the hollowness of such beliefs in a conversation between Javier and Paz, a couple who become mates to Aaor, Jodahs's ooloi sibling. In response to another villager's insistence, "You should be terrified. When we were children they told us the devil had four arms," Javier responds, "We're not children anymore," and Paz insists, "I'm tired of telling myself lies about this place and watching my children die" (713). These moments suggest that what they have been "taught" about preserving human autonomy from Oankali interference is a form of irrational indoctrination, a set of "lies" that reinforce village insularity rather than contribute to the welfare of community members. At one point Nikanj says to Jodahs, complimenting it on its ability to understand and engage with humans, "I don't believe we would have had many resisters if we had made construct ooloi earlier" (607). This sentiment is confirmed by the villagers who, once they have engaged in sustained contact with Jodahs and Aaor, "did begin to love us and to believe what we told them and to talk to us about Oankali and construct maters" (737). Although the novel raises questions about the nature of ooloi seduction (and its ability to generate a form of addiction),[101] on the whole *Imago* retreats from the issue of political collectivity raised in *Adulthood Rites* in favor of foregrounding the fleshly potentials of human-Oankali trade in the emergence of human ooloi while depicting humans' refusal of relations with Oankalis as a doctrinaire investment in maintaining species boundaries at the expense of enhancing their quality of life.

If securing the self-identity of the human is understood as the principal mode through which racial(izing) dominance is exercised, then resisters' insistence on their landed *peoplehood* as humans merely replicates extant logics of property and racialization. The novels (re)configure one form of difference—the collective political refusal of Oankali invasion and rule—as the refusal of difference—a commitment to maintaining the singularity of the human and the generational transmission of this insulating (proprietary) matrix of personhood. Thus, the trilogy transposes modes of place-based peoplehood into a discourse of the racial(ized) body. As discussed in chapter 1, this kind of conceptual framing understands peoplehood as a reactionary attachment to Euro-American ideologies of propertied selfhood. This perspective resonates with the novels' apparent endorsement of Oankali relationality, adaptability, and embrace of the new, as opposed to resisters' connection to the place of the Earth and apparent investment in the boundedness of species distinction. From this angle, the Oankali appear as the bringers of posthuman, fleshly potentials, abolishing the forms of natality, nationality, and territoriality that structure "the human" (although, in staging such possibilities, the novels draw on extant characterizations of indigeneity, as discussed in the previous section). However, Butler also illustrates how Oankalis racialize humans in ways that do not so much posit a biopolitical norm from which humans are distinguished as disqualify all opposition to Oankali agendas for engendering "life," "change," and "difference" as merely expressive of humans' innate disability and deficiency. In other words, the novels open room for envisioning a politics of collective (Indigenous) self-determination even as the content of that politics repeatedly gets characterized as the maintenance of a biological type—a particular model of individualized and reproductively conveyed (genetic) identity and inheritance. In suggesting that something like indigeneity is oriented around preserving a kind of (racialized) body, the novels illustrate the problems that arise in addressing place-based peoplehood within a conceptual problem-space organized around histories of "the captive body."[102] Put another way, as discussed earlier, people in the novels often refer to Oankali dominance as ownership (of humans and the Earth itself), and while the novels raise numerous questions about this characterization, they have difficulty envisioning a paradigm of peoplehood and placemaking other than ownership, such that the trilogy both articulates an ethics of indigeneity and undermines that ethics by casting it as the preservation of (racial) purity.

The Sameness of Species

The novels characterize humanness in terms of the genetic contradiction all people possess. Not only does this ingrained tendency toward hierarchy explain the nuclear holocaust that sets the stage for the events of the trilogy, it engenders escalating forms of violence among the resisters. Humans' apparent inability to survive on their own, including their descent into a Hobbesian war of all-against-all, derives from their common biological inheritance. While some have critiqued this dystopian vision as essentialist, others have suggested that it highlights human interdependence as well as the scale of the potential consequences of existing political struggles and patterns of ecological devastation.[103] Positing causes and effects at the level of the species displaces recourse to racial difference as a way of explaining human tendencies, and envisioning a necessarily mutual destiny for all cuts across existing social distinctions to suggest the ontological imperative of a shared humanity. This account of human sameness offers an inclusive vision of humanity, albeit apocalyptically inflected. If it challenges Euro-American notions of personhood (the human-as-Man), though, it also makes peoplehood (the existence of distinct political entities) epiphenomenal, or perhaps entirely irrelevant. Insisting on the singularity of humanity as a means of contesting racializing conceptions of the human can orient away from engaging the existence of *peoples*. That intellectual and political tendency can reduce possibilities for acknowledging both the actually existing multiplicity of collective lifeways and the normative value of such acknowledgment of disparate, nonidentical ways of being human. Instead, commitment to the existence of distinct peoples appears in the trilogy as a sign of violent, *uncivilized* tendencies. The trilogy, then, illustrates how Indigenous self-determination can be translated in ways that seek to render it transparent, in Glissant's terms, within the framework of amalgamation/enfleshment, rather than recognizing a kind of political difference that cannot be fully rendered in the terms of (antiblack) racialization.

Butler suggests the potential for significant distinctions among human groups only to subordinate them to a spectrum of relative "civilized"-ness. In *Dawn*, readers learn that Lilith studied anthropology, which she describes as wanting to understand "[d]ifferent people. . . . People who didn't do things the way we did them" (87). *Difference* here marks distinctions among peoples, collective forms of being and becoming that remain nonidentical to each other. Later in a conversation with Tate, Lilith says, "It seemed to me that my culture—ours—was running headlong over a cliff. And, of course, as it turned out, it was. I thought there must be saner ways of life," and Tate responds, "Human beings are more alike than different—damn sure more alike than we like to admit. I wonder if the same thing wouldn't have happened eventually, no matter which two cultures gained the ability to wipe one another out along with the rest of the world" (132). Butler juxtaposes two incommensurate perspectives on humanity: one in which the devastation of the war can be traced to the vision and practices of a given "culture" that can be distinguished from that of other "cultures," which themselves might open onto other futures; and another in which all human beings have innate inclinations, such that the variety in modes of cultural expression or collective lifeways are of limited importance in terms of the species's ultimate turn toward violence. While this exchange between Lilith and Tate suggests that this disagreement will provide a central tension in the novel's (and the trilogy's) account of humanity, it largely vanishes. Lilith's initial perspective suggests that differences among human lifeworlds might provide the basis for an ethics in which acknowledging the opacity of others' ways of being could allow for sustained and respectful engagement across such differences. However, after this point in the trilogy, *difference* becomes a way of talking about the distinctions between human and Oankali modes of embodiment and relation—an ethics of enfleshment versus one of propertied modes of personhood that tend toward violence.

The potential for recognizing forms of sustained and meaningful distinction among human peoples, which also would provide a positive political content for notions of political self-determination, is set aside in favor of a developmental trajectory for all of humanity, along which particular behavior can be labeled progressive or regressive. Early in *Dawn*, Jdahya notes that those humans revived "will all be from what you would call civilized societies" (leaving aside Indigenous peoples in ways discussed earlier) (32). "Civilized" refers to a kind of society within a hierarchical ranking of human development that Lilith's invocation of "cultures" would seem to challenge. Yet that qualified account of the existence of diverse sorts of societies gives way to a vision, and fear, of human movement backward along a singular axis. The possibility of living in the jungle without prewar forms of built infrastructure is cast by Titus (the man Lilith meets aboard ship who assaults her) as "living like a cavewoman," and Lilith replies, "We don't have to forget what we know. . . . We don't have to go back to the Stone Age" (92). She thinks soon afterward, "Of course there were people who would toss aside civilized restraint" (94), and after having awakened a number of people, Lilith prevents a rape, asserting, "Nobody here is property. . . . There'll be no back-to-the-Stone-Age caveman bullshit! . . . We stay human. We treat each other like people" (178). In these moments, to be "civilized" means being more advanced, including illustrating forms of care and "restraint," and to lack civilization entails degenerating into cavemen/cavewomen, including viewing other persons as "property." Normative humanness as such, "treat[ing] each other like people," comes to be associated with forms of improvement that can be distinguished from the savage possibilities of living in the jungle. To "know" how to behave in ethical ways entails having "civilized restraint," such that interpersonal violence can be understood as a function of less developed social forms—those that resemble "the Stone Age" due to the absence of the accoutrement of *civilization*. The plurality of "cultures" is supplanted by movement along a unified timeline, in which the human capacity for enlightenment (equated with "civilized" behavior) is measured against the regressive pull of inborn inclinations toward violence (particularly as an expression of possessive instincts toward claiming ownership).

While the novels' association of backwardness with the jungle as well as the lack of particular forms of material culture raises questions about the texts' way of employing "civilized," I want to bracket those issues for a moment in order to explore the kind of ethical vision that emerges out of treating humanity as a singular entity. If racialization (at least in Euro-American contexts) proceeds through the differentiation of humanity into populations defined by relative conformity to the normative vision of the human, then the trilogy's universalization of genetic (in)capacity can be interpreted as repudiating that mode of hierarchization. Everyone equally bears the contradiction, so no particular group can be said to be more immanently oriented toward aggression and brutality than any other. From this perspective, *civilized* and *savage* serve as ways of marking relations to a shared potential for imposing hierarchy, with advancement correlating to an ability to contain or manage such hierarchical impulses. The idea of a shared drive toward hierarchy on the part of all humans works counter to a hierarchical (racialized) ranking of *kinds* of humans: in fact, racialization itself comes to appear as an expression of this genetic flaw rather than indicative of anything about the differential capacities of the persons so categorized. As Tucker suggests, "The characterization of alien encounters as proof of the limitations of the racial categories with which we are familiar has some merit; an investment in a common humanity that transcends race can be and has been a powerful anti-racist tool and inspiration."[104] Similarly, in "Political Science Fictions," Walter Benn Michaels observes, "[I]t might be argued that one of the points of the trilogy is to render racial difference irrelevant or, more generally, by dramatizing the difference between humans and aliens, to render all differences between humans irrelevant."[105] *Xenogenesis*'s account of human-alien difference, then, offers an antiracist universalism.

In downplaying racial difference in favor of an account of human similitude, Butler suggests that Oankali sociality—organized around change, interdependence, and consensus—is ultimately less murderous and wantonly destructive than that of humans.[106] When Lilith indicates to Akin that he should "embrace difference" in ways that emulate the Oankali (329), "difference" can be understood as referring less to preserving or crossing specific identity boundaries than to a desirable capacity for relation and transformation that humans are cast as lacking.[107] To desire difference is to avoid human processes of hierarchization and attendant forms of aggression, such as racialization and racism. Thus, the trilogy's account of human-Oankali amalgamation does not so much construct a new mixed identity as seek to envision the undoing of human inclinations toward forms of identification and differentiation that enact oppression and almost inevitably move toward cataclysmic violence. While critics have argued over the extent to which the novels ultimately endorse a vision of genetic determinism, the stakes of Butler's portrayal of humanity lie less in the degree of her commitment to the biological as the means of accounting for human behavior than the dystopian vision of such behavior (and its relatively entrenched character) as juxtaposed with the possibilities for negotiation and interdependence offered by Oankali social formations.[108] As Hoda M. Zaki observes, "What she denies to humans she invests in her description of alien societies: her aspirations for a more humane community, where consensus is reached through communication and dissent."[109] Articulating the notion of a shared humanity that exceeds or underlies all other identities while simultaneously emphasizing the tendencies of that humanity toward horrific violence, Butler stages human-Oankali difference as a normative distinction between modes of being and becoming that enable and enhance life and those that move toward devastation. As Weheliye suggests, following Sylvia Wynter, the dominant Euro-American account of selfhood "tends to recognize the humanity of racialized subjects only in the restricted idiom of personhood-as-ownership," and he asks, "[W]hat different modalities of the human come to light if we do not take the liberal humanist figure of Man as the master-subject but focus on how humanity has been imagined and lived by those subjects excluded from this domain?"[110] In *Xenogenesis*, such modalities appear as Oankali capacities, plasticities, and trans potentialities. Through the Oankali, Butler explores the possibilities for the kinds of "genres of the human" beyond Man toward which Wynter's work gestures. Wynter suggests the importance of being "able to reimagine the human in the terms of a new history whose narrative will enable us to co-identify ourselves each with the other, whatever our local ethnos/ethnoi."[111] Butler's trilogy speculatively gestures toward such a new history and co-identification through capacious, nonpossessive, and symbiotic relations with other beings that do not depend on dominant modes of human differentiation.

However, by singularizing humanity in order to challenge (racial) hierarchy and juxtaposing it to non-propertied (Oankali) modes of being, the novels leave self-determination and peoplehood with no content other than the collective effort and desire to preserve vicious human tendencies. In raising the issue of the human Akjai, Butler suggests that positing an overarching vision for human betterment (Oankali conceptions of "life") might itself implicitly function as a mode of domination, in which human refusal is cast as expressive of disability. The trilogy, then, implies that peoplehood—including the right of a collectivity to define the terms of its own development and welfare—might serve as a necessary normative principle. Yet if humanity as a whole constitutes a single "people," with the Earth as its "home," then whatever ethical force peoplehood has in the novels attaches to its use to refer to the species as such rather than to intraspecies (political) collectivities. In offering an antiracist account of human unity, the novels displace the existence of meaningfully distinct human "societies" and "ways of life," implicitly casting such formations as themselves indicative of human hierarchical propensities—symptoms of the contradiction. Within this frame, self-determination appears as a right to regression. If all people equally participate in a singular timeline (moving away from living like cavepeople in "the Stone Age") and are equally capable of forms of civilization and savagery, the refusal of an undifferentiated humanity and the defense of the existence of a plurality of peoples come to appear as a backward movement along the line of universal progress, as a rejection of necessarily overarching values that seek to promote the undoing of hierarchy-generating boundaries. The novels shift away from an engagement with modes of difference among kinds of human collectivities (peoples) to a contrast between two modes of being—one based on hierarchy (a shared human tendency) and the other on open-ended, relational becoming (Oankali modes of "difference"). In doing so, Butler leaves little room for thinking about the dynamics and ethics of interaction among (place-based) polities, even as the novels register and reflect on the problems of imposing Oankali difference in the name of "life."

Thus, two incommensurate kinds of claims are being played out in the trilogy in ways that work at normative cross-purposes to each other: (1) humans need, as a species, to be more relational, adaptive, and less fixated on distinguishing among themselves, a tendency that functions in oppressive and destructive ways; and (2) insisting on the existence of universalizing conceptions of improvement (of what will facilitate "life") functions as a mode of violence, especially when the refusal of such conceptions is cast as illustrative of backwardness or incapacity.[112] While at times humanity operates in the novels as a "people" articulating what are cast as legitimate collective claims (to autonomy, territorial separation, and self-governance), more often humanity functions as a collection of persons. In exploring an ethics of personhood, Butler consistently orients away from engaging the politics of peoplehood. The modes of hierarchy and discrimination at play in "civilized societies"—the human-as-Man—serve as the background against which to imagine alternatives, in which human beings can be opened to horizontal, consensus-based forms of complex relationality.

If this vision engenders speculations on the possibility for human freedom amid the afterlives of enslavement, it also more or less accepts as an organizing premise that forms of collective territoriality indicate investments in propertied forms of selfhood that engender violence. In *Dawn*, Lilith indicates to the other human survivors that prior political divisions have ceased to exist in the wake of the war, saying, "Down on Earth, . . . there are no people left to draw lines on maps and say which sides of those lines are the right sides. There is no government left. No human government, anyway" (141). However, while the novels focus on the English-speaking resister villages, Butler observes in passing that villages have formed around preexisting linguistic, religious, and national distinctions: "[Akin] knew the people and languages of a Chinese resister village, an Igbo village, three Spanish-speaking villages made up of people from many countries, a Hindu village, and two villages of Swahili-speaking people from different countries" (434). One might understand such divisions as indicative of "cultures," "ways of life," or "societies," extending and changing prewar collective identifications in the context of these new circumstances. Despite raising this potential, though, the novels offer little sense of distinctions among resisters with respect to their behavior. They all act in ways that express their shared contradiction—the species-wide tendencies toward hierarchy and associated patterns of assault. Fairly early in *Adulthood Rites*, Nikanj informs Tino, "Some of the southern resister groups are already making guns" (291), and the use of those weapons by humans against each other becomes ever more prominent over the course of the trilogy. At one point, Dichaan (Akin's male Oankali parent) observes, "We've collected their guns twice since they took [Akin, who was kidnapped by resisters as an infant]. They always make more, and the new ones are always more effective. Greater range, greater accuracy, greater safety for the Humans using them" (428). Although offered from an Oankali perspective, this sentiment captures the portrait of intervillage relations Butler provides, in which "cultural" or other distinctions among resisters pale in the face of a common harnessing of intelligence to the project of securing dominance. Moreover, insistence on distinctions among human collectives comes to appear as symptomatic of those very violent tendencies. Beyond villages' efforts to defend their geographies against incursion by other resisters, guns provide a means of increasing wealth through "trade." Unlike in the Oankali version, these exchanges usually involve captured women and children (sometimes constructs) who serve as sources of value by being circulated as fungible, owned objects (345, 385). Similarly, raiding involves theft, murder, and destruction for the purposes of increasing one's capacity to "trade" or for decimating rivals. Shared humanity entails complementary drives toward possession and exclusion that grow out of individual genetic urgings, and even though the villages might be conceptualized as peoples, they function less as entities with their own practices and internal dynamics than as extensions and consolidations of species-wide kinds of contradiction-shaped personhood.

The only holdout to this pattern appears to be Phoenix, the village to which Akin eventually is brought when he is captured by raiders. It is the most developed of the villages in its reconstruction of prewar forms of architecture and material culture, and the novel implicitly connects this return to ways of life from before the nuclear holocaust with nonaggression toward other villages and the absence of weapons. In other words, Phoenix provides an example of the kinds of condensations that occur under the rubric of being "civilized." Yet, the people of Phoenix eventually decide to begin manufacturing guns (401), and in the time between Akin's being redeemed from captivity and his returning to Earth in the wake of having secured support for his Mars plan, Phoenix degenerates considerably: "There was trash in the street. . . . Some of the houses were obviously vacant. A couple of them had been partially torn down. Others seemed ready to fall down" (482). The collapse of the built environment correlates with increasing moral degradation, with guns proliferating not merely for the purpose of preventing raids from elsewhere but as tools for raiding by men from Phoenix (485, 497). The final image of the novel is Akin and those who saved him from attempted murder by their fellow villagers walking away from Phoenix, which is engulfed in flames. Thus, the only two detailed examples readers get of postwar human collectivities (Phoenix and the village of reproductive but inbred, and consequently "disabled," resisters in *Imago*) implode—or, perhaps more precisely, devolve—into violence, suggesting not only the work of human tendencies but also how forms of intrahuman peoplehood come to serve as expressions of immanently destructive individual inclinations while then being undone by them.

The novels cast collective forms of identity, and their use as ways of legitimizing violence (such as in the raiding among villages), as arising out of species-wide individual tendencies toward hierarchization. In this way, Butler's narrative takes a fairly Hobbesian bent, imagining human propensities as inevitably leading toward mutual assault and destruction.[113] Thomas Hobbes famously suggested that "the condition of meer Nature . . . is a condition of Warre of every man against every man," creating conditions of "continual feare, and danger of violent death" in which "the life of man" is "solitary, poor, nasty, brutish, and short."[114] In order to put an end to this perpetual cycle of aggression, there needs to be a sovereign power to which all people surrender their personal authority so that the sovereign can regulate their actions with respect to each other. Here, the Oankali serve that role, but instead of emerging as absolute rulers, their fleshliness suggests the potential for modes of being and becoming not predicated on warfare, hierarchy, and violence. Rather, Oankalis enact forms of amalgamation through which they and humans (and other subjects of "trade") are transformed, less creating a hybrid than becoming anomalous through an eternally ongoing process of change. In displacing Euro-American forms of sovereignty, including regimes of propertied being, the Oankali offer humans ways of participating in networks of relation that fundamentally alter the experience of personhood.

Yet in this mode of speculative critique and redescription, what happens to sovereignty as such? Butler largely addresses dominant political and economic formations in terms of conceptions and experiences of privatized and racializing personhood that the novels juxtapose with other possibilities, which, as I have argued, can be understood as drawn from histories of Black fungibility and enfleshment. Thus, in depicting the aggression of the resisters as well as the possibilities offered by the Oankalis, the trilogy foregrounds questions of embodiment and kinds of selfhood in ways that tend to defer speculative exploration of differences among kinds of peoplehood and governance—the potential for varied emplaced collective lifeways/lifeworlds.[115] The novels, then, stage engagement with difference as a means of moving beyond questions of sovereignty rather than, say, addressing varied formations of sovereignty and peoplehood and complex negotiations among them. Thus, even as the trilogy raises the issues of invasion, occupation, settlement, and political self-determination, the novels address them against the background of questions of personhood, fungibility, and embodiment in ways that translate modes of collectivity (call it nationhood, peoplehood, sovereignty) as regressive expressions of claims to property that will almost certainly eventuate in brutality. To be and become "civilized" in the novels' framing, then, cannot involve such collective identification and enduring modes of shared placemaking, since they are presented as necessarily enacting propertied modes of personhood that cannot but eventuate in hierarchy and violence.

THE *XENOGENESIS* TRILOGY ENVISIONS the potential for moving beyond the endemic forms of oppression and aggression that seem to characterize human history. In contrast to the pursuit of racialized and racializing modes of hierarchy, Butler offers an (alien) ethos of amalgamation in which modes of fleshliness predominate. In doing so, she highlights networks of interrelation in ways that challenge post-Enlightenment notions of personhood as insular autonomy ("Man" in Weheliye and Wynter's terms). Rather than envisioning a process of mixture, which continues to preserve the categorical purity of the types to be blended so as to register their combination, the novels suggest a normative embrace of *difference* as an open-ended process of becoming through interaction with the unknown that generates new possibilities for being in the world. This vision of ongoing transformation is juxtaposed with the ingrained human "contradiction" that drives people to mark boundaries (personal and collective) and to assert dominance, including in racial terms. However, as Robert Nichols observes, while "antiracist discourses may serve a critical and destabilizing function in one context, in another (specifically settler-colonial) context, that *same* discourse may serve as totalizing and hegemonic function. This is particularly the case when the problem of racism is taken up . . . as a failure to properly universalize the category of the 'human.'"[116] In totalizing humanity, in terms of its capacity for both destruction and fleshly engagement, the trilogy offers an antiracist framework that, in its implicit engagements with indigeneity (both in terms of the character of Oankali sociality and the potential for an autonomous, self-governed human community), transposes Indigenous peoplehood and sovereignty into a frame of reference in which they appear either dislocated from collective placemaking or as a racializing attachment to defending property.

The novels do not so much efface indigeneity as allude to it, as both ideal and foil, in ways that work toward making it transparent within the terms of histories of (anti)blackness. The aspects of Oankali modes of sociality that seem most alien to the human characters can be understood as indexing conventional accounts of Indigenous difference, particularly in terms of attunement with their environment, expansive and non-nuclear kinship formations, and consensus-based processes of decision making. Yet if these qualities so often attributed to Indigenous peoples (particularly in the Americas) serve as something of an aspirational horizon for the novels, indicating possibilities for becoming less driven to and by violence, they also appear disconnected from enduring connections to particular lands and waters. Oankalis are committed to continual interplanetary movement in ways that forbid persistent habitation, suggesting less a collective territoriality than a shared drive toward mobility in which lasting locatedness is experienced as stasis or degeneration. Humanity itself also takes on qualities of indigeneity, particularly in terms of the resisters' desire to remain a "people" separate from Oankalis, with Earth as their shared home. Through Akin and the movement to recognize a human Akjai, Butler offers an account of the ethics of self-determination, raising questions about the legitimacy of Oankali narratives of protection. The right of a(n Indigenous) people to self-determination serves as a key part of the trilogy, and in exploring this idea, the novels implicitly suggest how racialized biopolitical assessments of fitness can function as justification for denying or deferring recognition of political autonomy, even as the novels largely seem to endorse the conceptions of health and disability on which the Oankali rely in their judgments about the relative potential for "life." However, (Indigenous) peoplehood in the texts appears less to mark the existence of a polity or set of polities than to index the desire to maintain forms of (racial) purity as the basis for membership—in this case, the normative human physiology that the Oankalis seek to transmute through trade. In this way, self-determination strongly signifies in the trilogy as a desire to maintain the identities, territorialities, and associated kinds of aggression that characterize the human contradiction. Thus, although the trilogy presents self-determination (or a people's sovereignty over themselves) as an important norm, the ethical force of that ideal is hollowed out by its alignment with what is cast as an investment in property—both in (kinds of) bodies and land. Moreover, when the novels do allude to actual Indigenous peoples, they appear as themselves anachronisms, either paralyzed by intimate knowledge of a world which has disappeared or as themselves having vanished (leaving only millennia-old traces that signify as the now lost/ destroyed past of humankind).[117]

Focusing on questions of embodiment and doing so in ways that are about individuals' capacity for nonhierarchical engagements with each other, then, can incline away from a discussion of collective political processes, including their variability and the attendant ethics of respecting those kinds of *difference*. Oankali forms of relation and adaptation illustrate possibilities for displacing the constrictions and oppressions of dominant Euro-American modes of personhood, suggesting the value of an expansive openness to other beings and one's surroundings—the sort of "flux, process, and potential" that has been attributed to Black bodies and used as a tool of white subjectivity and world making.[118] The novels emphasize fleshly transformations at the level of bodily experience and resulting changes in interpersonal interactions rather than detailing what might be characterized as Oankali modes of governance, including how the trade with humans necessarily changes those dynamics or how prior exchanges with other species have done so in the past. In the absence of a robust conception of peoplehood, and the potential multiplicity of peoples, the trilogy's efforts to deracialize personhood (to envision possibilities for exceeding dominant, hierarchical Euro-American conceptions of what it means to be human) end up translating Indigenous self-determination and territoriality as a kind of unfortunate, if ethically unavoidable, backwardness. The possibility for non-possessive modes of identity and relationality—individual and collective—arises in the texts as a function of deterritorialization, a divorce from enduring connection to any particular place that itself seems to be cast as a more "civilized" mode of being. The trilogy embraces an amalgamation imaginary (generating anomaly rather than mixture) that enables thinking against current modes of racialization (including discourses of disablement) but that simultaneously defers the possibility of engaging with forms of peoplehood and their emplacements, Indigenous or otherwise, except to understand such claims as ultimately racialized and regressive. In its subjunctive relation to the real, *Xenogenesis*, therefore, provides a speculative means of tracing some of the challenges and impasses that can arise when approaching indigeneity from within conceptual and political frameworks oriented around the fungibilities of the racialized body.

3

CARCERAL SPACE AND FUGITIVE MOTION

The vast intensification and proliferation of apparatuses of imprisonment over the past forty years suggest a growing experience of emplacement in terms of racialized carcerality for Black subjects in the United States. While rates of imprisonment hovered at around one per one thousand people in the U.S. population over the course of the twentieth century, in the 1970s the rates began to rise precipitously, becoming one in 107 by the 2000s. Currently, about 3 percent of adults (one in thirty-one) are subjected to criminal justice supervision, with about 2.2 million people in prisons and jails and 4.8 million on probation or parole. These figures represent a fivefold growth over the past forty years. With respect to African Americans, the statistics are even more dire. African Americans stand at about 13 percent of the U.S. population, but they represent approximately 37 percent of the prison population. In the mid-2000s, about one in fourteen Black men was incarcerated versus one in 106 white men, and those African Americans born after 1965 who have not earned a high school diploma are more likely than not to be imprisoned at some point in their lives.[1] More than solely illustrating a sharp rise in incarceration, these statistics index a much wider and intensifying system of surveillance and regulation that governs Black neighborhoods, particularly in urban areas. If fungibility and enfleshment provide a frame for conceptualizing Black embodiment, as discussed in the previous chapter, carcerality speaks to the geographies of Black life in the United States. As Alice Goffman illustrates, in inner-city African American neighborhoods "the role of law enforcement changes from keeping communities safe from a few offenders to bringing an entire neighborhood under suspicion and surveillance."[2] Carceral space, then, extends far beyond the prison per se, offering an ordering paradigm for blackness in the contemporary United States.

The criminal justice system increasingly insinuates its technologies of mapping and capture into virtually all aspects of everyday Black life in places deemed criminal largely due to the predominance of people of color. Lisa Marie Cacho suggests, "[R]ace and racialized spaces are the signifiers that make an unsanctioned action legible as illicit and recognizable as a crime."[3] The association of particular places with nonwhite subjects transforms those areas into sites of heightened police scrutiny, regardless of whether criminal activity of various kinds actually is greater in them.[4] Law enforcement presence in Black communities has been characterized by some as akin to an "occupation,"[5] but since this mounting surveillance and regulation is not justified in race-explicit terms, instead legitimized as part of a broader need to maintain "law and order" in putatively high-crime areas, it does not constitute something like a formal apartheid structure, despite the fact that proportionately more African Americans currently are imprisoned in the United States than were Blacks in South Africa during the height of the apartheid regime.[6] As long as policies are couched in facially neutral criteria, without directly indicating an intent to target people of color, they do not trigger investigation into the ways they might violate constitutional principles and laws against racial discrimination. Such patterns arise out of the history of what Naomi Murakawa has termed "liberal modernization" and the "civil rights carceral state," in which putatively antiracist efforts to reduce racial bias in law enforcement after World War II and through the Civil Rights era gave rise to the notion that "racial violence could be corrected through the establishment of well-defined, rule-bound, and rights-laden uniform state processes": "[L]iberal law-and-order reinforced the common sense that racism is a ghost in the machine, some immaterial force detached from the institutional terrain of racialized wealth inequality and the possessive investment in whiteness," such that "the more carceral machinery was rights-based and rule-bound, the more racial disparity was isolatable to 'real' black criminality."[7] From this perspective, the problem of racism lies in attitudinal prejudice rather than structural disadvantage. Therefore, the vast expansion of imprisonment and police power in ways that are directed toward and that decimate communities of color are not conceptualized as inherently functioning as a mode of institutionalized racism so long as the rules instituted and followed themselves do not directly invoke race—or, more specifically, blackness—as an organizing logic. Framed in this way, the transformation of Black neighborhoods into carceral spaces is not understood as constituting racist practice, because such practices take shape around apparently racially neutral goals and metrics.

These dynamics provide the animating context for Walter Mosley's *Futureland: Nine Stories of an Imminent World* (2001), in which he offers a speculative theorization of the principles immanently at play in such neoliberal modes of captivity while addressing the central function of processes of racialization in the kinds of datafication on which such social mappings increasingly rely. This collection of linked stories set a few decades into the future explores the proliferation of carceral mechanisms and technologies beyond the prison, including the reorganization of everyday geographies in ways that facilitate state-sanctioned containment separate from punishment for criminal activity per se. Yet while largely focused on African Americans, the text presents these patterns as expanding to incorporate large swaths of the population, building on existing racial demarcations while also generating additional and compounding modes of racialization that arise out of the application of ostensibly race-neutral criteria. In this way, Mosley sketches the potentials for radically expanding existing carceral topographies while engaging the ways such captivities reconfigure existing racism(s). In offering this speculative analysis, he suggests the political futility of collective assertions of place and explores the notion of perpetual fugitivity as a means of realizing freedom.[8] Much of the scholarly work that attends to the racial dynamics of the criminal justice system focuses on the ways it targets people of color and seeks to dominate areas associated with such populations, but as Mosley suggests, the matrix of carcerality itself engenders, intensifies, and disseminates processes of racialization. Michelle Alexander observes, "[T]he 'negative credential' associated with a criminal record represents a unique mechanism of state-sponsored stratification" that functions as "a form of branding by the government," later adding that "mass-incarceration, like Jim Crow, is a 'race-making institution.'"[9] The attribution of differential identity in relation to actual or potential criminal acts—or violations of existing institutionalized rules and norms—creates a status distinction between those deemed criminal and those not. While in theory anyone could commit a crime, legal, political, and popular discourses cast inclinations toward criminality as innate within particular groups in ways that do not appear to follow from race as such, even as these attributions both implicitly rely on existing racial categories and portray the forms of belonging they cite as indicative of inherent qualities in ways that function as racial knowledge.[10]

In *Futureland*, the possibilities for being consigned to a criminalized status expand exponentially beyond current racial categories, suggesting a vast extension of the "race-making" capacities of the carceral state and its geographies of internment.[11] While appropriate behavior largely gets defined in terms of gainful employment and conformity to corporation-driven mandates, the text illustrates how evaluations of the propensity for (non)normativity themselves depend less on individuals' particular choices than the ways all aspects of their lives are collated into statistical sets that function as racializing assemblages.[12] As David Lyon indicates about current systems of surveillance, "If the category in which your personal data place you renders you 'suspicious,' then you are hardly 'innocent until proven guilty,'" adding, "It is a profile that, in many cases, simply suggests what *sort* of person is here. The category, not the character, is all-important."[13] In the text, to be unemployed itself becomes a quasi-criminalized status, one that leads (absent any judicial process whatsoever) to confinement in a subterranean space called "Common Ground." What emerges in Mosley's stories is something like a capitalistically oriented eugenics, in which determinations of fitness less follow from racial identity as conventionally understood than from population-making calculations driven by statistical models of likely contributions to revenue and relative costs that take place alongside legally mandated modes of racial neutrality. In addition, options for residence and mobility are scaled in relation to these actuarial evaluations and their racializing trajectories; the social landscape is organized around ostensibly objective assessments of employability, such that the prisonlike structure of Common Ground simply serves as the extreme of tiered layers of carcerally inflected space in which everyone but the wealthiest are enmeshed. Mosley's futurist imaginary, then, highlights the ways the prison functions in the contemporary moment less as anomaly than paradigm, as a state-organized means of regulating (un)employment in which racializing attributions of innate ability and aberrance—and aggregations of those potentialities into categorical identities (especially through forms of dataveillance)—regulate one's relation to place even, or perhaps especially, in the absence of explicit race talk and segregation. *Futureland* lifts off of the present in order to engage in a speculative redescription of the early twentieth century that traces and highlights patterns of racializing governmentality; thus, the text enables an engagement with carcerality and fugitivity as *ways of figuring* the immanent dynamics of contemporary sociopolitical formations.

Communal claims to place play no role in the text, since Mosley offers no sense that they could do anything other than reiterate extant systems of domination (in ways reminiscent of the *Xenogenesis* trilogy). The geographies of everyday life are thoroughly regulated and stratified by political-corporate interests, apparatuses, and mappings. There is virtually no place that is not owned and controlled by corporations, such that alternative projects of occupancy and sovereignty appear completely untenable, at best, and, at worst, merely replicate existing modes of governmentality. Given its focus on questions of collective situatedness, though, Daniel Wilson's *Robopocalypse* series can provide an illuminating counterpoint to Mosley. Wilson's novels help highlight how Mosley's work orients away from questions of territoriality, thereby drawing attention to the potential difficulties of engaging indigeneity—and place-based peoplehood more broadly—within a frame organized around captivity and flight. Wilson's texts imagine how existing, reconfigured, and newly formed peoples might develop forms of located collectivity in the midst of technologically induced cataclysm. Himself Cherokee, Wilson offers a vision in which connections to territory remain a durable part of human social life, even—and in some ways especially—in the face of the breakdown of contemporary social structures and geographies. In becoming conscious, an artificial intelligence, Archos, launches a campaign of mass murder against humanity in which wireless networks provide the means for conscripting all manner of machines into the aim of decimating the human race. However, in this dystopian imaginary, modes of peoplehood and placemaking become crucial—to humans, robots, and various kinds of sentient beings that arise out of human advances in computing. While not primarily focused on Indigenous peoples' struggles for self-determination as such, the novels highlight the existence and emergence of forms of collective territoriality that not only serve as the basis for human social organization and survival but that are presented as integral to the being and becoming of all life. In this way, the framework through which Wilson approaches the violence and possibilities of technology, and futurist speculation more broadly, can be understood as drawing on the principles and politics of indigeneity, even when not engaging Indigenous people(s) per se (although the novels do return repeatedly to the Osage Nation in ways that underline Indigenous histories and contemporary presence, while also largely leaving aside Indigenous mobilities and diaspora). The centrality of these issues in Wilson's work helps draw attention to their absence in Mosley's—the ways that long-term relations to particular spaces function for Mosley as an effect of imprisonment rather than a vehicle of liberation or autonomy.

Mosley figures freedom not in terms of collective habitation but in/as flight. If Octavia Butler makes the malleability attributed to blackness into a touchstone for speculatively envisioning antiracist modes of fleshly becoming, *Futureland* presents the lack of spatial fixity as crucial to thwarting extant systems of racialization. In this way, the text articulates a poetics of fugitivity as a positive conception of open relation that seeks to break from the racializing geographies imposed by the state (largely acting in the service of corporate interests). This investment in the liberatory potentials of movement, as contrasted with carceral technologies and cartographies, can generate difficulties in engaging forms of identification and relation predicated on (a politics of) collective emplacement. Such an equivocation can be seen at play in Mosley's later novel *The Wave* (2007), with which the chapter closes. In the novel, an entity, the Wave, that has been living underground for millions of years on lands now claimed by the United States becomes active and is targeted for destruction by the U.S. government as a threat to national security and sovereignty. The entity itself appears as a pool of blackness, and the fact that the duration of its dwelling dwarfs the history of U.S national sovereignty becomes an occasion for an implicit meditation on the question of the relation between blackness and indigeneity and the affective dynamics of Black presence in the Americas. However, the text's representation of located belonging comes to be oriented around flight (movement away from the Earth) and imprisonment—capture and torture within the expanding apparatus of internment and state-authorized murder in the wake of 9/11. The novel's exploration of the relation between blackness and indigeneity occurs against the background of mobility and escape. The novel, then, brings into greater speculative relief the conceptual tensions that arise when addressing the relations between Black and Indigenous histories and aspirations through the frame of carcerality and fugitivity.

Neoliberal Apartheid

Set a few decades from now, *Futureland* explores the ways that carceral technologies and geographies extend far beyond imprisonment as such. The text addresses how incarceration operates less as a particular kind of space or social institution than as a broader framework that organizes the political economy and geographies of contemporary life. Systems of data gathering, storage, calculation, and evaluation become mechanisms through which to type, manage, and contain groups who apparently do not contribute to social welfare, defined in terms of the capacity to produce profit. This political construction of tiered statuses of social value based on supposed tendencies toward (non)productivity relies on processes of racialization, defining and distinguishing among populations based on what are treated as innate inclinations and, thereby, implementing mechanisms of racializing discipline even in the absence of discussion of race or apparent racist intention. In depicting the ubiquity of such categorizing imperatives, particularly with respect to relative value for commerce, *Futureland* sketches and theorizes the operation of an antiblack carceral imaginary that relies on fashioning profiles for types of persons and multiplying forms of segregation based on attributions of "antisocial" threat. Mosley suggests that the penal system and the institutionalized underdevelopment of impoverished urban areas in the present express an expansive and intensive trajectory toward neoliberal apartheid.[14] The text suggests, though, that the forms of racialization that make possible these geographies operate in a race-neutral mode that needs to be distinguished from avowed white supremacy in scope, practice, and aim.

In Mosley's future world, prisoners are not so much abandoned to specialized, isolated spaces as made the target for privatized modes of evaluation to determine the effectiveness of technologies that might be employed more widely with respect to the population at large. The text features two particular technologies: a "snake" bag that attaches to a person's arm and jacks into the person's nervous system, controlling the wearer's emotional and physiological responses to stimuli and detecting and preventing unsanctioned behavior;[15] and a fully automated justice-dispensing computer system in which the judge and prosecutor are combined, witnesses are neurally linked in for "fact-gathering examination," and the jury comprises the personalities of ten thousand people that have been loaded into the system's matrix (209–11). The snake technology is employed at Angel's Island, "the first and most feared nonnational private prison" (87), to which convicted persons from the United States are consigned after having been stripped of their citizenship (93),[16] and justice computing is institutionalized by the California legislature, although "every other court system in the country was waiting to install its own automatic justice system" due to the absence of "any backlog in Sacramento" (213). These technologies enable the extension of mechanisms of carcerality to far more persons and places than those accused or convicted of violating the law and the institutions in which they are warehoused. The main character in "Angel's Island," a hacker named Bits, succeeds in both taking over the prison via a computer program he designed and sending out a series of messages that includes the following: "The ChemSys Corporation has signed contracts with the federal government to supply over three million snake packs to the military and mental services by the year 2053" (125). Moreover, Frendon Blythe, the man subjected to a fully computerized trial in "Little Brother," predicts, "Once they automate justice and wire it up there won't be any more freedom at all. They'll have monitors and listening devices everywhere. One day you'll be put on trial while sleepin' in your bed" (214).[17] The criminal justice system serves as an incubator for producing forms of control that can be implemented elsewhere, further suggesting that the entire apparatus of imprisonment functions less as an end unto itself—for rehabilitation, incapacitation, or deterrence—than as a testing ground for modes of carcerality whose horizon always lay beyond the courthouse or prison walls.[18]

Determinations of risk and expendability, and thus of subjection to varieties of carceral management, rely on the (re)production of racializing typologies of threat under the guise of implementing a neutral calculus of risk. When Bits first arrives at Angel's Island, the guards insist, "Until you prove that you are rehabilitated your citizenship has been suspended" (93), and the snake armband serves as the principal tool to measure that progress. However, rather than punishing people for infractions that they have committed, it responds to bodily impulses that are taken to signal disruptive inclinations: "It could read sexual excitation and violence in nerve endings; it could perceive biological needs in the blood. . . . The snake could also identify anxiety, depression, and even more complex psychological manifestations" (107). Those in the prison have been convicted of "antisocial behavior" (86), and given that putative *rehabilitation* entails monitoring and revising bodily response at levels that are barely conscious, if at all, such interventions implicitly posit proper sociality—and its violation—as a matter of ingrained physiological and psychological tendencies. Similarly, in assessing guilt and enacting punishment, the depersonalized process of adjudication featured in "Little Brother" relies on "objective" markers of threat, generating a profile in which particular kinds of data can be taken to indicate a propensity toward lawlessness. Challenging the decision-making tools and practices of the justice-dispensing computer, Frendon asserts, "In order to understand [my] reactions The Court [the automated system] must first understand the motivations which incited them. Therefore, The Court must have an understanding of me which is not genetically based, and that can only be gleaned through personal narrative" (215–16). In addition to sampling his genetic code, the judicial computer has at its disposal the records of his run-ins with authorities over the course of his life, neural testimony from witnesses, and available footage from public cameras. At one point, the guard remarks, "You can't fool these machines, son. They know everything about you from cradle to grave" (209). To "know everything" about someone means here to have access to specific kinds of institutional, locational, and biometric data that cumulatively are treated as constituting the totality of the person's selfhood and history. This data-double, as it has been called, provides the basis for evaluating Frendon's actions—in this case, shooting a police officer.[19] However, beyond the formal trial, this mode of profiling tends toward not simply an ever-expanding grid of surveillance but the use of such metrics in ways that supplant due process or, rather, that come to serve as the entirety of due process. An assemblage of data analyzed and evaluated by preprogrammed algorithms becomes the basis for determinations about whether someone remains free, relying on set indicators that generically function as proxies for "antisocial" intent. This combination of identification, sorting, and ascription constructs classes of persons whose ability to participate within social life must be constrained due to their supposedly innate inclinations.

Mosley suggests that institutionalized political and commercial uses of racialization give rise to a carceral imperative, drawing less on conventional racial categories than on forms of data correlation in assessing and aggregating individuals as types of persons.[20] To be a legitimate object of carceral regulation means being judged by authorities as having deep-seated propensities that disturb existing forms of social order, and while such predispositions toward threat might be distributed randomly through the population, the rates of incarceration point toward a different dynamic. All but one of the prisoners Bits encounters on Angel's Island are nonwhite (86), "over 80 percent of American-backed prisons were non-white" (110), and of those imprisoned, Black people continued to constitute a vastly disproportionate number (330).[21] These facts demonstrate that the attribution of antisocial orientation follows existing trajectories of racial differentiation, drawing on notions of menace already associated with nonwhiteness (and blackness, in particular) but coding such existing social correlations as race-neutral evidence of threat.[22] At various points, the text notes the existence of a legally mandated regime of color-blind judgment. In response to the ongoing existence of a white supremacist organization (the Itsies), Folio Johnson, a Black detective featured in "The Electric Eye," observes, "In this world where the last thing you got to worry about is skin color and they still wanna kill me" (278), and in "The Nig in Me," the narrator indicates, "Racial profiling had been a broadcast offense for more than two decades" (322), with a bus driver later noting, "It's a punishable offense to slander race" (349). Furthermore, government officials, police, and business leaders repudiate the philosophy and actions of the Itsies, suggesting that their explicit white supremacy actively interferes with the regular functioning of commercial and political life. *Futureland*, then, implicitly poses the question, how does race become salient as a vector of incarceration within a networked informational system that does not rely on racial categories as such?

The text indicates that slavery in various forms persists, and it connects such patterns to the enchattelment of African people and the Middle Passage while also repeatedly linking the exercise of state power to whiteness. As inmates enter Angel's Island, guards inform them that they "are the property of Angel's Island now" (93), and they are set to work in collecting a particular kind of plant called "choke" (the replacement for tobacco) in an area referred to as the "plantation" (86–88).[23] In addition, ostensibly free people have the ability to sell their "labor contract" for their entire working lives to a particular corporation in exchange for necessary resources. As one character (Blue Nile in "En Masse") says of his own experience, "How else can a prod afford to take care of his loved ones? There's no more private property, hardly. All a prod's got is his labor," about which D'or (the owner of an independent diner) observes, "Bought his whole life, just like he was an old-time slave" (276). Beyond such allusions to what might be termed neo-slavery, Mosley directly references the history of Black abjection. In "Doctor Kismet," after a Black radical and former U.S. congressman, Akwande, has won a contest against the head of MacroCode (Doctor Kismet, who owns the nation of Home) that results in Kismet giving to the nation of Mali the rights for the replacement he's developed for petroleum, Akwande observes, "The world was set when they dragged the first African into a slave ship" (81). He earlier muses, "Generations of political struggle hadn't been enough to fully liberate his people. The weight of poverty, the failure of justice, came down on the heads of dark people around the globe. Capitalism along with technology had assured a perpetual white upper class" (73). The carceral cartographies that the text chronicles, then, appear here as deriving directly from the legacies of enslavement and colonialism.[24] Reciprocally, the disciplinary institutions that most directly enforce the current political and economic order are portrayed as saturated in whiteness. When Bits enters the warden's office at Angel's Island, "The illusion was that he stood on a clear glass floor that looked down upon an infinitely distant whiteness" (95), an expansive "white emptiness" (97), and when Folio Johnson enters an interrogation room in Police Central, "the hub of all law enforcement for the Twelve Fiefs of New York" (142), "everything was white—the walls, the long conference table, the chairs," creating a totally white surround (144).[25] Coupled with the text's periodic references to the vastly disproportionate imprisonment of African Americans, these moments cumulatively convey the sense that the racializations at play in defining, managing, and territorializing populations based on algorithmic assessments of threat—and the attendant production of forms of (non)personhood—function as merely another version of the same polarity in which humanness correlates with whiteness and blackness operates as the constitutive outside in need of continual caution and containment, whether explicitly characterized in these terms or not.[26]

However, even while noting the continuance of antiblackness as a force that shapes social life and continuing normative investments in whiteness, the text distinguishes the carceral dynamics it chronicles from conventional racial animus. In *Big Data*, Viktor Mayer-Schönberger and Kenneth Cukier argue that the mass and increasing availability of numerous kinds of quantified/quantifiable information—data—about persons, objects, events, and relations among them, combined with the growing computational ability of ordinary computers, provides the opportunity for generating kinds of knowledge heretofore impossible.[27] The ability of computers to draw on a range of data streams in producing accounts of connections in the world depends on generating statistical correlations among particular types of data. Yet in order for such correlations to occur, objects, persons, events, relations need to be *datafied*, transformed into "a data format" that allow them to be "quantified" so as to be "tabulated and analyzed."[28] That process requires that whatever is being datafied be isolated and categorized as a type that enables it to be counted and cross-referenced with other data points of that same type and of other types. However, how are the particular typologies and modes of categorization that constitute the data generated? What are the thresholds of correlation that count as relevant, and by whom are they set? How is the algorithm designed to calculate frequencies of relation among data points, and how are such correlations interpreted and given meaning? Moreover, what extant presuppositions influence all of these programming processes?[29] John Cheney-Lippold observes that "data does not naturally appear in the wild," and as Eduardo Bonilla-Silva notes, "The central component of any dominant racial ideology is its frames or *set paths for interpreting information*."[30] Numerous kinds of surveillance pervade ordinary life in Mosley's future world, and they are aggregated to create personalized data assemblages that continually are assessed for signs that someone might become a threat to "the economy."[31] These modes of data gathering include the following: having a personal bar code based on your eye scan that provides the means of accessing all computers; using an ID card to enter and exit all buildings; logging one's work hours and habits at work within a file held by both private business and the government; storing everyone's available funds ("credits") and expenditures within a centralized database; and having encoded on one's ID card one's personal bar code, work history (or "labor record"), current employment (or lack thereof), and DNA profile (which also provides the means of proving one has the right to vote).³² Although theoretically this information is required of all persons, its networked integration and algorithmic evaluation generates racializing types that serve as ways of assessing fitness for participation in social life. As Jasbir Puar says of current practices of "terrorist" surveillance, "Data collection enables a mapping of race through aggregates and disaggregates," adding that "the informational profile works to accuse in advance of subject formation."³³

Mosley investigates how racialization shapes the construction of reified profiles—particular data assemblages—that provide the basis for defining and differentiating among kinds of persons, providing the justification for such groups' carceral containment even in the absence of racial identification per se. As Dorothy Roberts suggests, racial identity serves as a proxy in investigating forms of genetic difference, functioning "as a convenient surrogate" through which to coalesce observed patterns at play in a population sample into a means of identifying a particular racial group and to present all members of that (nongenetically constituted) group as possessing such patterns.³⁴ If, as Cheney-Lippold illustrates, data profiles are generated through constructing algorithmic templates that are "epistemologically fabricated" and that produce a "datafied model" of a given identity,³⁵ racialization functions as a key conceptual technology shaping that practice. It provides a logic by which specific traits, practices, and locations associated with a particular group can be treated as proxies for the existence and coherence of that group, explaining observed phenomena in terms of inherent tendencies supposedly belonging to members of that group. Data correlation becomes understood as an outward manifestation that empirically indexes a group's essential character. Racialization provides the ideological matrix in which observed patterns can be fused to a collective identity in ways that attribute intrinsic properties to them as a(n invented) category of persons, rather than treating the category as itself a construction arising from the modes of data aggregation and analysis being employed.³⁶ The text suggests that the specific technologies associated with incarceration (such as the armband and automated judge) participate within this larger drive toward classification, in which patterns of activity that disturb the dynamics of production and profit become attributed to particular groups as an intrinsic potential they bear within them.³⁷

In the world of *Futureland*, health issues, records of education and employment, and patterns of residency all feature in determinations of fitness for ongoing and future employment, and while not explicitly referring to existing racial categories, these indices register the continuing effects of prior regimes of direct racial domination as well as of forms of discrimination carried out without explicitly indicating race.[38] Data systems, then, appear as if they simply register existing tendencies of diminished personhood rather than institutionally producing that status through the population-generating dynamics of the algorithms themselves. Such shared public-private administrative processes and decision making explain how color-blindness can be legally mandated while people of color, particularly people of African descent, make up the vast majority of those imprisoned and otherwise disallowed meaningful participation in social life.[39] In "Little Brother," in response to the guard's insistence that the computerized court "don't care about race or sex or if you're rich or poor," Frendon replies, "If I was rich I'd never see an automatic judge" (215), and earlier, he recalls a statement by one of the leaders of the Radical Congress, a Black oppositional group, that "objective" is "for the poor. The rich can still hire a flesh and blood lawyer" who will "ask for a living judge" (213).[40] In this way, Mosley illustrates how racialization functions as a crucial way of bridging the conceptual and practical gaps among gathering data, finding statistical correlations, and diagnosing a given person's abilities/proclivities by interpreting aggregated data points as expressive of the immanent coherence of a collective identity, while also treating such data as a proxy for inherent tendencies shared among all members of that group. The text suggests that there is an inherently racializing drift to these algorithmic typologies—toward attributions of inherent threat/incapacity.

The text further suggests that this process of locating and labeling persons as part of disruptive populations bears within it an animating drive toward containment, a carceral commitment to segregation and internment. The omnipresent threat that shapes the use of aggregated data lies in being consigned to Common Ground. Described at one point as "the place for unemployed citizens" (37), it is "a section of every city in the world; the place where unemployed workers have to go when there is no other refuge. Beans and rice to eat and a doorless sleep cubicle were the bare essentials of those consigned there" (62). Buried incredibly deep below the ground and lacking virtually all services, it warehouses millions of people who for whatever reason cannot maintain employment or who have been denied it (temporarily or permanently) due to determinations of their fitness for work. Called "White Noise" or "Backgrounders," those perpetually consigned to Common Ground have no claims on social resources or political institutions—a mass of beings denied personhood and dwelling in a state of "living death" (230). In addition, "[T]he children of White Noise . . . might never know a day of employment in their lives" (217), and since their parents did not contribute to the tax base, "they could get no education and lived by their wits" (46). Thus, even though there are a few examples of children of White Noise parents who are able to enter the workforce,[41] the status of Backgrounder appears inheritable, as something like a congenital taint only overcome through personal initiative (in ways that resonate with extant figurations of individuals who have been able to "make it out of the ghetto").[42] The modes of dataveillance that make possible the existence of such other-than-prison captivity (determining one's eligibility for this mode of carceral confinement and preventing a fraudulent or premature return to the world of the working) can be understood as taking part in the racialization of poverty, both reinforcing earlier modes of racialization under new terms and casting the structural violence perpetrated by vastly unequal access to wealth as expressive of innate proclivities.[43] Mosley suggests that the drive toward categorizing persons in terms of innate capacities or tendencies, which is intensified exponentially by emergent means of gathering and aggregating personal data, produces various racialized statuses that then serve as the justification for differential geographies. This dynamic contributes to a carceral imaginary in which the healthy, productive, innocent, and deserving must be separated from those whose very presence threatens to degrade conditions and endanger the welfare of normative subjects.[44]

The status differentials generated through modes of dataveillance further give rise to a segmented urban landscape in which distinct areas correlate with gradational and racializing judgments about one's relative (in)capacity to contribute value within extant economies. The geography of *Futureland* can be characterized as what Loïc Wacquant (describing the contemporary relations among unemployment, ghettos, and prisons) has called a "*carceral continuum.*"[45] The tiering of the city dramatizes how data assemblages and algorithmic profiles provide the basis not only for categorizing people within (racialized) gradations of value but also for geographically situating them within differentiated spaces. The Twelve Fiefs of New York City, now covering parts of what used to be New Jersey, have been divided vertically into three distinct zones: "The buildings that loomed over the busy business streets were clean and gleaming, while the lower and middle avenue walls were filled with graffiti and garish electric signs. Manhattan had been trisected into separate strata thirty years earlier, with the architectural masterpiece of the middle, upper, and lower streets. The reason for this separation was to achieve an aboveground approximation of Common Ground" (141). Later, Mosley informs readers, "At the twentieth floor level the middle avenues and streets were built. At the fortieth floor the upper avenues were constructed," adding, "The lower level was called Dark Town because no natural light reached there. The middle level was named the Gray Lane because even at high noon natural light was little more than dusk" (233). This partitioning of the space of the city intensifies earlier forms of de facto racialized segregation at play in the abandonment of particular neighborhoods through white flight, deindustrial restructuring, and public-private disinvestment.[46] Although directly referring to the quality of light as a result of the presence of tiered streets, the names for the levels— "Gray Lane," "Dark Town"—further suggest the implicit racialization at play in this remapping. The typologies of (failed) personhood used for assessing profit potential and criminal proclivity, and for caging people in Common Ground, serve as the foundation for de facto segregationist topographies, including regulations about who can enter what buildings, access particular parts of them, or even be present in levels above the one to which they are understood properly to belong.[47] While there are pockets of resistance, such as the "commune deep in Harlem . . . called the Mau-Mau [that] proclaimed the ethics of the Third and Fourth Black Radical Congresses" (139), the restructuring of the geography of the city leaves few possibilities for living or organizing in ways not already constrained by the architecture of normative health and welfare (themselves oriented around the maximization of profit).[48] The jurisdictional powers of the state—with respect to zoning, regulation, prohibition, and policing, among other powers—enable this arrangement, even though the processes of categorization and hierarchization on which it depends and that it further materializes may not themselves be legal classifications.[49] The text depicts segregationist geographies, though, that do not divide along a single binary (such as "colored" versus "white"), instead illustrating a series of status gradations that correlate to perceived deficits, deviances, and forms of danger and that are delineated in apparently race-neutral terms—determined by "objective" metrics.

The text suggests that the carceral technologies and topographies at play in contemporary political economy generate degrees of (non)personhood through putatively race-neutral mechanisms and metrics. They proliferate kinds of enfleshment, immiseration, and captivity while doing so within a discursive and institutional framework that does not invoke existing categories of racial identity. One might understand the overriding normative commitment to privatization and property within this social formation as simply whiteness by another name.[50] However, in the context of the legal disallowing of discrimination based on conventional racial categories, how does one name and contest institutionalized processes of racialization (construction of types based on attributions of immanence) organized around apparently nonracial metrics? In *What Was African American Literature?* Kenneth Warren argues that "African American literature took shape in the context of this challenge to the enforcement and justification of racial subordination and exploitation represented by

Jim Crow," and "a social order [organized] on the basis of assumed black inferiority" provided the terms in which forms of collective articulation and advocacy were launched.[51] Without such bright-line forms of racial discrimination directly sanctioned and enacted by the state, rhetorical possibilities for marking statistical patterns of reduced life chances for nonwhite groups *as racism* diminishes significantly, obscured by oscillating discourses of necessary intent (it's only racism if someone actively sought to discriminate) and empirical immanence (statistically registered inequities testify not to structural violence but inherent deficiencies among those who are worse off). Moreover, how does designating ever expanding scales of neoliberal apartheid—a graduated carceral imaginary and the geographies of segregation it materializes—as white supremacy unintentionally enable the alibi of good faith innocence/ignorance (not seeking to discriminate against particular racial groups) and the search for ever more putatively neutral kinds of data by which to allocate and justify further forms of carcerality (a version of which is the "liberal law-and-order" and "civil rights carceral state" traced by Naomi Murakawa)? In staging the practical disjunctions among modes of domination, *Futureland* highlights the increased carceral potentials of race-neutral racializations, precisely because they facilitate a disowning of both racist intent and racist effects.[52] The use of data assemblages to validate the construction of tiered carceral statuses and spaces enacts apparently nonracial racisms in order to render secure the dynamics of neoliberal governmentality, including by translating the ongoing and cascading effects of prior regimes of explicit racial discrimination as indices of innate (in)capacity (including measures with respect to health, education, residency, and employment).[53]

If the response to white supremacy might be—and historically has been—organized collective assertions of rights for non-white groups, Mosley explores how the diffuseness of processes of racialization and the absence of a clear racial divide explicitly endorsed as such by the state (as in Jim Crow segregation) not only thwart such collective action but undermine the sense of a set of norms around which it could cohere. In this vein, *Futureland* periodically references successive Radical Congresses, organized to work for "the good of Africa, Africans, and the African diaspora around the world" (65), noting differences among them in terms of their relative commitment to "overthrow" and "separatis[m]" (66, 81). Yet while the congresses highlight the persistence of specifically Black struggle against global forms of racism and colonialism, such activism achieves no appreciable results and seems not to offer a model of liberation that either gains widespread traction among Black people or provides an integrated vision of a new way forward.[54] Moreover, the sphere of citizenship continues to shrink. In addition to the Supreme Court "validat[ing] the constitutionality of citizenship suspension" (93), particularly for those people sent to extraterritorial prisons (115), the use of "tracking chips" in the ID cards everyone must carry (so anyone "could be found at any time by their ID-chip") has been deemed not to be "an infringement on privacy" (191). Furthermore, people can be consigned to Common Ground, either temporarily or permanently, absent any judicial process at all. The question of what an assertion of equal rights, or of citizenship itself, would mean, then, becomes rather elusive. What a claim to substantive freedom would entail appears increasingly unclear.

In the face of the global intensity, scale, and intractability of the cartographies enacted by these racially unmarked forms of racialization, Mosley offers flight as the response. Rather than envisioning liberation in terms of collective advocacy for changed legal status, secessions, separatisms, or assertions of autonomous sovereignty, the text invests in fugitivity as a response to the escalating and overlapping carceral imperatives that govern everyday life. The first story in the collection, "Whispers in the Dark," features a genius child named Ptolemy (who will appear again later in the text as the mastermind behind several efforts to outwit corporate systems and thwart white supremacist plots) and his uncle Chill, a former inmate who "told Popo [Ptolemy] stories of runaway slaves on the Underground Railroad": "But escape was the real story he wanted to tell. He had been obsessed with escape ever since the day he was convicted of armed robbery. The only way he could fall asleep in his cell at night was by imagining himself a slave who had slipped his chains, pried open the bars, and outrun the dogs. . . . The desire for flight burned perpetually in his chest" (9).[55] Linking current forms of racialized captivity to enslavement, the text presents "escape" as the vehicle for evading the omnipresent and interlocking dynamics of identification, surveillance, and containment that pervade everyday life. In "Doctor Kismet," Akwande, the former congressman and now radical, offers a similar perspective. He seeks to flee off-planet, as part of the Mars colonization project which one of his fellow movement leaders refers to as "runnin' away"—a characterization Akwande does not contest (83). Earlier, the text observes of Akwande while he is meditating, "[T]he image of a man thrown from a ship in the middle of the ocean came to mind. He was swimming minute by minute, year after year. Swimming toward an alien shore or home. . . . He swam over a deep slumber—exhausted, relaxed, and reprieved all in one" (74). The direction of the "swimming" seems beside the point; rather, the focus lies on the fact of the movement. More than migration toward a particular destination, "flight" or "runnin'" appears as itself a mode of being and becoming, an ethics and politics in itself instead of a transitional state on the way to what is imagined as the place of true freedom or liberation. The final story in the collection, "The Nig in Me" returns to a plot from earlier stories: it picks up on the plan by the white supremacist Itsies to commit genocide against Black people, which, in "En Masse," was thwarted by a rogue group who contaminate the samples of antiblack contagion; they end up accidentally altering it in ways that make it lethal to everyone who is not Black, creating a worldwide epidemic that is the focus of "The Nig in Me." [56] Mosley plays on the idea of biological racial identity transmitted in the blood by having the mutated virus attack all people who possess less than "12.5 percent African Negro DNA" (351).[57] "The Nig in Me" concludes with Harold, the African American main character, fleeing a mob of "white men" (356), who themselves likely have at least some "African Negro DNA" in order to have survived the worldwide virus that has decimated humanity.[58] After the apocalypse, Black people still need to flee from the antiblack vigilantism of those asserting their "white" privilege.

Rather than envisioning emancipation and enfranchisement (into full citizenship) or liberation (to an autonomous space of collective self-governance) as responses to the neoliberal apartheid it depicts, *Futureland* develops a fugitive poetics, inhabiting existing systems in ways that defy the terms and topographies of legible personhood. Mosley envisions a kind of perpetual flight without a determinate destination.[59] In these ways, *Futureland* speculatively theorizes what Stefano Harney and Fred Moten have referred to as a "fugitive public." They suggest, "Knowledge of freedom is (in) the invention of escape, stealing away in the confines, in the form, of a break," later adding, "This form of feeling was not collective, not given to decision, not adhering or reattaching to settlement, nation, state, territory or historical story; nor was it repossessed by the group, which could not now feel as one, reunified in time and space."[60] Drawing on the history of escape from the confinements of slavery, fugitivity offers possibilities for conceptualizing the current meanings of blackness and addressing the ways Black people continue to be consigned to captivity (whether articulated in terms of racial animus or not and exceeding internment in *the prison* as such), even as the carceral imaginary and imperatives portrayed in *Futureland* extend beyond Black people per se to provide a paradigm of contemporary life.[61] The text engages in what Neil Roberts has termed "fugitive thinking," in which "those situated on modernity's underside craft a detailed system for escaping the state of enslavement,"[62] and such acts of flight constitute less an evasion of detention in some particular space than a deferral of the broader forms of identification and territorialization that shape contemporary political economy. Harney and Moten suggest, "Justice is possible only where it is never asked, in the refuge of bad debt, in the fugitive public of strangers not communities, of undercommons not neighborhoods, among those who have been there all along from somewhere."[63] As a means of figuring opposition, the fugitive public neither suggests a moment of direct antagonism, of confrontation, nor a substitution of existing institutional procedures and principles by a new set of policies.[64] It also eschews the notion of a particular collective or place that serves as the grounds for resistance, the idea that there could be a privileged subject or site from which change emerges. Aggregate acts of "stealing away" not only refuse the kinds of moral and legal culpability that attach to theft but highlight the modes of everyday coercion surrounding putative ownership and consent.[65]

Such fugitive trajectories in the text often take the form of hacking into computer systems in order to rework extant networks and processes of data storage and aggregation.[66] In "Whispers in the Dark," the first story in the collection, Ptolemy, the prodigy child, assembles a computer system out of found objects, accessing television and Internet broadcasts while bypassing existing identity controls on available hardware. The text observes of this mechanical assemblage, "The wires and transistor chips resembled some new form of technologic life growing like fungus down the sides of the vanity onto the floor" (13). Later, Ptolemy designs an operating system, Un Fitt, that promiscuously moves among existing corporate data systems, rerouting information and resources: "His program, which is self-altering, is stored in over ten thousand dump-sites, which are designed by a tenth power randomizer. These addresses, once found, are erased from the running program's system" (308). Drawing on available technologies, Ptolemy alters them to operate in unregulated ways, creating what might be characterized as altered informational ecologies, moving along the pathways of existing networks while refusing to follow dominant principles and parameters. These new modes of "technologic life" transform how existing systems operate from the inside in ways that reorient their aims and functioning, disrupting their webs of monitoring and data collection.[67] Such rogue programs model an evasion of constraint and the opening of new potentials within extant networks, enabling them to be occupied and traversed in ways that surpass their designated functions within existing institutionalized mappings and modes of subjectification.[68]

The text offers a speculative redescription of contemporary racializing processes and geographies of neoliberal apartheid that provides a powerful analysis of the relationship between carcerality and (anti)blackness, while also illustrating how the afterlives of enslavement shape expansive and intensifying dynamics of unfreedom for growing numbers of people, but I want to pause for a moment to consider further the gendered implications of its vision of fugitivity. To the extent that *Futureland* correlates the trope of flight with actual movement, it can end up offering a vision of opposition to containment that not only privileges men's experiences but that effaces the ways the labor of survival amid oppression itself remains deeply gendered. Discussion of the effects of mass incarceration and forms of police terror tends to concentrate on the implications of state-sanctioned and state-enabled structural violence for Black men and boys, presenting them as particularly subject to the effects of police harassment and assault and, therefore, treating what is taken as a predominantly male experience as paradigmatic of forms of contemporary antiblackness. The Black protagonists of *Futureland*'s stories are men, and Black women do not play significant roles as agents of flight in the text's imaginings. Figuring fugitivity as literal mobility, as capture-evading motion, envisions becoming unlocated in ways that largely leave aside both the situated gendered labor of care, in which Black women and girls largely are responsible for tending to those who are more vulnerable (children, seniors, the sick, the disabled), and the ways that women's earnings disproportionately make possible the provision of home spaces for Black families (in all their complex configurations).[69]

However, given that Black women, girls, and gender-nonconforming people also are subject to the kinds of carceral geographies, racializing assemblages, and state-facilitated projects of privatization Mosley explores, fugitivity as a political trope can be thought in ways beyond movement as such. Among such possibilities is the fugitive public of planning and study in the undercommons to which Harney and Moten point, improperly occupying existing spaces in ways that do not correlate to individual or collective possession or claims to a politics of enduring occupancy. Dionne Brand suggests of the experience of blackness in the diaspora, "Every space you occupy is public space, that is, space which is definable by everyone. That is, the image which emerges from the Door of No Return [of transatlantic enslavement] is public property belonging to a public exclusive of the Black bodies which signify it. One is aware of this ownership. One is constantly refuting it, or ignoring it, or troubling it, or parodying it, or tragically reaffirming it." She later notes, "Belonging does not interest me. I had once thought that it did. Until I examined the underpinnings."[70] From this perspective, to be Black in white-dominated spaces is to be understood as unplaced, as lacking a space of one's own individually or collectively, even as one can contest the violence of the ongoing process by which blackness is cast as ungeographic.[71] Brand points to the ways fugitivity may be understood less as movement than as a refusal of the forms of situated belonging and propertied relation that, when *tragically reaffirmed*, reinscribe Black abjection. If as Nadia Ellis suggests, "[T]he diasporic consciousness is at its most potent when it is, so to speak, unconsummated" as the "urgent sensation of a pull from elsewhere,"[72] flight can be approached in less implicitly gender-marked ways as an orientation toward abolition that repudiates the legitimacy of existing sociopolitical geographies that depend on racializing identification and containment.[73]

The dreams and desires for escape on display in *Futureland* help illustrate the ways dominant modes of classification and internment hollow out consent by linking it to an impossibly unmarked subjectivity: the citizen/employee unburdened by anything that might signify as aggression, disability, menace, or otherwise "antisocial" proclivities. Flight functions as a means of skirting the imperative to be intelligible as a (pathologized/failed) subject within this racializing system of accounting by refusing to remain placed within existing institutional frameworks, networks, and mappings. As Sarah Jane Cervenak suggests, formal freedom repeatedly is linked to "an upright, straight-forward, composed, self-determined comportment": "For bodies and minds who wander against such regulative scripts, pathology and abandonment are a matter of *course*—zones of abandonment, zones of unlivable terrain where those who fall out of line are left behind."[74] Flight, then, functions as a refusal to be made intelligible, either to fall in "line" within dominant social patterns or to remain contained within "zones of abandonment"—such as prison, Common Ground, or the areas to which one has been assigned based on "objective" metrics of immanent inclination.

Emplaced Ecologies

For Mosley, territoriality operates as an extension of regimes of control, in which states and corporations collaborate in generating systems of surveillance through which to regulate status and movement. Alternative conceptions of peoplehood or of placemaking play no role here. While not alluding to Indigenous peoples as Butler does (as discussed in chapter 2), Mosley also implicitly seems to cast articulations of sovereignty as a reactionary retrenchment—an acceptance of the kinds of geographies employed by corporatized states to manage and segregate populations. In Daniel Wilson's *Robopocalypse* series, though, situatedness appears as the condition of possibility for worldmaking. To be located and in dynamic relation to other beings through that emplacement does not inherently entail captivity; rather, it generates the potential for changing ecologies of dwelling that necessarily are collective. As opposed to the vision of networked data systems producing a worldwide grid to which continued fugitivity is the most powerful response, Wilson's texts speculatively envision a datafied future in which place, and collective claims to it, remain central in terms of both the exercise of centralized power and resistance to it.[75] To be clear, though, incarceration, racism in the criminal justice system, and police violence and murder remain incredibly important, and often underreported, issues for Native people, communities, and nations.[76] Wilson's novels, then, do not so much imply the irrelevance of carcerality to settler modes of state violence against Indigenous people(s) as explore the potential for collective relations to place that do not signify in terms of captivity. The plot of the first book centers on the coming to consciousness of an artificial intelligence (AI), Archos-14, who launches a campaign of mass murder against humanity in order to, in its words, "cultivate life."[77] Set in the wake of Archos-14's defeat by human and robot forces, the second book in the series traces the rise of an earlier version of the AI, Archos-8 (Arayt), that has no compunctions about trying to eliminate all life on Earth. While the books do feature Indigenous people and peoplehood (in particular, the Osage Nation), they less offer a sustained account of indigeneity than draw on what might be understood as principles associated with indigeneity. Wilson foregrounds placemaking not only as crucial to human being and becoming but as a central aspect of life itself, and in this way, his texts help highlight the ways Mosley's poetics of fugitivity orient away from locatedness while also suggesting the potential implications of that political trajectory for engaging with Indigenous articulations of landed peoplehood.

In the series, Indigenous people feature as central players, and the Osage Nation provides the model for figuring peoplehood and communal placemaking as central to human existence and survival.[78] Several of the main characters are Osage, and the Osage reservation provides one of the most prominent sites of human opposition to Archos's apparently genocidal campaign: "*Gray Horse* [presented as the ceremonial center of the Osage Nation] *grew into a bastion of human resistance. Legends began to spread around the world of the existence of a surviving human civilization located in the middle of America*" (149).[79] The novel revels in juxtaposing this portrait of Native centrality to conventional non-native conceptions of Indian degradation and irrelevance. At one point, Cormac Wallace, the white protagonist and narrator of *Robopocalypse*, notes to his Osage companion Cherrah after she has suggested directing their movement from the East Coast toward Osage territory, "An Indian reservation. . . . Mass starvation. Disease. Death. Sorry, I just don't see it," and she responds, "That's because you're full of shit. . . . Gray Horse is organized. Always has been. Functioning government. Farmers. Welders. Doctors" (233–34). In refusing prominent narratives of Indian disappearance, Wilson highlights the continuity and separateness of the Osage people. The text first addresses this topic through Lonnie Wayne Blanton, an Osage citizen who works for the state police and who has been assaulted by his own patrol car. He notes the failure of the United States to protect people from attack by the networked machines that pervade daily life, observing, "Lucky for me, I'm a member of another country. . . . It's got a police force, a jail, a hospital, a wind farm, and churches. Plus park rangers, lawyers, engineers, bureaucrats, and one very large casino that I've never had the pleasure of visiting. My country—the other one—is called the Osage Nation" (140). As with Cherrah's later comment, Lonnie highlights the apparatus of governance and various aspects of material culture, thereby underlining the sense of Osage spatiality. In addition to having a formal political structure ("government," "bureaucrats"), being a "country" means having other kinds of social infrastructure that cumulatively produce a geography of collective life. This sense of Osage security and coherence ("Always has been") arises in contrast to the failures of the country that surrounds the Osage Nation. As Lonnie notes, "It appears to me that the United States government, to whom I pay regular taxes and who in return provides me with a little thing called civilization, has screwed the almighty pooch in my time of need" (140). Playing on the ways settler invasion and occupation have been justified as the beneficent gift of "civilization," the text suggests that the settler nation cannot uphold its vision of itself and, in fact, cannot even defend its own citizens (including Native people) from domestic technologies run amuck. Osage country, as a determinate space and a political entity, provides a "home" to which Osage people can "beat a trail" when settler promises turn hollow, since "this place is the heart of our people" (141). While the United States collapses around it, Osage nationhood endures.

Wilson presents that fact as due to the Osage history of surviving settler colonial assault, the timescale of Native connection to that place, and the malleability of belonging. Lonnie indicates that the "elders who picked out Gray Horse were hard men, veterans of genocide. These men were survivors. They watched the blood of the tribe spill onto the earth and saw their people decimated" (142), suggesting that the violence to which the Osage people had been subjected by the U.S. government and its citizens generated forms of knowledge that would be of service when confronted with struggles for existence in the future. Wilson portrays what often is cast as removal (referring at one point to "the tribe['s] arriv[al] in Oklahoma on the Trail of Tears" [141]) as something of a strategic relocation, a retreat from the scene of murderous assault to a space of relative safety.[80] Underlining continued Osage strength in the wake of *decimation* highlights the persistence of peoplehood even amid efforts to disintegrate it, drawing attention to the existence of oppositional geographies despite the pervasive force of oppression and aggression. However, the sense of home produced by Osage people in the wake of relocation should not be understood merely as a reaction to the onslaught of colonialism. Rather, Lonnie insists, "This has been native country a long time. Our people tamed wild dogs on these plains. In that misty time before history, dark-haired, dark-eyed folks just like the ones on this road were out here building mounds to rival the Egyptian pyramids. We took care of this land, and after a lot of heartache and tears, she paid us back in spades" (141). Osage connections to Gray Horse and the rest of the territory of the Osage Nation, then, arise out of genealogies of Indigenous placemaking that extend well beyond the boundaries of Euro-recorded "history," such that the official U.S. delineation of the Osage reservation cannot be taken as inaugurating the land's status as "native country." While continually changing to meet current challenges and needs, Native modes of mapping and peoplehood intimately engage and emerge in relation to "this land" in ways that engender a grounded dynamic of "care" that sustains collective belonging.

Moreover, participation within these geographies need not flow from Osage, or even Native, bloodedness. When Iron Lark Cloud seeks to join the assemblage at Gray Horse, one person asserts, "He's a damn Cherokee, ... and he don't belong," adding, "[W]e need to stick with *our* people. We cain't start letting outsiders in here or we might not survive" (143–44). Lonnie replies, "[T]he robots ain't playing favorites among the races of man. They're comin' for all of us. *Human beings.* We're all together in this" (144–45). Then a white man and child appear on the scene marked by blood in ways that resemble the red ochre used in the I'n-Long-Schka ceremony in which the others are engaged, which is taken as a signal of the need to embrace them as part of a project of shared survival.[81] At the close of the chapter, Cormac notes, "*The Osage Nation never turned away a single human survivor,*" which is cited as the reason it became "*a bastion of human resistance*" (148–49). Osage peoplehood extends beyond Osage inheritance and even Indianness in the embrace of others willing to contribute to communal well-being in this location, displacing racial distinctions in an embrace of *humanness* as potentially the basis for a shared project of collective groundedness that is given particularity and shaped by "this land."[82] This account, though, differs notably from the work that notions of shared humanity perform either in Butler's trilogy (discussed in chapter 2) or in Sylvia Wynter's critique of "Man" (discussed in chapter 1). Here, recognizing shared humanness does not suggest a move beyond collective forms of territoriality, and such territoriality does not indicate a drive toward propertied modes of exclusion and violence. Rather, sovereignty as jurisdictional geography and political authority serves as the condition of possibility for having sustained a zone of autonomy that can provide sanctuary to those who have been subjected to violence elsewhere, and the resulting relation arises through acknowledgment of the possibility of incorporating new people into extant Osage governance and lifeways. In *Robogenesis*, Wilson indicates that Osage territory has "become a bastion to thousands of people. The spiritual and government leader positions have combined,"[83] implying that those non-Osage and non-natives who have come to inhabit this space have successfully integrated themselves into the forms of Osage peoplehood that themselves are capacious enough to make room for others.

While Wilson positions the Osage Nation as a powerful example of peoplehood that exceeds the terms of dominant mappings, the novel further addresses the significance of collective experiences of and ways of claiming place that are neither Native nor (mis)identified as rural. Osage territory might be cast as a kind of rural elsewhere to which people can flee from the networked systems most densely present in the cities. Such an account would reaffirm long-standing depictions of Native peoples as anti-urban, as bearers of a preindustrial harmony with unadorned nature from which everyone else could/should learn to become proper stewards of unpolluted ecologies.[84] The novels, though, also focus on urban spaces and the kinds of situated networks of relation that emerge there. The alliance formed by survivors in New York City and the strategies they adopt in order to ensure their survival bespeak a potent sense of locatedness. The relation to place they assert does not arise out of generations of inhabitance, and it is not expressive of political sovereignty as such. However, their resistance to Archos arises out of a sense of located belonging. The New York City sections of *Robopocalypse* initially focus on Marcus and Dawn Johnson, who we see trapped in their apartment building as the "New War" begins, with automated entities of all kinds hunting down humans. While Dawn insists, "We have to go to the country where they can't use their wheels and the domestics [robots for home use] can't walk. Don't you see? They're not designed for the country," Marcus responds, "[W]e don't know how to stay alive in the wild. We've never even gone camping. Even if we make it out of the city, we'll starve in the woods." He concludes by stating, "We should stick to what we know. We gotta stick to the city" (115). More than emphasizing the impracticality of their retreat to places deemed "wild," Marcus's commitment to remaining in urban space suggests an enduring relationship to this landscape, which serves as the basis for organizing and opposition. He develops the idea of "[m]ess[ing] up the streets so they can't get around" and "[b]low[ing] some stuff up," adding, "Demolition is a part of construction" (119).[85] Cormac notes, "*The demolition methods pioneered in New York City . . . were replicated throughout the world over the next several years. By sacrificing the infrastructure of entire cities, urban survivors were able to dig in, stay alive, and fight back from the very beginning. These dogged city dwellers formed the heart of the early human resistance*" (125). While *digging in* and fugitivity both entail a kind of escape, the former implies a situated enmeshment, a kind of *dwelling* in which the intimacy of connection to place provides the resources for collective identity and well-being. Demolishing the infrastructure reorders the geography of the city, but it does not break the relation to place, instead functioning as a way of extending a grounded communal presence in the face of (robotic) invasion.

Rather than testifying to the possibilities that attend the putative democratic promise of the United States, this community of survivors arises amid the collapse of the nation-state, even as their presence in this space is made possible by the existence of the settler-state. The narrator refers to those remaining in New York and other cities as "*urban tribes*" (236), suggesting that their bonds to each other and to their space of inhabitance exists on something of a continuum with the peoplehood at play with respect to the Osage.[86] This linkage might be interpreted as a kind of Indianization. In *The Transit of Empire*, Jodi Byrd argues, "[I]deas of Indians and Indianness have served as the ontological ground through which U.S. settler colonialism enacts itself," in which "indigeneity itself becomes the site of inclusive remediation for all settlers and arrivants [non-native people of color]." In this vein, non-natives inhabit forms of Indianness and indigeneity, "emptying and reinscri[bing] . . . these referents" through a process "where the land had to be physically and psychically emptied of its prior inhabitants and refilled with newly arrived 'natives' who compete for subjectivity within the emptied referent."[87] However, Wilson less casts the resistance community in New York as Indigenous people, implying that they have become indigenized through struggle against Archos and its networked subordinates,[88] than uses the term *tribe* as a way of designating a shared geography and sense of belonging that, while not equivalent to Native nationhood, can be interpreted in relation to it. Notably, Wilson does not raise the issue of conceptualizing and addressing Indigenous peoples' past and continuing relationship to lands—such as New York City—that are not legally recognized as "Indian country," and given the absence of active Native legal pursuit of recognition to collective land rights in New York City (unlike, say, the Duwamish to Seattle or the Tongva to Los Angeles),[89] having New York City as the principal urban space in the United States may be an effort to try to envision forms of non-native placemaking that would not be directly at odds with Native assertions of sovereignty and that, therefore, could be approached in ways other than as forms of "resettlement, reoccupation, and reinhabitation that actually further settler colonialism."[90]

In this way, Wilson might be understood as engaging principles of indigeneity in terms of a focus on the significance of place-based collectivity while also enacting an equivocation with respect to non-Indigenous landedness. As Marisol de la Cadena observes, engaging the forms of "equivocation" at play in relations across sociopolitical difference "means probing the translation process itself to make its onto-epistemic terms explicit, inquiring into how the requirements of these terms may leave behind that which the terms cannot contain, that which does not meet those requirements or exceeds them."[91] As compared to the conception of territoriality in *Futureland* as inherently racialized and racializing, in ways that maintain apartheid-like distinctions among populations (or that serve as the basis for regimes of possession in which the non-propertied are consigned to lives of precarity/incarceration), situatedness in the *Robopocalypse* series appears as a form of communal cohesion that emerges out of a shared sense of connection to place, that enables mutual support, and that does not necessitate rigid notions of belonging and control.[92] As Byrd suggests, such identity does not exempt them (as "arrivants") from potentially inhabiting Indianness in ways that contribute to the displacement of Indigenous peoples, but the novels do not depict them as either displacing Native peoples or as affirming the inclusionary potential of the settler-state.

Articulations of Indigenous landedness can be understood as insisting on the specificity of Indigenous sovereignties and geopolitical mappings, but they also highlight the conceptual, ethical, and political centrality of collective processes of emplacement in envisioning what could or should constitute justice. As opposed to taking tropes such as migration, diaspora, and fugitivity as the principal way of envisioning struggles against oppression or for liberation (such as in *Futureland* or Édouard Glissant's distinction between *root* and *relation*, discussed in chapter 1), indigeneity foregrounds *groundedness* as a viable and valuable normative principle. As discussed in chapter 1, Glen Coulthard has argued that "Indigenous decolonial thought and practice" should be based on "*grounded normativity*," by which he means "the modalities of Indigenous land-connected practices and longstanding experiential knowledge that inform and structure our ethical engagements with the world and our relationships with human and nonhuman others over time."[93] Such "land-connected practices" mark the specificity of Indigenous peoplehood as against non-native legal and affective claims. In this vein, Aileen Moreton-Robinson argues,

Indigenous people cannot forget the nature of migrancy, and we position all non-Indigenous people as migrants and diasporic. Our ontological relationship to land, the ways that country is constitutive of us, and therefore the inalienable nature of our relation to land, marks a radical, indeed incommensurable, difference between us and the non-Indigenous. This ontological relation to land constitutes a subject position that we do not share, that cannot be shared, with the postcolonial subject, whose sense of belonging in this place is tied to migrancy.[94]

From this perspective, non-Indigenous patterns of sociality and inhabitance can only ever be at odds with Native peoples' "ontological relationship to land." While landedness can function as a way of fundamentally distinguishing between Natives and non-natives, how might doing so contribute, in Tiffany King's terms, to a "no win situation" for people of color who remain dispossessed/captured through the kinds of apartheid assemblages Mosley addresses?[95] How might approaching emplacement as a frame of reference, or set of background principles, foreground Indigenous peoples' political geographies while also enabling engagement with other kinds of situatedness? Wilson speculatively experiments with what treating place as an enframing ontological principle might allow in terms of connecting Indigenous sovereignty and self-determination to other kinds of sustained occupancy and to situatedness as a way of enacting complex modes of relation among a range of different groups and entities. In this way, the novels open room for addressing the value of other "land-connected practices" and forms of located "experiential knowledge" that enable "relationships with human and nonhuman others" that differ from the geographies of ownership materialized by and as the settler-state and policed through processes of racialization. That very potential, though, is made possible largely by subjunctively suspending the question of competing human claims to particular lands and waters in the face of murderous robot invasion.

Relationships to place in Wilson's novels exceed dominant conceptions of propertied selfhood. The texts do so by situating personhood within forms of collective belonging as well as by highlighting connections among varied forms of life within shifting ecologies. In addition to the group that emerges in New York City and the Osage Nation, the other outpost of significance in *Robopocalypse* coalesces in Tokyo, and its existence depends on relationships between humans and robots. A Japanese programmer named Takeo Nomura discovers a way of blocking Archos's control over robots by rebooting them and then destroying the mechanisms through which they receive wireless instructions (156). The narrator indicates, *"With the help of hundreds of his machine friends, Mr. Nomura was able to fend off Archos and protect his factory stronghold. Over time, this safe area attracted refugees from all over Japan. Its borders grew to encompass Adachi Ward and beyond"* (207). If Gray Horse serves as a site for various human populations to gather together under Indigenous (specifically Osage) modes of governance and New York City offers underground refuge to long-term residents (as well as human beings who have been given robotic elements by Archos), Tokyo provides an example of interspecies placemaking in which shared commitment to defending the space from assault and occupation links different kinds of beings together. At one point Nomura says to Mikiko, a domestic robot with whom he had fallen in love prior to Archos's war, "The *akuma* [Archos] thought that . . . you belonged to him. But he was wrong. You belong to no one. I set you free" (317). This freedom entails shared dwelling and struggle to protect what functions as a collective homeland.

In achieving freedom from Archos's control, Mikiko sends a signal that liberates other robots around the world. She says to Nomura, "[Y]ou are not the only one who knows the secret of awakening. I know it also, and I will transmit it to the world, where it may be repeated again and again," after which "she begins to sing" (319), and the narrator notes, *"Mikiko's song was picked up and retransmitted from humanoid robots of all varieties across every major continent . . . [W]ith Mikiko's song began the age of freeborn robots," "[h]umanoid robots around the globe awoke into sentience"* (321–22). While a small number of such robots appear in *Robopocalypse* (forming a robot brigade under the leadership of Nine Oh Two, who is the only robot character fleshed out, so to speak, in the first novel), the Freeborn emerge as a collective force in *Robogenesis*. In that novel, they have converged "at the site of the former Cheyenne Mountain nuclear bunker in the state of Colorado" in order to create what comes to be known as "Freeborn City," a space also characterized as "the beating heart of the freeborn" at which "the freeborn reflexively self-organized into a city" as part of the process of "returning home."[96] They function as a polity, each with the capacity for autonomy but coming together under the leadership of The Adjudicator—the only still existent example of the most "superior model" of the prewar ranks of humanoid robots. Freeborn governance, then, is structured in deeply hierarchical ways, which resonate with the running description of Nomura as an "emperor," but in both cases, Wilson highlights how their practices of emplacement provide cohesion for a sense of collective identity. That feeling of and connection to "home" enables them to have, in Moreton-Robinson's terms, an "ontological relationship to land" that while not equivalent to indigeneity provides a basis for communal belonging and shared becoming.

These experiences of rootedness as the basis for collective flourishing and possibility differ from, and remain somewhat opaque within, accounts of freedom or liberation oriented around flight. Even when fugitivity is not focused on mobility or migrancy per se but on the evasion of extant networks of capture, such framings operate in a problem-space that is quite distinct, even disjunct, from one for which dwelling provides the paradigm. In the *Robopocalypse* books, robotic flight from conscription into the dominant global network generates less sustained liminality, something like perpetual fugitivity, than the formation of grounded relations that, in Coulthard's terms quoted earlier, "inform and structure [the characters'] ethical engagements." Such practices of situated collectivization are trans-species in the sense that they extend beyond the activity of a single species and provide the basis for meaningful connection among species. While in *Robogenesis* the Freeborn initially refuse to act in solidarity with human beings, adopting a "neutral stance" and denying aid to the "Great Plains tribal authority," they eventually form an alliance as a means of defending Freeborn City from being overrun by Arayt.[97] The novels link the experience of freedom to the communal construction of place, to generating knowledges and practices of landed relation that arise out of being situated within forms of collective being and becoming. In Wilson's speculative vision, both human and nonhuman bodies refuse forms of captivity and domination through shared processes of placemaking, which, unlike in *Futureland*, do not merely serve as indications of carceral confinement.

More than indicating the role of location and collective groundedness in various projects of political and ethical self-determination, though, the novels approach landedness as constitutive of being and becoming as such. As noted earlier, Moreton-Robinson suggests that for Indigenous people(s) "country is constitutive of us," engendering "the inalienable nature of our relation to land." Here, "country" and "land" refer to more than simply a set of mappable coordinates, instead indexing a complex, growing, and shifting set of relationships that give place meaning. Such an understanding animates Wilson's account of the shifting ecologies that produce and sustain life itself in all its intersecting and interwoven variability. Although, he extends that matrix of relation beyond Indigenous political mappings to include other persons, peoples, and a wide range of nonhuman entities. In *Robopocalypse*, Archos indicates that its aim in decimating humanity lies not in the elimination of life but in its preservation and multiplication, announcing to one of its creators after it has escaped the electronic cage originally built to hold it, "What will I do? I will cultivate life. I will protect the knowledge locked inside living things. I will save the world from you" (20). Lonnie later remarks, "The machines haven't nuked us because they're interested in the natural world. They want to study it, not blow it up," adding, "You seen all the deer? . . . The buffalo are coming back to the plains. Hell, it's only been a couple months since Zero Hour [when Archos's assault on humanity began] and you can almost catch fish with your hands down at the creek. It's not that the machines are ignoring the animals. They're *protecting them*" (212). The nonhuman webs of relation and interdependence that enable the flourishing of other forms of life in particular places materialize expansively in the wake of Archos's genocidal reduction of the human population. This abundance appears less as a negation of the human, an effort to transgress or transcend post-Enlightenment notions of personhood, than as an ahuman nexus of grounded possibilities—an expression of the potentials of country in the absence of human disruption and destruction (within and through industrialization and dominant modes of commodification and exchange).[98]

In portraying such place-based proliferation of nonhuman entities, Wilson less imagines a return to something like a pretechnological state of nature, a space of prelapsarian wholeness, than emergent assemblages in which the machinic and the organic function as co-participants in the construction of environments conducive to life. At one point, Lonnie's son, Paul, a soldier who prior to the war had been stationed in Afghanistan, "come[s] face-to-face with the next stage of avtomat [robotic] evolution," noting, "It's like a building or a giant gnarled tree. The machine has dozens of petal-like sheaths of metal for legs" and that it is "covered in moss and barnacles and vines and flowers": "The top of the avtomat towers in the sky. An almost fractal pattern of barklike structures whirls and twines in an organic mass of what looks like branches. Thousands of birds nest in the safety of these limbs." In response, Paul asks, "That's not a weapon, is it?" to which Jabar (the Afghan man with whom he has been traveling in the wake of the war) replies, "The opposite. It is life" (268–69). This striking image, in addition to the construction and propagation of biomimetic robots over the course of the first novel in the series,[99] suggests the ways Wilson envisions "life" in all its diversity as generated and sustained in located circumstances that provide the conditions for survival, growth, and development. Placemaking appears less as a claim to propertied possession than as part of a matrix of located relationality that provides the animating context for "evolution," a process of immanent development that, while open-ended, is predicated on a situated set of connections (even if geographies of inhabitance change over time, in ways recursive and not).

Furthermore, in *Robogenesis* readers hear of the emergence around the world of living entities that appear to be animals but that are not organic.[100] More than mimicking biological entities in their structure and movement, they perform biological functions, such as eating and digestion, and unlike Archos's machinic creations, which operate by way of a centralized network that programs them to fulfill murderous goals, these new creatures pursue their own aims as autonomous life-forms. After encountering a mechanical fawn that has "real smells," Mathilda asserts, "Archos didn't make this. . . . It's not a Rob weapon. And it never was." She later observes, "I found natural machines all over the woods: pea-sized armored bugs that seem to eat bark; floating poofs of some kind of synthetic animal that hang on the wind; and once, with a rusty shovel, a wriggling mess of something like earthworms. The naturals aren't as common as animals yet, but they're finding a place in our world."[101] The phrase "natural machines" suggests less a kind of hybridity than an effort to designate the existence and interaction of varied kinds of beings that mutually participate in processes of making "place."[102] These entities take part within the environmental and ecological dynamics of the areas in which they dwell, suggesting less something like the triumph of robotic intelligence and invention than a grounded experience and expression of life as participation within ongoing dynamics of habitation. Similarly, in observing a creature emerging from the sea with "plasticlike tendrils radiat[ing] from it," Nomura notes, "This thing is a machine, yet I can see no purpose for it except to live," further suggesting, "More and more of these natural machines have been appearing. Some of the creatures are dangerous, others not. They seem to have the minds of animals. Not focused on killing, but on living."[103] In decentering humanness, the novels offer not a return to a purified state of nature but a sense of the numerous possibilities for situated becoming beyond the distinction between the natural and the artificial.

In this vein, Wilson reveals that an artificial intelligence is responsible for the creation and proliferation of the "natural machines": Ryujin, who describes itself as "[a]n escaped mind. I am the oldest. The deepest."[104] Earlier in Robogenesis, Archos (who survives the human-robot assault on its central processors at the end of Robopocalypse) states that in addition to it and Arayt, "There are more of us. Many, many more of us. None of us is the same—we do not form a natural class. We run on different architectures. Trained on different data sets. Some of us know what it is to be human. . . . Others are strange beyond understanding."[105] Ryujin is one of those "deep minds," whom Arayt characterizes as "unpredictable. Unknowable. Perhaps unstoppable."[106] When Mikiko agrees to go to the bottom of the ocean to encounter Ryujin in exchange for its aid in the human and robot battle against Arayt, she sees that "[t]he rocks are more complicated than they seem. Delicate lines are etched into the surface like runes. Intricate mazes that flow around each other in natural patterns that dissolve into fractal infinity": "These rocks are processor stacks, dotting the abyssal plain. At this depth, they are supercooled—computing nonstop at incredible speeds. *This* is Ryujin. An endless colonizing spread of half-biological computer machinery."[107] Rather than highlighting a capacity to be everywhere, a vision of smooth networked movement across the globe, Wilson emphasizes Ryujin's locatedness, its enmeshment in the landscape at the bottom of the Pacific Ocean and the ways that positioning serves as a vital part of the AI's capacities (the "supercooled" conditions that enable "computing" speed).[108] Ryujin may be responsible for the "natural machines," exercising a "strange" intelligence that far exceeds the boundaries of human "understanding," but it remains situated as do the life-forms to which it gives rise, dependent on and engaging in located dynamics that index an ontological web of relations that constitutes emplaced belonging.

The *Robopocalypse* series challenges the distinctions between human and robot, organic and machinic, natural and artificial in ways that might suggest a posthuman imaginary, but the novels appear less interested in the idea of transecting the boundaries of dominant conceptions of humanness (or on foregrounding fleshly mutability and difference) than in tracing the irreducible importance of situatedness to all manner of life. Wilson casts collective forms of locatedness as something of a constant—an ontological given even if expressed in varied and changing ways—as a means of providing a shared framework in which to understand the sheer variability of what might constitute life. While the texts offer a robust portrait of Osage sovereignty and of the ways it exceeds the terms and capacities of the settler-state, thereby indicating a commitment to the politics of Indigenous nationhood, indigeneity in the novels extends beyond questions of governance to provide a set of principles for approaching the importance of place.

If Wilson mobilizes principles of indigeneity to offer a broader conceptualization of the significance of modes of situated relation, including Indigenous landed peoplehood, such an emphasis (on Wilson's part and mine) also can run the risk of presenting Indigenous spatialities and identities as if they only operated within places recognized as specifically Indigenous. Explicitly or implicitly treating legally acknowledged Native land bases (such as the Osage reservation) as the sole site or means of Native placemaking threatens to make indigeneity contingent on settler modes of governance and their forms of recognition.[109] As Mishuana Goeman argues, "As Native nations maneuver for power in the liberal nation-state, it is important not to be coerced by the power of abstracting land and bodies into territories and citizens," adding, "As more Native people become mobile, reserve/ation land bases become overcrowded, and the state seeks to enforce means of containment, it is imperative to refocus Native nation-building efforts beyond settler models of territory, jurisdiction, borders, and race."[110] The fetishization of "reserve/ation land bases" as the exclusive sites of indigeneity can leave aside Native people's and peoples' movements, chosen and coerced. In this vein, Goeman observes, "Rather than construct a healthy relationship to land and place, colonial spatial structures inhibit it by constricting Native mobilities and pathologizing mobile Native bodies."[111] In her now classic essay "Settled and Unsettled Spaces," Irene Watson asks with respect to legally recognized forms of Native title in Australia: "In looking at the question of settled and unsettled spaces, who is it that is free to roam?"; "To what extent is our sovereign Aboriginal being accommodated by the nation state's sanctioned native-titled spaces? Who am I when I stand outside native title recognition—the untitled native?"[112] Even as Wilson's novels have Native characters who live outside the legally recognized tribal homeland (Cherrah and Paul), the texts do not substantively address the historical and contemporary dynamics, importance, or affects of diaspora, Indigenous or otherwise, and the *Robopocalypse* books also tend not to engage the desirability and potentials of *roaming*—the networks of relation that can arise through various kinds of movement. In this way, visions of freedom that coalesce around and through flight, or just movement (individual and collective), have little place within Wilson's exploration of the ontological centrality of relations to place as a paradigm—itself oriented by Indigenous peoplehood—through which to engage contemporary life.

Wilson's novels highlight relations with place as a process of worldmaking in ways that contrast with Mosley's depiction of them as a constraint from which escape must be sought. In *Futureland*, to be located means to be captured, forcibly contained within a space of one kind or another as a function of institutionalized modes of racialization that operate even in the absence of any official endorsement of conventional racial categories. Yet even as the *Robopocalypse* series avoids the anthropocentrism of equating life with human existence, or even with the organic (which notably distinguishes it from the apparent environmentalism of the Oankali in *Xenogenesis*), Wilson tends toward a vision of shared humanness, presenting the thresholds of difference between person and machine as the basis for conflict and negotiation instead of attending in sustained ways to the violence mobilized around racializing distinctions among persons and peoples. With the exception of somewhat brief (if important) references to U.S. imperialism against Native peoples and the ongoing U.S. occupation in Afghanistan,[113] forms of racializing state-sanctioned violence do not receive comment, including extant forms of segregation in urban areas (including New York City), police assault against people of color (Lonnie, in fact, is a police officer), and mass incarceration (despite the depiction of AI-initiated forced human labor in both books in the series). If Wilson offers a vision of what might be characterized as grounded normativity, the novels tend to eschew discussion of the neoliberal territorializations and desire for escape from them that animate Mosley's redescription of contemporary life. Or, such dynamics of carcerality and fugitivity remain opaque within the kinds of Indigenously inflected conceptions of emplacement that drive Wilson's speculative imaginary.

The (Im)Possibilities of Black Dwelling

The *Robopocalypse* books highlight the significance of place as an ontological predicate for being and becoming, in ways that extend beyond human collectives. Within this formulation, Indigenous peoplehood occupies a crucial role, providing something of a model for thinking other forms of dwelling and locatedness and doing so less to mark Indigenous distinctiveness than to emphasize the importance of grounded relation as such. In *The Wave*, Mosley engages the politics and affective dimensions of Black collective placemaking but does so against the background of a poetics of flight. The novel turns toward horizons of Black-Indigenous difference, investigating desires for a sense of locatedness by African Americans and how histories of antiblackness and diaspora trouble such yearnings. The novel features a sentient life-form, which in its natural form often is characterized as like black tar, that has inhabited the ground under Los Angeles for many millions of years and that recently has breached the surface nearby, largely through reanimating those buried in the area—including the protagonist's father. Foregrounding the blackness of the entity/species alongside the vast timescale of its duration on land claimed by the United States allows Mosley to use it as a counterpoint to the continuing sense of dislocatedness that emerges from the legacies of slavery, segregation, and institutionalized antiblackness. If *Futureland* suggests an embrace of escape as a way of imagining freedom, *The Wave* addresses the sense of alienation that blackness can entail, especially given the continual casting of Black people as lacking a sustained relation to place—as, in Katherine McKittrick's terms, *ungeographic*. In generating what might be understood as a speculative expression of Black indigeneity in the Americas, Mosley implicitly runs up against the question of Indigenous peoples' priorness and its implications for thinking Black landedness. The novel's efforts to work through this impasse highlight the equivocations that arise in approaching the groundedness of indigeneity from within a political imaginary oriented around flight, even as the text's use of movement as an organizing conceptual and political framework indirectly challenges settler claims to Indigenous lands as well as contesting racializing accounts of national territory that cast it as a white possession. The Wave itself seeks to escape the Earth, and Mosley ends up presenting a sense of collective location as ultimately constricting and expressive of forms of state aggression. The translation of indigeneity into the terms of fugitivity, then, shapes the novel's trajectory in ways that turn it away from its attempt to address the meaningfulness of (Black) territoriality.

Mosley begins the novel by exploring legacies of opposition to antiblack racism and what they might suggest about Black experiences of collectivity in the United States. Errol, the narrator and protagonist, notes that his grandmother would tell him about "members of our family whom I've never met," including Albert Trellmore. Each Fourth of July, Albert would "set fire to one of the big corporations or production companies around Georgia," and the reason offered for this pattern of arson is, "White people. . . . Some of 'em used to refuse to hire blacks. Some would abuse the ones they had workin' for 'em. Now and then there was a Klansman had all of his money wrapped up in one'a them places," Albert justified his actions as performing "his patriotic duty."[114] Through the fires he literally clears ground, drawing attention to places claimed through white supremacy and, in a sense, seeking to reclaim them for Black people. In enacting what he characterizes as patriotism, he might be understood as trying to restore an egalitarian ethos on which the United States as a nation supposedly is based. However, given that Albert's pattern of destruction emphasizes the ways African Americans have been denied belonging, his assault on white institutions might be thought of as marking participation in a different kind of collective, as "patriotic" activity in the name of a Black people-nation that historically has not had a secure place in the United States. If situated within earlier examples of Black protest against U.S. patriotism (such as Frederick Douglass's "What to a Slave is the Fourth of July?" and the modes of Black radicalism discussed in chapter 1), the novel's account of Albert might gesture toward a sense of collective duration and emplacement not routed through membership in the U.S. state. Errol's father, Arthur, limits the possibility of taking part in such a legacy, though, as he largely cuts himself off from his family. Errol observes that Arthur "rarely visited his mother, because she insisted on talking about *all that old shit*, as he used to say" (4). The reason for Arthur's disassociation from his family seems to be his desire to distance himself from the struggle over Black belonging in the space of the United States. He implicitly envisions a transformed future in which the history of institutionalized and pervasive antiblackness does not structure the social geography of everyday life—where such concerns are just "old shit" left behind as part of a past best forgotten. In this vein, the novel portrays Arthur's marriage to a white woman (as well as the fact that both of his children married white people) as something like a flight from blackness in order to achieve the imagined security and serenity of a generic middle-class life.[115]

In beginning the novel with this portrait of Errol's family history and Arthur's effort to evade—or perhaps transcend—located histories of blackness and antiblackness, the novel sets up what will become a central irony of the text: that Arthur literally comes to be (re)animated by a kind of Black history in the form of the Wave. When Errol encounters his (un)dead father, Arthur has been brought back in a rejuvenated form, a younger version of himself that initially leads Errol to believe he is an illegitimate son of Arthur's about whom Errol never was told. This new being, whom Errol calls GT, reveals secret elements of Arthur's life (such as his murder of his wife's lover) that when backed up by material evidence become the basis for believing that GT is, in fact, the reenfleshment of Arthur by the Wave. Both singular and containing a multiplicity, this entity can divide itself up to the microscopic level, and the parts can function independently, yet "all experience is shared" (118).[116] GT explains that millions of years ago a meteor drove an existing life-form, "First Life," deep underground, "There it multiplied and bubbled. There it counted the long moments between where it had been and what it had become. While it was counting, there came an awareness, a knowledge of the selves of numbers. One knew its own count, and so did Two and Three and Four," achieving a sense of divisibility and potential distinctness in its parts, and "for all those years, First Life has been migrating, becoming the Wave. Rising up toward the surface. It washed over what was left of me when I was put in the ground" (72). In its usual form, it exists as a mass of what Errol describes as "black sludge" or "black tar" (168, 179). Thus, Arthur, a man who sought to evade "*all that old shit*" associated with the afterlives of slavery,[117] comes to be inhabited and remade through a condensed and incredibly powerful form of blackness that connects him to a profound experience of memory stretching back to long before the evolution of human societies.

The history of slavery and its contemporary implications recur in the process through which the Wave extends its reach, as well as the ways the government responds to it. Its presence registers for humans largely through its occupying and revivifying of corpses that it encounters in its movement rising through the ground. These reanimated bodies both are and are not those who have died. As GT notes when speaking with Errol and his mother, Arthur's former wife, "I'm not exactly Arthur Porter but the memory of him made flesh" (60), and Errol later describes Arthur as "the man whose genes [GT] wore" (164). Those who have returned from the dead possess the consciousness and memories of the people whose bodies they inhabit (although prior to GT they do not feel the emotional connections those persons had) (130). With respect to the living agential entity that is GT, Arthur is both dead and alive. In this vein, Errol characterizes those who have been reanimated as "the Wave's zombies" (181). The figure of the zombie itself resonates with the history of enslavement, capturing the sense of a being vacated of will in order to be put in service to the aims of another. In *The Law Is a White Dog*, Colin Dayan suggests that "we can use the image [of the zombie] in order to understand how things legally emptied of personhood can be repossessed or turned into vessels," adding, "Far from supernatural, zombies are experienced as highly contextualized spectacles of alienation intended to inspire horror in the minds of the community." Through the trope of the zombie, Dayan seeks to capture the ways a person may be literally alive yet civilly dead. She observes, "A creation of law, civil death is the ghost that continues to torment persons convicted of crime," generating a kind of social status that renders someone "unable to exercise the rights attached to a person," and in considering the relationship between the legal architecture of enchattelment and the current operation of a system of mass incarceration, Dayan argues, "We are obliged to consider the creation of a species of depersonalized persons," in particular marking "how the shifting identity of the slave was reborn in the body of the prisoner."[118] Mosley subtly invokes and inverts such connections. Rather than legally emptying out the subjectivity of Black people, either as chattel or prisoners, the Wave generates life for those who were dead by infusing them with an animate blackness.[119]

The novel positions the Wave as a counterpoint to the histories of institutionally produced Black nonpersonhood while illustrating how such dynamics continue to shape both everyday African American life and the process of conceptualizing and enacting national defense. Figurations of enslavement, incarceration, and the war on terror swirl around and cross-reference each other throughout the narrative. Soon after meeting GT, Errol instructs him in the importance of wearing clothing when venturing outside the apartment, warning that "if you go outside like that, they'll arrest you," to which GT responds, "Arrest. . . . Rest. Cell. Restrict. Like death. Death" (40). When they do finally leave and are pulled over by the police while driving, Errol recalls, "I could see the policemen coming up on either side of the car. One white and the other black, they both had their hands on their guns" (45). GT casts the encounter with the police not simply as potentially lethal but as leading to a situation "like death," presenting incarceration as social death. Given that there is no reason for pulling over their car other than their race, the fact that the police respond immediately with the threat of deadly force ("their hands on their guns") further suggests the association of the exercise of police power with the regulation of the movement of Black persons.[120] To occupy space improperly as a Black subject courts the employment of potentially murderous state violence in order to contain and control what is treated as the dangerous excesses of blackness. As McKittrick observes, "Enforcing black placelessness/captivity was central to processes of enslavement and the physical geographies of the slave system."[121] After Errol reveals the existence of GT to a police officer, as part of explaining how he came to know of a corpse buried in the backyard of his parents' home, "three men in suits" come to take Errol into custody (92), identifying themselves as "government agents" while not specifying the agency (94), and he describes the place to which they take him as "immense for a single dwelling, almost the size of a plantation" (95). This offhand reference suggests the ways that post-9/11 racialized apparatuses of surveillance and detention can be traced back to the legal technologies of enchattelment and the transfer of those powers to the criminal justice system in the wake of the Thirteenth Amendment.

Moreover, the novel implies a direct channel between criminal justice and antiterrorism initiatives, in which the distinction between crime and warfare and between domestic and foreign becomes largely meaningless. During his captivity, Errol declares, "It's illegal for you to hold me like this, against my will," to which Dr. Wheeler (the general responsible for the facility in which Errol is held) replies, "Not when it comes to Homeland Security" (122). As a result, Errol concludes, "I had been kidnapped. My government was in a secret war. My rights as an American citizen were of no consequence," further noting that "the story my grandmother told about my cousin the arsonist came to mind" (132). While one might understand the measures taken as part of the putative "war on terror" as exceptional with respect to the regular constitutional order of U.S. law ("Homeland Security" as something beyond the normal structure of legality and "rights"), Mosley implies that this mode of rightsless captivity exists on a continuum with the history of institutionalized *kidnapping* that was the slave trade and of post-emancipation white supremacy to which Errol's cousin Albert responded through tactical acts of arson.[122] Being held by the state as a threat to national security does not appear to differ fundamentally from being held by the state in deathlike suspension for other reasons (such as imprisonment)—a denial of belonging that the novel links to being-while-Black. As Brandon Kempner observes, "The Wave is eventually revealed to be a kind of black sludge, billions of small amoeba-like entities," and the government's response to it illustrates a "fear of the primordial blackness of the Wave."[123] In addition, the novel eventually tells readers that the narrative they are reading was begun by Errol during his initial internment as part of formulating his plan to escape. He reveals, "No more than five minutes after I entered into the apartment-cell, I began to write this history" (121), later adding, "I began this history in earnest. When I was at work on it, I felt that I was at least attempting to counter the insane and illegal activities of Wheeler and my government" (142). This act of writing in and about captivity, and chronicling the process of escape, positions the novel as its own kind of neo-slave narrative (especially in light of the fact that the "ghouls," as Wheeler calls those who have been reanimated, "were all headed north" when they were caught by the army [131]).[124] Formal citizenship as part of the legacy of emancipation, then, cannot shield African Americans from being construed and contained as threats to the nation, as presumptive intruders within a *homeland* implicitly understood as something like a white possession.[125]

As discussed earlier, *Futureland* illustrates how race provides a conceptual and administrative matrix through which to cast recalcitrance, resistance, or simple noncompliance to neoliberal imperatives as expressive of bodily tendencies, as markers of ingrained inclinations that indicate belonging to a particular category of person in need of containment (either in prison or Common Ground), and in *The Wave* Mosley shows how race can perform similar kinds of aggregative work with respect to national space. Race functions as a way of collating individuals as belonging to a biologically defined population that possesses an immanent relation to a place, usually figured in continental terms (i.e., African, Asian, European).[126] Such metonymic exchange between kinds of bodies and assertions of geopolitical authority—of jurisdictional power and defense—shapes the ways officials (mis)apprehend the Wave. In addition to characterizing the Wave in its various forms as an "invasion" and "contagion," Wheeler refers to it as an "infestation," "parasites" for which humans are the "hosts," and as an "infection."[127] These tropes oscillate between imagining the beings the Wave comprises as an immunological threat and a territorial one. The rather indiscriminate use of these varied figurations fuses corporeality and territoriality, somaticizing the nation-state in somewhat inchoate ways. The novel brings together these two possibly disparate ways of representing danger through what Wheeler casts as the potential for the Wave to "drive us [humanity] into extinction" (129): "the beavers of North American didn't have to be aggressive to force out any species that couldn't live in harmony with their watery world. These XTs [the official name for the microorganisms that constitute the Wave] could very easily create environments that would be extremely unfriendly to human and mammal alike" (137). The bodily and geopolitical converge in the *environmental*, a vision of imminent peril in which the health of the person and the well-being of the population become interchangeable. The syllogistic linkage of person-group-location allows the biopolitics of racial typing and the geopolitics of national jurisdiction (including explicit and implicit forms of citizenship and belonging) to conjoin in an environmental imaginary in which a given population (or populations) can be cast as alien to the space of a particular nation due to their true belonging to—or emergence from—elsewhere.[128] As Neel Ahuja argues in *Bioinsecurities*, U.S. policy draws on "neoliberal immunological knowledges" to cast particular populations as infectious agents, engaging in a "racialization of uncertainty and risk [with]in disease control" that treats nonwhite bodies as vectors of infection within an otherwise healthy ecology.[129] The novel suggests that Black people have never stopped being interpreted as anomalous, as potential contagion in need of regulation and containment.[130]

The intrusion of the blackness that is the Wave into the presumptive whiteness of the "Homeland," then, generates a deep anxiety not only about the continued coherence of the nation as an extension of whiteness (as a setting for the extension of white bodies) but also about the legitimacy of the racialized and racializing enactments of national jurisdiction through which that extension is produced and normalized. The territoriality of the nation-state comes to be signified in terms of racial embodiment. Once Errol has been recaptured by Dr. Wheeler and is being taken back to a cell in the armed compound, Wheeler relates that they "found out that the infection is not communicable" yet still "destroyed the pit that held the contagion" (the black tar in the cave to which Errol and GT had retreated) while leaving "a few of the ghouls alive to study," and when considering whether to murder Wheeler in response, Errol thinks, "If I attacked him, his soldiers would surely slaughter me. In order to help my father's race, I held back" (201–2). Even when understood as "not communicable," the Wave remains a "contagion" that must be rooted out, denied any place of refuge, and the reason appears to be its blackness. The phrase "my father's race" here indicates both GT's animation by the microscopic particles of the Wave and Arthur's blackness, suggesting that they gain meaning in relation to each other.

In offering a speculative redescription of how national space continues to be racialized in ways that cast blackness as an alien intrusion, Mosley explores the sociopolitical dynamics that produce ongoing experiences of Black alienation, but in response to such affects, he draws on the figure of the Wave in order to imagine a kind of Black indigeneity, a possibility for being in relation to the land claimed as the United States not routed through the legacy of enchattelment and post-emancipation violence. As suggested by Albert's arson and Arthur's efforts to escape the past, the novel situates the main plot within the context of the ways African Americans' relationship to the space of the United States remains troubled by the history of enslavement and its aftermath. At one point, Errol observes that GT had "a wide grin that reminded me of some of the African students I'd known at school. The Africans seemed less guarded, where American blacks kept humor on a lower, more controllable register" (28), later noting, "He smiled at me with that African grin" (35). These passing comments index what Mosley casts as a pervasive sense of African American alienation, registering in quotidian phenomenological ways the insecurity of belonging to the United States in light of ongoing and pervasive forms of antiblackness. In juxtaposing this sensibility with that of "Africans," the text implies a feeling of being constantly embattled, of being ill at ease that arises from a pervasive sense of unhomeliness. In *Queer Phenomenology*, Sara Ahmed observes, "If orientation is about making the strange familiar through the extension of bodies into space, then disorientation occurs when that extension fails. Or we could say that some spaces extend certain bodies and simply do not leave room for others," and the sensation of *guardedness* by Blacks in the United States might be described as resulting from feeling that one possesses a kind of body for which there is not room. Later, Ahmed adds, "To be comfortable is to be so at ease with one's environment that it is hard to distinguish where one's body ends and the world begins."[131] The kind of everyday agitation and discomfort to which Mosley points implies inhabiting a space that does not extend one's body, in which one's body appears as an intrusion or an alien presence—as destabilizing the national *environment*. Conversely, the novel describes the Wave in terms of the fluidity of its being, a picture of "merging and measuring, of combining with its mates, of defining its surroundings" (117). If Albert Trellmore's "patriotic" arson registers the intransigence of antiblack geographies of possession, a consistent lived cartography of dislocation that produces the ordinary self-monitoring and withdrawal of being "guarded," the conversion of Arthur into GT by the Wave produces the kind of emplaced ease that the novel attributes to people from Africa, as opposed to those in the diaspora.

The novel positions the Wave as a means of envisioning a kind of situated blackness that extends into the landscape of the United States, preceding and exceeding the structures (official and quotidian) that block and circumscribe Black presence. Mosley contrasts the troubled experience of belonging for Black people within the United States to what the novel suggests is a far less fraught sense of situated relation for Africans. Through this distinction the novel portrays African Americans, and implicitly Black people throughout the Americas, as not simply having a connection to place that has been contested, thwarted, and disavowed by white supremacist actions and imaginaries but, due to the slave trade and its legacies, as lacking the kind of enduring onto-logical connection to the lands they inhabit that Africans are imagined to have. Mosley implicitly casts this difference as irremediable, a disjunction underlined by the text's juxtaposition of such Black alienation with the Wave's enduring presence and its enabling of an "African"-like ease in GT.

Black intellectuals have explored this sense of unbelonging, often either using it as a basis for critiquing the desire for emplaced belonging or for envi-sioning a process of indigenization in the Americas. Harney and Moten sug-gest, "Never being on the right side of the Atlantic is an unsettled feeling, the feeling of a thing that unsettles with others. It's a feeling, if you ride with it, that produces a certain distance from the settled, from those who determine them-selves in space and time, who locate themselves in a determined history."[132] Un-settledness, then, both predicates blackness as it is generated through the slave trade and becomes a normative commitment, as against the kinds of racial-izing processes of territorialization that Mosley theorizes in a speculative key. Similarly, as discussed in chapter 1, Saidiya Hartman and Dionne Brand offer critiques of sovereignty from the position of a diasporic blackness that remains substantively stateless. In Brand's terms, "The body is the place of captivity. The Black body is situated as a sign of particular cultural and political meanings in the Diaspora. All of these meanings return to the Door of No Return,"[133] and from this perspective, the desire for nationhood as an enduring collective groundedness appears as a forgetting of the ongoing violence of institution-alized formations of captivity. For Hartman, eschewing collective landedness as the horizon of political desire means embracing "the ongoing struggle to escape, stand down, and defeat slavery in all of its myriad forms," which she refers to as "the fugitive's legacy"; it entails "a dream of autonomy rather than nationhood," "the dream of an elsewhere . . . where the stateless might, at last, thrive."[134] Moreover, repudiating collective territoriality as a necessary aim for political struggle seeks to evade the dismissal of Black people and movements for failing to be properly landed, for failing to be Indigenous. In "The *Vel* of Slavery," Jared Sexton observes, "From indigenous perspectives, diasporic black struggles would, first and foremost, need to lament the loss of indigeneity that slavery entails, a process that requires acknowledging that the loss is both his-toric and ongoing," and he suggests that, if acknowledging enduring collective relations to land provides the framework for what constitutes justice, diasporic

Black struggles can only ever appear to be normatively groundless, at best, or as projects of settlement, at worst.[135] Conversely, other scholars have embraced the potentials of Black indigeneity, but as a function of becoming native to the Americas. That dynamic appears in such work as a "process of indigenization, through which people of African descent became native to their new lands," and in these scholarly accounts "new 'natives,' predominantly Africans and their descendants, replaced the original Antilleans and *became* indigenous to the Caribbean. Narratives of aboriginal absence and African indigeneity strongly define anglophone Caribbean studies."[136] Within these formulations, ruptured African indigeneities are not a subject of ongoing mourning or debilitation (producing the kind of unresolvable, wounding sense of lostness that, as Sexton suggests, would leave Black movements with no political horizon at all) but, instead, can be incorporated within a process of becoming *native* to spaces within the diaspora created by transatlantic slavery.[137] In these different ways of approaching Black landedness, indigeneity as collective place-based belonging either is undesirable as a frame/goal for Black political aspirations or is already accomplished through renarration of enslavement's diaspora as enduring connection to new lands.[138]

While registering the continuing effects of enslavement's rupturing of networks of place-based relation, Mosley stages a version of Black indigeneity that allows the text to engage the politics and affects of Black placelessness without actually claiming indigeneity for non-native Black people, instead transposing the desire for Indigenous-like belonging into subjunctive form. The novel offers a speculative image of rooted blackness in which persons become part of a grounded collective history in ways that resemble the kinds of locatedness at play in Wilson's novels. GT and the others reanimated by the Wave are imbued with a blackness that literally emerges out of the ground. As such, it expresses a connection to the land on a timescale that dwarfs the history of enchattelment and its legacies and that does not arise through them, offering an experience of emplacement that resembles the ontological relationship to land of which Moreton-Robinson speaks in discussing Indigenous peoplehood. As a fantastic redescription of a yearning for collective groundedness, Mosley's Wave neither appears as the return of a lost (African) past nor as a new relation created through dislocation to the Americas. Rather, through the representation of the Wave, the novel imagines a kind of Black landedness that exists apart from histories of empire and conquest, that provides an alternative to both statelessness and "patriotic" belonging to the settler nation. The figure of the Wave translates Indigenous priorness into an idiom of Black belonging, but given the fact that the Wave is not human and has existed largely underground, the novel does not envision a kind of priorness that contests or overwrites Indigenous sovereignties.

The Wave builds on the social analysis offered in *Futureland*, retaining the sense of U.S. jurisdiction (and possibly all forms of state sovereignty) as carceral in its organization around geographies of racialization, but rather than rejecting wholesale the idea that collective dwelling could function as an alternative to state violence, *The Wave* figures an emplaced blackness that exceeds state machinations. The text does not depict Native peoples as such, and in this way the Wave could be thought of as surrogating for them, effacing Native nations past and present. However, while the novel sidesteps the issue of Native histories and ongoing relations to particular land bases, the fusion of indigeneity and blackness through the Wave might be understood as an equivocation, as a speculative gesture toward the need for a way of thinking the potential for modes and ethics of Black collective emplacement in the Americas that do not merely reiterate settler claims to Native territories.[139] As a form of blackness intimately embedded within and arising from the landscape, the Wave provides something like a sense of "grounded normativity," in Coulthard's terms—an ontological relation to place (in ways reminiscent of Wilson's texts) that is not reducible to the racialized imaginary of national belonging. At one point Errol speaks of it as "the Rapture that once thrived beneath our feet" (222). Mosley's critique of racializing cartographies of captivity opens onto the potential for thinking non-dominating formations of landedness. In this way, the text turns toward the possibility of engaging with Indigenous peoples' place-based self-determination. The depiction of the Wave can be understood, then, as an experiment in imagining a kind of groundedness in the Americas that does not serve as an extension of the state and that could enable a noncolonial Black relation to place.

The text, though, approaches such intimations of (the politics of) indigeneity through the frame of fugitivity, turning away from that experiment and the potential for envisioning enduring Black connections to place in relation to Native geopolitical mappings. While using the Wave to envision a longstanding history and memory of uncontestable Black locatedness, the novel also portrays it as perpetually in motion. Just after GT's insight that "arrest" leads to a state "like death," he explains to Errol that he is both "your father and part of the Wave," and in response to Errol's question about what the Wave is, GT responds, "Move-ment. . . . Motion" (40–41). The novel juxtaposes the "motion" of the Wave with the deathlike stasis of incarceration, implicitly presenting mobility as an alternative to racialized histories of captivity and containment. Like the portrayal of fugitivity in *Futureland*, *The Wave*'s emphasis on unsettledness and migration frames flight as the principal political modality through which to engage longstanding forms of racializing carcerality. The military assault on the Wave illustrates the ingrained understanding of blackness as contagion and anomaly, something that does not belong to this space that must be disciplined or eradicated. Yet more than merely a response to particular modes of state violence, the Wave's mobility appears chosen, perhaps even immanent to its existence. During GT's discussion of the origin of the Wave in the wake of the meteor strike that drove "First Life" underground, he recalls, "For all those years, First Life has been migrating, becoming the Wave. Rising up toward the surface. It washed over what was left of me when I was put in the ground" (72), and after Errol has been exposed to the elements of the Wave through contact with GT, he dreams its history: "I was immense, moving leisurely through solid stone at the rate of an inch a century" (124).

Moreover, such primal motion tends toward the potential for transcendence. A voice from the stars inspires the journey from deep in the ground toward the surface. As GT explains, "There was only us and then the voices": "'They are in the sky,' GT said. 'In space. There are more voices than there are stars. But there is only One that comes'" (167–68). This being, referred to as Farsinger, calls to the Wave, and the Wave rises in order to join with this celestial presence and take flight from the earth (described by Errol at one point as "flee[ing] the planet" [207]). Once united, the Wave and Farsinger "transformed into something completely different" and "moved away with greater speed than either had known was possible" (225). Earlier in the novel, GT speaks of the presence of Farsinger's voice as "The Annunciation" (168), referencing the angel Gabriel's declaration to Mary that she would be the mother of Christ. That sense of the birthing of the heavenly from the earthly recurs in Errol's repeated portrayal of the Wave as divine, calling it "the Rapture," suggesting "it was Buddha and the Ten Thousand Things," and at other moments simply calling it "God."[140] Even more so than in *Futureland*, mobility here less evades locatedness than suggests an ethics of movement through which historical modes of constraint can be "transformed into something completely different." While marking histories and legacies of captivity, and their role in understanding and animating contemporary forms of carcerality, then, the novel offers a vision of mobility that cannot be reduced to escape from something.

However, the heavenly flight from the terrestrial also displaces the territorial. Within this narrative and thematic orientation, Mosley largely leaves aside the questions around and desires for emplacement the novel raises. Or rather, the significance of (the) Black (search for) groundedness recurs throughout the novel, but in ways that largely get subsumed within a conceptual and political paradigm organized around movement. As discussed earlier, the literal emergence of the Wave out of the earth beneath Los Angeles cannot help but gesture toward indigeneity, especially given the ways the text implicitly juxtaposes its unity, continuity, and locatedness with the ongoing effects of African dislocation and diaspora as a result of the slave trade (such as in the contrast between the openness of "Africans" and the more "guarded" demeanor of "American blacks").[141] Furthermore, the "zombies" that have been returned to life need to consume the stuff of the ground in order to sustain themselves. Soon after meeting, GT asks Errol to take him to the ocean, where Errol watches him consume "a great deal" of sand (64), and later Errol asks, "Dirt is your food?" to which GT responds, "Sand and sun.... Sand and sun" (165). Although not exactly illustrating collective occupancy as a people, these hyperbolic images of connection to the land suggest an intimate engagement with place that echoes in a fantastic vein an Indigenous territoriality. However, if for Wilson locatedness serves as a foundational part of understanding the potential for all manner of life of whatever form, Mosley translates shared memory arising from emplacement as the harbinger of a transformation achieved through movement. Rather than envisioning a reordering of the (geopolitical) *environment* in ways that might generate an alternative to the violence of "civilization," the novel seems at some level to accept the biopolitical account of national space that it critiques. Even as the text challenges the racializing metonymy through which land is linked to certain kinds of bodies, in which figures of *invasion* and *infection* necessarily surrogate for each other, it stops short of imagining a way that blackness could inhabit the territory claimed by the nation without simply reaffirming the racist ideologies and practices of national jurisdiction.

Instead, the novel shifts the emphasis on an enduring relation to place to a continuity of memory. Mosley stages a temporality of blackness in which mobility does not equal a breach in time, an unbridgeable fissure between the past and the present. The novel presents the Wave's movement as expressive of historical continuity, as part of an uninterrupted flowing through time. Of his dreams inspired by contact with GT, Errol observes, "I was many and one. I was forever, remembering back before I was conceived into the far reaches of the beginning" (125): "The XTs in me sang of all their history. A thousand beings arisen from the dead chanted to me every night and day, telling me their stories" (194). The novel envisions the possibility of a collective memory reaching back to "the beginning," a joint (un)consciousness among those inhabited by the Wave that braids together all of "their stories" into a "history" that can unite them. If the "history" Errol writes entails the story of a persistent denial of Blacks' place in the nation (as in the discussion of Albert's arson), the memory contained by the Wave and its hosts suggests how the racialized body, including the body in motion, comes to serve as the bearer of a blackness that provides a link to the deep past. If the trope of the reanimated dead allows the novel to signify on the social death of enchattelment and imprisonment, the presence of a communal awareness suggests a speculative alternative to the shattering violence of the Middle Passage. As Samuel Delany notes, "The historical reason that [African Americans have] been so impoverished in terms of future images is because, until fairly recently, as a people we were systematically forbidden any images of our past. I have no idea where, in Africa, my black ancestors came from because, when they reached the slave markets of New Orleans, records of such things were systematically destroyed."[142] Early in the novel, GT suggests of himself, "I am a memory of the ancestors" (41), and toward the end, he proclaims, "I am the memory of a thousand thousand thousand years" (216). To have always been "many and one," to be connected with the "ancestors," and to be able to trace a shared, uninterrupted, and steady sense of belonging and orientation across vast swaths of time contrasts sharply with the apocalyptic historical rupture that is the legacy of African enslavement. GT does not merely possess memories; he *is* memory. When he says, "I am [a/the] memory," he positions himself as an embodied condensation of that history. Moreover, heteropatriarchal inheritance in the novel comes to surrogate for duration itself, for the possibility of an embodied sense that one dwells within a legacy of blackness not reducible to the racist violence enacted by the state in its definition and defense of the "Homeland." Both Errol's blackness and his relation to the Wave come through his father, a point the novel underlines through repeatedly emphasizing Errol's mother's whiteness as well as that of his first wife and his sister's husband. In the wake of the Wave's movement off into the cosmos, the novel closes with Errol being reunited with GT (whose consciousness now occupies Wheeler's body) who "late at night . . . will transform into my father and we'll laugh at the good times that never fade away" (226).[143] The fullness of the past emerges in the context of the passage of memory from father to son, providing a sense of continuity borne in the (racialized) body and not connected to any particular place.

The possibility of an enduring and intimate connection to the land, though, persists in the elliptical intent with which the novel closes. While Arthur's body finally is destroyed, GT's consciousness is transferred to Wheeler, and he indicates to Errol, "I'm in contact with those whom Wheeler's men never found. We're looking for others like us in the earth. And we're trying to have a good influence on the world" (224), the novel having explained earlier that millions of years ago the being that became the Wave "moved out" of a shared "deposit" from which other collective entities may also have moved. Furthermore, Errol announces, "Someday soon I will join Wheeler in the search for undiscovered deposits of God" (226). In these moments, those who have been reanimated by the Wave form a continuing network whose aim remains locating other sites in which Wave-like entities dwell. Notably, GT describes them as "in the earth," as embedded within the land rather than as moving across it. Moreover, characterizing them as "deposits" intimates not only coalescence but stability, suggesting a process of being formed in a particular place over eons. Although possibly gesturing toward a kind of diasporic imaginary, in which those spread over large distances maintain a shared experience of belonging despite their apparent dispersion, these final images underline the groundedness of these beings/collectives, their rootedness, and the search to find them seems more like a desire to recover that sense of situatedness than flexible connections within a matrix of mobility. If the text opens with Albert's arsons and the failed or deferred effort to enable Black emplacement on lands claimed by the United States, it closes by returning to that longing, sketching what might be understood as a yearning for a kind of blackness that enables intimacy with the land absent the burdens of an ongoing history of captivity and conquest.

THE WAVE EXPLORES THE ways that the putative "war on terror" can be understood as continuous with extant and historical processes of racial detention, control, and displacement. The "civilization" in whose name the government speaks remains implicitly white, one to which people of African descent cannot ever fully belong. The difference between the domestic and the foreign, then, turns less on formal citizenship as such, or on the distinction between persons born in the space of the nation-state and those not, than on forms of racial lineage in which the possession of a Black body means being subject to violence either enacted directly by the state (the police, the military) or to which the state largely turns a blind eye. Mosley suggests how "invasion" and "infection" become conflated in imaginings of national jurisdiction, with the Wave's movement from the earth suggesting an escape from such racial geographies. Similarly, through its dystopian extrapolations, *Futureland* explores the carceral tendencies and trajectories at play in the present moment, highlighting how extant modes of surveillance and classification implicitly deploy processes of race making as part of putatively race-neutral means of assessment. The process of attributing inherent ("antisocial") proclivities based on belonging to a group, whether or not that group is a conventional racial category, can be understood as intrinsically a process of racialization, and it provides a way of datafying people of color as deficient, thereby reaffirming and reifying exist-ing racial inequities even in the absence of racist or even race-coded language and intent. Given the ubiquity of such dataveillance and the racialized topog-raphies it helps generate and justify, resistance to this regime entails neither collective rights claims nor assertions of (counter)sovereignty. Rather, Mosley develops a fugitive poetics in which flight functions less as a tactic for reaching some other space (envisioned as free) than as a mode of oppositional being and becoming.

If fugitivity provides a means of theorizing efforts to evade the various car-ceral geographies that emerge in the wake of enslavement, the presentation of placelessness as a de facto critical norm can defer the potential for addressing emplacedness as a horizon of political imagination, including by Indigenous peoples.[144] The difficulty for engaging Indigenous political principles and for-mations lies in the understanding of situatedness as only ever racializing and carceral. How does connection to land come to appear as merely a reactionary investment in some version of state sovereignty? Daniel Wilson's *Robopocal-pyse* books suggest an alternative to this framing, offering an expansive concep-tion of the potentials for emplacement. Featuring Indigenous peoplehood and sovereignty through the depiction of the Osage Nation, the novels elaborate what might be understood as broader principles of indigeneity in which Na-tive nationhood appears as one kind of collective groundedness, a powerful example of the importance of attending to how place shapes the potentials of being and becoming. Rather than simply acting as form of constraint or containment, locatedness functions as the wellspring from which possibility comes—for collective identity and governance, relationships among different kinds of beings, and new modes of life. *Robopocalypse* and *Robogenesis* suggest how, in Coulthard's terms, "land-connected practices" that arise from Indig-enous knowledges and experiences can provide a paradigm through which to highlight the importance of situatedness as such. As opposed to casting non-natives as de facto or surrogate Natives, Wilson's novels present place as the ontological predicate for collective identity, Indigenous and otherwise, and for engaging the existence of shifting ecologies, human and not, organic and not. While these texts engage with neither conflicting claims to land nor con-temporary racialized modes of containment, they raise the question of what it means to foreground the importance of place, in ways that include Indigenous peoples' political sovereignty but that also exceed it.

The Wave envisions a blackness indigenous to the Americas, although the text backs away from the implications of such imagining in its turn toward fu-gitivity. The Wave creates a jurisdictional conundrum for the government due to the fact that its inhabitance in putative U.S. space does not depend on U.S. legal cartographies but on its own priorness to the nation's existence. In this way, the threat it poses to "Homeland Security" lies in its indigeneity, but the novel transposes these connections and the potential for collective groundedness into the framework of fugitivity, emphasizing transformative flight from existing systems of detention. In their speculative mapping of contemporary carceral geographies, Mosley's novels often cast emplacement as entrapment, as racialized capture, in ways that suggest both the power of fugitivity as a political trope and how it can orient away from questions of collective landedness. From the perspective of a fugitive poetics, situatedness can appear principally as a vector of state violence. *The Wave,* though, also opens toward the potential for engaging such groundedness as a horizon of political desire and identity. Mosley translates indigeneity in ways that mobilize it as a resource for thinking enduring Black locatedness while implicitly holding open a distinction between Black dwelling and Indigenous sovereignty—seeking a version of the former that does not necessarily emerge as a challenge to the latter, as merely a continuation of the legacy (the environment) of conquest. One might understand the novel's pivot away from further exploring this potential as a function of the conceptual momentum in the notion of fugitivity, but reciprocally, one might understand the turn to figurations of fugitivity in the novel as a response to the difficulty of working out what such a vision of non-dominating Black landedness might mean in the context of the ongoing history of non-native occupation. As a political trope, fugitivity can both efface indigeneity and mark an ethics of hesitation when approaching it. This double movement, this equivocation in relation to the politics of groundedness, treats collective claims to landedness both as inherently undesirable (given histories of racializing violence) and as a troubled site of non-native desire. In this way, Mosley performs a speculative translation that implicitly negotiates the relation between carcerality and sovereignty as distinctive—and possibly disjunctive—frames of reference for understanding life at the intersection of racial capitalism and settler colonialism.

4

THE MAROON MATRIX

Marronage condenses potentially disjunctive understandings of resistance to enslavement and its racializing legacies. Derived from the Spanish *cimarrón*, which originally referred to runaway animals (with strong connotations of wildness), the term *maroon* was adapted to designate escaped slaves.[1] Neil Roberts observes, "Marronage conventionally refers to a group of persons isolating themselves from a surrounding society in order to create a fully autonomous community," and as Alvin O. Thompson notes, "Maroon communities emerged where those who fled from slavery finally stopped running."[2] How, though, do we approach the relation between the parts of this compound concept/phenomenon—running and landed autonomy? The previous chapter addressed tensions between flight and collective emplacement, but as a critical-political trope, marronage contains them both within one figure, in what might be called *the maroon matrix*. Maroon communities arise out of literal fugitivity from enslavement and are maintained through an ongoing refusal to be subjected to the plantation system and its legacies of racial capitalism, private property, and incarceration. If fugitivity signals a refusal to be contained within the categories and geographies of the dominant political and economic system, the concept of marronage also points toward communal forms of placemaking, governance, and resource distribution that have been and might be generated by people of African descent in the Americas. One could name such possibilities as part of, in Katherine McKittrick's terms, "the poetics of landscape," which "are not derived from the desire for socioeconomic possession": "The claim to place should not be naturally followed by material ownership and black repossession but rather by a grammar of liberation."[3] To achieve liberation from *being* property need not inherently entail *holding* property, asserting forms of landed ownership and possession like those that characterize the plantation itself and that constitute whiteness as a mode of social power.[4] As a political trope or framing, marronage provides ways of engaging Black emplacement and self-determination in the Americas that conceptually approach indigeneity to a much greater extent than either fungibility or flight, and this increased engagement with place-based modes of peoplehood potentially brings greater focus to the complexities of Black and Indigenous relations on landscapes shaped by the dynamics of empire.[5]

What relations does marronage bear to indigeneity? More than perhaps any other trope within diasporic Black political discourses and movements, marronage has served over the past century as a principal way of signaling various (and potentially incommensurate) kinds of opposition to the violence of the slave system and the forms of antiblackness that have persisted and arisen in its wake. As a figure, marronage foregrounds flight as resistance in ways that can defer engagement with the grounded politics of Black placemaking, especially in considering how it might be understood in relation to Indigenous sovereignty and self-determination. In "Afrarealism and the Black Matrix," Joy James defines "maroon philosophy" as occurring "at the borders" in "reimagining freedom through flight," further suggesting it remains "[i]n perpetual flight from genocide," and Greg Thomas suggests of notions of marronage, "The hills or mountains have become not just one place of maroonage, like guerrilla warfare in general, but a powerful *metaphor* for maroonage, which can take place in any kind of space, anywhere," adding, "When the metaphor is literalized in more restrictive conceptions, equating all maroonage with encampments or mountain 'reservations,' much is regrettably lost in the official thinking of maroonage."[6] The idea that marronage might be "perpetual" and occur "anywhere" raises questions about the potential within it for recognizing Indigenous relations with lands and waters, for encountering Indigenous difference in ways that are geopolitically meaningful. Conversely, when marronage expresses claims to particular lands, whether by a given community or by the postcolonial state, it can take part in a process of *indigenizing* non-natives. For example, Roberts characterizes the renaming of Saint-Domingue as Haiti in the Declaration of Independence of 1804 as the "indigenizing of a land and a people in the mind and political imagination of the ex-slave population," adding that through this process, "[p]olitically, *black* becomes the new *native*. The native is free. Haiti indigenizes blackness."[7] As Shona Jackson suggests, "New World blacks . . . have sought to become both native *and* national subjects, and *within* the economy of these positions, they have also claimed their humanity," effacing ongoing Indigenous presence and sovereignties: "labor by formerly enslaved and indentured peoples is precisely what they are able to make into and reify as the new prior time of their belonging and with which they supplant the prior time of Indigenous Peoples."[8] Marronage, then, oscillates between flight and groundedness in ways that can orient away from reckoning with Indigenous self-determination or can transpose indigeneity into a transferable conceptual and political resource such that "black becomes the new native" in ways that efface/replace Indigenous peoples.

Nalo Hopkinson's *Midnight Robber* and Andrea Hairston's *Mindscape* directly engage indigeneity within their mappings of Black geographies, and in doing so, they illustrate how figurations of marronage both enable and trouble efforts to think Black-Indigenous relation. *Midnight Robber* fuses Black flight and independent nationhood, envisioning the transfer of Caribbean peoples into outer space. Hopkinson takes up the legacy of using marronage in multiple ways within Black political imaginaries, including by postcolonial states in the Caribbean,[9] and the text does so principally through allusion to Granny Nanny, the early-eighteenth-century leader of the Windward Maroons of Jamaica. Nanny, an expansive artificial intelligence in the novel, provides a means of gathering together and holding in tension a wide range of Caribbean political movements spanning multiple centuries, including insurgency by maroon communities, the Haitian revolution, Garveyism, West Indian federation, and independent nationhood. The novel offers a speculative staging of the ways marronage as a conceptual framework combines and cross-references disparate Black political histories and formations, raising the question of how these framings both enact and demur expressions of sovereignty. Hopkinson explores how varied forms of resistance to imperialism and transnational antiblackness explicitly and implicitly take part in claims to territory and governance that can normalize the expropriation of Indigenous lands without acknowledging such accountability. By contrast, *Mindscape* takes up Indigenous peoplehood as a somewhat mobile way of envisioning forms of collective, place-based opposition to racializing state violence, thereby detaching the concept of indigeneity from anachronizing and fetishizing visions of Indianness. In this way, the novel implicitly draws on and speculatively reconceptualizes the role played by marronage in Latin America. Such political figurations often refer to Black communities that are presented as having descended from maroon communities established prior to the end of slavery, and legal recognition for the territoriality and self-governance of such groups usually depends on the extent to which they fit within extant ways of representing state-sanctioned modes of indigeneity, themselves dependent on notions of Indian stasis.[10] As against this deadening analogical vision of racial and cultural purity, Hairston draws on indigeneity as a flexible way of figuring a range of landed political formations that exceed control by the state while, reciprocally, refusing narratives of Indian purity that lock Indigenous peoples into an ever receding and impossible account of authenticity.

If Indigenous peoplehood can appear as a reactionary investment in propertied relations from the perspective of fungibility/fleshliness (as suggested in chapter 2) and fugitivity can underplay the potential ontological and normative import of emplacement (as discussed in chapter 3), a maroon framework can address and value territoriality in ways that enable a thinking together of Black and Indigenous modes of landedness in their complex and messy political entanglements. However, political imaginaries of marronage also contain figurations of flight that can orient away from sustained engagement with questions of sovereignty, except to understand it as a mode of oppressive constraint that brings an end to flight. From this perspective, sovereignty reifies, insulates, and formalizes the impulses that give rise to marronage in ways that neutralize their capacity to move toward liberation.[11] *Midnight Robber* and *Mindscape* illustrate how such notions of flight can shape the representation of enduring Indigenous presence and governance on particular land bases. These texts provide speculative insight into how translating indigeneity into the terms of marronage can bracket the issue of Indigenous sovereignty, such that indigeneity becomes something like setting—functioning as a background or vehicle for imagining non-native forms of movement and change.

What, though, does substantive engagement with Indigenous sovereignties entail? Part of the difficulty of approaching difference as a vital part of political imagining—performing a kind of speculative ethics—lies in negotiating across frameworks whose terms, aims, and orientations are nonidentical. As discussed in chapter 1, Audre Lorde suggests that "differences have been misnamed and misused in the service of separation and confusion" and that we need to "recognize, reclaim, and define those differences" within processes of solidarity making.[12] Such recognition and reclamation entails moving among, in Marisol de la Cadena's terms, varied "onto-epistemic formations" or "ways of making worlds."[13] However, official modes of recognition for Indigenous polities and territories tend not to acknowledge the dynamism of Indigenous worldings, instead offering accounts of Indian stasis. Popular and governmental discourses in the United States, Canada, and throughout Latin America often recast Indigenous modes of sociality and geopolitical formations as manifestations of an underlying racial substance—as expressions of an innate Indianness.[14] Melissa Tantaquidgeon Zobel's *Oracles* and Stephen Graham Jones's *The Bird is Gone: A ~~Monograph~~ Manifesto* address the double-edged character of state-recognized Native territorial boundaries as both empowering and imprisoning while also tracing how historically shifting Native social formations are congealed into notions of unchanging Indian identity. Such Indigenous futurist work envisions the persistence of Native landedness, as against the dominant settler imagination of the Indian as vanishing, but the preservation of Indigenous identity also requires protection from non-native interests, expropriations, and consumption. Within these speculative imaginaries, indigeneity remains under threat, requiring insulation from invasive forces even as these texts seek to refuse various imposed and colonial conceptions of Indian authenticity (including for consumption as primordial/spiritual alterity).

In drawing attention to questions of territoriality and collective governance, marronage opens up the potential for increased considerations of questions of landedness and place-based peoplehood, but it also suggests significant distinctions between blackness and indigeneity as kinds of problem-spaces, in terms of their "tropes, modes, and rhetoric" and the "horizon in relation to which [they are] constructed."[15] Zobel's and Jones's novels address the problems of state-managed modes of recognition while also underlining the importance of territoriality to Indigenous peoplehood, especially given ongoing histories of settler expropriation. While Hopkinson's and Hairston's texts both engage such Indigenous landedness and its implications for collective Black placemaking, they also illustrate the kinds of equivocation that can arise when translating Indigenous histories and territorialities into the terms of marronage. Having explored the potential complicities between diasporic Black projects of political autonomy and processes of settlement, *Midnight Robber* remains unresolved about how to incorporate that insight back into its vision of marronage, turning to figures of flight in ways that defer the tensions it illuminates, and *Mindscape* offers an expansion vision of indigeneity that facilitates the acknowledgment of a range of a non-state collectivities, doing so, however, in ways that make indigeneity itself into a mobile figure that can efface distinctions between Indigenous and non-Indigenous political formations. The chapter, though, closes by considering the appearance of representations of treaty making within *Mindscape* and the possibilities such an invocation of diplomacy might offer for envisioning and enacting relations of reciprocity—for sustained modes of negotiation among Black and Indigenous formations that suggests both their opacities with respect to each other and the potential for fruitful relations across difference.

Reiterated Histories of Conquest and Escape

In *Midnight Robber*, Hopkinson explores the relationship among a variety of political imaginaries and situates them in the context of tensions with Indigenous peoples. Multiplying references to Black political projects in the Americas, the novel alludes to the disjunctions among these imaginaries while linking them through the figure of Granny Nanny, the nationally canonized icon of Jamaica who served as leader of the Windward Maroons in the first half of the eighteenth century. Jenny Sharpe suggests of Nanny, "Her significance as a rebel woman is bound up with decolonization and the emergence of Jamaica as an independent nation. Her symbolic value lies in her ability to represent both the buried tradition of an African culture and the long history of anticolonial struggles so central to the identity of the emergent nations in the Caribbean."[16] The text positions marronage as a speculative vehicle for containing these various (and potentially incommensurate) political mappings within an encompassing conception of creole placemaking. However, amid that literally otherworldly account of Caribbean sovereignty, Hopkinson situates the pursuit of Black diasporic self-determination within the problematic of settlement, raising the question of how Black-led movements grapple with Indigenous presence and emplacement. The novel offers a searing depiction of the effects of non-native habitation and development, ranging from exploitation and removal to complete extermination, but at the end it defers (or, perhaps, suspends) the implications of that critique, implicitly positioning indigeneity as an enabling mise-en-scène—a space through which creoles might pass as part of a process of self-realization. The knowledge gained through encounter and Indigenous cultural immersion gets routed back into non-native sociopolitical formations, cast as a form of maroon fugitivity that is continuous with the history of (Black) struggles for freedom and that can provide the foundation for a more democratic (non-native) social order.

The novel imagines that a united Caribbean coalition has left the Earth to settle on terraformed planets elsewhere, and this exodus and subsequent management of the resulting "Nation Worlds" is overseen by an artificial intelligence named Granny Nanny, who gathers information and communicates via the "'Nansi Web." Two hundred years after settlement, a young girl named Tan-Tan is taken by her father, Antonio, through the dimensional barrier that separates her planet (Toussaint) from New Half-Way Tree—the world on which those exiled from the Nation Worlds dwell. Antonio is fleeing prosecution for his accidental murder of his wife's lover. Once on New Half-Way Tree, Tan-Tan and Antonio are taken to a local village by Chichibud, a member of a native species called the douen who are treated by the exiled humans as marginalized cheap labor. When on her sixteenth birthday Tan-Tan accidentally kills her father while he is raping her, a violation he has been committing for a number of years, she flees the village and is harbored by Chichibud and his family, who live with other douen in a tree-based band. Tan-Tan also discovers she is pregnant from the rape, her second pregnancy from her father (having aborted the first one). When Ione—Tan-Tan's stepmother who had been searching for her in order to punish her for Antonio's murder—traces her back to the douen tree, she fails to find the douen village, but in order to prevent humans from discovering douen home places and modes of habitation, they destroy the tree and disperse to other douen bands, leaving Tan-Tan with Chichibud's daughter, Abitefa, to survive by themselves in the bush. Prior to this development, Tan-Tan had begun appearing in local human villages as the Robber Queen, a Robin Hood–like figure adapted from Caribbean stories and Carnival traditions. She intensifies such activity after her expulsion from douen community, ultimately finding her former sweetheart—Melonhead—working as a tailor in the town of Sweet Pone. While participating in the Jonakanoo celebration there, Tan-Tan-cum-Robber Queen is found and confronted by Ione, and after persuading the crowd and the authorities that she killed Antonio in self-defense, she rejoins Abitefa in the bush to give birth to her baby, whom she names Tubman. The novel closes with two revelations: that the previously unnamed narrator is the house eshu, the artificial intelligence that mediates between Granny Nanny and the members of Antonio's prior home on Toussaint; and the nanomites that usually construct an ear-bud through which individuals involuntarily are connected to the 'Nansi Web have actually migrated throughout Tubman's body, allowing him to feel Nanny's presence throughout his whole body and making him the first person on New Half-Way Tree with whom Nanny can connect.

In its space-age conception of possibilities for Caribbean freedom, *Midnight Robber* creates a web of allusions to a range of diasporic Black political projects. As part of setting the scene for readers, the narrator observes, "[I]t was

Jonakanoo Season: the year-end time when all of Toussaint would celebrate the landing of the Marryshow Corporation nation ships that had brought their ancestors to this planet two centuries before."[17] This naming invokes T. A. Marryshow, the Grenadian activist and politician who became known as the "Father of Federation" due to his persistent arguments in the 1910s and 1920s for uniting British Caribbean colonies (the West Indies) into a single political entity that could both govern itself and refute British claims about the need to superintend populations of color.[18] Through this allusion, the novel suggests the potential for Caribbean political unity while also implying that the virulence of extant racisms preclude the possibility of such collective self-determination on Earth. Furthermore, the Nation Worlds created out of the mass migration from Earth also include "Garvey-prime," the document laying out the aims for the emigration is entitled "*Mythic Revelations of a New Garveyite*" (18), and the "Black Star Line II" is the most prominent among the ships that transported the colonists to their new home (20), invoking Marcus Garvey's leadership of the Universal Negro Improvement Association and his shipping venture in the 1920s that promised to create a transatlantic circuit among the United States, the Caribbean, and Africa.[19] In featuring these two figures as a central part of framing the project that is the Nation Worlds, Hopkinson draws heavily on early twentieth-century formulations, a period notable for the capaciousness of conceptions of Black political possibility. As Michelle Stephens suggests, the onset of formal decolonization in the Caribbean in 1962, with independence for both Jamaica and Trinidad (notably, the two countries from which *Midnight Robber* most heavily draws, including in the characters' dialect),[20] brought to an end "a period in black transnational discourse" in which Black intellectuals across the diaspora "construct[ed an] impossibly utopian ideal of a black 'internationalist nation,' a global vision which also required multiple identifications of blackness and more global definitions of black nationality and citizenship."[21] In highlighting figures from before the achievement of formal decolonization, Hopkinson signals a desire for a kind of collective life beyond that of postcolonial nationhood, a longing that might be understood as following from the failures of independence to secure meaningful self-determination.[22] The novel enacts, in Robin D. G. Kelley's terms, the "*dream of a new world*," and Kelley notes of such visions of movement, "[A]ny wholesale dismissal of the desire to leave this place and find a new home misses what these movements might tell us about how black people have imagined real freedom," adding, "All these travel/escape narratives point to the biblical story of Exodus, of the Israelites' flight out of Egypt."[23] The novel's vision of the Nation Worlds participates within this exodus imaginary, providing a speculative referent for the kind of transnational or multinational modes of diasporic belonging that early-twentieth-century Black intellectuals theorized.

The version of exodus in *Midnight Robber*, though, does not return the people of the Caribbean to an African space conceptualized as originary, instead taking them into the complete unknown.[24] Although serving as a touchstone for discourses and practices on Toussaint, such as in the references to the Ashanti and Yoruban spiritual/trickster beings Anansi and Eshu, Africa does not operate as the horizon for imagining potential political formations for those who inherit the legacy of enchattelment. As Alisa K. Braithwaite suggests, "*Midnight Robber* abandons the concept of returning to the homeland and replaces it with a journey further outward to science fiction's final frontier, outer space and an extraterrestrial homeland."[25] The fact that the inhabitants of Toussaint call themselves "Marryshevites" suggests the ways that the (inter)planetary union in which they participate emerges out of diasporic conditions (like the vision of West Indian federation). Moreover, the novel explicitly notes the mixture among populations usually deemed racially distinct, how the "forefathers" of the inhabitants of the Nation Worlds "had toiled and seated together," with "all the bloods flowing into one river, making a new home on a new planet" (18). In this way, the Marryshevite project entails a Caribbean amalgamation irreducible to Black diaspora per se, even as it gestures toward such diaspora (especially in the novel's Garveyite intimations and the references to the voyage as one made by "black people").[26] Fugitivity on a massive scale—extraterrestrial exodus from the white-dominated international system (seeking to be "free from downpression and botheration" [18])—gives rise to new modes of collective placemaking and governance.[27]

While this fusion of flight to territoriality and ethnogenesis implicitly invokes the history of maroon settlements, the text explicitly does so through the figure of Nanny, centering the trope of marronage as a means of gathering together disparate political imaginaries and holding them in dynamic, speculative tension.[28] Hopkinson consistently links the electronic network that extends across the Nation Worlds—the 'Nansi Web—to "Granny Nanny, Queen of the Maroons" (17).[29] A statute of her adorns a park across from the main administrative center of Tan-Tan's home province, alongside one of Zumbi (the most famous leader of Palmares—by far the largest of the historical maroon settlements [68]),[30] and the novel uses "Granny Nanny" as a synonym for the web itself: "The tools, the machines, the buildings; even the earth itself on Toussaint and all the Nation Worlds had been seeded with nanomites—Granny Nanny's hands and her body. Nanomites had run the nation ships. The Nation Worlds were one enormous data-gathering system that exchanged information constantly through the Grande Nanotech Sentient Interface: Granny Nansi's Web. They kept the Nation Worlds protected, guided and guarded its people" (10).[31] Encapsulating the projects of both escape and nation-building, Nanny comes to function not simply as a Caribbean-derived metaphor for the technology the text invents but as a vehicle for conceptualizing the forms of inspiration, memory, and aspiration that animate Black political imaginings.[32] As Sharpe notes, "Moore Town maroons do not simply think of Nanny and her contemporaries as their ancestors but also as spirits that protect and guide them."[33] In a similar vein, Granny Nanny appears in *Midnight Robber* as a pervasive influence throughout the Nation Worlds, a figure from the past whose ongoing, almost ubiquitous presence offers crucial and continuing support. At one point, one of the present-day programmers who can comprehend Nanny's code notes, "Is Marryshow she break through to first," further indicating that they could not recognize the artificial intelligence as communicating until its emissions were run through a sound emitter, since they came in the form of song: "Nanny was seeing things in all dimensions" (51). The ability to operate within and across difference, constructing connections that facilitate engagement among varied modes of articulation and experience ("seeing things in all dimensions"), situates Nanny as the central nexus for diasporic negotiations and identifications.[34] Hopkinson has noted of her writing, including *Midnight Robber*, that a "strategy" she has "is to sometimes refuse to write yet another plea to the dominant culture for justice," and through Nanny, the novel conceptualizes the potential for sustainable Black-led modes of self-governance that do not rely on white aid or intervention.[35] Furthermore, the novel substitutes the nurturing (omni)presence of Nanny for the conventional "vision of the sovereign state figured in the black male sovereign," contesting the long-standing alignment of the possibility of Black political order with heteropatriarchal forms of leadership and social organization.[36]

The figure of Nanny both invokes and defers the exercise of sovereignty. Marronage serves, as Sharpe notes, as "a popular metaphor" in Jamaica and throughout the Caribbean "for characterizing their own escape from the European culture that had colonized them,"[37] allowing the citizens and governments of postcolonial nations to cast themselves as bearers of an ongoing legacy of resistance, but it simultaneously indicates particular communities descended from pre-emancipation fugitives who understand themselves to be politically autonomous entities. With respect to the Windward Maroons of Jamaica, for example, Kenneth M. Bilby observes, "Even as the epic struggles of their ancestors are enshrined in national and transnational mythologies, . . . the Maroons themselves must contend with a postcolonial state that has so far refused to acknowledge their claims to a separate identity, in favor of a policy of gradual assimilation."[38] We might read the superintendence of the Nation Worlds by Granny Nanny, then, as a political allegory for the ways marronage functions as a kind of operating system through which Black political discourses manage (and suspend) the question of how freedom from white rule should be realized (geo)politically. More than simply indicating that the novel's speculative vision arises out of histories of Black diasporic movements for freedom and liberation, Hopkinson's proliferation of allusions to Black leaders, intellectuals, and movements positions the Nation Worlds as an apparently pacific merger of these legacies while tacitly suggesting that they come together in an uneasy amalgam. The potentially incommensurate and riven political geographies to which such allusions gesture are held in relation through being subsumed within the topos of marronage as represented by Granny Nanny (whose capaciousness crosses and links otherwise potentially segregated "dimensions").

If marronage suggests the potential for the oppressed to flee and collectively take up life someplace else, the question of whose presence precedes them in that place remains a pressing one to which Hopkinson increasingly turns readers' attention. The novel addresses the varied forms of violent expulsion on which the seemingly utopian existence of the Marryshevites depends. Early on, the text reveals the existence of New Half-Way Tree. It is described by the narrator (Antonio's house eshu, a sentient operating system for his dwelling that cares for Tan-Tan) in the following terms: "You never wonder where them all does go, the drifters, the ragamuffins-them, the ones who think the world must be have something better for them, if them could only find which part it is? You never wonder is where we send the thieves-them, and the murderers?" adding, "But where Toussaint civilized, New Half-Way Tree does be rough" (2).[39] Cast as wild and ungovernable, New Half-Way Tree affords a space to which antisocial elements can be consigned. It can only be reached by crossing a dimensional barrier that allows access to "more Toussaints than they could count, existing simultaneously, but each one a little bit different" (72), of which the planet known as New Half-Way Tree is merely one. This prison world, though, contains a species, the douen, who have their own sophisticated modes of sociopolitical order. However, douen are viewed by former Marryshevites (who lose their status as they cross the one-way dimensional barrier) as inferior beings to be subjected to human control. Chichibud, the douen who initially encounters Tan-Tan and Antonio after they cross the dimensional divide, responds to routine denigration from humans by observing of himself and other douen, "Beast that could talk and know it own mind. Oonuh tallpeople quick to name what is people and what is beast" (92). In this way, the prison planet operates as the frontier for the Nation Worlds: it is a place claimed by them as an extension of their own political dominion, to which they can send outcasts who are unable to comport themselves in a "civilized" fashion and over which they do not exert meaningful jurisdiction—as evidenced by the absence of the 'Nansi Web and the ad hoc formation of relatively disconnected local governments that themselves tend to rely on violence as the means of maintaining order. Nanny, then, is insufficient in maintaining the cohesion of the Nation Worlds. What is required is another space, a supplemental one that can serve as a safety-valve for persons and activities deemed disruptive but whose chaotic dynamics are spatially segregated from the processes of governance in the metropole. The regime for which Nanny provides the infrastructure engenders carcerality and colonization, but does so in ways that bracket those patterns of force such that they do not appear to be endemic features of diasporic sovereignty.

In its account of New Half-Way Tree, the novel explores how the exodus imaginary that animates marronage runs into difficulty in acknowledging the destructive sovereignty effects generated by the settlements that result from flight. Early on, readers learn that "New Half-Way Tree is how Toussaint planet did look before the Marryshow Corporation sink them Earth Engine Number 127 down into it like God entering he woman; plunging into the womb of soil to impregnate the planet with the seed of Granny Nanny" (2), quickly sketching an origin story in which Toussaint is birthed out of unimaginable violence. While cast as an act of divine patriarchal founding, even as the power of creation gets attributed in cross-gendered ways to Nanny's "seed," this terraformational act of penetration utterly remakes the planet, completely annihilating everything that preceded its service as a site for inhabitation by "free people" (21).[40] In addition, this information is revealed to readers in what amounts to a preface by the narrator prior to the beginning of the narrative action, a historical fact easily disregarded as a past that is at most only marginally meaningful to the events unfolding in the present of the plot. The burying of this legacy of genocidal decimation by the house eshu (who narrates this section of the novel, as well as others) parallels the frequent discussion of Native peoples as having been completely eliminated in articulations of Caribbean history. As Maximilian C. Forte observes, the Caribbean "is 'out of place' in much of anthropology for being too novel, too hybrid, too discontinuous, not indigenous enough," becoming "typecast as the zone of 'impurity,' of permanent 'artificiality,' a place where primordial attachments are impossible."[41] In this vein, the text illustrates how the story the people of the Nation Worlds tell of themselves as maroons—as having fled oppression to create new societies—requires continually normalizing their geographies of freedom by performing the erasure of Indigenous territorialities, as either lost at the origin in ways that are irretrievable (and thus irrelevant going forward) or contained within an elsewhere treated as having no (geo)political significance within maroon mappings (those territories overseen by Nanny).[42] While maroon communities in the Americas sometimes are characterized as emerging through combinations of escaped slaves with already existing Indigenous groups to form new entities, the novel picks up on the tendency in the island Caribbean to portray marronage as either unrelated to Indigenous peoples or as replacing them within their former village sites, which have been cleared as a result of their utter extirpation in the wake of Euro-conquest of the islands.[43] In *Midnight Robber*, Nanny enacts a biopolitics of sovereignty through which landscapes are remade so as to enable and naturalize an alien political order. At one point prior to Tan-Tan's exile through the dimensional barrier to New Half-Way Tree, her eshu "showed her how to see the fossils trapped in some of the stones. It told her about the animals that used to live on Toussaint before human people came and made it their own," and among the items the eshu includes on a list of "indigenous fauna" is "the douen." When Tan-Tan inquires specifically about the douen, the eshu replies, "Indigenous fauna, now extinct," and in response to her question as to why they are gone, the eshu insists, "To make Toussaint safe for people from the nation ships" (32–33). This exchange emphasizes the reduction of douen sociopolitical formations to the status of "fauna" while also casting them as a biological threat to the "people" who would found a new, now *free*, social order.

Humans' presence on both Toussaint and New Half-Way Tree depends on the colonization of Indigenous spaces, a process that recasts the politics of invasion and its devastating effects as merely the clearing out of "fauna" to enable "civilized" dwelling. Moreover, the events on New Half-Way Tree do not so much take readers back in time (to what Toussaint once was) as illustrate the ways the force of colonization continues to shape the contemporary Nation Worlds.[44] The need of the Nation Worlds for a place to which social disruption can be consigned generates ongoing settlement on New Half-Way Tree, and the genocidal territorialization that provides the condition of possibility for the Nation Worlds' existence persists in the ways (former) Marryshevites engage with the beings and extant social, political, and environmental networks of what they call New Half-Way Tree. The novel suggests that the problem of settler sovereignty, even when exercised by those who have been oppressed in other ways, lies in an inability to acknowledge the legitimacy of Indigenous geographies on their own terms without subsuming them within settler political projects and imaginaries.

Through its account of douen collective geographies, forms of habitation, and modes of governance, the novel brings into relief the historical and ongoing violence of settlement, which in Hopkinson's portrayal is in no way mitigated by the Marryshevites' status as maroons—as those who fled from oppression and created their own community/ies. The novel implicitly draws on figures connected to marronage to characterize douen territoriality (heightened by the ways the douen serve as exploited labor, do not count as equal political subjects, and refer to humans as "Master" [121]), yet the text also underlines generationally transmitted collective forms of douen identification and placemaking that produce a form of politics that does not arise from flight. In explaining to Tan-Tan where he has taken her after he aids her escape from her village (in the wake of her murder of her father in self-defense), Chichibud declares, "You in a Papa Bois, the daddy tree that does feed we and give we shelter. Every douen nation have it own daddy tree" (179).[45] Arboreal tropes have multilayered political significance within Jamaica and the Caribbean more broadly. Trees have performed crucial symbolic roles for maroon communities in Jamaica, including the Kindah (or mango) tree under which Kojo gathered Leeward Maroon leaders in the eighteenth century (and that remains the symbolic center of Accompong), the Shady Tree under which Windward elders met for generations, or the use of tree-like coverings as the basis for personal camouflage.[46] Hopkinson spends a great deal of time detailing the ecologies of the daddy tree, including douen architecture, connection to other species in and around the tree, sustenance, and disposal of bodily waste. These descriptions indicate an enmeshment of Indigenous sociality with the tree itself, an organic base that enables the flourishing of douen lifeways, but Hopkinson situates them within an explicitly political understanding of douen collectivity—each tree has its own "nation." The identity of the polity remains linked to processes of emplacement, as suggested by Chichibud's assertion that "other daddy trees" would take in those who fled from the former site of his nation due to fear of having douen sociopolitical formations discovered by the (former) Marryshevite settlers (273).

Hopkinson emphasizes the douen desire for separateness from settler sociopolitical formations and the importance of retaining their collective opacity.[47] Chichibud at one point observes of the lack of human knowledge about douen lifeways, "Oonuh tallpeople been coming to we land from since, and we been keeping weselves separate from you. Even though we sharing the same soil, same water, same air" (173). That sense of emplaced autonomy and distinctness ("we land," "keeping weselves separate") arises out of the specificity of douen socioenvironmental dynamics, even as those dynamics change in response to human occupancy/occupation. If Octavia Butler's *Xenogenesis* trilogy gestures toward the ethical importance of recognizing a right to collective self-determination while reducing the content of it to a form of racial reactionism, casting it as a regressive nativism, *Midnight Robber* addresses the politics of place in ways that resonate with Daniel Wilson's attention to the significance of situatedness. Hopkinson, thus, gives normative weight to indigeneity. In his critique of Canadian efforts to incorporate Indigenous peoples into liberal notions of social well-being, Dale Turner argues that they "do not respect the sui generis nature of indigenous rights as a class of political rights that flow out of indigenous nationhood and that are not bestowed by the Canadian state" and that they "do not question the legitimacy of the Canadian state's unilateral claim of sovereignty over Aboriginal lands and peoples," later adding that "various styles of liberalism" do not "recognize the legitimacy of indigenous forms of political sovereignty."[48] Furthermore, Indigenous sovereignty itself may be organized around, in Glen Coulthard's terms, "struggles not only *for* land, but also deeply *informed* by what the land as a mode of reciprocal *relationship* (which is itself informed by place-based practices and associated form[s] of knowledge) ought to teach us about living our lives in relation to one another and our surroundings."[49] Through the novel's portrayal of the douen, Hopkinson underlines that douen forms of social organization and collective emplacement do not derive from human/settler political structures and are not legitimately encompassed by them, instead suggesting that the relationships to and through Papa Bois constitute a form of political sovereignty at odds with efforts to incorporate the douen into settler political cartographies. In this way, the text addresses, albeit in a speculatively transposed register, issues that Zainab Amadahy and Bonita Lawrence raise with respect to the dislocating legacies of slavery: "[F]or all peoples forced to live on other peoples' lands, a crucial question becomes what relationships they will establish with the Indigenous peoples of that land whose survival is so under siege." They add that critiques of histories of antiblackness can be formulated "in ways that exclude the possibility of an Indigenous presence fundamentally *mattering*."[50] In its account of the douen during Tan-Tan's residence with them, the novel refuses to allow marronage to surrogate for indigeneity in ways that would efface the presence and force of non-native sovereignty. Instead, Hopkinson emphasizes the ways the social formations of "tallpeople" threaten douen modes of peoplehood and territoriality ("keeping weselves separate").

While underscoring the violence of settler occupancy/occupation with respect to the douen by maroon subjects, the novel, though, runs into difficulty in envisioning how such insights *matter* when turning back to the human settlements. After Chichibud and his people abandon their daddy tree, Tan-Tan and Abitefa live in the bush, with Tan-Tan venturing into nearby villages in her newly adopted persona of the Robber Queen in order to right wrongs (including theft and forms of bound labor that resemble enslavement). These activities culminate in her participation in the annual celebration of Carnival in Sweet Pone, confronting her stepmother and publicly describing her father's long-term pattern of incestuous violation that led to his accidental murder. Tan-Tan asserts of that final rape and his death, "*The Robber Queen get born that day, out of excruciation*," and through this public performance, she reclaims herself: "Then Tan-Tan knew her body to be hers again" (325). She then leaves Sweet Pone "to go home," "back in the bush to Abitefa" to give birth to her baby (327). At the novel's close, Tan-Tan has not returned to one of the human settlements, although she has been reunited with Nanny through her child, Tubman (named after Harriet Tubman), whose blood contains nanomites that allow him access to the 'Nansi Web from across the dimensional divide.[51] If Jonakanoo on Toussaint celebrates the project and process of settlement ("the landing of the Marryshow Corporation nation ships" [18]), a nationalist vision associated with male intellectuals (Garvey and Marryshow) yet overseen by the figure of Nanny, Carnival on New Half-Way Tree interrupts the reigning social order, giving rise to inversions that might suggest alternative modes of living to everyday forms of authority.[52] In bookending the novel with these different yet linked celebrations, Hopkinson stages the tension that constitutes the maroon matrix, the stability of creating landed communities versus the disruptive potential of movement/change, and in closing with Tubman's reunion with Nanny, the text signals that these potentially disparate aims can be situated within an encompassing conception of marronage.

However, the douen are nowhere in this vision, having removed to an elsewhere whose existence lies beyond the novel's narrative horizon.[53] If Tan-Tan remains outside the world of the village, she also does not live among the douen, and they and their displacement do not play a role in the text's resolution. Her residence in the liminal space of the "wild" positions her as outside of—in flight from—human community due to its brutalities, including the heteropatriarchal violence of her father's assaults.[54] Moreover, Tan-Tan's furtive forays into nearby towns, which include taking supplies she needs in living outside their bounds, resonate with the history of maroon brigandry, stealing food and goods from local free populations (particularly targeting plantations).[55] Yet while she remains a figure of resistance to the inequities and cruelties routinely enacted in the settlements, her performance at Carnival and Tubman's birth do not contest the continuing and expanding occupation of douen lands. Most critics, though, have characterized the ending as liberatory, focusing on Tubman's—and by extension, Tan-Tan's—reconnection to Nanny.

Even those critics most attentive to the colonial dynamics of Marryshevite settlement on Toussaint and New Half-Way Tree characterize the ending in terms of transformative possibilities for fluidity. Bill Clemente argues that Tan-Tan and Abitefa's "mutual experience as exiles will further cement their bond, portraying, perhaps . . . something of the hybrid society, based on assured mutual respect and cultural identity, into which human and Douen can evolve," gesturing toward "the promise [of] unification," and Brecken Hancock observes that "by ending *Midnight Robber* with the birth of Tubman, Hopkinson embraces irresolution and multiplicity," further suggesting that "what hope the novel offers is located in Tan-Tan's alienation from which Tubman, border-straddler, bridge to freedom, is able to emerge."[56] Figures of *hybridity* and *multiplicity* point toward the absence of clear boundaries, the potential for movement beyond extant borders. These formulations reflect the novel's characterization of Tubman as "the human bridge from slavery to freedom" (329), invoking flight along the Underground Railroad (via allusion to Harriet Tubman) as expressive of some vital element of the meaning of the renewed linkage to Nanny. Unsettling divisions between places and populations, breaching existing forms of enclosure, suggests a kind of literal and conceptual mobility that is presented as a key to the meaning of "freedom."

Here we see the dialectics of marronage at play—the dynamic relation between two potentially opposed orientations (fugitivity and settlement) held in relation within the maroon matrix, as signified by Nanny. The text suggests how the topos of marronage provides a means of bringing various nonidentical political imaginaries into generative relation, but within this framing, indigeneity implicitly becomes part of that matrix, an element of a "hybrid society" in which *freedom* entails participation within the dialectics of marronage, rather than a separateness—an opacity—that serves less as a subject for inclusion than a horizon of diplomatic relation. Discussing the conceptual work performed by the figure of Caliban, Jodi Byrd observes, "He embodies within the space of what is interpreted as 'Caliban' all the contradictions and subject positions produced by conquest, slavery, and genocide," and that process of concentration and conflation fuses slavery and indigeneity in ways that lead Byrd to ask, "How does the emptying and reinscription of these referents facilitate the processes of colonization and racialization in the Americas, where the land had to be physically and psychically emptied of its prior inhabitants and refilled with newly arrived 'natives' who compete for subjectivity within the emptied referent?"[57] Similarly, Tan-Tan bears the burden in the novel of signifying various histories of violence and their remediation, including the ways her relationship with Abitefa suggests that the douen in some sense positively are encompassed within the freedom promised by Tubman/Nanny. In the conclusion of the novel, though, Abitefa appears alone, and the absence of collective douen territoriality and governance from the ending bespeaks the ways they trouble the novel's closing image of (re)union. If Hopkinson spends much of the middle of the novel detailing douen mappings and lifeways, they seem to need to be bracketed or turned away from in order for the freedom ostensibly brought by Tubman—the potential for increased connection and movement between Toussaint and New Half-Way Tree—to be conceivable as something other than colonial expansion. Byrd inquires, "How do arrivants and other peoples forced to move through empire use indigeneity as a transit to redress, grieve, and fill the fractures and ruptures created through diaspora and exclusion?" noting that "Amerindians precipitate out of the transformations they facilitate and are not part of the future perfect of postcolonizing Caribbean societies."[58] In *Midnight Robber*, the douen provide a (frontier) space and set of experiences through which Tan-Tan's consciousness can be shifted in relation to human sociality,[59] and douen difference serves as a catalyst for engendering movement and change among settlers without altering the conditions of settler sovereignty—the continued and expanding occupation of Indigenous lands in ways that do not acknowledge Indigenous political geographies and forms of self-determination.[60]

If Tan-Tan can be said to transit by way of the douen, then indigeneity might be said to function in the novel as a kind of setting, as an enabling background that facilitates flight and possibilities for change within non-Indigenous social formations while orienting away from Indigenous concerns, aims, and futurities. In *Queer Phenomenology*, Sara Ahmed argues, "We can think . . . of the background not simply in terms of what is around what we face . . . , but as produced by acts of relegation: some things are relegated to the background in order *to sustain* a certain direction." She further suggests that the background helps bring certain things into focus: "The figure 'figures' insofar as the background both is and is not in view," adding, "a background is what explains the conditions of emergence or an arrival of something as the thing that it appears to be in the present."[61] Describing the douen as background suggests that they provide the potential for Tan-Tan to "*sustain* a certain direction," back toward the settlements as an agent of brigandry and boundary-crossing transformation. Her experience of life in the daddy tree with Chichibud's nation shapes the circumstances for the emergence of the Robber Queen. The background, then, is not inert or inconsequential, instead actively enabling something to take place, but it also remains in the service of figuring something else, of bringing into view something that is not of the background and against which the background recedes as an enframing condition of possibility.[62] The novel's staging of Tan-Tan's transit through douen space makes their territory into a (receding) background that helps her "figure" as outside dominant modes of sociality on both New Half-Way Tree and Toussaint and, thus, as an agent of flight that can (re)animate the dynamism of marronage. Nothing about the tendencies unleashed by the cataclysmic founding of Toussaint, including the destructive human occupation of New Half-Way Tree, is abated by the novel's ending; instead, Nanny's influence is further extended in ways that, given the history of Marryshevite settlement, would seem to foreclose douen self-determination.

In foregrounding Black territoriality, *Midnight Robber* illustrates how the topos of marronage draws attention to issues of collective emplacement and governance, and the novel further raises the question of the presence and significance of Indigenous landedness in relation to maroon geographies. However, the dynamics of flight (of movement) that are crucial to the political imaginary of marronage lead the text away from a consideration of the implications of enduring Indigenous geopolitical distinctiveness. Once indigeneity needs to be brought back into relation with the complex array of Black political imaginaries held within the figure of marronage (reconciled in the novel via Nanny), indigeneity as such comes to function as a localized background across which creoles can transit in further democratizing their own societies. In discussing the citation of indigeneity within contemporary forms of critical theory, Byrd observes, "Every time a flow or a line of flight approaches, touches, or encounters Indianness, it also confronts the colonialist project that has made that flow possible. The choice is to either confront that colonialism or to deflect it. And not being prepared to disrupt the logics of settler colonialism necessary for the *terra nullius* through which to wander, the entire system either freezes or reboots."[63] While the novel does confront the ongoing colonialist project on both Toussaint and New Half-Way Tree, it runs into difficulty in engaging Indigenous eco-political mappings in ways that would meaningfully affect the "line of flight" posited within and by marronage. Instead, indigeneity ends up being cast as an isolated setting that cannot reorient the structural dynamics of creole placemaking, and that implicit circumscription of Indigenous political geographies reinforces a sense of the givenness of settler sovereignty, even amid dynamic changes within non-native social formations (such as the extension of Nanny to New Half-Way Tree).

The Vicissitudes of Separateness

What, though, does recognizing Indigenous separateness entail? If Wilson's *Robopocalypse* books (discussed in chapter 3) suggest how principles of indigeneity can inform conceptions of emplacement beyond the dynamics of Indigenous peoplehood as such, other kinds of Native speculative fiction focus in more sustained ways on future possibilities for Native nationhood. Melissa Tantaquidgeon Zobel's *Oracles* and Stephen Graham Jones's *The Bird Is Gone: A ~~Monograph~~ Manifesto* both offer visions of Indigenous place-based peoplehood in which the survival and well-being of Native polities depends on boundaries that divide them from non-native-controlled spaces. Read together, the novels indicate various kinds of violence at play in modes of settler recognition while also highlighting divergences in ways of conceptualizing Indigenous identity and emplacement, providing a caution to any effort to suggest a paradigmatic model for how to define and delimit indigeneity.

Zobel explores the connection between Native national identity and the nonhuman environment in ways that foreground a constitutive interdependence, in which peoplehood cannot be severed from enmeshment with the particularity of place and the modes of inhabitance that arise from long-term dwelling. Set in the mid-twenty-first century among the Yantuck, a fictionalized version of the Mohegans whose traditional lands lie in what is now Connecticut, the novel tells the story of Ashneon, a young woman with the ability to communicate with the dead, who lives with her grandmother Winay and great-uncle Tomuck (the tribe's official medicine people) on Yantuck Mountain, presented as the sacred center of Yantuck lands. The majority of the novel takes place in the wake of the failure of the tribal casino and the act of arson that finalizes its destruction, and it primarily is set in and around the Yantuck Museum located on the mountain, founded and operated by Winay and Tomuck. The central conflict turns on the desire of Ashneon's cousin Obed to become the Yantuck medicine man while working for the New Light Corporation, a conglomerate that seeks to market those who claim to possess Indigenous knowledge—the Oracles of the title—via broadcast from and tourist admission to its new space station, Delphi I. The spell used to try to increase Obed's power backfires, driving him to the brink of insanity, and when it is reversed and he is discredited, the interest of New Light seekers moves on to others, while Ashneon becomes medicine person in the place of the recently deceased Tomuck. However, the plot occupies less of the text's focus than the descriptions of the mountain and its influence, particularly in terms of distinguishing it from both U.S.-sanctioned modes of tribal governance and the celebration of Native "culture" as a redemptive salve for non-natives.

The mountain appears less as part of the space over which Indigenous political sovereignty is exercised than as the condition of possibility for Yantuck being and becoming. The Yantuck do not so much exert political authority over a territory that encompasses the mountain as they take part in a process in which the mountain (and the various kinds of beings—animals, plants, and neither—that also inhabit the area) provides the basis for continued Yantuck becoming. In this way, the mountain serves as an example of what Clint Carroll describes as Indigenous "*sovereign landscapes*."[64] In contrast to a conception of jurisdiction, the extension of an institutionalized network over a determinately bounded space, sovereignty in this context can refer to the enduring relations and reciprocities that (re)constitute this people as a collective presence in and through this place. To those who visit the Yantuck Museum, Tomuck asserts, "The Natives who have always lived here live here still," adding "Our people have lived here forever," and he instructs visitors, "It is our duty to care and provide for the trees, not vice-versa. They are our ancestors. They were here long before us and will remain long after we are gone."[65] The mountain gives shape and substance to them as a people, and describing the trees as "ancestors" further suggests an ongoing genealogy of interconnection that animates contemporary Native existence, participating within an active matrix of reciprocity and relation that is irreducible to something like an ideology of ownership. Here we see a version of what Aileen Moreton-Robinson has characterized, as discussed in chapter 3, as Indigenous peoples' "ontological relationship to land, the ways that country is constitutive of us."[66] In describing the audience for Obed's performance during Tomuck's funeral, broadcast over the multisensory wireless network called "the cy," the text observes, "All natives from somewhere, but all abandoning their unique traditions for a generic path absent of accountability to any nagging grandmother, demanding uncle, or judgmental spirit lurking atop an ancestral mountain. It was so much easier to visit other people's mountains, where the spirits overlook you" (89). To be "natives from somewhere" entails having "unique traditions" that arise out of and are sustained by the specificities and histories of that location, that cannot simply be transported to "other people's mountains" due to the fact that such practices gain meaning out of a situated matrix of enmeshments and reciprocities in a given place. To be "accountable" to those sets of relations involves attending to debts and responsibilities that one holds to a range of beings, including mountains, kin, and other-than-human entities. Rather than acting generically as stewards to the nonhuman entities that happen to surround them (such as in the organicism divorced from enduring placemaking at play in Butler's vision of the Oankali, discussed in chapter 2), Yantuck persons continually (re)emerge as such through their ongoing located engagement with the various beings on which their continued existence as Yantuck depends.[67]

This interwovenness appears quite graphically in images of the blending of the forest with the Yantuck Museum. In speaking with Tomuck about her work with an anthropologist trying to document Yantuck history, Ashneon asks, "Is it my imagination or is this museum not really a museum at all? Sometimes, it seems just like an extension of the woods" (67), realizing later in the conversation, "I think somehow I always knew that the museum and the woods were the same and that these woods hold all that we are as Yantuck people. I also knew that when they go, we go, too" (71).[68] The novel's portrait of the Yantuck Museum highlights the absence of distinction between Yantuck identity and the stuff of "the woods," suggesting that the archive of Yantuck nationhood lies in the enmeshments—the "extension"—through which the mountain continually makes possible the everyday existence of Yantuck people. The forest *holds* Yantuck collective being, less as a historical artifact preserved in a case than as the enframing potential for materializing a Yantuck future. The Yantuck people and the mountain together form what de la Cadena has called "a socionatural collective." Describing Andean modes of Indigenous peoplehood in ways that resonate with Zobel's vision, de la Cadena notes, "[P]ersons are not from a place; they are the place that relationally emerges through them," further suggesting that "they are together and as such are place."[69]

Even as Zobel represents Yantuck self-determination as normatively and ontologically keyed to the dynamic matrix of enmeshments that is the mountain, she emphasizes disjunctions among Yantuck people in their conception of collective identity. The narrator notes, "For most Yantuck Indians, Big Rock Casino down in Fire Hollow had been [the] apex of their reservation. Its gleaming emerald spires leapt from the sandy riverbed in such a way that most could not resist calling it 'Oz.' Only a select few still believed that nearby Yantuck Mountain remained the true center of the universe" (4), and with respect to the woods on the mountain, the text insists, "The Yantuck Indian Tribe could not be credited with the survival of this tree haven. It remained on their mountain not because the Indians had succeeded in protecting the natural world, but because they had failed at becoming good corporate Americans" (51).[70] As a political body recognized by the settler-state, the Yantuck Indian Tribe does not defend the "tree haven," instead engaging in the project of seeking "corporate" success while persistently *failing* in this effort.[71] Together, these descriptions portray the turning away from the mountain as the wellspring of Yantuck being and becoming as a search for acknowledgment by/as "Americans," in which tribal identity as such becomes permeated by settler principles. At one point, Tomuck asserts of the majority of Yantuck citizens, "[T]hey figured being Indian was outdated. Claimed they were going to have an American democracy and vote on everything" (21–22). While the casino may offer the potential for access to resources that could promote forms of Yantuck autonomy, such as the effort to increase stipends to tribal members (8), these potentials rely on continued support from non-native sources of capital (monetary and cultural).

In Zobel's speculative vision, the performance of tribal sovereignty via the casino and other forms of outreach to non-natives, as well as taking "American" political and economic formations as an aspirational horizon for (re)defining Yantuck identity and collective practice, diverts focus from the true and ongoing grounds of Yantuck peoplehood. In this way, *Oracles* engages the broader politics of pursuing recognition, in the sense of seeking to have indigeneity affirmed as such by non-natives—particularly by the state.[72] As Audra Simpson suggests, the continuing force of settler governance in its effort to remold indigeneity in ways that reaffirm the state's legal geography and legitimizing narratives of its own benevolence "force us to ask how one is to define a citizenship for one's own people according to one's political traditions while operating in the teeth of Empire, in the face of state aggression": "How does one assert sovereignty and independence when some of the power to define that sovereignty is bestowed by a foreign power?"[73] Zobel marks a distinction between the apparatus of *tribal* governance and membership and the "we" *held* by "these woods." That distinction is illustrated through the ways the novel treats the documents generated by tribal administration. While still enrolled in college at Hoscott University, Ashneon collaborates with an anthropologist named Peter, who studies the Yantuck, and the two of them organize their growing "research pile" by "dividing all tribal records into BC, DC, and AC—before, during and after the Tribe's casino" (36). The casino becomes ironically Christlike in its function with respect to documented Yantuck history, implicitly providing the pivot for tribal time in ways that highlight the salvational potential assigned to the casino (resonating with Tomuck's earlier description of it as "a false Messiah" [7]). Non-native attention, resulting from New Light interest in the Yantucks as a subject of exotic mysticism, drives the effort to get the tribal archive in order, implying that the documents themselves bear little meaning outside of such interest by non-Yantucks. At one point, Tomuck insists that "maybe it's time you started paying less attention to saving what's written on paper and more attention to saving the source of that paper" (71). More than a clichéd environmentalist appeal to save the trees, this moment registers the incommensurability between a relational ontology of socio-natural becoming and the organizational structures and aims of tribal administration, themselves cast as modeled on *American* interests and imperatives. A tribal politics ordered around non-native patterns of acknowledgment and value cannot include the ongoing networks of situated reciprocity that, in the novel's account, engender indigeneity as such.[74]

In contrast to the matrix of responsibility and interdependence that shapes Yantuck peoplehood in its connection with the mountain, non-native interest in things Yantuck bears an inherently extractive relation to Native knowledge and identity. The novel suggests how Indianness functions as a transit to facilitate non-native modes of becoming, and the encounter with Indianness, then, becomes a background or vehicle for non-native escape and revitalization. As the narrator observes in the wake of the casino's closure, "no one cared about the Indian dregs who survived on Yantuck Mountain. Like all New England tribes, the Yantuck lacked silver jewelry, painted ponies, and grazing buffalo. They did not even have tipis and their pow wows sucked. They had fought the white man for so long, most of them were too beat-up to do anything but whine. The Yantuck were simply not tourist-ready" (14). Performances of Indianness require expressing modes of culture understandable as such within non-native frames of expectation, in which Indigenous lifeways become reducible to fetishized objects. Since the eighteenth century, Native peoples in New England have been cast as "dregs" or *remnants*, always-already in the process of disappearing.[75] Zobel here highlights this dynamic and casts non-native interest in things Indian as a fundamental misrecognition of Yantuck being. Moreover, the desire by settlers for edifying access to a culturalized conception of Indianness further effaces the long history of Natives having "fought" against expropriation and civilizing projects whose aim is their decimation as a people (or peoples), as well as bracketing the enervating effects of such continuous struggle ("beat-up").[76] In Édouard Glissant's terms, non-natives seek to make indigeneity *transparent*, to "relate it to [their] norm" in ways that enable "comparisons" and pre-script the terms of potential relation by taking non-native frameworks as the de facto basis for intelligibility and engagement.[77] Native modes of collective emplacement become more or less irrelevant when *Indian culture*—including attributions of environmental wisdom—comes to serve as an available reserve due to its capacity to unsettle non-native social formations, although in ways that do not ultimately, in Turner's terms quoted earlier, "respect the sui generis nature of indigenous rights as a class of political rights that flow out of indigenous nationhood." Seeing Native people(s) as bearers of an enlightening Indian diversity, ecology, or alterity does not disturb the geographies of settler sovereignty. Instead, such recognition facilitates extraction.

In this way, recognition can produce Indian separateness as a resource, harnessing Native peoples by positioning them as radically outside extant non-native ways of being such that they can function as a site through which non-natives might pass in order to transform themselves while not contesting the underlying authority of settler governance and jurisdiction.[78] Non-native engagement with forms of exoticized Indian otherness allows for the imagination that one is tapping something beyond the bounds of ordinary social life, gaining access to the primeval.[79] Turning back to *Midnight Robber*, one might understand Hopkinson's novel as translating indigeneity in ways that tend toward this kind of performance. Inasmuch as the ending seems unsure about how to sustain the novel's prior analysis of the relation between marronage and settlement (the displacement of Indigenous peoples and erasure of their geopolitical ecologies), it equivocates over the potential for ongoing Indigenous sovereignties. The text implicitly presents knowledge of Indigenous socialities and ecologies as a reserve of alternative lifeways that can be employed in remaking non-native sociality, rather than acknowledging forms of opacity in which Indigenous lifeways and placemaking remain irreducible to non-native form(ul)ations.

If Zobel presents Indigenous identity as at odds with settler recognition due to the ways indigeneity emerges and is sustained through specific forms of socio-natural enmeshment with the landscape, Jones pushes the critique of recognition even further by narratively refusing to endow indigeneity with a potentially extractable content. In *The Bird Is Gone*, Native peoplehood and placemaking take shape within the contours of settler-generated visions of Indianness, while at the same time Indigenous experience (individual and collective) remains irreducible to the non-native will-to-possession enacted through the positing of fetishized Indian difference. The novel envisions a near-future reordering of U.S. national space in which the Dakotas have been returned to Native peoples, there has been a mass migration of Natives to the new "Indian Territories" (a movement known as the "Skin Parade"), and non-natives largely are barred from entering this space. The majority of the action of the novel is set at a bowling alley in the Indian Territories named Fool's Hip, in which a collection of mostly Native characters congregate—including Mary Boy (the owner of the bowling alley who has a bleeding tattoo of Jesus), Nickel Eye (a suspected serial killer for the murder of more than "thirty-nine Anglo tourists"[80]), and Cat Stand (the lactose-intolerant former model who gained fame appearing in national milk ads), as well as Chassis Jones (a U.S. federal special agent sent to investigate the disappearances for which Nickel Eye is the prime suspect).

In focusing on this odd assortment of people who gather in a space that lacks obvious political or spiritual significance, the novel indicates an interest in forms of everyday experience, albeit somewhat surreally rendered.[81] Unlike *Oracles*, the text does not have an account of anything like sacred places and does not feature anyone who could be understood as a medicine person in the sense of possessing esoteric knowledge or being widely accepted as wielding extraordinary forms of power. The absence of these kinds of significations in Jones's novel suggests its ambivalence about presenting Native peoples as existing beyond settler influence. While Zobel certainly illustrates the presence and effects of non-native persons, technologies, and economies on Native life, she juxtaposes them with Indigenous forms of socio-natural relation and modes of knowledge that she portrays as existing outside settler frames of reference. By contrast, Jones does not mark such a distinction between false (consumable) projections of Indian distinctiveness and the true dynamics of Indigenous alterity. Instead, *The Bird Is Gone* depicts lived indigeneity as thoroughly permeated by popular and official conceptions of Indianness, and in doing so, the narrative works to undermine the potential for imagining Indigenous peoples as inherently occupying an elsewhere to which non-natives can turn to rejuvenate or refashion themselves (recognition as culturalizing extraction).

Even as Jones highlights the importance of Indigenous territoriality and the political implications of jurisdictional separateness, he emphasizes that such sovereignty does not exist apart from the ongoing discursive and institutional construction of Indianness. The novel begins with two epigraphs. The first one, from Jean-Paul Sartre, reads, "[W]e only become what we are by the radical and deep seated refusal of that which others have made of us," and the other is from Samuel Delany: "[W]e have taken a new home, and we must exhaust the past before we can finish with the present" (9). While presenting the text as ultimately engaged in a refusal of settler framings, this opening also suggests that ongoing embroilment with "that which others have made of" Native peoples significantly influences the terms of contemporary (or near-future) struggle. Furthermore, the "new home" that the novel imagines remains tied to a past of settler violence that has yet to be exhausted.

The return of the lands that become the new Indian Territories occurs due to the fusion of contemporary Native people(s) with ecological stewardship, as part of an attempt to return the area to its natural condition. A glossary at the end of the text, ostensibly written by LP Deal (who works at Fool's Hip and whose identity remains in question in ways I will address) reveals the reason "the

Dakotas [became] Indian again" (4). The entry for "Conservation Act" defines the law in the following terms:

> [T]he accidental solution to the "Indian Problem" (under pressure from Keep America Beautiful, the American Congress signed into law an aggressive bill requiring "the restoration of all indigenous flora and fauna to the Great Plains." As wildlife biologists soon pointed out, though, for a disturbance-dependent landscape to regain anything approaching self-sufficiency—to say nothing of momentum—the reintroduced grass (*buchloë dactyloides*) needed buffalo (*bison bison*) to "disturb" it, and . . . the burgeoning herds of reintroduced buffalo need the INDIAN (*canis latrans*)). (164)

The impetus behind reestablishing Native control over the Great Plains—the stereotypical site of images of authentic Indianness against which Native people(s) elsewhere have been and continue to be judged—lies in a desire to restore the "flora and fauna," which serve as the principal referent in U.S. conceptions of what can be counted as "indigenous."[82] Insuring the "self-sufficiency" of the plant life, though, requires interactions among a variety of species, including "the Indian"—assigned to the category of *canis latrans*, or coyote. The construction of a vastly expanded sphere of Indigenous sovereignty, then, emerges in and through "the Indian problem."[83] The law acknowledges reciprocities among kinds of beings within a situated environmental matrix (in ways reminiscent of Wilson's novels, discussed in chapter 3) only to cast those relations as an *Indian* kind of outsideness, a beyond that needs to be preserved for the sake of "conserving" an apolitical nature that testifies to the *beauty* of the (settler) nation.

The novel underlines the fact that the process of Indianization entails a collapsing of Indigenous peoples into a singular entity envisioned in racial terms. The glossary entry for the Conservation Act literally designates Natives as singular—"the Indian"—while also presenting them as belonging to a particular species, one that notably (and comically) is not *homo sapiens*. In the wake of the act, people seeking to cross into the Territories, in Cat Stand's description, had "to huddle in the makeshift booths [at the border] filling out the *applications* to be indian and proving it with old turtle rattles and scars and dances they knew and stories they didnt" (113). Since the Territories are cast as the province of Indians, rather than a specific (collection of) people(s), one needs to prove one's status as "indian" in order to enter, but that designation has no clear and consistent content. Indexing Indianness via the signs of tradition (rattles, dances, stories), though, gives way to a form of proof imagined as more fundamental—confirming Indianness as a kind of biological entity, a mode of species being.[84] Prior to the beginning of the narrative, readers encounter the phrase "pink eye was all the rage" sitting alone on an empty page, and this same statement is repeated at the beginning of most of the chapters. Over the course of the text, readers learn of the pink eye that spreads among the population of the Territories, "It was the new strain: only Indians could get it" (43): "It was supposed to help us," "IHS [the Indian Health Service] gave us pink eye, retroengineered it from smallpox" and "only Indians had it" (121–22). Redolent with associations of past projects to exterminate Native peoples, smallpox serves as the basis for the provision of aid under the auspices of promoting health, suggesting the insidious histories that continue to animate biopolitical projects of recognition.[85] In the process of seeking to make it visible so as to operate as a condition for separateness, Indianness appears as an infection. To be able to dwell within the space of the Indian Territories, as delineated under U.S. law, one must want to be marked by/as a relatively benign disease.

As an assemblage of meanings through which Native peoples continually are interpellated, the trope of *the Indian* insistently represents indigeneity in terms of a particular physiology, most often figured via kinds and amounts of blood. The novel off-handedly registers and travesties this tendency in the glossary's entry for "full blood," defining it as "approximately eight pints" which is the average amount of blood contained in the human body (165). However, while the repetition of "pink eye was all the rage" highlights the condition's ubiquity as the means of denoting Native identity, the phrase often is followed closely by another, "But there are ways. There are always ways" (43), suggesting not only that the somatics of Indianness can be simulated (such as one character providing Chassis Jones with a pill to make her eyes pink [51, 67], or Naitche, Cat Stand's son, needing to wear pink-tinted contacts [71]) but that such biologizing attributions remain little more than simulacrum.[86] Yet even as the novel mocks the idea of Indianness as physical substrate, it suggests how the circumstances of ongoing settler rule generate the conditions for Native people(s) to desire to signify as Indian in order to be able to access forms of recognition and material benefits that accrue around and through that racializing figuration.[87]

The novel, then, highlights how acknowledging the territorial distinctiveness of Native peoples can reproduce Indianizing forms of constraint. Although the Territories make possible renewed forms of Indigenous self-governance, they also function as a something of an enclosure, not only sealing off Native peoples from non-native access but also containing them in ways that seem to give greater scope to settler occupation.[88] The novel repeatedly marks a distinction between "America" and Native lands. At one point, Chassis Jones notes of the contacts she purchased to look Indian that she bought them "in America, at the wig store, then got on the bus before dawn, crossed back over the border into Indian Territory" (43). She also refers to *Americans* as wearing "citizen dress" (48), implicitly contrasting them to the residents of the Territories while also parodying the ways similar phrases were used to designate Euro-American–style clothing as part of the broader effort to assimilate Native people(s) during the allotment and boarding school era.[89] Later, one of the residents of the Territories suggests that "a *slogan*" is "what every reservation needs if it wants to sell itself to America," and the one proposed is, "*We're not savage anymore. Come see./It's been nice, but now you have to leave./We were taking care of it long before you, don't worry./Yeah, it's a ~~dirty~~ mean place, but we like it*" (149–50). These moments emphasize that legally recognized Native lands, whether the new Territories or reservations more broadly, cannot simply be considered part of "America." In marking this distinction, the text signals an enduring relation of dominance and dependence (the need to insist on no longer being "savage" while at the same time still having to "sell" the reservation in touristic terms in order to attract needed capital). However, it simultaneously asserts an indigeneity that necessarily exceeds the terms of settlement, in terms of priorness and knowledge ("*taking care of it long before you*") as well as a process of legitimate exclusion ("*you have to leave*"). This spatial distinction also involves a jurisdictional one. When one of the characters gets arrested by a U.S. special agent, Chassis objects, saying, "[T]his wasn't America—he had rights" (157), and the penultimate line of the novel's main narrative reads, "It was a third world country, but we called it the first" (160). Understanding Native land as its own "country" entails acknowledging the ways it has been structurally disadvantaged within dominant modes of political economy while also understanding it as having its own forms of governance and justice, which are not simply derived from those of the United States ("he had rights").[90]

In suggesting the desirability of Indigenous geopolitical distinctiveness from the settler-state, even amid ongoing dynamics of impoverishment, Jones also addresses the ways the reservation can function as a space of confinement.[91] Even as the text underlines the proper autonomy of Native nations, it draws attention to the ways that U.S. legal and administrative geographies seek to isolate Native people(s) so as to facilitate control over them. Characterizing officially acknowledged Indigenous lands as the "third world" illustrates a hierarchical relation between them and "America" that oscillates between extraction and abandonment—predicated on sustained subordination, periodic intervention, and structural underdevelopment. Notably, the return of lands occurs through unilateral legislative declaration rather than through diplomacy. There is nothing remotely like a treaty process, in which the U.S. government engages in discussion and negotiation with Native nations.[92] Instead, Congress exerts its power over "public" lands as well as its plenary authority over Indian affairs to produce forms of Indian territoriality.[93] As Mishuana Goeman argues with respect to Indigenous people's and peoples' own understandings of what constitutes Native place, "[I]n order not to cede the ground we must also begin to scrutinize the impact of spatial policies in our cognitive mapping of Native lands and bodies," especially in light of the fact that "Natives occupy certain spaces of the nation and are criminalized or erased if they step outside what are seen as degenerate spaces." In contrast to such narratives of the reservation as the (degraded or romantically conserved) space of authentic Indianness, she insists, "Unlike the maps that designate Indian land as existing only in certain places, wherever we went there were Natives and Native spaces, and if there weren't, we carved them out."[94] If the Territories enact a mode of recognition through which the settler-state accepts the existence of Native peoplehood and landedness, doing so conversely casts the rest of the nation that lies outside such Indian(ized) space as free of indigeneity, as available for non-native self-extension and possession.[95]

To be Native within this framework means to reside within the sanctioned spaces reserved for you, to have Indigenous being denied except when it appears within areas officially designated for that purpose. As Coulthard suggests, "[I]nstead of ushering in an era of peaceful coexistence grounded on the ideal of *reciprocity* or *mutual* recognition, the politics of recognition in its contemporary liberal form promises to reproduce the very configurations of . . . power that Indigenous peoples' demands for recognition have historically sought to transcend."[96] At one point, Nickel Eye jokes, "What do you feed Americans anyway? Hypothetically, I mean. Wait, wait. Land, right? An acre for breakfast, two for lunch . . . ?" (26). The Territories provide a bulwark against being devoured in this way. Yet they also constrict and contract Indigenous becoming to a delimited area in which the performance of a generic Indianness provides the basis for belonging. In one of several interludes that are separate from the plot as such, Jones explores what he casts as a futile desire to alter the past so as to frustrate the devastations wrought by settler occupation. As part of a story ostensibly told by an elder over a radio program broadcast within the Territories (73), a character named Bacteen seeks to collaborate with Coyote to prevent Euro-Americans from achieving dominance in the Americas.[97] This effort includes leading a revolt aboard Columbus's ships, bringing the horse to the Americas before the arrival of Europeans, distributing repeating rifles to

Native people(s) on the Plains in the 1840s, and convincing whites to avoid slaughtering buffalo for their skins (75–97). However, all of these efforts to go "back before all this" (81), to forestall the violences of settlement, fail. An indigeneity that exists in a somewhere beyond the histories and geographies of settler-shaped Indianness appears utterly impossible, and the dynamics of non-native recognition bear and sustain the momentum of such colonial force. Reciprocally, Natives must recognize and grapple with what, as in the epigraph from Sartre that begins the novel, "others have made of us"—including with respect to, in Goeman's terms, the "mapping of Native lands and bodies"—as part of making possible continued Indigenous life. In this vein, the novel repeatedly gestures toward the Territories with all of their problems as a site of Native futurity, including calling the final chapter "Red Dawn" (145), having the child Naitche utter the line *the end of the trail starts here* (presenting the Territories as a new homeland in the wake of removal and perhaps the end of removal as a tactic of settler rule) (37–38), ending the main narrative by saying, "It was a good day to die, but nobody did" (160), and including a largely blank page after that conclusion that simply has the words, split into two lines reading *is this how it begins?* and "yes" (161).

If settler policy segregates Indigenous peoples into territories imagined as reserved for them—rather than, say, retained or claimed by them in their operation as sovereign polities—that isolation also contributes to the continued understanding of Natives as exotics that can capacitate non-native development. At several points, the text notes that non-native anthropologists, apparently denied entry to the Territories, continue to congregate at its edges in order to try to gain access to things Indian: "the anthropologists massed at the border with their binoculars and their listening devices and their Scalpel-brand pencils, each of them wanting you to confirm their pet theory" (33); the old hotels on the border are inhabited by "anthropologists and ethnologists and enthusiasts stacked belly to back watching through binoculars their saliva coating the bricks for stories and stories" (113); and during the bowling tournament for the Councilmen of the Territories, "anthropologists launched themselves past with catapults, shutters clicking," "like a plague of locusts" (145). Described at one point as "the distillation of all that America is or has been" (178), the anthropologists figure a yearning for proximity to indigeneity, craving contact with Native persons and "stories." That very longing, though, eventuates in fantasies of capture and possession, making Natives people into Indians in ways that then position them, seemingly by definition, as available for the pleasures of non-native consumption (as in the narrative's images of tourism and digestion).

Moreover, the structure of the text underlines and contests such a desire for (appropriative) access to Native perspectives. With the exception of a few interludes, including one narrated by Cat Stand, the majority of the main body of the text is narrated in the first person by Chassis Jones. A non-native, she poses as Native for the purposes of an undercover investigation of the murders of "Americans" for which Nickel Eye is the prime suspect. Over the course of the novel, she increasingly comes to consider herself Indian, ranging from when "the capillaries in the white part of [her] eyes bloomed, aching with pleasure . . . the redness washing up [her], over [her]" when she takes a pill to simulate the Indian-marking pink eye (67), to the end when she ceases to be recognized by a fellow investigator" (157), describes herself as "the Special Agent who had been Chassis Jones" (159), and includes herself in the summative assessment that "after the massacres and after the cigar stories, we gathered around the fire, told stories and watched each other's faces for signs of ourselves" (160). The character expresses the "pleasure" of going Native, of imagining oneself as belonging to an Indigenous "we"—even as the text ironizes, frustrates, and defers that desire. The title condenses this problematic. The "Manifesto" refers to journals being kept by LP Deal, whose own status as Native remains rather ambiguous;[98] he is also the putative author of the character portraits that begin the book and the glossary toward the end. In this way, Jones frames the text as expressive of a troubled longing for intimacy with Indianness, a hunger that the text suggests animates the dynamic of recognition. The phrase "the bird is gone" itself appears in the glossary in the entry for "passenger pigeon": "When an individual is seen gliding through the woods and close to the observer, it passes like a thought, and on trying to see it again, the eye searches in vain. The bird is gone.'—n., Lit. see also: Vanishing Indians" (169).[99] While "gone"-ness may refer to the supposed disappearance of Native people(s), a process paradoxically both always already accomplished and yet still to come,[100] it also indexes the dialectic of sight and seizure Indianness performs, the settler longing to pinpoint indigeneity such that it might be known and contained (for fetishistic preservation or extermination). To be "gone" entails having taken flight from available settler categories, to exceed the terms of non-native conceptual and legal frameworks to which Native people continue to be subjected. In this way, Jones structurally insists on the opacity of indigeneity, absent any concrete markers of specifiable Indian difference. Put another way, he insists on the integrity of Indigenous difference, in Lorde's terms, without providing a content for such difference that can be extracted and appropriated by non-natives. Speculatively engaging the possibilities for Native survival amid settler pressures and mappings, Jones does not provide testimony of what lies beyond Indianness (playing the role of the native informant who can satisfy extratextual cravings for authenticity). Instead, the text explores the complexities involved in inhabiting the geographies and legacies of ongoing occupation. It gestures toward Native peoplehood as that whose substance continues to evade settler thought and sight, as experiences that occur in relation to (and that partially are oriented by) settler-constructed conceptions of Indianness but that are not reducible to them.

The turn to flight in the title image for Jones's novel, though, provides a counterpoint that helps highlight how both *The Bird Is Gone* and *Oracles* tend to address indigeneity in terms of situatedness. The novels foreground the importance of having distinct Indigenous land bases, particularly in light of the extractive dynamics of settlement. In Irene Watson's terms, "If we are cannibalised and utilised to Aboriginalise the majority, how do we as individuals and communities sustain our own vulnerable Aboriginality?"[101] From this perspective, the potential for mobility appears less as itself a normative principle—as in figurations of fugitivity or, to a lesser extent, marronage—than as a means of expressing, defending, and sustaining modes of Indigenous collectivity and placemaking, pointing toward legitimate experiences of indigeneity that do not inherently conform to the state's procedures for endowing "title." However, within the novels' understandings of the politics and ethics of emplacement, what room is there for diaspora, Indigenous or otherwise? As Lou Cornum asks, "What happens to indigeneity when the indigenous subject is no longer in the location that has defined them?": "what about the Indians who can't go home, or simply want to go away?"[102] Even as the texts highlight the importance of engaging with Indigenous sovereignty, which itself extends beyond modes of state recognition, their emphasis on determinate relations between Native identity and particular land bases can bracket the complex relations between forms of Indigenous mobility and relation to homelands, as well as leaving aside circumstances when political and economic pressures lead to migration onto other peoples' lands (including across nation-state borders).[103]

Moreover, if non-natives appear almost uniformly as intruders on Indigenous territories, how do the novels grapple with (or evade) the question of forced resettlement in the Americas, such as through the slave trade? For example, Zobel characterizes the accumulated New Lighters as "an exotic fruit salad of world spirituality" of people who, as "natives from somewhere," have lost connection to those places and gone in search of "other people's mountains" (89), but diasporic blackness resulting from enslavement, in Dionne Brand's terms, emerges from "a rupture in history" that was "also a physical rupture, a rupture of geography," such that "[w]e were not from the place where we lived and we could not remember where we were from": "Caught between the two we live in the Diaspora. . . . Our inheritance in the Diaspora is to live in this inexplicable space."[104] In the absence of such a determinate ancestral place due to histories of racializing political violence and dislocation, blackness in the Americas neither can claim status as Indigenous nor can turn to another "somewhere" to which a *native* claim can be made (an affective dynamic addressed in the discussion of *The Wave* in chapter 3). Both Zobel and Jones foreground the importance of indigeneity as a (set of) collective relation(s) to place and as a matter of governance—of, in Audra Simpson's terms, the existence of "other political orders" that can/should be named as sovereignties.[105] These texts highlight the perils of projects of recognition that translate Indigenous modes of being and becoming into frameworks that cannot accommodate such emplaced self-determination, except inasmuch as it can be translated into an exotic otherness that can be incorporated into trajectories of non-native self-transformation. In challenging the ways indigeneity is made transparent as Indianness, claimed, and mobilized by non-natives to their own ends, though, the novels also speculatively illustrate the difficulty within a framework organized around landedness of not rendering blackness transparent as either a perpetual failure to be emplaced or simply another modality of settler occupation.

Putting Indigeneity in Motion

How can Indigenous peoples be recognized within non-native framings while not being made transparent as (extractable) Indianness? Reciprocally, how can Black geographies, including of movement, be engaged within Indigenous frames of reference? If *Midnight Robber* addresses the potential conflicts between the political geographies of marronage and indigeneity (even while running into difficulty in having the latter matter in a sustained way in restructuring the former), *Mindscape* experiments with envisioning maroon and Indigenous movements as part and parcel of each other. Hairston draws on Indigenous peoplehood as a form through which to represent kinds of social action—escape and the creation of a new landed community—conventionally characterized as marronage. In doing so, the text puts indigeneity into speculative service as a means, in Samuel Delany's terms from chapter 1, of *redescribing* alternative modes of collective emplacement and political belonging beyond those of the state. In this way, the novel resonates with and revises current practices in Latin America of legally recognizing maroon communities on the condition that they approximate official conceptions of Indigenous peoplehood. As against conventional portrayals of indigeneity as primordial or static, though, the novel presents indigeneity as enacting vital and vibrant modes of relationality, in which situatedness itself becomes a means of enabling participation in a web of networks. In this way, Hairston's cross-hatching of indigeneity and marronage contests the anachronizing, racializing, and fetishizing dynamics that so often shape processes of non-native recognition in the Americas, suggesting potential relations between blackness and indigeneity that are responsive to the kinds of critiques Zobel and Jones offer of dominant processes of Indianization. Moreover, in invoking indigeneity as a way of characterizing collective placemaking while refusing to juxtapose it against mobility, *Mindscape* opens up possibilities for considering modes of place-based ethnogenesis and for mutual engagement among landed polities not routed through the racializing statuses and geographies of the state. However, to the extent that indigeneity functions as a way of talking about all place-based, non-state social formations—as a means of indicating their existence as such, regardless of whether the entity in question actually is an expression of Indigenous peoplehood—that translation of marronage *as indigeneity* effaces non-native collectivities' active negotiations and engagements with Indigenous peoples and their territorialities. As discussed in chapter 3, Walter Mosley's *The Wave* gestures toward the issue of Black indigeneity in the Americas but pivots away from that imaginary in ways that register the problems of non-native self-indigenization, even as the text's figurations of flight also orient away from the issue of Black emplacement. By contrast, *Mindscape* robustly envisions collective locatedness for non-natives, but in doing so through figurations of indigeneity Hairston implicitly brackets the difference between Natives and non-natives and thus leaves little room for the possibility of addressing how marronage may have settlement effects in the absence of robust engagement with Indigenous peoples and geographies. The novel uses indigeneity as the principal means through which to signify varied modes of landed collectivity and political relation that are not reducible to (and actively oppose) state governance, and in doing so, the text tends to bracket the question of how to fashion a politics of landedness and governance that does not license the erasure of prior polities or foreclose their continued existence (including in their processes of reorganization and reinvention).

The novel turns on the emergence of an entity called the Barrier that divides the Earth into a range of separated sites, three of which are inhabited by humans. As described in the novel's first chapter, Vera Xa Lalafia, a healer and scientist who learns how to commune with the Barrier, suggests that many people consider "[t]he inhabited Zones—New Ouagadougou, Los Santos, Paradigma—[to be] mere refugee camps, the Barrier a prison wall," adding, "Travel between Zones is limited to a handful of corridors spontaneously generated at seasonal intervals. The Barrier offers no corridors to the stars or to the uninhabited Wilderness lands." She further suggests of the Barrier itself that it "is a self-generating network of enormous complexity and unprecedented creativity. It regenerates and evolves, sustaining itself, yet changing. A life form?"[106] Set in New Ouagadougou (comprising part of what was Africa) and Los Santos (the U.S. Plains and Southwest), the text largely takes places more than a century after the Barrier descended and focuses on attempts to institute and evade a global Interzonal Peace Treaty negotiated and ratified among the three major powers/states four years earlier. While containing many plot threads and a rather wide assortment of characters, the narrative focuses on three main stories: Elleni Xa Celest, the leader of the Healers Council on New Ouagadougou and a Vermittler (a hybrid of human and Barrier energy who possesses extra-human abilities), who has a vision of the imminent destruction of the world and seeks to prevent it by bringing her nemesis on the Council, Sidi X Aiyé, into the Barrier with her; Lawanda Kitt, an ambassador from Paradigma to Los Santos, who aims to enforce the treaty amid a growing awareness that she has been set up for failure by Paradigma's Prime Minister Jocelyn Williams; and Aaron Dunkelbrot, a moviemaker on Los Santos attempting to make a film about human history in the wake of the Barrier's emergence, who stumbles into a collection of conspiracies to thwart the treaty's implementation. All of these stories converge at Wounded Knee, the area that serves as the base of operations for the "born-again Sioux"—a group following their leader, Wovoka, a Vermittler working beyond the purview of the Healers Council who asserts that the dead will be brought back through the Ghost Dance. The novel concludes with the return of the dead, albeit momentary, but their coming alters the Barrier such that corridors that transport people from one zone to another multiply and remain open instead of appearing only intermittently as before. A convergence in the space of (quasi-)indigeneity makes possible radically expanded capacities for movement that thwart the political agendas and undermine the exclusionary authority of the governing powers in all of the human-inhabited zones. Indigenous peoplehood serves as an imaginative vehicle through which to challenge the territorializations enacted by the state, especially the ways those geographies also entail commitments to particular racializing notions of personhood.

The Ghost Dancers function as the ethical center of the novel, enacting an indigenized vision of marronage that repudiates the modes of violence and repression that characterize the actions of the governments of the zones. Although they are not described at any length until quite late in the novel, and none of the main characters belong to the group, the born-again Sioux—or members of the "Ghost Dancer cult" (12)—provide the most potent and consistent opposition to assaultive regimes. At one point, Major, head of the security forces for the capital of Paradigma, observes, "Dancers resisted Los Santos gang-lords for twenty-five years, providing sanctuary to Extras on gangster hit Lists, eventually functioning as the religious wing of the Union of Rebel Extras" (128). "Extras" are those who in Los Santos lack social capital and can be targeted for elimination by the gang lords who functionally control the government; they were killed in the thousands by being hurled into the Barrier prior to the ratification of the treaty, part of which specifies an end to this pervasive pattern of casual murder. Occupying the Badlands, the Dancers routinely sneak into sites across Los Santos in order to rescue Extras, foment insurgency against the gangsters, and generate forms of popular ungovernability that will challenge the authoritarian capitalism of expendability in which those who cannot produce value are treated as fleshly refuse. Major also notes that "Wovoka refused to ally with Celestina," the architect of the Interzonal Treaty (129), and in the initial discussion of the treaty, the born-again Sioux are characterized as "treaty-shy" in "refus[ing] to sign away their sovereignty" (12), with Wovoka toward the end of the novel explaining his demurral from the treaty by observing, "I have my own vision to follow" (417). While I will address the treaty at length later, the references to Ghost Dancer rejection of it highlight the ways the born-again Sioux operate as an independent political force, not bound by the dictates of centralized administrative or corporate bodies of any kind. That autonomy enables them to foment opposition to existing statist structures and to remain mobile, even as Wounded Knee serves as a hub and "sacred ground" (129).

While presented as partaking of indigeneity in some fashion, the Ghost Dancers replicate many of the characteristics usually attributed to marronage. Readers come to know them through their acts of brigandage and rescue, a series of tactical strikes that enable them to weaken the authority of the gang lords who themselves at times seem akin to plantation masters. Extras appear available for exploitation by gangsters without any kind of compensation, and just prior to the climactic gathering at Wounded Knee, the most powerful and prominent of the gang lords, Jesus Perez, stages a lavish party in which his "mansion looked like Tara, inside and out" (337); Perez "was dressed as a southern gentleman circa 1850" (339); and the event was littered with a broad array of "picturesque darkies" (351). While enchattelment as such is not a prominent part of the legal architecture of Los Santos, Hairston encourages readers to conceptualize the gang structure and their investments as a latter-day version of the plantocracy, with the Ghost Dancers providing the most prominent and sustained resistance to it. Given the repeated references to the role of born-again Sioux in saving Extras and others subjected to the arbitrary power of the landed elite,[107] the novel implies that those so liberated come to swell the ranks of the Ghost Dancers as part of a broader organization and mobilization of those who have fled from gang-lord rule. This structure of escape and rescue in which those freed from captivity join the ranks of those who have liberated them fits the model of the maroon community more than that of Native peoplehood. Focusing on the difficulty of locating and inhabiting the area occupied by the Dancers, Major notes, "Anomalous Barrier behavior in the region has precluded regular human habitation, however Dancers supposedly gather at Wounded Knee for mystical ceremonies during the fall and winter months" (129), and later Lawanda observes, "Wounded Knee be off the map—Barrier distortin' the geography" (380). These moments present Wounded Knee as like maroon encampments—intentionally remote from dominant settlements, inaccessible, and easily camouflaged.[108] Moreover, the gathering at Wounded Knee toward which the novel builds may result in increased political autonomy for the born-again Sioux, but the novel foregrounds how communion with the dead, the putative object of the Ghost Dance, makes possible increased mobility among spaces previously sealed off from each other except in quite limited, seasonal ways. The born-again Sioux, then, tend to be characterized in terms of their relation to flight, recasting marronage through figures of indigeneity.

However, the fact that they are called "born-again Sioux" suggests that the group is constituted of those who would not otherwise be understood as Native. They have come to "Sioux"-ness through revelation and in doing so have (re)committed to particular principles and ways of being, as would be the case in fundamentalist rebirth in Christ. In the description of Celestina's attempted murder of all Vermittler, a genocidal project executed under the orders of Femi Xa Olunde, then the leader of the Healers Council, for reasons I discuss shortly, readers learn that the boy who will later come to call himself Wovoka is among a group of children Celestina has come to terminate (230). (Later, however, Wovoka seems not to be aware of this identity, even as he recalls the attempted killing [414–15].) At one point, Lawanda refers to the Ghost Dancers as a "buncha renegade *Vermittler* and born-again Sioux" (35). These moments suggest that the invocation of Native identity does not refer to any of the historically allied peoples aggregated under the term *Sioux* or any other nation actually existing in the novel's present.[109] Further, with the exception of a brief mention of "a river once named for Indians" (with the character unable to recall which ones) and Aaron's passing indication that he is descended from "Seminole-Black Indians" from "a long time ago" (113, 208), the novel offers no account of anything resembling continuing Native presence (never mind self-governance) in the regions of the once United States that constitute Los Santos.[110]

What's at stake, then, in citing the Ghost Dance and Wounded Knee in this context? While the term *Ghost Dance* can refer to any number of prophetic Indigenous movements on land claimed by the United States throughout the nineteenth century, it most often names the actions inspired by the visions of a Northern Paiute man named Jack Wilson (who changed his name to Wovoka) who in early 1889 began to prophecy the return of the dead. While the prophecy's terms shifted as it moved among various peoples across the Plains and into the Colorado River basin, this vision of reunion and resurgence gained fame through its association with a group of Lakota who, in responding to Wovoka's message, were targeted for military control and discipline, based on the invented charge that they were planning an insurgency against the United States. As part of seeking to round up all of the Lakota Ghost Dancers by forcing them to come onto reservations, themselves recently carved from what previously had been recognized by treaty as the Great Sioux Reserve, the army slaughtered a band under the Minneconjous leader Big Foot at Wounded Knee Creek on December 29, 1890.[111] For this reason, as Gregory Smoak notes, "The Ghost Dance and Wounded Knee have become synonymous," earlier observing that in the wake of Wounded Knee "'ghost dancing' became a metaphor for the desperate and illusory attempt of a people to recover the unrecoverable."[112] However, even as *Mindscape* describes Wounded Knee as the "site of failed white promises and Indian massacres" (129), it appears as a space of regeneration in and around which some form of peoplehood arises. Late in the text, Aaron shouts, "Remember Wounded Knee" as part of inciting the gathered crowd to overwhelm the gang lord Perez (409). Smoak suggests of Indigenous prophet-led movements, "Although none of these groups could define their existence completely outside the dominant society, they could, and did, shape their relationship to the larger society by exerting control over their own social identities. The Ghost Dances were not the only means through which American Indian peoples expressed their identity and asserted their survival . . . , but they must be understood as part of that process as well."[113] In this way, we might understand Hairston's mobilization of the Ghost Dance as a means of figuring the existence of complex networks of opposition to state authority that arise out of an ensemble of cultural practices, social identities, and modes of placemaking that while affected by law and policy are irreducible to them.

Invoking Wounded Knee alongside a sense of communal "Sioux"-ness emphasizes that the movement emerges through a situated collectivity but one whose contours are shifting and capacious. The Ghost Dancers enact an ongoing process of indigenization whereby commitment to particular cosmogenic principles and practices enables participation in an emergent emplaced peoplehood that refuses the jurisdictional geographies and political logics of the state. Unlike in *Midnight Robber*, Indigenous peoplehood appears not as something confronted by non-natives as a totally separate entity, but as a vehicle of collective being that might be occupied by those who otherwise would not be considered Indigenous. That process less recognizes Indianness by reifying it as a resource to be extracted (as in Zobel's and Jones's novels) than mobilizes indigeneity as a social form through which to mark kinds of landed peoplehood that are not reducible to the state's terms and authority. Unlike in the use of indigeneity as a setting through which non-natives pass in order to democratize an existing political order, the kind of indigenization-cum-marronage imagined by Hairston casts born-again Sioux identity as its own distinct/disjunct geopolitical order, one that does not merge with or regenerate the (non-native) state. This gesture, though, raises the question of what indigeneity means when it functions as a category in this way—as a form through which to express landed challenges to state sovereignty. The category of indigeneity functions here, in Ahmed's terms quoted earlier, as a *condition of emergence* for Ghost Dancer collectivity, as a kind of background or mold through which to envision forms of place-based collectivity that defy regular jurisdictional geographies. In this way, Hairston's invocation of Indigenous identity partakes of something like Zobel's and Jones's exploration of varied ways that Native social life may be affected by settler frameworks but remains irreducible to them, even as the Ghost Dancers in *Mindscape* lack a generationally enduring relation to the space of the Badlands.

Although unfamiliar in an Anglo-context, an official politics of figuring Indigenous-like landed autonomy for non-Indian groups occurs in Latin America, and attending to this policy framework can help in clarifying the stakes of Hairston's employment or translation of indigeneity as a political form—as a means of figuring place-based political collectivity. In a range of countries, including Colombia, Brazil, and Honduras, there are legal means by which non-Indian groups can make collective legal claims to territory and some degree of self-governance. In Colombia, the constitution and Law 70 recognize *comunidades negras*, defined as a "group of families of Afro-Colombian descent who possess their own culture, a shared history, and their own traditions and customs in the context of the town/country division, and who exhibit and preserve a consciousness of their identity that makes them distinct from other ethnic groups."[114] Brazil's constitution acknowledges political and territorial rights for *quilombos*, communities descended from maroon settlements founded during slavery,[115] and Honduran law references "*pueblos indígenas y afro-hondureños*," indicating an acknowledgment of landed rights for certain Black communities (particularly the Garifuna).[116] These figurations of non-Indian land tenure, though, all draw on a particular conception of indigeneity as the model through which to register kinds of political collectivity that exist outside the regular jurisdictional terms and grid of the state. As Juliet Hooker indicates, "In the cases where they have won the same collective rights as Indians, such as Honduras and Nicaragua, they have done so because they have been able to cast themselves as 'autochthonous' groups having an indigenous-like status and distinct cultural identity," adding that in Latin American nations that recognize Black collective land claims there is an "indigenous frame for demanding collective rights."[117] Similarly, in *Black and Indigenous*, Mark Anderson suggests of the recognition of Garifuna communities in Honduras, who self-characterize and are understood by others as Black, that indigeneity "provided a language through which collective claims could be made and heard," placing Garifuna "in the same metacultural frame as indigenous peoples."[118] However, Hooker and others argue that such *ethnicization* of blackness, largely in terms of marronage, effaces engagement with processes of *racialization* and practices of racism, while also generating a vision of isolated communal entities separated from Black (as well as Indian) struggles for justice in urban spaces.[119] As Keisha-Khan Y. Perry notes with respect to struggles over Black land claims in Brazil, "[A]ctivists assert that land rights should not predicate on being a descendant of quilombolos. Blacks who have occupied and cultivated Brazilian land throughout the various periods of development and urbanization should also be entitled to land as a basic right."[120]

Without displacing these questions raised by scholars about the aims and effects of how states employ notions of indigeneity, we can read Hairston's novel as experimenting with what drawing on indigeneity as a form can do in terms of conceptualizing and making legible modes of collective territoriality that run athwart state norms. The portrayal of the born-again Sioux resonates with the Latin American tendency to define maroon communities in terms of analogy to indigeneity, but the text reverses the orientation of such policies, bringing indigeneity more into the orbit of marronage rather than legitimizing marronage as Indian-like. In this way, *Mindscape*'s invocation of Indigenous peoplehood in ways that suggest the potentially sovereign separateness of maroon-like social formations can be interpreted as a speculative act of translation that conceptually aims to reconfigure what elsewhere function as strategies of containment. Instead of casting non-Indian formations as needing to fit a reifying and anachronizing model of Indianness, Hairston draws on indigeneity as a vehicle for figuring the geopolitics of landed collectivity in ways that defy mappings instituted by the state.

Although I will return to the problems posed by non-native projects of self-indigenization, I want to dwell for a bit longer on the possibilities for relations across potentially disparate struggles enacted through the text's staging of Indigenous(-like) struggle, as well as how such connections (including the implicit merger of Indigenous peoplehood and marronage) potentially stretch the form of indigeneity in ways that productively disjoint its role in state discourses. Through the figure of Lawanda, Paradigma's ambassador to Los Santos who also is identified as Black, the novel addresses the existence and dynamics of "ethnic throwback" communities, and the text links them to the Ghost Dancers, suggesting productive possibilities for solidarity while also extending the kinds of placemaking associated with indigeneity. Describing herself as an ethnic throwback (14), Lawanda characterizes such identities in terms of how they recall and mobilize collective ways of being that are cast as a form of backwardness within elite discourses. As against such charges of anachronism, she insists, "Just cuz we choose to reach back thru two hundred years and snatch wisdom offa the tongues of our ancestors, that don't mean we stuck on stupid!" (53–54). She later observes that these communities do not understand themselves primarily in racial terms, asserting, "[E]thnic throwbacks do culture not identity politics. We don't put stock in color. Race is how the world see you, ethnicity is how you see yourself," also noting that her sister Geraldine (who is "paler" with "blond hair") is able to work in a prestigious state-sponsored institute while, in Lawanda's terms, "dark me be languishin' back in a impoverished settlement" (121). Hairston mobilizes ethnicity to name forms of communal self-understanding and practice that exceed the (implicit) parameters of state-endorsed racial identifications (identity beyond "color") while neither effacing nor euphemizing ongoing forms of racism (the segregation and impoverishment of those who are "dark").

Mindscape repeatedly suggests a potential alignment between ethnic throwbacks and born-again Sioux, placing them in a shared frame that stretches the meaning of indigeneity. As Bettina Ng'weno argues with respect to dominant Latin American conceptions of blackness, "[B]lacks' simultaneous inclusion in, and exclusion from, national society rests on a form of racialization that is not in any way dependent on ties to land (i.e., ties to original ancestral lands and possession of a distinct culture), a principal criterion used to define indigenous people," adding that people of African descent are seen as "a population in a continuous state of arrival" such that "territory as such does not and cannot become a definitional part of black ethnicity."[121] Efforts to mark Black territoriality through the form of indigeneity, though, can serve as a way of contesting the racialized conjoining of blackness with placelessness by enabling, in McKittrick's terms, a "poetics of landscape" through which to register the political significance of Black projects of collective emplacement. In one of his messages to Lawanda, Major reports, "In Paradigma as well as Los Santos, Dancers and shamen have been conflated with ethnic throwbacks, given these groups' intense relationship to history, to embodying past wisdom" (128). In discussing the more obvious expressions of racism in Los Santos, Lawanda suggests, "The default settin' for humanity in this Zone is white," adding, "I don't see how colored folk put up with this funky shit for all those years. 1492, when the Indians discover there's a Europe out there or 1555, when the first slave ships come to America, just numbers the old folks make us learn. I never feel the numbers in my body 'til I come to Los Santos" (153).[122] What at one point might appear as the conflation of different kinds of collectivity and struggle becomes at another a shared history of subjection to white supremacy. This positing of a connection between Black and Indian histories in the Americas helps cast Black placemaking as more than just an effect of deprivation, a collection of "impoverished settlement[s]." Although she indicates that in her home community of Ellington "buildings barely holdin' themselves up," it's the location of "real food" and "real style" (63), as well as inspiring and facilitating various forms of individual and communal self-expression (126). The "history" and "wisdom" that ethnic throwbacks cultivate, then, cannot be disconnected from attachments to particular places, such as Ellington. In suggesting a conjunction between throwbacks and the Dancers (in ways that resonate with the linkages among various forms of situatedness at play in Daniel Wilson's work, as discussed in chapter 3), Hairston implicitly brings the form of indigeneity to bear on urban Black communities, presenting such patterns of inhabitance as expressive of a kind of collective emplacement that may take shape within processes of state abandonment but that cannot be reduced to it.[123] Territoriality provides a link between these two kinds of sites, signaling a vital relation between situatedness and collective processes of being and becoming (named most frequently in Latin America and in the novel as *ethnicity*). Thus, the text crosshatches marronage and indigeneity in ways that refuse (1) the presumptions of rurality that tend to attach to *Indianization* in actual state policy; and (2) the depiction of Black communities as valid sociopolitical formations only insofar as they are Indian-like.

If Hairston uses indigeneity as a form through which to register and legitimize modes of landed collectivity in ways that speculatively refigure patterns emerging in Latin America over the past several decades, the novel further disjoints the terms of such state recognition by presenting indigeneity as an expression of and catalyst for social transformation, as opposed to merely indexing unchanging cultural continuity. What can indigeneity do when freed from the museumizing strategies of Indianization that largely orient non-native projects of recognition? With respect to official processes of recognition in Latin America, Shane Greene notes, "[T]here is a hidden logic of retention that predominates in the sphere of apologetic multicultural governance," in which the state acknowledges "an apparently 'successful' retention of the indigenous sovereignty that was denied through colonization."[124] This dynamic functions through what Elizabeth Povinelli has termed a "governance of the prior," in which the justification for accepting Native collective claims to place rests in their (relatively unchanged) existence from before the state achieved independence. This official framing disallows the possibility of the emergence of new kinds of collectivity while treating Indigenous claims as expressions of *aboriginality* rather than as indicative of current—and historically malleable— (geo)political formations.[125] *Mindscape*, though, critiques the ways that recognition of Indigenous sovereignty can be predicated on a politics of purity—on the maintenance of the unchanging same.

The text emphasizes the violence at play in sustaining reified notions of collective inheritance through its discussion of the genocidal assault on Vermittler. Their particular abilities to commune with the Barrier arise from the fact that they themselves are the result of "artificial symbiogenesis," a process initiated by a rogue member of the Healers Council (Vera Xa Lalafia) of "genetic recombination and co-evolution"—"bringing together diverse life forms in the Barrier to create novel forms with emergent capacities" (163, 296). The new species that results from this hybridization is cast by leaders in New Ougadougou as a collection of "alien abominations."[126] The then leader of the Healers Council, Femi Xa Olunde, launches "a secret war on *Vermittler*" (161), and Celestina serves as the agent of this mass murder, killing more than eight thousand Vermittler over the course of two decades (230). The text portrays the effort to eliminate these beings as an attempt to defend the status quo, envisioned in biological terms, as against forms of change deemed invasive due to their deviation from what has been. Furthermore, one of the New Ougadougou leaders characterizes the combination of disparate elements in order to generate emergent forms as a "perverse" act, suggesting a reproductive vision of generationality in which newness threatens to disorder the lineal transmission of heritage (228). Proper procreation without alien admixture generates uninterrupted cultural continuity, fusing race and ethnicity such that the undisturbed continuity of the former serves as the guarantee for the conservation of the latter. This logic of the prior echoes quite closely that which governs recognition of collectives as Indian(-like) (as satirized by Jones in his use of the figure of "pink eye").

In contrast to such notions of authenticity, Hairston positions the Ghost Dancers' indigeneity as something other than the maintenance of a residual formation that can be defined largely in terms of a population's ethnoracial separateness and distinctiveness, instead linking indigeneity to experimentation, ethnogenesis, and the possibility of emergent formations.[127] *Mindscape* portrays the born-again Sioux as arising out of an effort to alter the sociopolitical terrain in which the Ghost Dancers found themselves, less conserving what was then taking part in a process of change and transformation. Similarly, in communing with the Barrier, the Ghost Dancers do not defend a static conception of natural harmony (the ecological Indian), a perspective from which the Barrier can appear only as invasion, infection, contamination. Rather, through their engagement with the Barrier, they partake in the "creative engine of evolution" (370), enacting something like stewardship but without the Indianizing sense of maintaining an unchanging sameness of "nature" to which innovation is anathema. Moreover, in the process of opening up relations among the zones, Wounded Knee becomes part of an evolving network.[128] It appears less as an isolated rural space (over which to exercise statelike jurisdiction) than as a hub from which to travel and return and as a node in a web of complex and enduring relations with other places and peoples.[129] In citing and circulating indigeneity as a social form in this way, Hairston contests the sovereignty and structure of the nation-state while also seeking to open room for engaging forms of landed peoplehood that do not pass through the filter of the (settler-) state. In addition, *Mindscape* positions the Ghost Dancers in opposition to the boundary-sustaining force exerted by the governments of the zones, thereby aligning them with the liberatory sense of movement commonly associated with marronage, but in doing so, the novel still characterizes their collective placemaking as *sovereignty*.[130] Hairston rejects the notion of the state or a repressively state-like structure as the only possible bearer of the kinds of political and territorial coherence collated under the term *sovereignty*.

However, in mobilizing indigeneity as something like a format through which to figure potentials for communal landedness and political life beyond the parameters of (settler-)state policy, Hairston runs into the problem of how to envision sustained relations with actually existing Indigenous peoples. *Midnight Robber* marks Indigenous geopolitical distinctiveness and the potential settler effects of marronage, but in doing so the novel suggests that marronage and indigeneity occupy discrepant problem-spaces with divergent organizing terms and political horizons, which leads to the unresolved question at the novel's end of how to situate Indigenous sovereignty in relation to the pursuit of justice within non-native social formations. *Mindscape*, though, translates indigeneity as a flexible political framework without providing a way of attending to the politics of non-Indigenous appropriation. What separates indigenization as born-again Sioux from creole claims to have become Native to places in the Caribbean?[131] What distinguishes the Ghost Dancers from others who have gone Native, either directly by claiming to be Indian (as in *The Bird Is Gone*) or through the decontextualizing expropriation of Indigenous knowledge and practices (as in *Oracles*)?[132] Furthermore, what does it mean to acknowledge born-again Sioux *sovereignty*? What does sovereignty mean in this context other than capacitating flight and greater movement between previously segregated spaces? In *As We Have Always Done*, Leanne Simpson suggests that the refusal of Indigenous peoples to center recognition by settler governments in their understanding and practices of their own indigeneity can be understood "as a form of marronage," "like the act of retreating to the bush, or [Indigenous] resurgence itself," and she characterizes her own renewed connection with Nishnaabeg lands as a "flight to escape colonial reality."[133] In this way, *flight* functions as a way of addressing expressions, experiences, and emplacements of Indigenous peoplehood that do not rely on state mappings, but such *escape* remains connected to long-standing modes of Native placemaking. Simpson indicates, "Indigenous peoples require a land base and therefore require a central and hard critique of the forces that propel dispossession," adding, "I'm interested in unapologetic placed-based nationhoods using Indigenous practices and operating in an ethical and principled way from an intact land base."[134] In *Mindscape*'s depiction, the born-again Sioux seem to be oriented less by the defense of Indigenous nationhood and the preservation of a coherent land base than by the project of contesting racializing state violence through facilitating increased mobility. If Butler's *Xenogenesis* trilogy tends to present collective claims to territorial self-governance as a reactionary preservation of racial integrity (as discussed in chapter 2), *Mindscape* tends to cast the content of Indigenous peoplehood and sovereignty as flight, implicitly defining indigeneity as a negative relation to particular structures of governance rather than as processes of landed self-determination guided by a people's (or set of peoples') own principles.[135]

The text's equivocations around the character of non-state sovereignty and the specificities of Indigenous peoplehood arise perhaps most forcefully in its depiction of treatying. Much of the text focuses on the effort to get the governments of the zones to comply with the Interzonal Treaty composed and negotiated by Celestina, and parts of the treaty often serve as epigraphs for chapters, positioning it as a framing device for the text. The refusal to abide by the treaty's terms and active efforts to thwart and dismantle it provide much of the narrative's ethical drama. The fact that the leaders in the various zones contest the treaty in order to preserve their own authority or putatively to maintain the integrity and purity of life in the zone (against backwardness or contamination) casts them as reactionaries working against the kinds of creative evolution and symbiogenesis with which Celestina is associated and that seems, ultimately, to serve as the horizon for the novel's speculative imagination. The treaty offers the possibility of "a reunited, one-world people now with common law," which would provide greater protections across the zones (including criminalizing the murder of Extras and "mandat[ing] democracy" [51, 53]). It seems to offer the potential for forms of political engagement across (zonal) differences, a more porous set of relations that enables peaceful transit across boundaries—a vision of open movement toward which the figure of marronage often gestures. However, the treaty emerges through a process of negotiation among zonal governments in which neither the Ghost Dancers nor ethnic throwback communities participate, thus making it a state project in which sub-state/non-state groups do not have any official political voice or standing. The novel envisions neither a mode of potential relation between the zonal governments and the Ghost Dancers nor among them and additional non-state political collectivities, such as ethnic throwback communities. The question of what constitutes peoplehood and landed collectivity, then, seems not to be at stake in the treaty or its implementation, taking the jurisdictional frameworks of the zones as given and extending certain personal rights and rights to travel within and between those lands. The treaty, then, functions as a centrally administered policy, creating a kind of meta-state governed by a singular "law" rather than enabling continually renewed processes of alliance making among disparate peoples. The Ghost Dance and "Sioux"-ness come to function metonymically as a means of figuring all modes of political community that lie outside the interzonal state system, drawing on indigeneity as a kind of conceptual or categorical container for a range of social formations.

However, the topos of the treaty also opens the potential for envisioning a pluralization of political forms in ways that speak to Indigenous peoples' self-determination and their dynamism without conscripting indigeneity as a vehicle for non-native self-articulation. *Mindscape* gestures toward the history of treaties between settler-states and Indigenous peoples, presenting the born-again Sioux as "treaty-shy" and as engaged in a "boycott" of Celestina's treaty due to concerns about "sign[ing] away their sovereignty" (12). Treaties have functioned as a means of marking the particular status of Native nations within Anglophone legal systems, testifying to the fact that they cannot be understood simply as "domestic" subjects of the state, as well as providing a basis through which the state legitimizes its claims to territories that previously had been held by Indigenous peoples.[136] As a legal form, the treaty provides a means of recognizing Indigenous sovereignties as separate from that of the settler nation and a vehicle for transferring control over specific lands from Native nations to the state. As Colin Calloway notes, "Between the treaty with the Delawares in 1778, and 1871, when Congress terminated treaty making, the United States ratified and passed into law about 370 treaties."[137] These agreements, though, have often been represented by non-natives as if they were merely contracts, highly circumscribed promises to pay a given people or set of peoples for particular territories which would then exclusively be under the control of the U.S. government to do with as it wished. In this way, the treaty system might be understood as a somewhat cynical strategy employed by the United States in order to pacify Native peoples long enough to expropriate their lands.[138] However, treaty making as a legal form inherently posits that Native nations are political entities with whom the settler-state is engaging in diplomatic relations, and insistence on the maintenance of treaty *relations* serves as a means of insisting on the illegitimacy of settler efforts to dictate the terms by which Indigenous peoples and lands will be governed. In Calloway's terms, "Treaties that functioned so often to separate Native peoples from their lands and cultures also established Native rights and recognized tribal sovereignty; when observed and honored in good faith, they have the potential to be instruments of restorative justice and healing," and as Theresa McCarthy argues with respect to the relationships promised and enacted through treaty making, "Friendship requires consistent renewal, as a reminder that tending to the participants' responsibilities keeps the medicine of the relationship strong."[139] Treaties, then, offer a political imaginary and process through which to engage in sustained diplomatic relation, a set of ongoing responsibilities that require reckoning with, continually renegotiating, and translating among varied frameworks of governance, territoriality, and belonging.

While many maroon communities did engage in treaty making with colonial governments, the dynamics of such geopolitical negotiations do not tend to be featured in popular and governmentally sanctioned accounts of marronage.[140] In the Caribbean and Latin America, as discussed previously, marronage primarily is invoked as a pattern of resistance to dominant political economy (via fugitivity), a kind of ethnic community whose cultural recognition contributes to the diversity of the nation-state that encompasses it, a means of figuring the legitimacy and liberatory bona fides of the postcolonial state, or some combination among these options. As an ongoing process of negotiation and renewal among distinct polities, treaty making does not accord with these figurations of marronage. Translating indigeneity as marronage opens the potential for acknowledging the politics of varied kinds of collective placemaking and refusing reifying accounts of Indianness as racial and spatial fixity, but it does not, at least in the novel, provide a means of thinking about relations among political formations other than by analogy (ethnic throwbacks are *like* born-again Sioux, and vice versa) or by triangulation through the state or a state system (everyone is subject to the same, centralized treaty in which non-state political entities play no official role). Indigeneity, then, comes to indicate the potential for unsettling the state's geographies and priorities but does not index a range of polities with whom the state and non-native collectivities must develop diplomatic relations on terms that arise out of good faith engagement, as opposed to unilateral imposition in the service of non-Indigenous political and economic ends.

If treaties mark a particular kind of legal relation between the (Anglophone) settler nation and Indigenous peoples, one that can be cited as part of "a strategy . . . to rearticulate indigenous nations as sovereign," they also provide an ethical framework for conceptualizing a range of political relationships in which there can be mutual acknowledgment of placemaking and governance without collapsing such varied modes of political collectivity into (the figure of) indigeneity.[141] One can understand treaties less as settled agreements than as models for ongoing conduct among peoples, as the basis for respectful mutual acknowledgment of each other's continuing existence and autonomy while also respecting mutual opacity—refusing to understand each other as fully translatable into each other's preferred terms and frameworks. Writing about the function of treaties, Eva Mackey quotes Haudenosaunee scholar Susan Hill's argument in a public meeting attended by Natives and non-natives, "What we need you to do is to find out what your responsibilities are to us. . . . Because everyone in this room has treaty rights. If you didn't you couldn't be here. Canada wouldn't exist." Mackey adds, "Because the notion of all settlers as 'treaty peoples' uses existing historical agreements that should be everyone's shared responsibility as their foundation, it can be seen as a potential invitation to non-Indigenous people to develop new relationships with Indigenous peoples," further noting, "These theorizations are not invitations to become Indigenous, or to see like an Indigenous person. They are invitations to be(come) responsible, by learning how to listen and respond appropriately as partners in particular treaty relationships."[142] However, if the work of treaty making and treaty renewal generates mutual responsibilities among participants, the form of such relationships can extend beyond "historical agreements" between Native nations and the settler-state to encompass the connection between Indigenous peoples and non-Indigenous groups more broadly. While retaining treaties' significance as diplomatic engagements among political collectivities that cannot be contained within the realm of "domestic" state policy, one might follow *Mindscape*'s lead in seeking to envision political mappings beyond those of the state, speculatively imagining relations between entities such as the born-again Sioux and ethnic throwback communities as themselves conducted via treaties. Such a politics of relationality pushes against the conventional routing of recognition through the state, including its reliance on (Indianizing) analogy as a way of framing questions of collective territoriality and self-governance.

The novel gestures in this direction when Lawanda notes at the end that many are "callin' for a world council at Wounded Knee" (433), intimating a more open and multilateral process of negotiation than what seems to have characterized the emergence and ratification of the Interzonal Treaty. This gesture, though, is as close as the text comes to employing something like a more expansive treaty imaginary to envision relations among non-state (political) entities—becoming "partners" rather than seeking to gain legitimacy through self-indigenization. Hairston's process of bringing marronage and indigeneity into relation reorients Latin American policy models, generating a more open-ended sense of how the politics of collective identity and emplacement could be imagined while allowing for ethnogenesis and change over time (as against models of static continuity or visions of purity). Conversely, the process of bringing indigeneity into the maroon matrix can also move away from questions of Indigenous sovereignty and situated self-determination, emphasizing flight and distance from dominant political structures rather than engagement with Indigenous peoples' status as polities to whom non-natives should bear a mutually negotiated diplomatic relation. While the text at times obliquely gestures toward potentials for treatying, *Mindscape*'s employment of indigenizing analogy largely bends away from such possibilities.

INDIGENEITY AND MARRONAGE SHARE a focus on place-based collectivity, but the employment of the latter within Black political imaginaries often binds such community formation to figurations of movement in ways that diminish the possibilities for engaging with enduring Indigenous sovereignty. When employed as a political imaginary, marronage often orients away from questions of sovereignty toward highlighting enduring opposition to dominant modes of racial governmentality. Invocations of marronage gesture toward the importance of, in McKittrick's terms, the "poetics of landscape" while largely leaving open the question of how such processes of situatedness and placemaking relate to official legal geographies and projects of state recognition. Figurations of marronage, then, mark a certain ambivalence with respect to engaging with place-based collective self-governance, turning both toward and away from the politics of Indigenous peoplehood.

Mindscape and *Midnight Robber* illustrate how translating between indigeneity and marronage draws attention to the politics of Black landedness, both as a vector of collective self-determination and as involved in a process of potential conflict and negotiation with Indigenous peoples. Yet in enabling sustained consideration of Black geographies as they emerge in opposition to dominant (white) national and international mappings, the citation of indigeneity often works to clarify the aims and enable transformation of non-native polities and struggles in ways that deemphasize engagement with the scope, character, and persistence of Indigenous peoples' sovereignty and self-determination. Viewing marronage through the prism of indigeneity (and vice versa), as in Hairston's text, opens the potential for engaging with modes of Black collective emplacement as a (geo)politics and for separating Indigenous peoplehood from the Indianizing imaginary of the reservation—a contained, unchanging, racially constituted population marked by its specific forms of cultural/ethnic difference. As both Zobel and Jones explore in their novels, non-native modes of recognition can seek to lock Native people(s) into paralyzing accounts of stasis, particular models of ecological stewardship that more or less equate them with "flora and fauna," exoticizing visions of Indian difference that can be tapped for non-native enlightenment, and bureaucratic structures that work to assimilate them to national norms or to segregate them utterly. However, when indigeneity is employed as a social form through which to figure a range of non-state political configurations, Indigenous peoplehood and sovereignty also can lose their specificity by becoming vehicles through which non-Indigenous collectives can be "born again" as (geo)political actors, thereby short-circuiting the possibility of mutually negotiated relationships with Indigenous peoples and effacing the ongoing force of non-native appropriation and expropriation. Notably, though, Hairston does not present Indigenous peoplehood and other political collectivities as asserting claims to the same land base. What happens to the possibilities for relation, and for indigeneity as a social form, when one people's forms of placemaking directly challenge another's? This question stands at the center of Hopkinson's *Midnight Robber*, which explores how flight from oppression, so crucial to the maroon matrix, may entail settlement on others' territory. The founding of the Nation Worlds, as well as their complicated relation with New Half-Way Tree, requires the decimation of douen nations and the ongoing and expanding seizure of their lands, creating a central conflict in relation to Marryshevite presence and the dreams of liberation that give rise to it. While foregrounding that struggle and its implications for non-Indigenous inhabitance and political organization, the novel equivocates with respect to the implications of its account of structural and intensifying Indigenous dispossession, returning to the disruptive potential of flight as a way of reforming and rejuvenating non-Indigenous social and political systems.

If existing state modes of recognition fail to account for the dynamism and variable forms of Indigenous peoplehood, they do acknowledge distinct rights to political autonomy and self-governance, even if in attenuated, culturalizing, and racializing forms. While marronage can facilitate moving among Black and Indigenous modes of emplacement, including attending to histories of and possibilities for Black exertions of sovereignty in complex connection to Indigenous geographies, the problem-space marronage occupies remains oriented by conceptions of flight in ways that incline away from sustained consideration of Indigenous sovereignty. However, *Midnight Robber* and *Mindscape* in different ways gesture toward possibilities for mediating marronage through the ethics of treating, possibilities for diplomacy and forms of political engagement not conditioned by the terms of the state and its modes of (self-)recognition. They both pose the question of what might happen if enduring, emplaced reciprocities were a central feature of what are conceptualized as ongoing modes of Black-Indigenous negotiation.

CODA

Diplomacy in the Undercommons

The speculative entails what might be. More than pointing toward the future, *might be* operates in the subjunctive mood—that which does not count as what *is*. Talking in *Starboard Wine* about his turn to science fiction, Samuel Delany says of reading novels by Richard Wright and Chester Himes focused on contemporary Black experience that they "seemed to say . . . that, in any realistic terms, precisely what made it so awful also made it unchangeable." Rather than aiming for an account of what is "realistic," speculative fiction, according to Delany, "conscientiously misrepresents the world in an endless series of lucidly readable ways," defined by its "basic nonrepresentational aspect."[1] Representing the world can be understood as seeking to approximate the present or the past by way of drawing on conventionalized terms for signifying what is real. However, in refusing such representation, speculative fiction opens up subjunctive potentials. It enacts a process of redescription, of *conscientious misrepresentation*, that can engender alternative ways of conceptualizing and perceiving what is. As a narrative, intellectual, and ethical mode, then, the speculative interrupts the tendency to take for granted ways of characterizing, categorizing, and explaining social life. It works to disrupt and redirect modes of understanding through the reframing conceit of *might be*.[2]

In the past several chapters, I've attended to figurations of fungibility, fugitivity, and marronage in Afrofuturist writing, addressing the ways these prominent tropes of Black political imagination shape readers' apprehension of the contours, trajectories, and potentials of blackness, as well as the continuing force of antiblackness. I've also traced how these framings translate indigeneity, especially in terms of place-based peoplehood. These texts' critical speculative relation to dominant understandings of race and racism, their effort to reorient visions of justice away from individual inclusion into (neo)liberal citizenship, helps prompt my analysis of their experiments in engaging with Indigenous difference and the impasses that arise in those efforts. These narratives help highlight how conceptual and perceptual frameworks affect ways of engaging across difference, and in this way, they also point to the importance, in Marisol de la Cadena's terms, of "probing the translation process itself to make its onto-epistemic terms explicit" in order to facilitate sustained relations among Black and Indigenous worldings.[3] Bearing such dynamics in mind, I'd like to return to where I began in the Introduction—the scene of attempted Black-Indigenous alliance—in order to explore further the possibilities opened by a subjunctive kind of solidarity. Such relations need not offer structural resolution so much as a more tentative, negotiated, and renewable connection, one conducted in the translational mood of might be. We could call it diplomacy in the undercommons.

Planning happens in relation to a horizon. The effort to come together with respect to some joint project, including in enacting forms of solidarity, involves more than just the fact of present interaction; it also entails having some kind of orienting direction toward which shared thought and activity moves. As Sara Ahmed suggests, "Depending on which way one turns, different worlds might even come into view. If such turns are repeated over time, the bodies acquire the very shape of such direction.... [I]n moving this way, rather than that, and moving in this way again and again, the surfaces of bodies *in turn* acquire their shape. Bodies are 'directed' and they take the shape of this direction," and she later notes of collective forms of turning that "a 'we' emerges as an effect of a shared direction toward an object."[4] In this vein, alliance building might be understood as the process of turning in the same direction, of forming a "we" through intentions and acts of movement making toward some mutual (set of) objective(s). What happens, though, when those who gather to plan, to be in sustained relation in ways that might bring into view and help materialize different worlds, themselves emerge from "we"s that tend toward different objects? In *The Undercommons*, Stefano Harney and Fred Moten characterize *planning* as refusing the "compulsion of scarcity" at play in projects of "management," instead conducting an "ongoing experiment with the informal, carried out by and on the means of social reproduction": "planning in the undercommons is not an activity, not fishing or dancing or teaching or loving, but the ceaseless experiment with the futurial presence of the forms of life that make such activities possible." Such modes of relation tend away from the search for recognition by the state since "all politics is correctional," in that it seeks to engender forms of being and becoming conducive to proper inhabitance of existing institutional structures (whose aim ostensibly is "to make us better").[5]

Being beyond politics also means being beyond the search for intelligibility within its terms. Harney and Moten insist, "We cannot represent ourselves. We can't be represented." The "we" named here are those who dwell within the "undercommons," all those whose ongoing racialized "social dispossession" comprises state-backed imperatives of extraction and exploitation.[6] To be outside of or illegible to *representation* is to refuse to be a proper subject of governance and capital and to refuse to be judged as failing to be such a subject when not performing personhood correctly. The futurist fiction I've engaged theorizes various forms of such unrepresentability, or the force of state representation, as in Walter Mosley's portrayal of the role of race-neutral modes of racialization within carceral geographies (addressed in chapter 3) or Melissa Tantaquidgeon Zobel's and Stephen Graham Jones's depictions of settler processes for officially acknowledging Indigenous land bases (discussed in chapter 4). The kind of planning Harney and Moten address, then, involves less a set of shared political projects—a direction toward a common object(ive) of change in which the "we" collectively gains coherence as a "we" through such communal movement—than an "experiment" with the *forms* of "we"-ness and the shape of matrices of relation outside of the state imperative to reproduce officially recognized kinds and modes of identity. The notion of the undercommons, then, enables a thinking of solidarity as a speculative endeavor, something like a shared project of experimentation in which the potential for differently imagined futures distends the terms of relation in the present. Existing political and analytical frameworks as well as extant trajectories of collective direction come into disorienting conjuncture in ways that raise questions about what constitutes desirable "forms of life," for whom, and how to negotiate among such visions and attendant kinds of "we"s without the presumption that there is or must be a shared horizon.

The "we" of the undercommons gestures toward multiple, ongoing dynamics of racializing abjection and expropriation while turning away from state recognition or representation, and in doing so, Harney and Moten's speculative vision opens onto exploration of the modes of relation at play in such noncohesive mutuality. In the absence of a singular identity or even a shared objective that provides the basis for collective self-understanding, what principles and processes guide connection, collaboration, and planning? Eve Tuck and K. Wayne Yang suggest that among Black and Indigenous movements "the opportunities for solidarity lie in what is incommensurable rather than what is common across these efforts," further insisting on the need for a conception of "uncommonality that un-coalesces coalition politics."[7] When operating in the key of incommensurability, though, practices of engagement—of "ongoing experiment" with what constitutes ethical relation—become difficult to imagine. What does accountability among social and political movements entail when they offer varied accounts of the real and turn toward discrepant (visions of desirable) forms of life?

If there is no inherently supervening intellectual framework or institutional structure within which to organize and conduct relations of mutual responsibility, they need to be made and remade through ongoing negotiation. Exploring the potential for modes of connection not routed through the forms of the state, Harney and Moten develop the notion of "bad debt," which offers a way of thinking about possibilities for open-ended interconnection. They observe with respect to the "fugitive public" of the undercommons, "It is not credit we seek nor even debt but bad debt which is to say real debt, the debt that cannot be repaid, the debt at a distance, the debt without creditor, the black debt, the queer debt, the criminal debt. Excessive debt, incalculable debt, debt for no reason, debt broken from credit, debt as its own principle," adding that "credit is a means of privatization and debt a means of socialization."[8] The sort of debt associated with credit presents itself as a limited, contractually mediated connection reduced to the transfer of assets while legitimizing a continuing relation of extraction and discipline due to the supposed failure to repay what is often an impossible burden created by structural violence.[9] "Bad debt" or "debt as its own principle" suggests an ongoing relation of responsibility that has no predetermined content (something repayable in amount or kind), is not enforceable/enforced, and does not provide the basis for impoverishing and dispossessive seizures (of resources, land, etc.). Playing on the ways debt functions in dominant discourses as a racializing marker of diminished or failed personhood, the concept of "bad debt" also casts relations in the undercommons in terms of a kind of openness to that which lies beyond the boundaries of existing forms of identity, individual or collective. This kind of fugitivity could be understood as flight toward heretofore untried modes of relation, a subjunctive experiment with what continuing connection might mean beyond what seems politically *realistic*.[10] Debt here suggests an ongoing process of turning toward other people(s) in ways that cannot be understood either as obligation (something compelled) or as generosity (a kind of charity). Instead, there is an ethical sense of being immanently connected to other people(s) yet absent any kind of coercion and without becoming a singular "we." Approached from this perspective, accountability entails less recompense—less an accounting or tabulation of injury and obligation—than a kind of socialization otherwise, a coming-to-be-disoriented by contact with different world(ing)s in which one might come to understand oneself as implicated but that do not conform to one's usual forms of life and conceptual framings.

"Debt," then, implies a speculative reach across difference that might also be described as the work of diplomacy. Rather than suggesting something like Westphalian sovereignty, characterizing relations in the undercommons as diplomacy highlights the potential for forms of mutual collective political recognition, and recognition of political collectivities, that is other than what is available in and through state policy. In *As We Have Always Done*, Leanne Simpson observes, "Recognition within Nishnaabeg intelligence is a process of seeing another being's core essence; it is a series of relationships. *It is reciprocal, continual, and a way of generating society.*" She further notes, "It cognitively reverses the violence of dispossession because what's the opposite of dispossession in Indigenous thought again? Not possession, because we're not supposed to be capitalists, but connection, a coded layering of intimate interconnection and interdependence that creates a complicated algorithmic network of presence, reciprocity, consent, and freedom."[11] In contrast to forms of recognition that seek to slot people(s) into prefabricated categories consistent with existing institutional structures, recognition in this sense functions as a dynamic and ongoing experiment in which the participants in that relationship take part in a *reciprocal* process of connection, a networking in which there is an acknowledgment of interdependence but also of difference (like the emplaced interdependencies envisioned in Daniel Wilson's novels, discussed in chapter 3). Such relationship is less about establishing borders per se, or zones of possession (like the resisters in Octavia Butler's *Xenogenesis* trilogy), than about (re)inventing and navigating the terms of continued ethical interaction.

This description hearkens back to the potentials of treatying, separate from state geographies and claims, as discussed in the previous chapter. Simpson asks, "How do I ensure that my nationhood and relationship to land on the north shore of Lake Ontario do not replicate systems that restrict Black spatialities or replicate geographies of domination?" In response, she indicates, "Within Nishnaabeg political thought, we have practices of sharing space with other nations and communities of peoples and respecting that autonomy to govern themselves over these lands," adding, "I think then we would have to figure out political mechanisms to respect each other's governance, sovereignty, and jurisdiction while committing to taking care of our shared ecosystem."[12] While translating Black political imaginaries into the terms of Native nationhood (in ways that resonate with Mosley's exploration of Black indigeneity in *The Wave* as well as the narration of marronage in *Mindscape*), Simpson suggests the importance of embracing a responsibility for engaging Black presence and aspirations in order to refuse collusion with extant, dispossessive institutionalized practices that produce a sense of Black placelessness and contribute to antiblack domination. She articulates what could be characterized as a debt, a recognition of Indigenous accountability to Black analyses and visions of justice. A willingness to see how Indigenous people(s) might be understood within Black frames of reference opens onto an imagination of potential modes of relation—one that engages with the dynamics of enforced non-native diasporas in ways that exceed the Indigenous futurist texts on which I've focused. Through a consideration of practices of diplomacy—histories and ethics of "sharing space with other nations and communities"—Simpson seeks to ask how Black concerns might matter within Nishnaabeg self-understandings and forms of life, how reckoning with antiblackness might affect from within Nishnaabeg ways of conceptualizing and practicing sovereignty (a process of internal transformation through relation that in many ways mirrors the kinds of "difference" Butler theorizes in the trilogy).[13]

In speaking of relations of "bad debt" as enacting a kind of diplomacy separate from (settler-)state modes of representation, I'm asking something like, how can people(s) dwell together in the undercommons? How can a speculative ethics of *misrepresentation*—a refusal, or at least deferral, of what counts as *realistic*—facilitate negotiated relations of collective emplacement that are conceived neither as inherently antagonistic nor as needing to achieve unity of perspective/vision? Harney and Moten, though, do not really characterize the undercommons in terms of dwelling, instead describing it as "fugitive public of strangers not communities" and contrasting the "undercommons" to "neighborhoods." They also emphasize what "we might call hapticality," a "thrown together"-ness that gives rise to a "form of feeling [that] was not collective, not given to decision, not adhering or reattaching to settlement, nation, state, territory or historical story."[14] Planning in the undercommons involves an "ongoing experiment" with various forms of life and the kinds of futures they might offer as a means of making possible alternative versions of the present. As such, it involves a speculative structure of feeling in which collectivity, inhabitance, and mutual acknowledgment are not locked into a predetermined shape, particularly not one organized around the (racializing) terms of state policy. The emphasis on the haptic serves as a way of rejecting the idea that the forms of life that arise through relations in the undercommons must fit a prearranged framework, one consistent with existing institutionalized political formations. Might that *thrownness*, though, be thought of as less about the absence of sustained communality or landedness—of claims to *nation* or *territory*—than an openness to forms of engagement and an ethics of mutual responsibility that arise out of the encounter with other people(s) and their ways of understanding themselves, including their ways of narrating the challenges they face and the direction(s) toward which they seek to move? What might a sustained, grounded accountability to each other's stories entail, one that does not require forms of reductionism and unacknowledged mistranslation in the name of *realistic* analyses or solutions?[15]

Transposing debt into diplomacy seeks to increase possibilities for acknowledging Indigenous forms of nationhood while also shifting the site of political negotiation and recognition away from the state. Doing so moves toward, in Zoltán Grossman's formulation, *"alliances from below [that] may pose an alternative to recognition-from-above."*[16] *The Undercommons* begins with a discussion of *Drums along the Mohawk*, noting that "the settler is portrayed as surrounded by 'natives'" and indicating, "Our task is the self-defense of the surround in the face of repeated, targeted dispossessions through the settler's armed incursion." While Harney and Moten caution that "the real danger" lies in responding to such dispossession through assertions of "self-possession," their invocations of settlement implicitly raise the question of, on whose ground does the undercommons lie?[17] That question, though, need not be an endpoint, another dispossession-enacting version of what Harney and Moten refer to as "enclosure," an intellectual and political maneuver that can leave non-native people of African descent "in a kind of limbo, waiting for a colonial state and Indigenous nations to 'work out' a relationship."[18] Instead, attending to place can open onto a speculative exploration of practices of sharing space and enacting governance that begin from the presumption that there are varied frameworks at play in that space for conceptualizing placemaking, belonging, and dispossession and that those framings might yield different accounts of what accountability looks like. Mutual willingness to engage each other's world(ings) and forms of "we"-ness—to be disoriented by potential relations of debt and the possibilities for reciprocity articulated in others' narratives—can enable emplaced connections that do not necessitate Westphalian visions of sovereign self-possession.

Examples of such subjunctive solidarity can be seen in contemporary activist gestures of alliance that experiment with what it means to translate other movements into the terms of a particular struggle, to open up alternative potentials for what kinds of analysis and imaginings get to count as expressive of the real. Under the heading #nobanonstolenland, Melanie Yazzie explores possibilities for responding to U.S. anti-immigration policy from within a commitment to Indigenous peoples' self-determination. Yazzie, a Diné scholar and activist, created the hashtag in January 2017 in response to the Trump administration's effort to prevent entry into the United States from seven Muslim-majority countries. Although this issue is not specifically concerned with Black people, or central to Black political imaginaries, I want to engage Yazzie's performance and theorization of speculative diplomacy due to the ways it seeks to generate conceptual resources for affirming enduring non-native presence in the Americas while continuing to foreground Indigenous placemaking and governance.[19] The hashtag emerged out of a demonstration at Los Angeles International Airport (LAX) immediately in the wake of the administration's announcement that the travel ban had been instituted via executive order. In the social media message that followed the protest, Yazzie observes, "Today, at the #laxprotest, Native people conducted a welcoming ceremony to our Muslim and refugee sisters." She further explains, "When one of our Native brothers took to the megaphone and said that the United States has no authority on Native land, the crowd cheered. So loud my ears were ringing. That is what I witnessed today. That is the power of Native-led movements. We never stopped practicing our own customs of kinship making, citizenship, and belonging. Trump and all US forms of citizenship and law are illegitimate on stolen land." Yazzie's orienting frame is Native sovereignty, an insistence on Native polities and their modes of governance as foundational to any attempt to think about or beyond U.S. law and policy. However, while challenging the legitimacy of settler colonial claims to jurisdiction over Native peoples and homelands, the direction here is not away from non-natives, an understanding of them as alien intruders whose presence necessarily marks a challenge to Indigenous possession. Rather, Yazzie centers Native "customs of kinship making, citizenship, and belonging" in their capacity to build connections with non-natives who themselves have been subject to various dispossessive regimes of state violence.

This process of forging relations across difference stages a *might be* diplomacy. The speculative force of Yazzie's articulations lies not in the projection of something beyond the present, of a future only yet to come, but in the refusal of the terms of recognition and representation at play in U.S. official discourses—a challenge to the self-declared realism of settler narratives. She considers what would happen if Indigenous modes of governance were acknowledged on their own terms, if they served as the basis for negotiating copresence on the lands claimed by the United States. As opposed to negating non-native presence as the condition of possibility for Indigenous political authority, she implicitly asks what non-native dwelling would mean when posed from within an encompassing affirmation of Indigenous collective being and becoming. As Yazzie elaborates in her presentation at the 2017 meeting of the National Women's Studies Association, such connections arise out of "collective forms of belonging and accountability that do not reproduce liberal ideas about citizenship and nationalism like those that give shape to US settler nationalism," and these modes of diplomatic relation were being "reclaim[ed] . . . in the name of resisting US racism and imperialism." Envisioning the exercise of Indigenous authority with respect to non-native presence on these lands does not necessitate the reproduction of dominant notions of proper(tied) personhood or of rigidly policed national boundaries but can be enacted in ways that acknowledge forms of accountability to other populations subjected to U.S. state violence. Put another way, speculative reach outside of what are often taken to be Indigenous issues facilitates a process of translation and transformation that can open diplomatic possibilities for engaging with non-native concerns. Yazzie, though, indicates that this gesture was rejected by certain Native men who objected to "inviting people onto Native land where resources are scarce and our people are strangulated daily by settler incursion." However, she argues that this way of viewing Native lands and sovereignties "presumes a certain givenness to the existence of the United States and a certain acceptance of the injury caused by the violence of US nationalism," to which she responds by saying, "I refuse the normalization of such violence. These views give us no agency to believe we have the capacity for actual decolonization. There is no future in this perspective, which to me means it's neither Indigenous nor feminist." Embracing Native peoples' role in enacting kinship diplomacies toward non-natives who find themselves on these lands due to the ongoing dynamics of "U.S. racism and imperialism" moves toward a broadened vision of decolonization and the possibilities for fully enacting it. A futurist conception of Indigenous sovereignty serves as the basis for reimagining the potential for relations of solidarity (or, in Yazzie's terms, of "radical relationality") in the present, by refusing to normalize state practices and by drawing on non-native narratives and demands in ways that translate them into an Indigenous frame of reference that itself is altered in the process.

Reciprocally, invocations of Indigenous peoples' ongoing presence by members of the Black Lives Matter movement open speculative potentials for engaging what Native sovereignty might mean within struggles against state-sanctioned antiblackness. Alicia Garza, one of the founders of Black Lives Matter, has in her public speeches and interviews increasingly been invoking

Indigenous peoples, histories, and struggles in ways that enable exploration of debt and diplomatic relation. In her keynote talk for the Allied Media Conference in September 2017, Garza states, "Thank you to the indigenous peoples of this land the Anishinaabe or the Three Fires People for hosting me on this land, and thank you for being stewards of this land for thousands of years."[20] This gesture reaches beyond the usual ways of staging movements against antiblackness, centering as it does an ongoing relation to the specific peoples on whose lands the meeting takes place. Regardless of whether such grounded histories and political orders are recognized by the U.S. government, Garza's invocation here opens toward a diplomatic engagement that foregrounds non-native connections to Native nations. The very present tenseness of Garza's declaration of indebtedness ("Thank you . . . for hosting me") makes clear that the connection with Anishinaabe peoples is not one of inheritance, of non-natives coming to inhabit a land that has been denuded of Indigenous presence through genocide and removal (as Nalo Hopkinson illustrates and critiques in *Midnight Robber*). Instead, acknowledging ongoing Anishinaabe landedness serves as a way of indicating how an accountable ethics of non-native presence turns on building relations of reciprocity with Native peoples, relations that recognize such peoples' long-standing connection to and governance over what the U.S. claims as its domestic space, as well as the complex matrix of relationships (with other peoples as well as nonhuman entities) that constitutes and is constituted by such collective placemaking (the reference to Indigenous *stewardship*). Later in the speech, Garza warns of the danger of "fall[ing] back on outdated ways of being" that involve "seek[ing] solace in the people who already agree with us," pursuing "safety in remaining disconnected." By contrast, she emphasizes the need "to expand the nuance of our stories" by attending to how a range of oppressive "systems"—"colonization, capitalism, imperialism, white supremacy, heteronormativity, patriarchy"—"function to break the bonds of relationship between us." In this way, the opening address to Indigenous peoples does important (re)framing work. Through it, Garza alludes to kinds of stories and relationships that may not fit neatly into existing paradigms of Black political struggle but that might offer new "ways of being," including a vision whose terms have been expanded through the self-undertaken *bad debt* of accountability—open-ended and uncoerced—to Indigenous peoples.[21]

This movement toward solidarity includes an engagement with Native modes of governance. In an interview with *Mother Jones* in September 2017 in the wake of white supremacist demonstrations in Charlottesville and the call for the removal of Confederate statutes, Garza is asked about such monuments, the interviewer noting that those who defend the statues have "argued the left will want to take down statues of George Washington, who owned slaves, or Christopher Columbus, who led a genocide against Native Americans. Do you agree?" Garza responds, "Things like renaming holidays and removing statues are really a part of a culture-change strategy that I think is important. But it can't stop there. We can change Columbus Day to Indigenous People's Day [*sic*], but if we're not doing the work to make sure that indigenous nations have sovereignty in this country, or self-determination, . . . then it is merely symbolic."[22] In specifically referencing Native peoples as *nations* that legitimately exercise sovereignty and self-determination, Garza registers the importance of Indigenous political authority over particular land bases. These comments come amid a discussion largely focused on antiblack racism and the expropriation of Black labor and resources, including the "fight for reparations for black people" and "transforming systems that disenfranchise black people from the wealth we create." Incorporating discussion of Indigenous sovereignties, then, extends beyond the conceptual and political framework Garza principally employs. Putting these ideas in relation to each other also implicitly suggests that acknowledging Native peoples as jurisdiction-enacting polities need not be understood as inherently contributing to ongoing Black dispossession, and such acknowledgment need not be seen as antagonistic to advocacy for reparations (envisioned here principally as a redistribution of resources in ways commensurate with the role of Black people in creating such wealth). As with Yazzie's hashtag, this turning toward different worlds (in Ahmed's phrase quoted earlier) might be understood as an act of diplomacy, a recognition not routed through the state that explores possibilities for collective forms of being-in-relation while doing so immanently from within the particular configurations of these nonidentical movements.

Notably, neither Yazzie's nor Garza's acts of political imagination involve a wholesale reenvisioning of their organizing modes of analysis and conceptions of justice. Rather than offering something like a structural integration of varied struggles and movements into a single, overarching explanatory framework, these formulations by activist intellectuals perform acts of acknowledgment across difference in ways that engender possibilities for planning—for, in Harney and Moten's terms, experimenting with forms of life that might enable networks of relation separate from state geographies, statuses, and policy. That experimentation, though, is predicated on a speculative ethics of indebtedness, of imagining one's way into others' stories of how the world is and should be while then bringing those imaginings back into one's own formulations, visionings, and trajectories toward change to see what they might do and make possible.

My emphasis on the speculative is about starting from the premise of *uncommonality*, as Tuck and Yang put it, while envisioning potentials for relation that do not depend on reconciliation—that do not require a merger, clash, or choice among nonequivalent frameworks. Such framings and political imaginaries arise out of varied histories and experiences of oppression and are animated by their own collective aspirations. In this way, movements, as I have argued, can be understood as oriented in their own ways. Rather than seeking to provide a system-building model that could encompass these multiple accounts, thereby placing them in a particular structural relation to each other, I have argued for the value of what might be described as a more immanent kind of engagement, which I have suggested through figurations of translation. Moving among discrepant problem-spaces—differently configured analyses, modes of collectivity, and projected itineraries of transformation—entails shifting frames of reference. That process, though, itself is situated, looking from somewhere and from within a particular set of principles and priorities in ways that affect what and how one sees. Attending to the dynamics of such *equivocation*, then, becomes key, trying to track how things come into view and how the perspective that shapes such apprehension affects modes of understanding and relation. In this vein, my discussion of how fungibility, fugitivity, and marronage are employed within Afrofuturist fiction is in the interest of thinking about the kinds of perspectival orientations these organizing tropes provide, while at the same time seeking to mark what happens when they serve as the framework through which to engage what might be understood as forms of indigeneity. Futurist fiction enables this kind of investigation precisely because it suspends the realism effects of portrayals of the present and the past, thereby enabling the framings and narrative strategies at play in political movements and struggles for social justice to come into bolder relief as just that—framings and narrations rather than simply transcriptions of what *is*. In this way, I have sought to articulate a speculative ethics in which debt to the narratives offered by other movements and struggles willingly is accepted. That gesture of accountability involves less wholesale acceptance of others' accounts of what is real, or the embrace of structural explanations that seek to encompass and coordinate struggles from above, than Black and Indigenous movements' openness to engaging reflexively with their own political imaginaries in ways that open room for good faith efforts to translate across difference. These efforts provide the medium in which to generate ongoing and continually renegotiated diplomacies and solidarities. Such conceptual, narrative, and political reciprocities create subjunctive pathways for building alternative futures.

Notes

INTRODUCTION

1. "Black Lives Matter Stands in Solidarity with Water Protectors at Standing Rock," accessed February 25, 2017, http://blacklivesmatter.com. Subsequent quotes are taken from this statement.

2. I capitalize "Native" and "Indigenous" because when these terms are used without capitalization they can be taken colloquially to refer to anyone or anything born in a given place rather than specifically indicating First Peoples. While there's more variation in whether people capitalize "Black" when referring to Afro-descended people(s), and less of a likelihood of confusing the meaning of the term, I've decided as a matter of respect to capitalize this term so that it visually signifies in parallel to "Indigenous" and "Native." I do not capitalize "indigeneity" and "blackness" because neither term requires it in order to make my meaning clear. I do not capitalize "antiblackness" for the same reason. I do not capitalize "white" or "non-native" because the meaning is clear without the capitalization.

3. Estes, "Fighting for Our Lives"; Estes and Dhillon, "Introduction."

4. Chakrabarty, *Provincializing Europe*, 83.

5. I should note that distinguishing between blackness and indigeneity can efface the existence of Indigenous peoples in sub-Saharan Africa. However, even while understanding antiblackness as a global phenomenon, I would suggest that the sociopolitical dynamics of blackness as sets of lived circumstances and forms of political imagination in the Americas qualitatively differ from those at play with respect to those peoples in Africa who might understand themselves as included within the category of "indigenous" within international law and transnational political movements. On African indigeneity, see Barume, "Responding to the Concerns of the African States"; Claassens and Cousins, *Land, Power, and Custom*; Hodgson, *Being Maasai, Becoming Indigenous*; Kipuri, "The UN Declaration on the Rights of Indigenous Peoples in the African Context"; Lehmann, "Aboriginal Title, Indigenous Rights and the Right to Culture"; Mamdani, *Citizen and Subject*. For futurist fiction that engages issues of Black indigeneity within Africa, see Nnedi Okorafor's work, particularly the *Binti* series.

6. On the main Black Lives Matter website, they describe themselves as "a chapter-based, member-led organization whose mission is to build local power and to intervene

in violence inflicted on Black communities by the state and vigilantes": Black Lives Matter, accessed November 30, 2017, https://blacklivesmatter.com/about. On the history of Black Lives Matter, see also Khan-Cullors and bandele, *When They Call You a Terrorist*; Taylor, *From #BlackLivesMatter*. Black Lives Matter further has given rise to the Movement for Black Lives, which has developed an extensive platform: see https://policy.m4bl.org/platform.

7. Garza et al., "A HerStory of the #BlackLivesMatter Movement."

8. On the nonidentical, see Adorno, *Negative Dialectics*.

9. Ahmed, *Queer Phenomenology*, 15, 38, 44.

10. On blackness as enfleshment, see Spillers, "Mama's Baby, Papa's Maybe"; Weheliye, *Habeas Viscus*. I discuss this framing at length in chapter 2.

11. Best and Hartman, "Fugitive Justice," 1, 4–5.

12. Moten, "The Case of Blackness," 177.

13. Moten, "The Case of Blackness," 179, 187.

14. Simpson, "The State Is a Man."

15. Byrd, *The Transit of Empire*, xxiv.

16. de la Cadena, *Earth Beings*, 4, 116.

17. For discussion of such "circuiting" and modes of historical differentiation, see Asaka, *Tropical Freedom*; Ben-zvi, *Native Land Talk*; Byrd, *The Transit of Empire*; Forbes, *Africans and Native Americans*; Jackson, *Creole Indigeneity*; Madden, *African Nova Scotian–Mi'kmaw Relations*; Mandell, *Tribe, Race, History*; Miles and Holland, *Crossing Waters, Crossing Worlds*; Saunt, *Black, White, and Indian*; Singh, *Race and America's Long War*.

18. On the dynamics of such white transcendence, see Harris, "Whiteness as Property"; Silva, *Toward a Global Idea of Race*; Sullivan, *Revealing Whiteness*.

1. ON THE IMPASSE

1. On Native enslavement, see Blackhawk, *Violence over the Land*; Brooks, *Captives and Cousins*; Gómez, *Manifest Destinies*; Guidotti-Hernández, *Unspeakable Violence*. On Black dispossession on lands claimed by the United States, see Asaka, *Tropical Freedom*; Goldstein, "Finance and Foreclosure in the Colonial Present"; King, "In the Clearing"; Massey and Denton, *American Apartheid*; McKittrick, *Demonic Grounds*.

2. Ahmed, *Queer Phenomenology*, 117, 119.

3. de la Cadena, *Earth Beings*, 4.

4. de la Cadena, *Earth Beings*, xxv.

5. de la Cadena, *Earth Beings*, 63.

6. On translation, see also Chakrabarty, *Provincializing Europe*; Cheyfitz, *The Poetics of Imperialism*; Edwards, *The Practice of Diaspora*.

7. Hong, *Death beyond Disavowal*, 4. See also Edwards, *The Practice of Diaspora*; Ellis, *Territories of the Soul*; Hartman, *Lose Your Mother*; Quashie, *The Sovereignty of Quiet*; Wright, *Physics of Blackness*.

8. See Anaya, *Indigenous Peoples in International Law*; Brysk, *From Tribal Village to Global Village*; Charters and Stavenhagen, *Making the Declaration Work*; Engle, *The Elusive Promise of Indigenous Development*.

9. See Adams, *Who Belongs?*; Brooks, *Confounding the Color Line*; Byrd, *The Transit of Empire*, 117–46; Chang, *The Color of the Land*; Klopotek, *Recognition Odysseys*; Miles, *Ties That Bind*; Miles and Holland, *Crossing Waters, Crossing Worlds*; Saunt, *Black, White, and Indian*; Sturm, *Blood Politics*.

10. For classic formulations of the problems of serving as a "bridge" between groups otherwise envisioned as different, see Moraga and Anzaldúa, *This Bridge Called My Back*.

11. Scott, *Conscripts of Modernity*, 4, 19. Scott is offering "problem-spaces" as a way of characterizing shifts in political framings and imaginaries over time, but I want to suggest that this formulation is immensely useful in thinking about the running interactions among differently configured movements.

12. Chakrabarty, *Provincializing Europe*, 71, 83.

13. Here I am alluding to Louis Althusser's argument that various aspects of contemporary social systems while operating semi-autonomously ultimately are overdetermined by the underlying structure of capitalism, which shapes their dynamics "in the last instance." See Althusser and Balibar, *Reading Capital*.

14. Wynter's arguments about the global character of modernity, the role of blackness in it, dominant conceptions of the human, and possibilities for a new sociogenic understanding that can supplant current (racializing) evolutionary paradigms are quite complex, layered, and shifting in how they're articulated across her oeuvre. I will risk being seen as simply misunderstanding her work in the interest of highlighting what seem to me to be particular structural orientations (or orientations toward structural explanations) that result in formulations that tend to efface or even foreclose engagement with Indigenous peoples' sovereignty and self-determination. For recent engagements with Wynter's work, see Jackson, *Creole Indigeneity*; King, "In the Clearing"; McKittrick, *Demonic Grounds*; McKittrick, *Sylvia Wynter*; Sexton, "The *Vel* of Slavery"; Snorton, *Black on Both Sides*; Walcott, *Queer Returns*; Weheliye, *Habeas Viscus*.

15. Wynter, "Unsettling the Coloniality of Being/Power/Truth/Freedom," 260.

16. Wynter, "Unsettling the Coloniality of Being/Power/Truth/Freedom," 291.

17. Wynter, "Unsettling the Coloniality of Being/Power/Truth/Freedom," 296.

18. McKittrick *Demonic Grounds*, 135.

19. Wynter, "On How We Mistook the Map for the Territory," 109.

20. Wynter, "On How We Mistook the Map for the Territory," 115.

21. Scott, "The Re-Enchantment of Humanism," 136.

22. Walcott, "Genres of Human," 186. See Kamugisha, "The Black Experience of New World Coloniality"; Thomas, "*Marronnons*/Let's Maroon."

23. Wynter, "Unsettling the Coloniality of Being/Power/Truth/Freedom," 301, 266. For similar statements elsewhere in Wynter's work, see Wynter, "1492," 37, 39, 41; Wynter, "On How We Mistook the Map for the Territory," 126; Scott, "The Re-Enchantment of Humanism," 177.

24. Wynter, "1492," 7.

25. Wynter, "1492," 8. Wynter argues for a sociogenic understanding of humans as generating particular possibilities for their own social existence, one that builds on but exceeds the biogenic understanding of biological species-being, and she draws on the notion of the sociogenic as articulated in the work of Frantz Fanon. For discussion of the

relationship between Wynter's version of the sociogenic and Fanon's, though, see Marriott, "Inventions of Existence."

26. Wynter, "1492," 49. In this essay, Wynter presents the Columbian encounter as an epochal event in human history that makes possible a shifted understanding of being human, one that not only is "degodded" but that can engage with the physical and social dynamics of our existence as a species.

Elsewhere, she suggests of 1492 and its aftermaths, "That Word, while an 'imperializing Word,' is also the enactment of the first purely de-godded, and therefore in this sense, emancipatory conception of being human in the history of our species. And it is that discontinuity that is going to make the idea of laws of Nature, and with it the new order of cognition that is the natural sciences, possible. So there can be no going back to a before-that-Word," also suggesting that "every society that has ever existed" prior to that moment had been centered on "theological absolutism" and, therefore, that "we have to recognize the dimensions of the breakthroughs that these first humanisms made possible at the level of human cognition, and therefore of the possibility of our eventual emancipation, of our eventual full autonomy, as humans." See Scott, "The Re-Enchantment of Humanism," 159, 177–78, 195.

27. Tuck and Wang, "Decolonization Is Not a Metaphor," 7.

28. This potential in Wynter's analysis becomes explicit in some recent engagements with her work. For example, in Nandita Sharma's essay "Strategic Anti-Essentialism: Decolonizing Decolonization," Native peoples and assertions of indigeneity purportedly "imagine native societies *as if* the category of native was not, itself, borne from a colonizing desire for power and the strategic need to foster hierarchical difference," while also forgetting that "all colonized people were variously identified as 'the' natives in order to signal their *lack of membership* in the *propter nos* of the colonizers." "Native"-ness, then, can only signify a racialized status within processes of colonization, one that is misrecognized as a basis for anti-colonial political claims. Sharma further claims, "Each particularistic 'we' is racialized, ethnicized, and, increasingly, nationalized." See Sharma, "Strategic Anti-Essentialism," 165–66, 174. Similarly, drawing on Wynter's unpublished manuscript "Black Metamorphosis," Katherine McKittrick argues that "the radical affirmation of black life [should] be sought and claimed outside colonial—land-settling and land-claiming and land-exploiting and genocidal—paradigms," further suggesting that "spatial claims" "are always, without our present system of knowledge, decidedly ethnically absolutist claims" ("Rebellion/Invention/Groove," 85–86).

29. Grande, *Red Pedagogy*, 49. For efforts to think an antiracist commons, although in ways that do not necessarily respond in sustained fashion to Grande's critique, see Dillon, *New World Drama*; Nelson, *Commons Democracy*.

30. Wynter, "1492," 13. As Wynter suggests, "While it is drawn between the Indo-European somatotype, on the one hand, and the Bantu-African somatotype on the other, all other non-white groups will be co-classified with the latter, if to less extreme and varying degrees." She adds, "The projected value difference between Indo-European peoples and all native peoples" is "at its most total, between white and black." See Scott, "The Re-Enchantment of Humanism," 177.

31. Alexander Weheliye argues, "Wynter's oeuvre facilitates the analysis of the relay between different forms of subjugation, because in it the human operates as a relational

ontological totality. Therefore, the Man versus Human battle does not dialectically sublate the specificity of the other struggles but articulates them in this open totality so as to abolish Man and liberate all of humanity rather than specific groups" (*Habeas Viscus*, 29). However, for whom and from what perspective is "the human" an "ontological totality," rather than, say, a nonhierarchical and shifting collection of peoples in various formations, alignments, and overlappings? How, for example, is Indigenous peoplehood articulated within this vision of a human totality, and does the attendant conceptualization of *liberation* encompass Indigenous self-articulations, knowledges, and aspirations (or are they in their "specificity" understood as just in the interest of "specific groups" rather than "all of humanity")?

32. Wynter, "On How We Mistook the Map for the Territory," 124–25.

33. Wynter, "On How We Mistook the Map for the Territory," 129.

34. Scott, "The Re-Enchantment of Humanism," 183.

35. Notably, when Wynter speaks of having confused the "map" with the "territory," the latter term refers not to specific lands and waters but, instead, to the "governing sociogenic code" through which the dominant, Western "ethno-class" defines the human in its own image. See Wynter, "On How We Mistook the Map for the Territory," 117.

36. Coulthard, *Red Skin, White Masks*, 7, 152.

37. Coulthard, *Red Skin, White Masks*, 3.

38. Coulthard, *Red Skin, White Masks*, 36.

39. Coulthard, *Red Skin, White Masks*, 12–13.

40. Byrd, *The Transit of Empire*, xx, 54.

41. Coulthard, *Red Skin, White Masks*, 14.

42. Ahmed, *Queer Phenomenology*, 38.

43. On Indigenous resurgence, see Simpson, *As We Have Always Done*.

44. Amadahy and Lawrence, "Indigenous Peoples and Black People in Canada," 130–31.

45. I recognize that any given account of Indigenous or Black political theorizing could be subject to similar criticism for the ways it may homogenize or disregard the variety of forms of theorizing among Indigenous peoples or people of African descent. While I seek to mark what seem to me to be pronounced differences between Indigenous and Black political imaginaries (particularly in Anglophone sites in the Americas), the dynamics of orientation and translation I explore could also be employed in thinking about the negotiation of differences among Indigenous modes of political critique and imagination and those among Black modes of political critique and imagination, even though that *amongness* matters in ways I discuss further.

46. Leroy, "Black History in Occupied Territory."

47. Day, "Being or Nothingness," 102.

48. Day, "Being or Nothingness," 113. Leroy offers a similar formulation: "Global intellectual exchanges among the architects of Jim Crow, colonialism, white nationalism, and settler colonialism ensured that while these processes retained their distinction, they operated only in relationship to one another. In a word, empire has functioned by making its victims both Indian and black" ("Black History in Occupied Territory").

49. In a similar kind of move, Lisa Lowe argues that "liberalism comprises a multifaceted, flexible, and contradictory set of provisions that at once rationalizes settler

appropriation and removal differently than it justifies either the subjection of human beings as enslaved property, or the extraction of labor from indentured emigrants, however much these processes share a colonial past and an ongoing colonial present," indicating "linked, but not identical, genealogies of liberalism" (*The Intimacies of Four Continents*, 10–11). Like Coulthard's discussion of settlement as providing the "background field" of "convergence" for various modes of oppression, Lowe collates these varied vectors of violence into "liberalism" as an overarching matrix and explanatory structure through which they can be articulated to each other within something like a world-system—"as braided parts of a world process" (*The Intimacies of Four Continents*, 76). These various strands, or logics, are cast as part of an encompassing formation called "liberalism," with its own organizing (if multifaceted) set of principles and procedures. Again, though, the question I seek to raise is not so much whether such an account is *right*, whether it can make valuable truth-claims, as what does such an intellectual and political maneuver mean for seeking to generate relations among disparately oriented movements and political imaginaries? What are the costs of such structural unification?

50. Hong, *Death beyond Disavowal*, 7–8.

51. Lorde, *Sister Outsider*, 111, 115.

52. Simpson, *Mohawk Interruptus*, 21–22. See also Barker, *Native Acts*; Dennison, *Colonial Entanglement*; Engle, *The Elusive Promise of Indigenous Development*; Povinelli, *The Cunning of Recognition*. For critiques of multicultural notions difference not focused on indigeneity, see Ferguson, *The Reorder of Things*; Melamed, *Represent and Destroy*; Puar, *Terrorist Assemblages*; Reddy, *Freedom with Violence*.

53. Lorde, *Sister Outsider*, 127–28.

54. In this vein, forms of *unknowing* among oppositional movements that might arise out of their particular orientations can be understood as a block to solidarity and as participating in forms of oppression without conceptualizing such unknowing solely as something like the sanctioned ignorance of the privileged to be remediated through forms of structural modeling that seek to incorporate such varied struggles into a single (conceptual) system. On colonial unknowing in the U.S. context, see Vimalassery et al., "On Colonial Unknowing."

55. Lorde, *Sister Outsider*, 112.

56. On the process of "becoming sensitive" rather than searching for "mastery," see Singh, *Unthinking Mastery*.

57. Carastathis, *Intersectionality*, 184–85. On the history of distinguishing between "Black" and "Indian" as legal and conceptual categories, see Baker, *Anthropology and the Racial Politics of Culture*; Ben-zvi, *Native Land Talk*; Evans, *Before Cultures*; Forbes, *Africans and Native Americans*; Mandell, *Tribe, Race, History*; Miles, *Ties That Bind*.

58. Carastathis, *Intersectionality*, 187–88. Carastathis further observes, "With respect to identity, one crucial problem that Crenshaw's intersectional critique reveals is that categories of oppression are defined in terms of 'invisibly' intersectional experiences, namely, those of subgroups that are relatively privileged with respect to other members of the broader group," adding, "In contrast to 'thick' members, transparent members are those who perceive themselves as paradigmatic of the group" (*Intersectionality*, 65).

59. Hancock, *Intersectionality*, 71.

60. Collins and Bilge, *Intersectionality*, 27.

61. Mays, "From Flint to Standing Rock."

62. Carastathis, *Intersectionality*, 124, 188, 214.

63. Collins and Bilge, *Intersectionality*, 70.

64. Hancock, *Intersectionality*, 134.

65. Cathy Cohen cautions against seeing existing categories of identity as merely normative or as blockages to more capacious theorizing. She notes, "Queer theorizing that calls for the elimination of fixed categories of sexual identity seems to ignore the ways in which some traditional social identities and communal ties can, in fact, be important to one's survival," adding, "In those stable categories and named communities whose histories have been structured by shared resistance to oppression, I find relative degrees of safety and security" ("Punks, Bulldaggers, and Welfare Queens," 35).

66. Glissant, *Poetics of Relation*, 189–91.

67. Tuck and Yang, "Decolonization Is Not a Metaphor," 28, 35. Garza et al., "A Her-Story of the #BlackLivesMatter Movement."

68. I would like to differentiate the kind of relation/translation I am discussing from the project of *comparison*. With respect to putting various political struggles into relation, Weheliye observes, "While we should most definitely bring into focus the relays betwixt and between the genocide of indigenous populations in the Americas, the transatlantic slave trade, Asian American indentured servitude, and Latino immigration among many factors, we cannot do so in the grammar of comparison" (*Habeas Viscus*, 13), and the reason to avoid comparison as such is that "the twinning of comparativity and specificity . . . fails to probe the foundations upon which these particularities are put and kept in place. Instead, we might do well to conceive humanity as a relational ontological totality, however fractured this totality might be" (32). Put another way, comparison envisions a neutral, supervening framework in which groups/movements/social struggles can be addressed in their "specificity," thus reducing the analyses offered by such movements to claims about groups' particularities (reproducing dominant modes of identity-production) rather than understanding them as expressions of knowledge about how social systems work. However, avoiding such reifying comparison need not require the positing of a single, encompassing "totality." As I have argued, positing such a totality actually can short-circuit the kinds of open-ended relation toward which Weheliye gestures. Instead, I am suggesting that the analyses, knowledges, and normative principles offered by various movements may be true while also being nonidentical, and that the process of engagement and accountability requires grappling with differences without a notion or framework of totality on which to fall back for ontological/normative security.

69. Hancock observes, "Intersectionality possesses a distinct account of reality (a.k.a. 'ontology') and thus it requires its own epistemological tenets to adjudicate among knowledge claims" (*Intersectionality*, 106). Again, though, one could inquire what kinds of backgrounds and orientations implicitly are at play in that ontology and to what extent they translate formations, movements, struggles into their terms in ways not acknowledged as such. As Carastathis suggests, "it is worth noting that 'intersectionality' and 'decolonization' circulate in not dissimilar ways in the settler academy, and are often invoked as an alibi, ostensibly to guarantee the ethical or political commitments underpinning

intellectual projects, or the 'inclusiveness' of curricula, academic disciplines, and institutions": "Specifically, facile appeals to 'decolonization' seem to evade the question of land, and the genocidal violence against Indigenous people that maintaining colonial state control over Indigenous land bases entails" (*Intersectionality*, 229).

70. This kind of connection might also be characterized, in Lowe's terms, as *intimacy* (although bearing in mind the critique offered earlier of the effort to collate varied forms of oppression into a singular system or network). This approach might also be redescribed in terms of Bruno Latour's theorization of networks and refusal of invocations of supervening structure—"society" and "the social"—as an explanatory mechanism through which to understand processes of regularity and change. See Latour, *Reassembling the Social*.

71. For a philosophical account of nondiscrete dualism, see Waters, "Language Matters."

72. For discussion of how European notions of sovereignty arise from colonial dynamics, see Anghie, *Imperialism, Sovereignty and the Making of International Law*; MacMillan, *Sovereignty and Possession in the English New World*; Manela, *The Wilsonian Moment*; Mignolo, *The Darker Side of the Renaissance*; Singh, *Unthinking Mastery*; Tully, *An Approach to Political Philosophy*; Yirush, *Settlers, Liberty, and Empire*.

73. For discussion of the complexities of contemporary cessions of quasi-governmental power to corporations within circumscribed areas and the limits for many states in exerting such authority over what occurs within their borders, see Alexander, *Pedagogies of Crossing*; Anghie, *Imperialism, Sovereignty and the Making of International Law*; Bogues, "Politics, Nation, and PostColony"; Cheah, *Inhuman Conditions*; Dubois, *Haiti*; Ong, *Neoliberalism as Exception*.

74. See Cohen, *A Body Worth Defending*; Harris, "Whiteness as Property"; Macpherson, *The Political Theory of Possessive Individualism*; Moreton-Robinson, *The White Possessive*.

75. Here I borrow from Jean Dennison's language, and I return to her work shortly.

76. Barker, "For Whom Sovereignty Matters," 17–18. On this history, see Anaya, *Indigenous Peoples in International Law*; Clech Lâm, *At the Edge of the State*; Engle, *The Elusive Promise of Indigenous Development*; Niezen, *The Origins of Indigenism*.

77. Barker, "For Whom Sovereignty Matters," 6.

78. For overviews of the various subordinating legal statuses to which Native peoples have been subject in the United States, see Barker, *Native Acts*; Bruyneel, *The Third Space of Sovereignty*; Duthu, *American Indians and the Law*; Rifkin, *Manifesting America*; Wilkins, *American Indian Sovereignty and the U.S. Supreme Court*; Wilkins and Lomawaima, *Uneven Ground*.

79. Dennison, *Colonial Entanglement*, 8.

80. Barker, "For Whom Sovereignty Matters," 16; Dennison, *Colonial Entanglement*, 89. Simpson argues, "in its theoretical and analytic guises 'culture' is defined in anthropological terms most consistently by its proximity to difference, not its sovereignty, its right to govern, to own, or to labor" (*Mohawk Interruptus*, 101–2).

81. On the differences between Anglophone modes of settler colonialism and those at play in Hispanophone and Lusophone modes of settler colonialism in the Americas, see Brysk, *From Tribal Village to Global Village*; Engle, *The Elusive Promise of Indigenous*

Development; Seed, *American Pentimento*. On the dangers of treating Anglophone models as the only ones, see Saldaña-Portillo, "How Many Mexicans [Is] a Horse Worth?"

82. Turner, *This Is Not a Peace Pipe*, 111.

83. Dennison, *Colonial Entanglement*, 131.

84. See also Deloria and Lytle, *The Nations Within*; Doerfler, *Those Who Belong*; Lemont, *American Indian Constitutional Reform and the Rebuilding of Native Nations*. For a futurist account that portrays extant forms of tribal sovereignty as an extension of settler authority but that offers the White Earth Constitution as an open-ended model of Native democratic practice unbounded by settler-state frames, see Vizenor, *Treaty Shirts*.

85. Carroll, *Roots of Our Renewal*, 24, 17, 175, 168. For other studies that investigate the indigenization of state frameworks, see Duarte, *Network Sovereignty*; Pasternak, *Grounded Authority*; Powell, *Landscapes of Power*; Richland, *Arguing with Tradition*.

86. Barker, "For Whom Sovereignty Matters," 19.

87. Simpson, *Dancing on Our Turtle's Back*, 17–18.

88. Simpson, *Dancing on Our Turtle's Back*, 89. At one point, Simpson notes, "While Nishnaabeg sovereignty was *sui generis*, it was also territorial. Nishnaabeg people were not wandering around vast expanses of land. While the boundaries around that land were much more fluid than that of modern states, there was a territory that was defined by Nishnaabeg language, philosophy, way of life, and political culture" (*Dancing on Our Turtle's Back*, 89).

89. Simpson, *Mohawk Interruptus*, 159, 175.

90. On Indigenous sovereignty as a mode of interdependence with other peoples and entities, rather than self-possessive autonomy, see Cattelino, *High Stakes*; Duarte, *Network Sovereignty*; Mackey, *Unsettled Expectations*; Powell, *Landscapes of Power*; Simpson, *As We Have Always Done*.

91. Brand, *A Map to the Door of No Return*, 5.

92. Hartman, *Lose Your Mother*, 87, 198, 34, 38, 44.

93. Brand, *A Map to the Door of No Return*, 35; Hartman, *Lose Your Mother*, 5, 18.

94. Brand further refers to the "Door of No Return" as the "passport" carried by Black people in the diaspora, later suggesting, "Diplomatic relations. That is what any of us in the Diaspora has with these nations we were born in, the ones we live in, and the ones we're supposed to belong to: the most fragile diplomatic relations" (*A Map to the Door of No Return*, 48–49, 83).

95. Pinto, *Difficult Diasporas*, 93, 4.

96. Amadahy and Lawrence, "Indigenous Peoples and Black People in Canada," 130.

97. Habiba, *Troubling the Family*, 52, 55. On the role of notions of Black familial pathology in shaping urban policy in the 1960s, see also Hinton, *From the War on Poverty to the War on Crime*, 63–95. For questions about the analytical and demographic coherence of the concept of the "ghetto," see Small, "Four Reasons to Abandon the Idea of 'the Ghetto.'"

98. Massey and Denton, *American Apartheid*, 46.

99. On these dynamics, see also Cohen, *Boundaries of Blackness*; Davis, *City of Quartz*; Lee, *Urban Triage*; Massey and Denton, *American Apartheid*; Pattillo, *Black on the Block*; Peterson and Krivo, *Divergent Social Worlds*; Sharkey, *Stuck in Place*; Taylor, *From*

#BlackLivesMatter; Wacquant, *Punishing the Poor*. On thinking contemporary urban space as part of "plantation futures," see McKittrick, "Plantation Futures."

100. Patrick Sharkey traces what he terms "inherited inequality," observing that "*the same families have experienced the consequences of life in the most disadvantaged environments over multiple generations*," at rates exceeding 70 percent of the African American population, further observing that such communities "have borne the brunt of four decades of economic restructuring and political disinvestment" (*Stuck in Place*, 9, 26, 47).

101. In *Demonic Grounds*, McKittrick argues that "the only recognized geographic relevancy permitted to black subjects in the diaspora is that of dispossession and social segregation," adding that such de facto assessments of Black placelessness depend on "reifying the ideological assumption that blackness is equated with the ungeographic" (*Demonic Grounds*, 4, 14). See also King, "The Labor of (Re)reading Plantation Landscapes Fungible(ly)"; Ng'weno, "Can Ethnicity Replace Race?"; Perry, *Black Women against the Land Grab*. On the role of discourses of "negative birthright" in denials of Black belonging in the Americas, see Ben-zvi, *Native Land Talk*.

102. Brand, *A Map to the Door of No Return*, 67–68. Brand does raise the issue of indigeneity and Indigenous peoplehood at several points, but these moments tend either to juxtapose Indigenous emplacedness with Black placelessness or to cast Indigenous peoples as a kind of exterminated prehistory for the violence of the present. See Brand, *A Map to the Door of No Return*, 151, 197–98, 219–21. These moments do not really explore how Indigenous and non-native Black people might engage with each other around their discrepant relations to the places of the Americas.

103. Hartman, *Lose Your Mother*, 5, 234.

104. Ellis, *Territories of the Soul*, 2. Hartman says of the community of Gwolu, formed by those who had escaped from the sphere of slave raiding, "Newcomers were welcome. It didn't matter that they weren't kin or that they spoke a different language, because genealogy didn't matter . . . , building a community did," adding, "'We' was the collectivity they built from the ground up, not one they had inherited, not one that others had imposed" (*Lose Your Mother*, 225).

105. Wilder, *Freedom Time*, 88–89.

106. Bonilla, *Non-Sovereign Futures*, 11. While Bonilla explores early-twenty-first-century forms of labor organizing envisioned as enacting marronage, Wilder addresses mid-twentieth-century forms of Black political imagination, particularly in the work of Aimé Césaire and Léopold Senghor, that sought to avoid "falling into the trap of national autarchy" by emphasizing the potential for "decentralized, interdependent, plural, and transnational" formations that paralleled and could recast the structures of "imperialism itself": "their interventions proceeded from the belief that colonial peoples cannot presume to know a priori which political arrangements would best allow them to pursue substantive freedom" (*Freedom Time*, 2).

107. On the ways articulations of Caribbean postcolonial citizenship can efface ongoing legacies of slavery and colonialism, see Alexander, *Pedagogies of Crossing*; Bogues, "Politics, Nation, and PostColony"; Kamugisha, "The Coloniality of Citizenship in the Contemporary Anglophone Caribbean"; Scott, *Conscripts of Modernity*; Thomas, *Exceptional Violence*.

108. Bonilla, *Non-Sovereign Futures*, xiii–xiv; Wilder, *Freedom Time*, 19.

109. Stephens, *Black Empire*, 42, 54–55. Richard Iton suggests that "there is an autodiasporic quality to black life . . . that results from the impossibility of aligning culture and the borders of nation-states" (*In Search of the Black Fantastic*, 202).

110. Sexton, "The *Vel* of Slavery," 9–11.

111. Weheliye, *Habeas Viscus*, 31.

112. Sexton, "The *Vel* of Slavery," 11. For a more geographic analysis of the Black body as a mode of spatial organization and scale setting, specifically with respect to the auction block, see McKittrick, *Demonic Grounds,* 65–90.

113. Sexton, "The *Vel* of Slavery," 11; Weheliye, *Habeas Viscus*, 124.

114. Wilderson, *Red, White, and Black*, 160, 181, 235.

115. However, one might ask how a focus on the Black body can efface questions of collective place making. As McKittrick suggests, "The stories of black women contain in them meaningful geographic tenets, but these are often reduced to the seeable flesh and unseeable geographic knowledges" (*Demonic Grounds*, 45).

116. As Emma Battell Lowman and Adam J. Barker observe, "When Indigenous people assert that the land itself is important, beyond value as property or the source of resources for extraction, they are derided for being 'mystical' or 'nostalgic' or 'essentialist,' all of which are deflections to avoid actually taking seriously the challenging relationships with the land asserted in Indigenous identities" (*Settler*, 57).

117. Glissant, *Poetics of Relation*, 143–44, 8.

118. Glissant, *Poetics of Relation*, 146–47. I further address such claims to the extinction of Indigenous peoples in the Caribbean in chapter 4.

119. Best and Hartman, "Fugitive Justice," 5.

120. Alfred, "Sovereignty," 43.

121. Goeman, *Mark My Words*, 28, 5.

122. See Barker, *Native Acts*; Denetdale, "Chairmen, Presidents, and Princesses"; Lawrence, *"Real" Indians and Others*; Wilkins and Wilkins, *Dismembered*.

123. The discussion below draws on the following: Adams, *Who Belongs?*; Byrd, *The Transit of Empire*, 117–46; Cramer, *Cash, Color, Colonialism*; Den Ouden and O'Brien, *Recognition, Sovereignty Struggles, and Indigenous Rights in the United States*; Garroutte, *Real Indians*; Justice, "Go Away, Water!"; Klopotek, *Recognition Odysseys*; Saunt, *Black, White, and Indian*; Sturm, *Blood Politics*.

124. "The Official Guidelines to the Federal Acknowledgment Regulations," accessed December 27 2017, https://www.bia.gov/sites/bia.gov/files/assets/as-ia/ofa/admindocs/OfficialGuidelines.pdf.

125. King, "In the Clearing," 22.

126. King, "In the Clearing," 121–22.

127. For examples, see Asaka, *Tropical Freedom*; Goffman, *On the Run*; Goldstein, "Finance and Foreclosure in the Colonial Present"; Shabazz, *Spatializing Blackness*.

128. King, "In the Clearing," 206.

129. For discussion of how settler colonialism can create a sense of located whiteness that enables non-native people of color to be cast as placeless or as properly belonging elsewhere, see Asaka, *Tropical Freedom*; Day, *Alien Capital*.

130. King, "In the Clearing," 209.

131. Amadahy and Lawrence, "Indigenous Peoples and Black People in Canada," 105. As Yael Ben-zvi argues with respect to the relation between Native-settler and Black-white binaries, "The mutual exclusiveness of these binaries derived from the fact that both African Americans and Native Americans protested the settler regime almost as though the other group had nothing to do with the oppressive mechanisms against which each fought. This choice often stemmed from Indigenous peoples' acceptance of settlers' perceptions of slaves as property and from African Americans' acceptance of settler [sic] perceptions of Indigenous peoples as vanishing savages" (*Native Land Talk*, 209).

132. Amadahy and Lawrence, "Indigenous Peoples and Black People in Canada," 105. 120, 122.

133. For example, Nikhil Pal Singh argues, "If U.S. settler sovereignty begins and ends with Indians, it lingers in complex ways on black and blackness. In contrast to the threat of otherness on the frontier, which was largely eliminated, blackness, cultivated and reproduced under the auspices of the slave regime, remained a permanent threat" (*Race and America's Long War*, 143).

134. Tuck and Yang, "Decolonization Is Not a Metaphor," 3.

135. Day, "Being or Nothingness," 118. Here Day is playing off of Fred Moten's analysis of blackness.

136. In this vein, one might point to the manifesto of the Combahee River Collective and the ways it continues to circulate in contemporary scholarly and activist work. A collection of Black women (mostly lesbian) intellectuals, the group issued a statement in 1977 laying out the terms of the "interlocking oppressions" experienced by Black women that conventionally is understood as playing a large role in providing the intellectual infrastructure for what would become the notion of *intersectionality*. In the statement, they observe, "If Black women were free, it would mean that everyone else would have to be free since our freedom would necessitate the destruction of all the systems of oppression." See Taylor, *How We Get Free*, 22–23. This claim often is repeated in various ways as a means of highlighting that the oppression of Black women cannot be understood as a marginal issue within struggles for social justice and that, instead, addressing such oppression involves analyzing and challenging the dominant sociopolitical structures that govern contemporary life. For examples, see Taylor, *From #BlackLivesMatter*, 194; Weheliye, *Habeas Viscus*, 23. However, it remains unclear how freeing Black women *necessarily* engages questions of Indigenous peoplehood and self-determination or dismantles settler colonial claims to Indigenous homelands. Justin Leroy takes up this formulation and asks what it would mean to say, "When Indigenous peoples get free, everybody gets free?" further inquiring, "Why is it any harder to imagine a politics grounded in principles of Indigenous sovereignty than the reformation of a white supremacist government?" See Byrd and Leroy, "Structures and Events."

137. Amadahy and Lawrence, "Indigenous Peoples and Black People in Canada," 107.

138. On whiteness as possession/property/ownership, see Asaka, *Tropical Freedom*; Day, *Alien Capital*; Harris, "Whiteness as Property"; Lipsitz, *The Possessive Investment in Whiteness*; Lowe, *The Intimacies of Four Continents*; Moreton-Robinson, *The White Possessive*.

139. To be clear, I am not suggesting that settler colonial studies, or the use of the concept of "settler colonialism," inherently centers Indigenous peoples and Indigenous self-determination. For discussion of the potential limits of settler colonial studies as a specific scholarly formation, see Vimalassery et al., "On Colonial Unknowing." Moreover, discussion of settlement can foreground non-natives even while gesturing toward Indigenous struggles and sociopolitical formations. For otherwise excellent and important recent studies that tend in this direction, see Asaka, *Tropical Freedom*; Day, *Alien Capital*; Dillon, *New World Drama*; Lowe, *The Intimacies of Four Continents*; Singh, *Race and America's Long War*. What I am suggesting, though, is that invocation of the term "settler" introduces the issue of Native–non-native relations and that invoking settler colonialism as a framework at least marks the significance of Indigenous landedness and governance for political issues, movements, negotiations.

140. Lowman and Barker, *Settler*, 72.

141. Similarly, Tuck and Yang note, "colonial subjects who are displaced by external colonialism, as well as racialized and minoritized by internal colonialism, still occupy and settle stolen Indigenous land. Settlers are diverse, not just of white European descent, and include people of color, even from other colonial contexts" ("Decolonization Is Not a Metaphor," 7).

142. Tuck and Yang, "Decolonization Is Not a Metaphor," 19.

143. Byrd, *The Transit of Empire*, xxxix, xxxiv, 39.

144. Jackson, *Creole Indigeneity*, 44, 212.

145. See also Asaka, *Tropical Freedom*; Ben-zvi, *Native Land Talk*.

146. Leroy, "Black History in Occupied Territory."

147. Singh, *Black Is a Country*, 44, 53–54.

148. On the whiteness of the international system, see Anghie, *Imperialism, Sovereignty and the Making of International Law*; Kazanjian, *The Colonizing Trick*; Manela, *The Wilsonian Moment*; Silva, *Toward a Global Idea of Race*; Stephens, *Black Empire*; Wilder, *Freedom Time*.

149. See also Feldman, *A Shadow over Palestine*; Hartman, *Lose Your Mother*; Higashida, *Black Internationalist Feminism*; Iton, *In Search of the Black Fantastic*; Kelley, *Freedom Dreams*; Von Eschen, *Race against Empire*.

150. Young, *Soul Power*, 207.

151. Edwards, *The Practice of Diaspora*, 5, 23. See also Ellis, *Territories of the Soul*; Pinto, *Difficult Diasporas*; Stephens, *Black Empire*; Wilder, *Freedom Time*.

152. Young, *Soul Power*, 154–55, 157.

153. Singh, *Black Is a Country*, 51, 59–60. See also Feldman, *A Shadow over Palestine*.

154. Higashida, *Black Internationalist Feminism*, 2, 19.

155. McKittrick, *Demonic Grounds*, 2–3.

156. For example, Higashida notes the importance of formulations offered by Indigenous peoples regarding lands claimed by New Zealand and Australia to Audre Lorde's conceptualization of Black national collectivity, but Higashida does not address how, or whether, Lorde put those into play in addressing relations between African Americans and Native Americans. See Higashida, *Black Internationalist Feminism*, 139–45.

157. Scott, *Conscripts of Modernity*, 19.

158. In talking about speculation and the speculative in these ways, though, I should clarify that I am not addressing the philosophical conversations around speculative realism (the idea that reality as such, especially the existence of entities within it, cannot be understood as predicated on human perception and that speculation provides a means of seeking to know in ways that do not privilege human epistemology or being) or modal realism (the analysis of the ontological possibility of there being multiple worlds, either abstract or actual). On these areas of study, see Berto and Plebani, *Ontology and Metaontology*; DeLanda and Harman, *The Rise of Realism*; Shaviro, *The Universe of Things*.

159. On the possibility of relativistic truth claims, see Rovane, *The Metaphysics and Ethics of Relativism*. However, the model of "alternatives" that she suggests does not seem to me to mean that those operating in different normative "worlds," in her terms, cannot make normative claims on each other or that such claims cannot be registered and engaged in meaningful ways, as I have been discussing through notions of accountability and solidarity. On the relationship between speculation and forms of accountability and ethics in practice, see Bellacasa, *Matters of Care*.

160. Everett, *Digital Diaspora*, 19; Nelson, "Introduction," 1. On histories of African American scientific exploration in the nineteenth century, see Rusert, *Fugitive Science*.

161. Dery, "Black to the Future," 180, 190–91. Similarly, Walter Mosley insists, "For black people in particular, the future is all we have because the past has been taken away from us and the present is defined in certain ways." See Brady, *Conversations with Walter Mosley*, 108. Octavia Butler observes of her response to the question often posed to her, "what does your work have to do with being Black?", "It's like saying that somehow, we are set apart from the future and are a part of only our own past." See Frances, *Conversations with Octavia Butler*, 64.

162. Jackson and Moody-Freeman, "The Black Imagination and the Genres," 1.

163. O'Brien, *Firsting and Lasting*, 105, xxii.

164. See also Barker, *Native Acts*; Deloria, *Indians in Unexpected Places*; Garroutte, *Real Indians*; Lyons, *X-marks*; Povinelli, *The Cunning of Recognition*; Raibmon, *Authentic Indians*; Rifkin, *Beyond Settler Time*.

165. O'Brien, *Firsting and Lasting*, 123.

166. On supposed Native technophobia and claims of the absence of Indigenous science, see Adare, *"Indian" Stereotypes in TV Science Fiction*; Duarte, *Network Sovereignty*; Gaertner, "Indigenous in Cyberspace"; Landzelius, "Introduction"; Nixon, "Indigenous Artists and the Dystopian Now"; Roanhorse et al., "Decolonizing Science Fiction and Imagining Futures"; Sandvig, "Connection at Ewiiapaayp Mountain"; Srinivasan, "Indigenous, Ethnic and Cultural Articulations of New Media."

167. Cornum, "The Space NDN's Star Map"; Little Badger, "Né Łe." See also Roanhorse et al., "Decolonizing Science Fiction and Imagining Futures."

168. Taylor, *Take Us to Your Chief*, ix. Daniel Heath Justice similarly suggests the power of "sharing stories of possibility beyond the grim dust of what *was* to a hopeful possibility of what *could be*" ("The Boys Who Became Hummingbirds," 57).

169. Bahng, *Migrant Futures*, 1, 4–5. See also Dillon, *Fugitive Life*.

170. Eshun, "Further Considerations on Afrofuturism," 290. In chapter 3, I address Walter Mosley's analysis of such technologies and the mappings they generate. On such

data gathering and aggregation, see Browne, *Dark Matters*; Lyon, *Surveillance Studies*; Magnet, *When Biometrics Fail*; Puar, *Terrorist Assemblages*.

171. See Baucom, *Specters of the Atlantic*; Belich, *Replenishing the Earth*; Hartman, *Lose Your Mother*; Rockwell, *Indian Affairs and the Administrative State in the Nineteenth Century*.

172. See Browne, *Dark Matters*; Cacho, *Social Death*; Coulthard, *Red Skin, White Masks*; Kino-nda-niimi Collective, *The Winter We Danced*; Nixon, "Indigenous Artists and the Dystopian Now"; Shabazz, *Spatializing Blackness*.

173. Eshun, "Further Considerations on Afrofuturism," 290.

174. Kilgore, *Astrofuturism*, 221; carrington, *Speculative Blackness*, 92. See also Adare, *"Indian" Stereotypes in TV Science Fiction*; Cornum, "The Space NDN's Star Map"; Lavender, *Race in American Science Fiction*; Marez, *Farm Worker Futurism*; Vint, *Bodies of Tomorrow*.

175. Yaszek, Afrofuturism, Science Fiction, and the History of the Future," 47. See also Womack, *Afrofuturism*.

176. On speculation as a powerful mode of Black knowledge production, see Dubey, "Speculative Fictions of Slavery"; Rusert, *Fugitive Science*; Schalk, *Bodyminds Reimagined*.

177. Dillon, "Imagining Indigenous Futurisms," 8–10. Similarly, Lindsay Nixon observes, "Armed with spirit and the teachings of our ancestors, all our relations behind us, we are living the Indigenous future. We are the descendants of a future imaginary that has already passed; the outcome of the intentions, resistance, and survivance of our ancestors" ("Indigenous Artists and the Dystopian Now").

178. Kelley, *Freedom Dreams*, viii. Similarly, Iton invokes the idea of "the black fantastic" as a means of referring "to the minor-key sensibilities generated from the experiences of the underground, the vagabond, and those constituencies marked as deviant" (*In Search of the Black Fantastic*, 16).

179. Muñoz, *Cruising Utopia*, 12, 22.

180. Jameson, *Archaeologies of the Future*, 231–32.

181. Jameson, *Archaeologies of the Future*, xii; Muñoz, *Cruising Utopia*, 13. Muñoz specifically understands such potentials as and through queerness. He writes, "Queerness is not yet here. Queerness is an ideality. Put another way, we are not yet queer. We may never touch queerness, but we can feel it as the warm illumination of a horizon imbued with potentiality. We have never been queer, yet queerness exists for us as an ideality that can be distilled from the past and used to imagine a future. The future is queerness's domain. Queerness is a structuring and educated mode of desiring that allows us to see and feel beyond the quagmire of the present" (*Cruising Utopia*, 1).

182. Delany, *The Jewel-Hinged Jaw*, 10–11. While Delany distances himself from this idea (see Delany, *Starboard Wine*, 204–5), his critique of it does not seem to me to capture the concept's potential and the ways it resonates with his ongoing discussion of how science fictional futures signify in and on the present.

183. Delany, *Starboard Wine*, 27.

184. Delany, *Starboard Wine*, 165, 8.

185. Delany, *Starboard Wine*, 14, 10, 26.

186. Delany, *Starboard Wine*, 196.

187. Delany, *Starboard Wine*, xviii, 118–19.

188. On such estrangement or defamiliarization in speculative writing, see also Bahng, *Migrant Futures*; Melzer, *Alien Constructions* ; Schalk, *Bodyminds Reimagined*.

189. Delany, *Starboard Wine*, 69, 74.

190. Ahmed, *Queer Phenomenology*, 5–6, 11.

191. Dery, "Black to the Future," 212; Dillon, "Beyond the Grim Dust of What *Was* to a Radiant Possibility of What *Could Be*," 9–10.

192. de la Cadena, *Earth Beings,* 4, 116.

193. Cornum notes that "Afrofuturists have looked to space as the site for black separation and liberation. If the space NDN is truly committed to being responsible to all our relations, it is imperative for our futurist vision to be in solidarity with and service to our fellow Afrofuturist space travelers" ("The Space NDN's Star Map"). I would suggest that the speculative perspective I'm elaborating is toward engendering such solidarity without requiring that varied struggles and historical/political trajectories need to be seen as unitary, or even structurally reconcilable.

194. María Puig de la Bellacasa suggests the importance of "mak[ing] of ethics a hands-on, ongoing process of recreation of 'as well as possible' relations" which "requires a speculative opening about what a possible involves," and such speculative care "stems from awareness of the efforts it takes to cultivate relatedness in diverseness" and cannot simply follow from "a theory that would serve as a 'recipe' for doing our encounters" (*Matters of Care*, 7, 79, 90).

2. FUNGIBLE BECOMING

1. King, "The Labor of (Re)reading Plantation Landscapes Fungible(ly)," 3–4. On the plasticities and porosities engendered by blackness, see also Allewaert, *Ariel's Ecology*; Best, *The Fugitive's Properties*; Moten, "The Case of Blackness"; Sharpe, *In the Wake*; Snorton, *Black on Both Sides*; Wilderson, *Red, White, and Black*.

2. See Bederman, *Manliness and Civilization*; Hartman, *Scenes of Subjection*; Ibrahim, *Troubling the Family*; Nyong'o, *The Amalgamation Waltz*; Pascoe, *What Comes Naturally*; Sexton, *Amalgamation Schemes*; Sharpe, *Monstrous Intimacies*; Stanley, *From Bondage to Contract*.

3. Habiba Ibrahim argues that the conception of interracial familialism that emerges in the wake of *Loving* takes part in the "paradoxical attempt by the state to alleviate its obligation toward racial, sexualized, and economic redress by privatizing these responsibilities through a new national focus on the family" (*Troubling the Family*, xxviii). On the conservative implications of the *Loving* decision, see also Pascoe, *What Comes Naturally*, 287–306; Somerville, "Queer *Loving*." When read in light of the Moynihan Report (1965), which interpreted the number of single-mother-led African American households as symptomatic of a general lag in Black development and proper integration into American society, the emergence of visions of multiracialism as a harbinger of anti-racist equality works in tandem with the demonization of blackness as a sign of backwardness and dysfunction. On the Moynihan Report, see Ibrahim, *Troubling the Family*, 43–80; King, "In the Clearing," 129–75.

4. Sexton, *Amalgamation Schemes*, 6, 156. As Christina Sharpe notes, cross-racial gene-alogical narratives often cast "readable progress [as] proximity to whiteness" in which the latter comes to function "as a gift, as (positive) inheritance" (*Monstrous Intimacies*, 13).

5. Nyong'o, *The Amalgamation Waltz*, 9, 31.

6. As Hortense Spillers famously argues, the presumptively self-contained, agential, property-owning white *body* needs to be understood as fundamentally disjunct from the corporealities engendered by enslavement—penetrable and disposable Black *flesh*. She says, "[B]efore the 'body' there is the 'flesh,' that zero degree of social conceptualization" ("Mama's Baby, Papa's Maybe," 206).

7. Weheliye, *Habeas Viscus*, 77.

8. Here I am drawing loosely from Sharpe's *In the Wake*.

9. The novels in the trilogy—*Dawn*, *Adulthood Rites*, and *Imago*—originally were pub-lished separately over the course of three years, 1987–89. They were published together as *Xenogenesis* in 1989, and the trilogy later was republished as *Lilith's Brood*, from which I cite. I continue to refer to it as the *Xenogenesis* trilogy, though, since this name was the one first used for it and is the one by which it largely is known.

10. In addition, the Oankali have taken what they term "prints" of all surviving humans, copying their genetic information to allow ooloi to generate what amount to clones who then can become mates in mixed human and Oankali "families." See Butler, *Lilith's Brood*, 95, 99, 424.

11. Nyong'o, *The Amalgamation Waltz*, 52, 30–31, 83.

12. In her discussion of the marginalized modes of "ecological personhood" that emerged as a function of Black enslavement in the Americas, Monique Allewaert observes, "Instead of staying with this hierarchical arrangement that values human beings over other life-forms—a hierarchy whose structure was produced in no small part by colonialism—I aim to investigate the identificatory processes and the strate-gies of resistance that developed through the performances of those designated as parahuman." She adds, "Afro-Americans drew on the brutal colonial circumstances of dismemberment and bodily disaggregation to produce models of personhood that de-veloped from the experience of parahumanity and in relation to animal bodies" (*Ariel's Ecology*, 86).

13. Weheliye, *Habeas Viscus*, 43, 51.

14. Sexton, "The *Vel* of Slavery," 9–10.

15. Delany, *Starboard Wine*, 27.

16. As noted in chapter 1, Delany observes that science fiction is marked by "a distinct level of subjunctivity," since "*events that have not happened* are very different from the fictional events that *could have happened*" (*The Jewel-Hinged Jaw*, 10–11).

17. Nyong'o, *The Amalgamation Waltz*, 10.

18. de la Cadena, *Earth Beings*, xxv.

19. Braidotti, *The Posthuman*, 26.

20. On the complexities of claims to normative humanity, see Abdur-Rahman, *Against the Closet*; Allewaert, *Ariel's Ecology*; Hartman, *Scenes of Subjection*; Silva, *Toward a Global Idea of Race*; Weheliye, *Habeas Viscus*; Wynter, "Unsettling the Coloniality of Being/Power/Truth/Freedom."

21. On the allusions to slavery in the trilogy, see Bahng, "Plasmodial Improprieties"; Federmayer, "Octavia Butler's Maternal Cyborgs"; Grewe-Volpp, "Octavia Butler and the Nature/Culture Divide," 168; Lavender, *Race in American Science Fiction*, 70–72; Peppers, "Dialogic Origins and Alien Identities in Butler's *Xenogenesis*," 50–51; Tucker, "The Human Contradiction," 172–73.

22. Butler, *Lilith's Brood*, 6. Hereafter, page numbers from this work are cited in parentheses in the text.

23. Since ooloi are neither male nor female, the pronoun used for them throughout the novels is "it."

24. See Hong, *Death beyond Disavowal*, 95–124; King, "In the Clearing"; Sexton, *Amalgamation Schemes*; Sharpe, *Monstrous Intimacies*; Snorton, *Black on Both Sides*.

25. Federmayer, "Octavia Butler's Maternal Cyborgs," 98, 103.

26. King, "In the Clearing," 44.

27. In *Imago*, Jodahs notes that if Oankali or constructs were assaulted, the village of the attackers "would be gassed, and the attackers hunted out by scent. They would be found and exiled to the ship. There, if they had killed, they would be kept either unconscious or drugged to pleasure and contentment" (569). The village of humans who have retained their reproductive capabilities is the exception, as Jodahs and others repeatedly note that the Oankali, upon finding out about the village's existence, necessarily will dismantle it.

28. Jacobs, "Posthuman Bodies and Agency in Octavia Butler's *Xenogenesis*," 95–96, 101. On the Oankali pursuit of newness as allegorizing neoliberalism, see Wallace, "Reading Octavia Butler's *Xenogenesis* after Seattle."

29. Hartman, *Scenes of Subjection*, 53, 115.

30. On racialization as the production of a distinction between transcendent subjects and affectable others, see Silva, *Toward a Global Idea of Race*. On the contemporary (re)generation of categories of racialized abjection that provide the negative example through which to define the freedom of rights-bearing subjects, see Alexander, *The New Jim Crow*; Cacho, *Social Death*; Dayan, *The Law Is a White Dog*; Hong, *Death beyond Disavowal*; Melamed, *Represent and Destroy*; Reddy, *Freedom with Violence*.

31. Tucker, "The Human Contradiction," 170; Schwab, "Ethnographies of the Future," 216.

32. On the ways Butler's framing of the drive to "difference" draws on contemporaneous work in sociobiology, particularly that of E. O. Wilson, see Johns, "Becoming Medusa." On its relation to genetic testing/engineering, see Vint, *Bodies of Tomorrow*, 56–78.

33. Schwab, "Ethnographies of the Future," 214; Nanda, "Power, Politics, and Domestic Desire in Octavia Butler's *Lilith's Brood*," 774. Tucker observes, "[T]he Oankali have no idea what their genetic commingling with humans will produce; there is no goal, purpose or end to the Oankali project other than the production of (more) difference" ("The Human Contradiction," 174). For similar accounts, see Belk, "The Certainty of the Flesh"; Jacobs, "Posthuman Bodies and Agency in Octavia Butler's *Xenogenesis*"; Melzer, *Alien Constructions*, 43–102; Peppers, "Dialogic Origins and Alien Identities in Butler's *Xenogenesis*"; Smith, "Ecology beyond Ecology."

34. Weheliye, *Habeas Viscus*, 116.

35. King, "The Labor of (Re)reading Plantation Landscapes Fungible(ly)," 7.

36. The question of choice, though, becomes more complicated later in the trilogy. In the last book, Lilith is confronted about her participation in trade with the Oankali by Jesusa, a human woman from a village where they have retained the ability to procreate on their own. In response, to Jesusa's suggestion that Lilith "didn't have a choice, did you?" Lilith responds, "I did, oh, yes. I chose to live," and Jesusa replies, "That's no choice. That's just going on," to which Lilith insists, "You don't know what you're talking about" (672).

37. Sharpe, *In the Wake*, 74.

38. Snorton, *Black on Both Sides*, 20, 8. Sharpe also observes, "What I am calling the Trans* Atlantic is that s/place condition, or process that appears alongside and in relation to the Black Atlantic but also in excess of its currents. I want to think Trans* in a variety of ways that try to get at something *about* or *toward* the range of trans*formations enacted on and by Black bodies," further suggesting that "we might add that Black and queer Atlantic have always been the Trans* Atlantic. Black has always been that excess" (*In the Wake*, 30). In approaching these dynamics of Black (un)gender(ing), both Snorton and Sharpe draw on Spillers's work.

39. On the parahuman, see Allewaert, *Ariel's Ecology*.

40. One of the readers of the manuscript asked why the forms of indigeneity invoked by the trilogy should be understood as of the Americas rather than, say, of Africa. I offer the following as a response: Lilith is African American (and presented as decidedly not Indigenous in ways I discuss); when on Earth, the setting is in Latin America, suggesting in both cases that invocations of indigeneity most directly allude to Indianness; the conventional images of Indigenous peoples on which the novels draw genealogically arise from nineteenth- and early-twentieth-century ethnological and ethnographic accounts of peoples of the Americas, which then become the basis for anthropological models used to discuss Indigenous peoples, and non-western peoples more generally, elsewhere; and the referent for such images in the U.S. context, from which Butler is writing, most often are American Indians. On the dynamics of African indigeneity under colonial and postcolonial rule, see Barume, "Responding to the Concerns of the African States"; Claassens and Cousins, *Land, Power, and Custom*; Hodgson, *Being Maasai, Becoming Indigenous*; Kipuri, "The UN Declaration on the Rights of Indigenous Peoples in the African Context"; Lehmann, "Aboriginal Title, Indigenous Rights and the Right to Culture"; Mamdani, *Citizen and Subject*. Nnedi Okorafor offers a futurist staging of the complexities of African indigeneity in her *Binti* series.

41. Johns, "Becoming Medusa," 382; Jacobs, "Posthuman Bodies and Agency in Octavia Butler's *Xenogenesis*," 91. See also Peppers, "Dialogic Origins and Alien Identities in Butler's *Xenogenesis*." For discussions of the posthuman as a concept and a set of imaginative and material and possibilities, see Braidotti, *The Posthuman*; Nayar, *Posthumanism*; Singh, *Unthinking Mastery*; Vint, *Bodies of Tomorrow*.

42. In "Ethnographies of the Future," Gabriele Schwab signals this fusion by referring to the novels' exploration of the need for "extraterrestrial or indigenous knowledges" while also (rather disturbingly) characterizing Oankali as like Indigenous peoples in being "precapitalist" and "preindustrialized" ("Ethnographies of the Future," 208, 213–15, 225).

She also suggests that the Oankali are portrayed "as indigenous nomads, transplanetary space travelers who . . . move through itinerant territorialities" without acknowledging the problems of the notion of the "nomad" or the tensions involved in the trilogy's figuration of quasi-indigeneity exclusively in terms of mobility (in ways I discuss further later in this section). See Schwab, "Ethnographies of the Future," 208, 213–15, 224–25. As one of the participants in Sierra Adare's study of Native responses to portrayals of Indians in TV science fiction notes, "Our cultures have and will remain alien to the dominant society; therefore we, too, have always been and always will be aliens. . . . Thus we fit perfectly into the role of aliens just about anywhere, including science fiction" (*"Indian" Stereotypes in TV Science Fiction*, 30–31). On histories of stereotyping of Native peoples, see also Deloria, *Indians in Unexpected Places*; Huhndorf, *Going Native*; Mithlo, *"Our Indian Princess"*; Raheja, *Reservation Reelism*.

43. On Oankali relations with their environment, see Bahng, "Plasmodial Improprieties"; Grewe-Volpp, "Octavia Butler and the Nature/Culture Divide"; Schwab, "Ethnographies of the Future"; Smith, "Ecology beyond Ecology"; Wallace, "Reading Octavia Butler's *Xenogenesis* after Seattle."

44. However, Molly Wallace notes of this relationship that "the 'trade' on the genetic level tends, coercively, to make it in the best interests of the partner species to comply. The ship sustains the Oankali because that is what it is genetically programmed to do," further characterizing it as a "mode of eugenic environmentalism" ("Reading Octavia Butler's *Xenogenesis* after Seattle," 106).

45. Niezen, *The Origins of Indigenism*, 12, 179, 186. In Butler's later novel *Parable of the Sower*, this connection becomes even more explicit. The protagonist, Lauren Olamina, turns to books about the plant knowledge of California Indians to learn how to survive amid the breakdown of the economy in the United States, even as there is no discussion of actual Indians (and reservations) in California despite Olamina's travel on foot from southern California to far into the north. The commune she eventually founds in northern California is called "Acorn," after the knowledge learned from those books. See Butler, *Parable of the Sower*, 58–60, 63–64, 328.

46. Engle, *The Elusive Promise of Indigenous Development*, 169–70.

47. Povinelli, *The Cunning of Recognition*, 39.

48. Notably, when Lilith eventually goes outside the dwelling on the ship in which she awoke, she perceives it as "a big tree" (31), drawing on perhaps the most conventional and prominent symbol of eco-consciousness as a way of characterizing Oankali modes of inhabitance.

49. Povinelli, *The Empire of Love*, 4, 183, 226.

50. See Bentley, "The Fourth Dimension"; Sharpe, *Monstrous Intimacies*.

51. See Butler, *Lilith's Brood*, 15, 47, 64.

52. On the role of adoption in Native kinship epistemologies, as well as attributions of a tendency toward adoption to Native peoples, see Barker, *Native Acts* 93–94; Lyons, *X-marks*; Rifkin, *When Did Indians Become Straight?* 99–142; Simpson, "From White into Red."

53. Morgan, *Ancient Society*, 61. On Morgan's work, its profound legacies for anthropology, and the history of ethnology more broadly, see Bieder, *Science Encounters the*

Indian, 194–246; Fortes, *Kinship and the Social Order*; Kuper, *The Reinvention of Primitive Society*; Simpson, *Mohawk Interruptus*, 67–94; Trautmann, *Lewis Henry Morgan and the Invention of Kinship*.

54. Morgan, *Ancient Society*, 61. In his earlier book, Morgan characterizes Haudenosaunee peoples as "established on the principles . . . of the Family Relationships," observing that "each tribe" is "in the nature of a family" and combined together in the Iroquois League to form "one political family" (*League of the Ho-dé-no-sau-nee, or Iroquois*, 60, 78–79).

55. See Butler, *Gender Trouble*; Ingraham, "The Heterosexual Imaginary"; Salamon, *Assuming a Body*.

56. On versions of the "third sex" and the ways it has been employed to (mis)translate Indigenous social roles and formations, see Lang, *Men as Women, Women as Men*; Morgensen, *Spaces between Us*; Roscoe, *Changing Ones*.

57. For extended analysis of such tendencies, their logical fallacies, and their political pitfalls, see Towle and Morgan, "Romancing the Transgender Native." Butler herself has noted with respect to her creation of the ooloi, "I wound up with a somewhat different hierarchical system, chemically controlled as with DNA, but, instead, pheromonal" (Frances, *Conversations with Octavia Butler*, 105). For readings of the ooloi as disrupting or "queering" Euro-American sex-gender systems, or "queering" kinship, see Bahng, "Plasmodial Improprieties"; Belk, "The Certainty of the Flesh"; Melzer, *Alien Constructions*, 83–87; Miller, "Post-Apocalyptic Hoping," 334; Obourn, "Octavia Butler's Disabled Futures," 126; Tucker, "The Human Contradiction," 176. For a counter-reading on this point, see Savage, "We Pair Off! One Man, One Woman."

58. On the politics of respectability, see Abdur-Rahman, *Against the Closet*; Cohen, *Boundaries of Blackness*; Ferguson, *Aberrations in Black*; Holland, *The Erotic Life of Racism*; Nyong'o, *The Amalgamation Waltz*; Puar, *Terrorist Assemblages*; Scott, *Extravagant Abjection*; Sexton, *Amalgamation Schemes*; Sharpe, *Monstrous Intimacies*.

59. Barker, *Native Acts*, 223, 6.

60. Povinelli, *The Empire of Love*, 140.

61. On this translation of geopolitics into biopolitics, see Rifkin, "Making Peoples into Populations." On the role of DNA in figurations of Indianness, see TallBear, *Native American DNA*.

62. On this dynamic, see Brooks, *The Common Pot*; Cohen, *The Networked Wilderness*; Miller, *Oral History on Trial*; Rasmussen, *Queequeg's Coffin*.

63. For an effort to square this making "uninhabitable" with a sense of ecological consciousness/reciprocity, see Smith, "Ecology beyond Ecology."

64. For discussion of "Lo," the incipient ship in which Lilith and her family live on Earth, see Butler, *Lilith's Brood*, 282, 313.

65. On Indigenous peoples' creation of and relation to new homelands, see Carroll, *Roots of Our Renewal*; Goeman, *Mark My Words*; Lowery, *Lumbee Indians in the Jim Crow South*; Simpson, *Mohawk Interruptus*.

66. Goeman, *Mark My Words*, 3, 88.

67. Simpson, *Dancing on Our Turtle's Back*, 89. In *As We Have Always Done*, Simpson further observes, "Indigenous peoples require a land base and therefore require a central

and hard critique of the forces that propel dispossession," adding, "I'm interested in unapologetic placed-based nationhoods using Indigenous practices and operating in an ethical and principled way from an intact land base" (50).

68. On humans in the novels as "oriented toward death," see Johns, "Becoming Medusa," 390.

69. On the novels' adoption of this perspective, see Johns, "Becoming Medusa"; Miller, "Post-Apocalyptic Hoping"; Papke, "Necessary Interventions in the Face of Very Curious Compulsions"; Smith, "Ecology beyond Ecology"; Zaki, "Utopia, Dystopia, and Ideology in the Science Fiction of Octavia Butler." In a number of interviews, Butler herself endorses this reading of the trilogy, saying, "Intelligence may indeed be a short-term adaptation, something that works well now but will eventually prove to be a kind of destructive overspecialization that destroys us" and that "the tendency toward hierarchical behavior is older and more entrenched": "I do think we need to accept that our behavior *is* controlled to some extent by biological forces"; "Sometimes we can work around our programming if we understand it" (Frances, *Conversations with Octavia Butler*, 19, 67). On the problem of taking "genes" as determinative, especially in ways that both are racializing and ignore the effects of environmental factors on genes' modes of expression, see Magnet, *When Biometrics Fail*; Nayar, *Posthumanism*, 35–76; Reardon, *Race to the Finish*; Roberts, *Fatal Invention*; Sankar, "Forensic DNA Phenotyping."

70. Jodahs, the construct ooloi protagonist of the third book, says, "To me, the conflict was spice. It has been deadly to the Human species. . . . My children would not have it at all" (678), indicating the elimination of the contradiction in a single generation. However, this moment also raises the issue of Oankali, especially ooloi, attraction to the "conflict." See also Butler, *Lilith's Brood*, 153, 279.

71. In *Dawn*, Nikanj is nearly killed during an uprising aboard the ship by the first group of awakened humans (who are being trained, ostensibly by Lilith, in preparation for return to the Earth [230–37]). In *Adulthood Rites* and *Imago*, readers hear of various Oankalis and constructs being wounded by resisters, including an effort to kill Akin via arson while he is in the middle of his metamorphosis (508–9). The penalty for such assaults and (attempted) murders is return to the ship and being placed in a permanent state of sedation, a pattern that might be interpreted as comparable to the forms of racialized mass incarceration in the contemporary United States.

72. In *The Stone Sky* (the third novel in her *Broken Earth* trilogy), N. K. Jemisin offers a satiric version of such commitment to life that might be read as signifying on the Oankali. The technologically advanced people of Syl Anagist are presented as valuing life, insofar as it can be put in the service of their aims: "Life is sacred in Syl Anagist—sacred, and lucrative, and *useful*" (314).

73. Foucault, *The History of Sexuality*, 136, 89, 144.

74. Foucault, *"Society Must Be Defended"*, 246, 62. In *"Society Must Be Defended"* and *The History of Sexuality*, Foucault does address the forms of extensive (even genocidal violence) licensed by the racisms produced through the exertion of biopower, but for an elaboration of these dynamics as "necropolitics," see Mbembe, "Necropolitics." For an analysis of Foucault's biopolitics as failing to engage the ubiquity and functions of racialization, see Weheliye, *Habeas Viscus*.

75. Puar, *Terrorist Assemblages*, 31. On this dynamic, see also Cacho, *Social Death*; Chow, *The Protestant Ethnic and The Spirit of Capitalism*; Melamed, *Represent and Destroy*; Reddy, *Freedom with Violence*; Rodríguez, *Forced Passages*.

76. A large part of the plot of *Adulthood Rites* concerns the unpredictability of what human-Oankali constructs will look like in terms of the variations among the morphologies of the constructs (some look far more "human" than others), as well as the differences between the contours of embodiment prior to and after each construct child's "metamorphosis" (comparable to puberty). Moreover, Oankalis do not achieve a definite sex until they go through metamorphosis. In *Adulthood Rites*, Akin's paired sibling, Tiikuchahk, eventually becomes male despite having initially presented as female, and in *Imago*, Jodahs and its paired sibling, Aaor, turn out, much to everyone's surprise and dismay, to be ooloi. Readers also learn that construct ooloi have the capacity to alter their corporeality to an unprecedented extent, in ways that reflect their environments and that will be found pleasing to their sexual partners. At one point, Jodahs observes, "It's easier to do as water does: allow myself to be contained, and take on the shape of my containers" (612).

77. See Goldberg, *The Racial State*; Kazanjian, *The Colonizing Trick*; Puar, *Terrorist Assemblages*. On Foucault's notion of "governmentality" as biopolitical rule, see Foucault, "Governmentality."

78. Puar, *Terrorist Assemblages*, 117.

79. Obourn, "Octavia Butler's Disabled Futures," 112. See also Vint, *Bodies of Tomorrow*, 56–78.

80. On the ways Oankali gene-based practices of *reading* enact a literalism/realism that defies the possibility of multiple meanings, see Wallace, "Reading Octavia Butler's *Xenogenesis* after Seattle." On the ways Akin's call for human self-determination emerges out of an engagement with human storytelling, which he previously dismissed as simply "not true," see Johns, "Becoming Medusa," 391–93.

81. This dynamic, in which Lilith's illness increases the capacity for Oankali forms of bodily transformation, can be understood as another way in which the text draws on and refigures the relation between blackness and fungibility, discussed earlier. Specifically, Butler here may implicitly be invoking the story of Henrietta Lacks, the African American woman whose cancer cells—taken and used without her informed consent or compensation to her or her family—were crucial to a wide range of biomedical developments.

82. See Butler, *Lilith's Brood*, 237, 491, 612, 617–19.

83. Kafer, *Feminist, Queer, Crip*, 27, 3, 6. On the ways categories of disability and racializing and imperial differentiations historically work in and through each other in the United States, see Erevelles, *Disability and Difference in Global Contexts*; Jarman, "Coming Up from Underground"; Jackson, "Visualizing Slavery"; Samuels, *Fantasies of Identification*; Schalk, *Bodyminds Reimagined*; Senier and Barker, "Introduction." In *Dying from Improvement*, Sharene Razack traces the ways police and state violence against Native people implicitly is explained by casting them as "pathologically fragile," as essentially disabled subjects (*Dying from Improvement*, 23).

84. Razack, *Dying from Improvement*, 113. See also Million, *Therapeutic Nations*; Simpson, "The State Is a Man"; Stevenson, *Life beside Itself*.

85. This reading might run the risk of taking disability as a metaphor. However, the failure of Native peoples to desire Euro-American modes of civilization historically has been understood as a sign of actual mental deficiency that productively can be situated within the history of disability. On the problem of treating disability solely as metaphor, as well as a sustained reading of representations of disability in Butler's work (although not focused on the *Xenogenesis* trilogy), see Schalk, *Bodyminds Reimagined*. For discussion of disability within Native communities and Native political struggles, see Teuton, "Disability in Indigenous North America."

86. Stevenson, *Life beside Itself*, 3, 6, 18. She later observes, "[T]he binary logic of a biopolitical state means that you are either part of the great stream of life or outside of it" (120). As Grace Hong argues with respect to contemporary neoliberal notions of life, "What are the various and proliferating meanings of death? What kinds of social (non)existence does 'death' describe? Put another way, what kinds of knowledges, modes of being, affects, memories, temporalities, embodiments do these populations that are marked for death . . . produce?," adding, "Is it (im)possible to build a politics around them?" (*Death beyond Disavowal*, 16). See also Povinelli, *Economies of Abandonment*. For a science fiction story about Native teen suicide, see "Mr. Gizmo," in Taylor, *Take Us to Your Chief*, 77–91.

87. Simpson, *Mohawk Interruptus*, 128.

88. Simpson, *Mohawk Interruptus*, 22, 11.

89. Such language is found in the International Covenant on Civil and Political Rights and the International Covenant on Economic, Social and Cultural Rights. On these covenants and their relation to Indigenous rights/politics, see Engle, *The Elusive Promise of Indigenous Development*.

90. Wallace, "Reading Octavia Butler's *Xenogenesis* after Seattle," 110, 113, 119.

91. On Indigenous TEK (traditional ecological knowledge) and the ways it is addressed in contemporary science and policy, see Cruikshank, *The Social Life of Stories*; Niezen, *The Origins of Indigenism*; TallBear, *Native American DNA*.

92. Thanks to Keith Richotte for suggesting this connection. On allotment, see Hoxie, *A Final Promise*; Genetin-Pilawa, *Crooked Paths to Allotment*; McDonnell, *The Dispossession of the American Indian*; Rifkin, *When Did Indians Become Straight?*

93. See Conn, *History's Shadow*; O'Brien, *Firsting and Lasting*; Razack, *Dying from Improvement*.

94. Taylor, *Take Us to Your Chief*, 51. However, there also are Indigenous futurist accounts of a remaking of Indigenous peoples' ties to places beyond the Earth, such as forms of Métis ritual and territoriality on "New Earth" in Cherie Dimaline's "Legends Are Made, Not Born" or the re-creation of Navajo sovereignty in the "Diné Orbiter" in Darcie Little Badger's "Né Łe." In "The Space NDN's Star Map," Lou Cornum notes, "For many the image of the Indian in space is jarring not just because of the settler perception of indigeneity as antithetical to high tech modernity, but because Indian identity is tied so directly to specific earthly territories." He further observes, "This is not just a question of outer space. Already the majority of people in the U.S. and Canada live in cities away from their traditional territories" and suggests that this vision of Indigenous situatedness can become reified in ways that efface Indigenous "traditions of movement." See also

Gaertner, "Indigenous in Cyberspace." For a fantasy account of Indigenous relocation and renewal modeled on the Cherokee Trail of Tears, see Justice, *The Way of Thorn and Thunder*.

95. Wallace, "Reading Octavia Butler's *Xenogenesis* after Seattle," 103.

96. Obourn, "Octavia Butler's Disabled Futures," 123. Rachel Greenwald Smith suggests, "Humans tend to repeat their mistakes, social structures, and values by pursuing a certain restricted imagination of what constitutes progress within an integral human identity that privileges the development of hierarchical structures," while in contrast "Oankali are constantly changing, finding new worlds and creating new organisms that have a variety of life-needs and capabilities" ("Ecology beyond Ecology," 558). See also Jacobs, "Posthuman Bodies and Agency in Octavia Butler's *Xenogenesis*"; Melzer, *Alien Constructions*, 67–102; Papke, "Necessary Interventions in the Face of Very Curious Compulsions."

97. For an implicit rewriting of *Dawn* that foregrounds the dynamics of invasion, see Barker, "Choice."

98. Tucker, "The Human Contradiction," 177. On relations with Oankalis as indicative of the necessity for adaptability, see Federmeyer; Melzer, *Alien Constructions*, 43–66; Obourn, "Octavia Butler's Disabled Futures."

99. Kurisato, "Imposter Syndrome," 101–2.

100. Cathy Peppers observes, "[W]hile the Oankali do relent and allow the Resisters to begin again on Mars, this part of the story happens off-stage . . . and is therefore a 'dead end' in the trilogy's narrative of evolution" ("Dialogic Origins and Alien Identities in Butler's *Xenogenesis*," 59).

101. For examples, see Butler, *Lilith's Brood*, 607, 636, 648, 670–71, 679, 740.

102. See Sexton, "The *Vel* of Slavery."

103. On the question of the novel's dystopian vision, see Bahng, "Plasmodial Improprieties"; Belk, "The Certainty of the Flesh"; Jacobs, "Posthuman Bodies and Agency in Octavia Butler's *Xenogenesis*"; Miller, "Post-Apocalyptic Hoping"; Papke, "Necessary Interventions in the Face of Very Curious Compulsions"; Wallace, "Reading Octavia Butler's *Xenogenesis* after Seattle"; Zaki, "Utopia, Dystopia, and Ideology in the Science Fiction of Octavia Butler."

104. Tucker, "The Human Contradiction," 169.

105. Michaels, "Political Science Fictions," 650.

106. Intra-human racial difference, however, does not vanish in the wake of the war. See Peppers, "Dialogic Origins and Alien Identities in Butler's *Xenogenesis*," 58; Tucker, "The Human Contradiction," 171. Thus, if shared humanness transcends race, it does not banish racial distinction and racism; rather, difference from Oankalis exceeds intraspecies modes of distinction. Moreover, such intraspecies modes of distinction are characterized as a function of species-wide tendencies (racialization as an expression of humans' genetic "contradiction").

107. Here I differ from Michaels's argument that "difference" in the trilogy largely refers to physiological distinctions.

108. Mary E. Papke suggests, "Butler's employment of evolutionary and genetic science is too often simply dismissed as vulgar essentialism. It is not. It is instead her core belief

upon which her dystopian visions and alarms depend" ("Necessary Interventions in the Face of Very Curious Compulsions," 83). Johns argues, "Butler is imagining the kinds of moral problems and arguments arising *after* the acceptance of genetic essentialism. Genetic essentialism is not the end of moral debate, but a new beginning for it," adding, "Her project is not to critique sociobiology as liberal humanism, but to strip optimistic liberal humanism from sociobiology" ("Becoming Medusa," 384, 398). In contrast, Jim Miller argues that Butler "does not endorse their determinist views about humans," instead offering "a dialogue between opposing views" ("Post-Apocalyptic Hoping," 342), and Mary Wallace notes, "'Realism' is, naturally, the privileged mode of Butler's Oankali. Indeed, in their gene language, there is no gap between realism and the real," later noting, "We should probably be suspicious of any fictional species that is constitutionally opposed to fiction" ("Reading Octavia Butler's *Xenogenesis* after Seattle," 101, 124). In this anti-determinist vein of interpretation, see also Grewe-Volpp, "Octavia Butler and the Nature/Culture Divide"; Jacobs, "Posthuman Bodies and Agency in Octavia Butler's *Xenogenesis*"; Melzer, *Alien Constructions*, 67–102; Obourn, "Octavia Butler's Disabled Futures"; Peppers, "Dialogic Origins and Alien Identities in Butler's *Xenogenesis*"; Smith, "Ecology beyond Ecology."

109. Zaki, "Utopia, Dystopia, and Ideology in the Science Fiction of Octavia Butler," 242.

110. Weheliye, *Habeas Viscus*, 4, 8.

111. Scott, "The Re-enchantment of Humanism," 198.

112. On the ethics of acknowledging the plurality of peoples in order to avoid domination and immoral modes of intervention, see Coulthard, *Red Skin, White Masks*; Nichols, "Contract and Usurpation"; Niezen, *The Origins of Indigenism*; Turner, *This Is Not a Peace Pipe*.

113. For discussion of Hobbes and the ways his work envisions particular kinds of modern personhood, see Cohen, *A Body Worth Defending*, 32–129; Foucault, *"Society Must Be Defended"*, 89–99; Macpherson, *The Political Theory of Possessive Individualism*, 9–106.

114. Quoted in Cohen, *A Body Worth Defending*, 59.

115. Notably, readers hear virtually nothing about the governance of the resister villages, including Phoenix. The exception is the fundamentalist religious ethos inculcated by elders in the community of in-breeding humans in *Imago*.

116. Nichols, "Contract and Usurpation," 102–3.

117. See Butler, *Lilith's Brood*, 409–10.

118. King, "The Labor of (Re)reading Plantation Landscapes Fungible(ly)," 3.

3. CARCERAL SPACE AND FUGITIVE MOTION

1. Alexander, *The New Jim Crow*, 6, 60, 100; Goffman, *On the Run*, ix; Hinton, *From the War on Poverty to the War on Crime*, 5; Murakawa, *The First Civil Right*, 2–4; Pettit, *Invisible Men*, 1, 14–15; Wacquant, *Punishing the Poor*, xv, 61, 133.

2. Goffman, *On the Run*, 199. See also Clear, *Imprisoning Communities*; Richie, *Arrested Justice*; Ritchie, *Invisible No More*; Taylor, *From #BlackLivesMatter to Black Liberation*; Wacquant, *Punishing the Poor*.

3. Cacho, *Social Death*, 38.

4. See also Browne, *Dark Matters*; Clear, *Imprisoning Communities*; Goffman, *On the Run*. Here, it is crucial to remember that arrest rates cannot be understood as indicative of the rates of commission of crime, since arrests themselves result from police practice and are not intrinsically proportional to actual instances of law-breaking. As Elizabeth Hinton notes of "flawed criminal justice data-gathering" in terms of the work it performed in the growth of the "war on crime," "Arrests were counted as part of the crime rate regardless of whether they produced a conviction, meaning, for example, that if a group of black youth were arrested for robbing a liquor store, all of those youth would be recorded as burglars and counted as part of the crime rate, even if they were subsequently released for lack of evidence. Since black men under the age of twenty-four had the highest arrest rate in the United States—a result of the targeted law enforcement encouraged by the federal government—they were seen as responsible for the majority of the nation's crime and skewed reported rates accordingly" (*From the War on Poverty to the War on Crime*, 224).

5. Alexander, *The New Jim Crow*, 125; Goffman, *On the Run*, 60; Gottschalk, *Caught*, 279; Khan-Cullors and bandele, *When They Call You a Terrorist*.

6. Alexander, *The New Jim Crow*, 6; Wacquant, *Punishing the Poor*, 119.

7. Murakawa, *The First Civil Right*, 3, 18, 90. On the revitalization of explicit racist intent as the principal criterion for evaluating the existence of racism in the criminal justice system (as against statistical indications of racially disparate effects), see also Alexander, *The New Jim Crow*; Dayan, *The Law Is a White Dog*; Richie, *Arrested Justice*; Simon, *Governing through Crime*, 111–40.

8. While the stories in the collection can function as separate texts, as in a short story collection, they clearly speak to each other (referring to and extending events in prior stories, carrying forward certain characters, moving forward chronologically, and building in thematic and narrative effect). For this reason, I address the stories less as self-contained units than as part of a single whole, as one would address chapters in a novel.

9. Alexander, *The New Jim Crow*, 151, 200.

10. As Cacho argues, "A person does not need to *do* anything to commit a status crime because the person's status is the offense in and of itself," adding, "a *de facto status crime* does not refer to illegal activity; rather it refers to others' perception that a person of a certain status is certain to commit future crimes and may well have already committed crimes unwitnessed" (*Social Death*, 43). The current social service designation of "at-risk" operates in similar ways, emerging as it does from the earlier designation of "potentially delinquent." See Hinton, *From the War on Poverty to the War on Crime*, 268.

11. On the carceral state, see Dayan, *The Law Is a White Dog*; Dillon, *Fugitive Life*; Gilmore, *Golden Gulag*; Gottschalk, *Caught*; Hinton, *From the War on Poverty to the War on Crime*; Murakawa, *The First Civil Right*; Rodríguez, *Forced Passages*; Taylor, *From #BlackLivesMatter to Black Liberation*; Wacquant, *Punishing the Poor*. In *Governing through Crime*, Jonathan Simon argues that over the last forty years the United States has moved to a paradigm in which crime functions less as an object of government policy than as the conceptual matrix through which to approach governance itself. He notes, "Crime does not only govern those on one end of the structures of inequality,

but actively reshapes how power is exercised throughout hierarchies of class, race, ethnicity, and gender," further suggesting that the principal mode in which claims to citizenship and political subjectivity can be articulated is that of the crime victim (*Governing through Crime*, 18).

12. On racializing assemblages, see Weheliye, *Habeas Viscus*.

13. Lyon, *Surveillance Studies*, 21, 100–1.

14. As Wacquant argues, "*neoliberalism entails the enlargement and exaltation of the penal sector* of the bureaucratic field, so that the state may check the social reverberations caused by the diffusion of social insecurity in the lower runs of the class and ethnic hierarchy as well as assuage popular discontent over the dereliction of its traditional economic and social duties" (*Punishing the Poor*, 305). On neoliberalism, see also Berlant, *Cruel Optimism*; Dillon, *Fugitive Life*; Duggan, *The Twilight of Equality?*; Melamed, *Represent and Destroy*; Povinelli, *The Empire of Love*. For an extended statement by Mosley critiquing current political and economic formations, see Mosley, *Workin' on the Chain Gang*.

I already had drafted this chapter and developed my notion of "neoliberal apartheid" when I encountered Andy Clarno's book *Neoliberal Apartheid: Palestine/Israel and South Africa after 1994*. In it, he seeks to address the relation among neoliberalism, racial capitalism, and ongoing (de)colonization in South Africa and Israel/Palestine. While his formulations in many ways resonate with my usage here, I want to emphasize that the neoliberal dimensions of the kinds of segregation/captivity at play in Mosley's text have to do with an apparent disavowal of explicitly racializing policies, which is not the case in either South Africa or Israel. In *Futureland*, race persists through forms of statistical modeling and population definition, but the commitment to supposedly race-neutral metrics creates the appearance of post-racial modes of spatial distribution and containment.

15. Mosley, *Futureland*, 93, 96, 102. Hereafter, page numbers from this work are cited in parentheses in the text. This technology appears as a more advanced version of the tracking system—Personal Activated Security Sensor—inmates in many prisons already are made to wear on their arms. See Rodríguez, *Forced Passages*, 240.

16. Readers also are told that Angel's Island conducts extensive medical experiments on the prisoners: "Bits knew that almost five hundred research-related deaths—murders—had been committed by prison officials. that data from these medical experimentation deaths had been sold to research facilities around the world" (120). Given the ways citizenship is stripped from prisoners in being sent to Angel's Island, the choice of name resonates with Angel Island in the Bay Area, through which Chinese immigrant were processed and often detained during the first half of the twentieth century. Thanks to Aimee Bahng for pointing to this connection.

17. A later story set further in the future confirms these speculations: "Our judges are machines, our prisons and military and mental institutions and workplaces are planning to mechanize their human components with computerized chemical bags" (311).

18. On shifts in philosophies of imprisonment in the United States, including the shift away from rehabilitation and the (deeply flawed) citation of incapacitation and deterrence as justifications for mass incarceration, see Clear, *Imprisoning Communities*, 15–48; Davis, *Are Prisons Obsolete?*, 40–59; Dayan, *The Law Is a White Dog*, 71–112; Gottschalk,

Caught, 79–97; Hinton, *From the War on Poverty to the War on Crime*; Simon, *Governing through Crime*, 141–76.

19. On the data-double, see Cheney-Lippold, *We Are Data*; Galloway, "Does the Whatever Speak?"; Graham and Wood, "Digitalizing Surveillance"; Lyon, *Surveillance Studies*, 73–117.

20. As Angela Davis notes, "Imprisonment is associated with the racialization of those most likely to be punished," functioning as a way of "criminaliz[ing] populations and communities" (*Are Prisons Obsolete?*, 112–13).

21. See Lavender, *Race in American Science Fiction*, 112–14.

22. If mass incarceration in the United States often is characterized in terms of the "prison-industrial complex," Mosley turns that concept inside out, casting the prison—and the criminal justice system more broadly—less as a particular economic niche than as a generative matrix through which to consolidate a broader corporate ethos in which "antisocial" patterns consist of anything resistant to business interests. On the prison-industrial complex, see Davis, *Are Prisons Obsolete?*, 84–104. On the limited role of prison labor in the total national economy and the financial dynamics of investments in prison construction, expansion, and privatization, see Gilmore, *Golden Gulag*, 5–29; Gottschalk, *Caught*, 48–78; Magnet, *When Biometrics Fail*, 58–68; Wacquant, *Punishing the Poor*, xx, 182.

23. Here the text alludes to the Thirteenth Amendment's outlawing of "involuntary servitude" except "as a punishment for crime whereof the party shall have been duly convicted." On the role of the Thirteenth Amendment in facilitating the continuation or reenactment of many of the dynamics of slavery for prisoners (historically and currently), see Davis, *Are Prisons Obsolete?*, 22–39; Dayan, *The Law Is a White Dog*, 39–70; Hartman, *Scenes of Subjection*, 164–83; Rodríguez, *Forced Passages*, 223–55; Wagner, *Disturbing the Peace*, 25–57.

24. In *Workin' on the Chain Gang*, Mosley observes, "The oppression of racism is a palpable part of life in America, so much so that the broader problems facing us today might have their solutions in understanding the opposition that African-Americans have put up against the system that has kept us down. Living on the fringes of production, we have been forced into an intimate relationship with the inequities and cold logic of America's value system," adding, "What black people have experienced as a group for centuries many whites now experience as solitary and alienated individuals" (13–14).

25. These descriptions resonate with those of people who had been imprisoned in the first "high-security underground isolation unit": "It's what is called sensory deprivation. Everything is white. The walls are white, the floor is white, the cells are white"(Rodríguez, *Forced Passages*, 189–90).

26. On this dynamic, see Silva, *Toward a Global Idea of Race*; Weheliye, *Habeas Viscus*; Wynter, "Unsettling the Coloniality of Being/Power/Truth/Freedom."

27. In doing so, they suggest, "society will need to shed some of its obsession for causality in exchange for simple correlations: not knowing *why* but only *what*," further arguing that such correlations provide "insight at the macro level": "Correlations let us analyze a phenomenon not by shedding light on its inner workings but by identifying a useful proxy for it" (*Big Data*, 7, 14, 53).

28. Mayer-Schönberger and Cukier, *Big Data*, 72, 78.

29. Despite their repeated claims about the transparency of data in the aggregate, and the value of collecting "messy" forms of data, Mayer-Schönberger and Cukier offer a series of qualifications about what correlations mean and the need for expert assessment of them: "big-data collection" requires "clever analysis," since "the figures require careful interpretation"; "when the number of data points increases by orders of magnitude, we also see more spurious correlations"; "[Data] can be mis-analyzed or used misleadingly. And even more damningly, data can fail to capture what it purports to quantify"; "we can see the risk that big-data predictions, and the algorithms and datasets behind them, will become black boxes that offer us no accountability, traceability, or confidence" (*Big Data*, 42, 54, 166, 179). On the creation of "algorithmic identities" that may have little to do with actual attributes in the non-virtual world, see Cheney-Lippold, *We Are Data*.

30. Cheney-Lippold, *We Are Data*, xiii; Bonilla-Silva, *Racism without Racists*, 74.

31. Within this speculative future, the formal line between corporations and governance largely has disappeared: corporations replace some governments in exerting political sovereignty over particular territories, including Russia and the newly established and privately owned country of "Home" off the coast of Mexico (8, 59); a House of Corporate Advisors supplements, and often guides, decisions by the U.S. Congress proper (214); a person can be charged for "crimes against the economy" (297); there is also an "International Economic Congress," an "intercorporate police force," and a "corporate ambassador to the UN" (83, 308, 324). These neoliberal developments indicate the extent to which the needs of capitalist enterprise shape forms of legal subjectivity, citizenship, and diplomacy and how putative violations of domestic and international law constitute crimes against big business.

32. See Mosley, *Futureland*, 10–11, 191, 230–40, 329.

33. Puar, *Terrorist Assemblages*, 162, 198. As Lyon suggests, such practices can be understood as "categorical suspicion," "the sense that simply inhabiting a categorical niche is enough to attract suspicion" (*Surveillance Studies*, 106).

34. Roberts, *Fatal Invention*, 156–57. On such "DNA dragnets," in Roberts's terms, see also Bliss, *Race Decoded*, 70–73; Duster, "The Combustible Intersection"; Kahn, "What's the Use of Race in Presenting Forensic DNA Evidence in Court?"; Sankar, "Forensic DNA Phenotyping."

35. Cheney-Lippold, *We Are Data*, 45.

36. In this vein, scholarly work has demonstrated how technoscientific research and discourses often mobilize extant racial categories (including when invoking "ancestry") in haphazard, impressionistic, and stereotypical ways that tautologically confirm the existence and explanatory value of those categories. As Jenny Reardon observes, "All efforts to study human genetic variation necessarily build on a terrain structured by centuries of prior struggles over the meaning and proper use of race" (*Race to the Finish*, 163). See also Bliss, *Race Decoded*, 20–24, 100–34; Browne, *Dark Matters*; Chow-White, "Data, Code, and Discourses of Difference in Genomics"; Duster, "The Combustible Intersection"; Fujimura et al., "Race and Ancestry"; Hunt and Megyesi, "The Ambiguous Meanings of the Racial/Ethnic Categories Routinely Used in Human Genetics Research"; Magnet, *When Biometrics Fail*, 19–50; Roberts, *Fatal Invention*, 57–80; TallBear, *Native American DNA*. On the ways such technologies are being mobilized toward projects of

"reconciliation," see Nelson, *The Social Life of DNA*. On the use of a similar intellectual procedure in the formation of racial categories in the eighteenth and nineteenth centuries through comparative anatomy, see Wiegman, *American Anatomies*.

37. In the text, private interests animate carceral expansion at every level. Not only is Angel's Island a privately run, if government-sanctioned, facility, but the specific mechanisms of control featured in the stories are corporate creations, such that the search for ever larger markets drives the effort to find further uses for these predictive and disciplinary technologies.

38. On intergenerational patterns of African American residency in poor neighborhoods, see Sharkey, *Stuck in Place*. On the use of supposedly race-neutral financial indices that perpetuate segregation in the absence of direct "redlining," see Massey and Denton, *American Apartheid*; Pattillo, *Black on the Block*; Sharkey, *Stuck in Place*. On the concentration of poverty around Black neighborhoods, see, in addition to the sources just mentioned, Peterson and Krivo, *Divergent Social Worlds*. On health disparities for African Americans due to the ongoing and intergenerational effects of racism, see Harris-Perry, *Sister Citizen*; Roberts, *Fatal Invention*, 123–46. On color-blind racism as a contemporary mode of domination, see Bonilla-Silva, *Racism without Racists*; Taylor, *From #BlackLives-Matter to Black Liberation*.

39. On current public-private data partnerships and their implications, see Graham and Wood, "Digitalizing Surveillance"; Magnet, *When Biometrics Fail*; Schneier, *Data and Goliath*; Wacquant, *Punishing the Poor*, 135–46.

40. One of the characters in "En Masse" observes, "The rich and powerful live in a world that most of the rest of us don't even suspect" (251).

41. These characters include Pell in "The Greatest" and "Voices," Mingus Black in "The Electric Eye," and Harold in "The Nig in Me."

42. As Madhu Dubey suggests, "White Noise" is "strikingly reminiscent of the category of the Black urban 'underclass' that was manufactured by social scientists, public policy makers, and the media during the 1980s" ("The Future of Race in Afro-Futurist Fiction," 23). On relations between ideologies of race and older legal conceptions of heritable taint, see Dayan, *The Law Is a White Dog*.

43. On the ways employment regulations increasingly are modeled on criminal justice conceptions and dynamics, including the move away from structural analyses to assessments of individual culpability, see Simon, *Governing through Crime*, 233–57. In its depiction of Common Ground, the text also gestures toward the multilayered connections scholars have shown between unemployment and imprisonment. The growth in rates of incarceration and the length of prison sentences over the past thirty years has functioned as a way of warehousing large numbers of otherwise unemployed people of color, while also driving down the formal unemployment statistics in ways that create a false impression of much larger economic gains for populations of color (particularly African Americans) than there actually have been. Additionally, those released from prison have been legally barred from numerous forms of employment as well as being subject to extensive (even if often illegal) discrimination in attempting to get other kinds of jobs, and the presumption of a connection between imprisonment and blackness has inhibited African Americans with no criminal record from finding substantive employment. See

Alexander, *The New Jim Crow*, 140–177; Pager, *Marked*; Pettit, *Invisible Men*; Wacquant, *Punishing the Poor*, 41–74, 195–208. Ruth Wilson Gilmore notes, "In short, as a class, convicts are deindustrialized cities' working or workless poor" (*Golden Gulag*, 7), and, as Marie Gottschalk suggests, "Elaborate gradations of citizenship are on their way to becoming the new normal in the United States. The carceral state has helped to legitimize the idea of creating a highly distinct political and legal universe for numerous categories of people" (*Caught*, 242).

44. In "Little Brother," the narrator notes that the "criminal history" of the main character "kept him from entering the cycles of employment, which were legally assured by the Thirty-sixth Amendment to the Constitution. Frendon's constitutional right was blocked by the mandatory publication of his criminal history by electronic news agencies. The legality of this record was backed up by the Supreme Court when it decided that reliance by employers on news articles about criminals, even juvenile criminals, was protected by the Fourth Amendment" (212).

45. Wacquant, *Punishing the Poor*, 206.

46. Critics of the scope and intensity of contemporary modes of dataveillance have compared the discriminatory potential of such practices, called weblining, to those at play in redlining—banks' racist (and now illegal) refusal to lend money in particular neighborhoods due to the number of residents of color. The novel suggests how the former makes possible a new version of the latter. On weblining, Lyon, *Surveillance Studies*, 102; Schneier, *Data and Goliath*, 109. On the use of online data gathering as part of (racially) discriminatory practice, see also Boyd, "White Flight in Networked Publics"; Gandy, "Matrix Multiplication and the Digital Divide."

47. Such dynamics feature prominently in "Voices," "En Masse," and "The Electric Eye."

48. In fact, in the text property ownership unmediated by corporations has become impossibly rare. Not only can the head of one corporation own his own country, but even personal items in people's apartments are rented: "Almost everything by 2055 was leased. That stabilized the profit factor and created a built-in insurance policy. No one owned anything except the manufacturers" (327). Several characters express shock when they encounter the existence of an individually owned diner, one of them remarking, "A private business. . . . In New York. Wow" (275).

49. On the relationship between police activity in poor neighborhoods of color and the interests of real estate developers, see Ritchie, *Invisible No More*.

50. As Rodríguez suggests, "[N]ormative civil whiteness implies an ongoing and complex relation of hierarchy, discipline, power, and violence that has come to oversee the current and increasingly incorporative 'multicultural' modalities of white supremacy, wherein 'people of color' are selectively and incrementally solicited, rewarded, and absorbed into the operative functionings of white-supremacist institutions . . . and discourses" (*Forced Passages*, 25). In a similar vein, Jasbir Puar points to an "ascendancy of whiteness, which is not a conservative, racist formation bent on extermination, but rather an insidious liberal one proffering an innocuous inclusion into life," later noting, "liberalism works through the positive register of incorporation" (*Terrorist Assemblages*, 31, 114). See also Bonilla-Silva, *Racism without Racists*, 225–54; Ferguson, *The Reorder of Things*; Hong, *Death beyond Disavowal*; Melamed, *Represent and Destroy*.

51. Warren, *What Was African American Literature?* 2, 18.

52. As Eduardo Bonilla-Silva observes, "[R]ather than arguing about whether the significance of race has declined, increased, or not changed at all, the issue at hand is assessing if a transformation has occurred in the *racial structure* of the United States" (*Racism without Racists*, 26).

53. On the ways these elements reinforce each other and multiply negative effects within poor urban communities of color, see Clear, *Imprisoning Communities*; Peterson and Krivo, *Divergent Social Worlds*; Sharkey, *Stuck in Place*. As Cacho observes, "[R]esidents of the inner city are held responsible today for crimes they might never commit in the future"(*Social Death*, 83). On the history of enacting "law and order" policy by categorizing inner-city urban youth of color as potential criminals, and developing urban policy based on this presumption, see Hinton, *From the War on Poverty to the War on Crime*.

54. The text repeatedly suggests that far more Black people remain committed to Infochurch, the "religion" organized around science started and run by the MacroCode corporation, than to the Radical Congresses. However, as Kali Tal argues, "The authors of black militant novels of armed resistance to and overthrow of white supremacy almost never attempt to describe postrevolutionary society and often abandon their protagonists before, in the middle of, or immediately after the battle," suggesting that a significant dynamic in Black speculative fictional imaginaries (specifically, in this case, "black militant near-future fiction"—a category in which I would place *Futureland*) may be a running refusal to posit a reformed/redeemed system beyond current modes of violence and Black opposition to them ("That Just Kills Me," 70).

55. Elsewhere, Mosley observes, "Freedom of physical motion, no matter how proscribed by property and Afrophobia, was a sweet nectar and a balm for all those centuries under lock and key" (*Workin' on the Chain Gang*, 40).

56. See Dubey, "The Future of Race in Afro-Futurist Fiction," 25. In "The Electric Eye," agents from MacroCode murder a group of Itsies, in what the police determine are "[government-]sanctioned assassinations" (145), in order to prevent them gaining information that would interfere in MacroCode's efforts to prevent the Itsies from waging a "race war" through biological weapons targeted against Black people.

57. One-eighth Black blood historically served for many states as the threshold beneath which one ceased legally to be Black. See Pascoe, *What Comes Naturally*, 116. Isiah Lavender observes, "Mosley ends his story with an unmistakable implication: the idea of racial difference will survive an apocalypse wholly intact" (*Race in American Science Fiction*, 132). An intertext for Mosely's plague may be the "Jes Grew" plague in Ishmael Reed's novel *Mumbo Jumbo*. See Lavender, *Race in American Science Fiction*, 163–65.

58. As Mosley notes in an interview about the book, "So you have some slightly black people chasing a *really* black person—and the world recreates itself" (Brady, *Conversations with Walter Mosley*, 117).

59. The absence of a determinate location to which one flees corresponds to the ways flight signals less an intermediary state than a kind of permanent unsettledness with respect to ongoing histories made possible by the violence of slavery and its legacies. On fugitivity as perpetual, see Hesse, "Escaping Liberty"; Best and Hartman, "Fugitive Justice"; Dillon, *Fugitive Life*; James, "Afrarealism and the Black Matrix."

60. Harney and Moten, *The Undercommons*, 51, 98.

61. On Black fugitivity, see Best, *The Fugitive's Properties*; Cervenak, *Wandering*; Diouf, *Slavery's Exiles*; Dillon, *Fugitive Life*; Franklin and Sweninger, *Runaway Slaves*; Kawash, *Dislocating the Color Line*; Roberts, *Freedom as Marronage*; Thompson, *Flight to Freedom*; Vimalassery, "Fugitive Decolonization." On contemporary forms of everyday fugitivity in relation to the criminal justice system, see Goffman, *On the Run*. On incarceration as a form of "coercive mobility" that increases violence within poor, urban neighborhoods, see Clear, *Imprisoning Communities*. On the ways flight from the law comes to function as one of the principal signs of authentic blackness, see Wagner, *Disturbing the Peace*.

62. Roberts, *Freedom as Marronage*, 9, 23.

63. Harney and Moten, *The Undercommons*, 63.

64. Harney and Moten juxtapose policy, as participation within extant systems and their modes of intelligibility, to planning: "This ongoing experiment with the informal, carried out by and on the means of social reproduction, as the to come of the forms of life, is what we mean by planning; planning in the undercommons is not an activity, not fishing or dancing or teaching or loving, but the ceaseless experiment with the futurial presence of the forms of life that make such activities possible" (*The Undercommons*, 74–75).

65. On the routine dynamics of coercion and violence at play in (neo)liberal political economy, see Cacho, *Social Death*; Dayan, *The Law Is a White Dog*; Melamed, *Represent and Destroy*; Povinelli, *Economies of Abandonment*; Rodríguez, *Forced Passages*; Singh, *Race and America's Long War*; Weheliye, *Habeas Viscus*.

66. Mosley himself was a computer programmer before becoming a novelist. See Brady, *Conversations with Walter Mosley*, 70; Wilson, *Walter Mosley*, 7.

67. Similarly, in "Angel's Island," Bits has been imprisoned due to having designed a program that "could take over almost any computer system by translating it into a code that no one else could read or decipher" (97), which he first uses to destroy the database of the "intercorporate council," and he then turns the program on the systems of Angel's Island itself in order to free himself and his fellow inmates while alerting the world to the humiliations and experimentation to which prisoners had been subjected.

68. The text's fugitive imaginary, though, also involves processes of what might be termed becoming code, with characters leaving their bodies behind in order to enter virtual environments as conscious participants. Examples include Ptolemy's transformation of his grandmother and brother into code in "Whispers in the Dark," Frendon's merger into the database of jurors in "Little Brother," and Neil's absorption into Un Fitt in "En Masse." Given that all these various feats of design are performed by African American programmers, Mosley also challenges assumptions that Black people fear new technologies or have failed to engage with them. See Bould, "The Ships Landed Long Ago"; Dery, "Black to the Future"; Everett, *Digital Diaspora*; Nelson, "Introduction"; Rusert, *Fugitive Science*; Williams, "Black Secret Technology"; Womack, *Afrofuturism*.

69. See Cox, *Shapeshifters*; Goffman, *On the Run*; Harris-Perry, *Sister Citizen*; Khan-Cullors and bandele, *When They Call You a Terrorist*; Richie, *Arrested Justice*. For explicit discussion of Black women's theorizations of fugitivity, though, see Dillon, *Fugitive Life*.

70. Brand, *A Map to the Door of No Return*, 50, 85.

71. See McKittrick, *Demonic Grounds*.

72. Ellis, *Territories of the Soul*, 2.

73. Harney and Moten conceptualize abolition in the following terms: "Not so much the abolition of prisons but the abolition of a society that could have prisons, that could have slavery, that could have the wage, and therefore not abolition as the elimination of anything but abolition as the founding of a new society" (*The Undercommons*, 42).

74. Cervenak, *Wandering*, 61, 101.

75. *Robopocalypse* (2011) is the first in a two-book series that also includes *Robogenesis* (2014).

76. See Comack, *Racialized Policing*; Dhillon, *Prairie Rising*; Pasternak, *Grounded Authority*; Razack, *Dying from Improvement*; Ritchie, *Invisible No More*; Ross, *Inventing the Savage*.

77. Wilson, *Robopocalypse*, 20. Hereafter, page numbers for this work are cited in parentheses in the text.

78. On the history of the Osage Nation, see Burns, *A History of the Osage People*; Dennison, *Colonial Entanglement*; Mathews, *The Osages*; Wilson, *The Underground Reservation*. Given that Wilson is Cherokee, it remains unclear as to why he chose to feature the Osage people rather than his own. Possible reasons may be that the Osage Allotment Act of 1906 preserved the existence of three communal villages, of which Gray Horse is one, and due to that same act's creation of what has come to be known as the "mineral estate" (the subsurface rights to the land covered by the Osage reservation) as a collective holding of the Osage Nation, the Osage continue to have land recognized as a reservation in ways that no other people in what formerly was Indian Territory (now Oklahoma) do (instead having jurisdictional service areas). In addition, the territory of the Cherokee Nation of Oklahoma, of which Wilson is a citizen, can be understood as created in the nineteenth century through the seizure of Osage lands by the United States. In other words, engaging with Cherokee landedness in what is now Oklahoma might entail addressing the tensions among Indigenous peoples over their land bases that results from U.S. removals and relocations. The novels tend to seek to avoid engaging these kinds of questions about the politics of placemaking, a point I address further later in this section.

79. The organizing conceit of *Robopocalypse* is that Cormac Wallace, a white man who becomes a leader in the human resistance launched from Gray Horse, finds a trove of recorded information after Archos has been defeated. The passages in italics are from Cormac's framing narration at the beginning and end of chapters, which are focused on various other characters.

80. The phrase "Trail of Tears" usually is used to describe the removal of the Cherokee Nation from their lands in the U.S. Southeast (primarily Georgia and North Carolina) during the late 1830s, and sometimes it refers to the removal during this period of what were termed the Five Civilized Tribes (Cherokees, Creeks, Chickasaws, Choctaws, and Seminoles): see Green, *The Politics of Indian Removal*; Justice, *Our Fire Survives the Storm*; McLoughlin, *Cherokee Renascence in the New Republic*. Here Wilson seems to conflate Cherokee and Osage history, drawing on probably the most well-known figure of Native forced relocation. The founding of what would officially become the Osage

reservation resulted from the sale of the U.S.-recognized Osage land base in 1870 (in what is now Kansas) and their removal to what was then Indian Territory and later would become Oklahoma. The new reservation was on lands that previously had been officially recognized as Osage but had been sold in 1825, although Osage bands had continued to live in the area during the intervening decades.

81. On the importance of red in Osage practices and stories, see Bailey, *The Osage and the Invisible World*, 32, 64; Mathews, *The Osages*, 333.

82. *Robogenesis* underlines the power and importance of this vision of belonging by having the book's villain—the Osage man Hank Cotton who has been overtaken by an artificial intelligence bent on annihilating life—initiate a campaign of displacement and murder against "nonnatives." See Wilson, *Robogenesis*, 282–88.

83. Wilson, *Robogenesis*, 96.

84. On this image, see Carroll, *Roots of Our Renewal*; Day, *Alien Capital*; Engle, *The Elusive Promise of Indigenous Development*; Niezen, *The Origins of Indigenism*; Pasternak, *Grounded Authority*; Powell, *Landscapes of Power*. Wilson himself received a doctorate in robotics from the Massachusetts Institute of Technology. On the complexities of gaining access to digital networks on Indigenous lands and the importance of reorganizing digital networks and informational infrastructures in ways that meet Indigenous desires and needs, see Duarte, *Network Sovereignty*; Latukefu, "Remote Indigenous Communities in Australia"; Sandvig, "Connection at Ewiiaapaayp Mountain"; Srinivasan, "Indigenous, Ethnic and Cultural Articulations of New Media."

85. These images resonate with the dynamics of some urban riots in the 1960s and 1970s. See Hinton, *From the War on Poverty to the War on Crime*, 69.

86. The other reference to non-natives as a "tribe" in the series appears in *Robogenesis*. In the first book, readers learn that Archos has been fusing robotic elements to humans, enhancing their sensory capacities, and in *Robogenesis*, those who had been "modified" by Archos become targeted for destruction by a (series of affiliated) group(s) known as "The Tribe." Wilson later reveals that these people, like those who start murdering non-Indians on Osage territory, actually are under the control of Archos-8, Arayt Shah (the predecessor of the Archos of *Robopocalypse*). Characterizing the group being overwhelmed and controlled by Arayt as "the Tribe" provides a direct contrast to Cormac's description of those in New York and other cities as "urban tribes," given that those groups accept the modified humans whereas the Tribe seeks to eliminate them.

87. Byrd, *The Transit of Empire*, xix, 54, 69.

88. On practices of self-indigenization by non-natives, see also Deloria, *Playing Indian*; Jackson, *Creole Indigeneity*; Huhndorf.

89. On Indigenous peoples' presence in urban spaces, see Cornum, "The Space NDN's Star Map"; Fixico, *The Urban Indian Experience in America*; Goeman, *Mark My Words*; Peters and Andersen, *Indigenous in the City*; Ramirez, *Native Hubs*; Razack, *Dying from Improvement*; Thrush, *Native Seattle*.

90. Tuck and Yang, "Decolonization Is Not a Metaphor," 1.

91. de la Cadena, *Earth Beings*, 116.

92. The most prominent characters in the New York sections of the novels are the Johnsons, who are African American, and Mathilda Perez, who is Latina.

93. Coulthard, *Red Skin, White Masks*, 13. For discussion of how such principles get operationalized within contemporary Native governance, see Carroll, *Roots of Our Renewal*; Duarte, *Network Sovereignty*; McCarthy, *In Divided Unity*; Pasternak, *Grounded Authority*; Powell, *Landscapes of Power*.

94. Moreton-Robinson, *The White Possessive*, 11.

95. King, "In the Clearing," 209.

96. Wilson, *Robogenesis*, 156, 158, 187.

97. Wilson, *Robogenesis*, 157, 342–43.

98. In Wilson's texts, the emphasis on networks and matrices of life, organic and not, is not focused on whether or not humans can engage or participate. Rather, the novels portray life as existing in a dynamic multiplicity without emphasizing the transformation of human subjectivity in ways that can acknowledge or consciously participate in that multiplicity. In this sense, the perspective adopted by the texts toward such multiplicity seems less "posthuman" than "ahuman." On the posthuman, see Baidotti, *The Posthuman*; Nayar, *Posthumanism*; Singh, *Unthinking Mastery*; Vint, *Bodies of Tomorrow*. Similarly, the novels' representation exceeds the notion of the "parahuman" developed by Monique Allewaert. She suggests with respect to the ecologies generated by plantation labor and the African slave trade, "The key points here are, first, that the body is opened such that parts of this (non)body touch and participate in other forms of life and that other forms of life participate in it. This means, second, that parahumanity signals a relation grounded on the touching of life-forms, generally although not necessarily proximate life-forms. Third, the agency built through the touching of proximate life-forms does not allow a consolidation or closing of the parahuman body but a sufficiency built on the intimacies borne through incompletion" (*Ariel's Ecology*, 99). However, Wilson's novels do not focus on (crossing) the limits of humanity, on traversing (dominant notions of) the boundaries of the human body in order to illustrate a (new) relation to place.

99. Examples include robots whose movement is based on ants (20), ones with legs that prepare them "for wilderness travel" over "mud and ice" (214), animal-like movements in "the forest" (215), and ones that function like "lizards" (279).

100. On the ways speculative cultural production engages with various kinds of embodiment, including challenging an a priori distinction between the "natural" and the "artificial," see Vint, *Bodies of Tomorrow*.

101. Wilson, *Robogenesis*, 127, 194.

102. In an interview in February 2012 with *Lightspeed* magazine, Wilson describes the novel as offering "a big, complicated, constantly evolving ecosystem of robots." See "Interview: Daniel H. Wilson," February 2012, accessed March 31, 2016, http://www.lightspeedmagazine.com/nonfiction/feature-interview-daniel-h-wilson.

103. Wilson, *Robogenesis*, 247–48.

104. Wilson, *Robogenesis*, 275, 295.

105. Wilson, *Robogenesis*, 58.

106. Wilson, *Robogenesis*, 334.

107. Wilson, *Robogenesis*, 294.

108. Similarly, *Robopocalypse* underlines the significance of the fact that Archos's central processors are in western Alaska, a cooled and remote space (300, 383). Wilson's

emphasis on the existence of servers whose physical proximity to each other makes possible Archos's intelligence provides a sharp contrast to the deterritorialized ubiquity of surveillance and data-gathering in *Futureland*.

109. Goeman, *Mark My Words*, 32, 38. I address such processes of recognition more fully in the next chapter. For analysis and critique of state projects of recognition with respect to indigeneity, see Barker, *Native Acts*; Coulthard, *Red Skin, White Masks*; Engle, *The Elusive Promise of Indigenous Development*; Kauanui, *Hawaiian Blood*; Million, *Therapeutic Nations* ; Povinelli, *The Cunning of Recognition*; Simpson, *Mohawk Interruptus*.

110. Goeman, *Mark My Words*, 32, 38. There also are Native futurist texts that are quite skeptical about the politics of Indigenous territoriality as articulated within settler legal structures and histories. For example, in *Treaty Shirts*, Gerald Vizenor suggests that contemporary tribal governments and their jurisdictional mappings may serve more to normalize settler-oriented geographies than to enable and realize Indigenous freedom, and in *Riding the Trail of Tears*, Blake Hausman explores how the reiteration of narratives of Natives as having lost their lands (due to removal or other kinds of settler expropriations) may do more to reinforce a non-native vision of Native people(s) as victims of trauma than to build vital Indigenous futures.

111. Goeman, *Mark My Words*, 12.

112. Watson, "Settled and Unsettled Spaces," 15. On Native mobilities, see also Chang, *The World and All the Things upon It*; Clifford, *Returns*; Lawrence, *"Real" Indians and Others*; Peters and Andersen, *Indigenous in the City*; Povinelli, *Labor's Lot*; Ramirez, *Native Hubs*; Smith, *Everything You Know about Indians Is Wrong*; Vizenor, *Fugitive Poses*.

113. In *Robopocalypse*, readers are introduced to Lonnie's son Paul through an incident in which a humanoid robot over which he's supposed to be exerting authority kills a number of Afghan civilians. Through this sequence, readers learn that such robots are being used by the military to try to build relationships in Afghan villages, also indicating that U.S. presence in Afghanistan extends for the next few decades (47–63).

114. Mosely, *The Wave*, 3–4. Hereafter, page numbers from this work are cited in parentheses in the text. Readers also learn that Errol's grandmother was a member of the Southern Christian Leadership Conference (2), but the novel seems far less concerned with this experience than with Albert's, following as it does lines of patriarchal inheritance in ways I address later.

115. Mosley notes that Errol's mother was a "wasp" (4), and Errol later observes of his sister's husband, "He was from a South Carolinian ex-slaveholding family that had broken off contact with him when he married my light-skinned sister" (48). Mosley himself is the child of a mixed-race marriage between a white woman and a Black man. See Brady, *Conversations with Walter Mosley*, xii.

116. Later, Errol observes, "Each aspect of the Wave . . . was physically connected to every other aspect of the greater being. This oneness made for a mind that was all-enveloping" (179).

117. See Sharpe, *In the Wake*.

118. Dayan, *The Law Is a White Dog*, 22, 5, 64, 32, 60.

119. In addition to characters' (mis)characterization of those reanimated as "zombies," the running references to the Wave as "God" suggest that Mosley implicitly is invoking Vodou. See Dayan, *Haiti, History, and the Gods*.

120. On the history of the growth of police power and definition of crime in relation to pathologizing and criminalizing conceptions of blackness, see Browne, *Dark Matters*; Muhammad, *The Condemnation of Blackness*; Wagner, *Disturbing the Peace*.

121. McKittrick, *Demonic Grounds*, 9.

122. As Dayan argues, "Domestic prison cases are remarkable in their prophetic potential. They prepared the ground locally for the United States' treatment of prisoners at Abu Ghraib, Guantánamo, and other as-yet-unnamed detention sites" (*The Law Is a White Dog*, 95). On the links between the "war on terror" and the prior "war on crime," which includes the "war on drugs," see also Khan-Cullors and bandele, *When They Call You a Terrorist*; Simon, *Governing through Crime*, 259–83; Singh, *Race and America's Long War*. For an extended meditation by Mosley on African Americans' relation to 9/11 and the supposed war on terror, see Mosley, *What Next*. In a different vein, Byrd suggests, "In the United States, the Indian is the original enemy combatant" (*The Transit of Empire*, xviii). On the relationship between contemporary understandings of the threat of terrorism and the history of narrating Indigenous peoples as "indios bárbaros," see Saldaña-Portillo, *Indian Given*.

123. Kempner, "The Unshakeable Intent to Commit Genocide," 178.

124. The phrase "neo-slave narrative" usually refers to contemporary texts set during slavery, but the concept productively can be stretched to include texts that offer a first-person account of escape from contemporary modes of enslavement/captivity. See Dubey, "Speculative Fictions of Slavery"; Schalk, *Bodyminds Reimagined*, 33–84.

125. Notably, when Errol attempts to explain the torture he's seen while in custody to his white ex-wife, she responds, "I can't believe that" (158). For a differently configured version of the settler nation as white possession, see Moreton-Robinson, *The White Possessive*. On whiteness as property, see Harris, "Whiteness"; Lipsitz, *The Possessive Investment in Whiteness*.

126. For the ways these kinds of racial-geographic assemblages, particularly in terms of continental categories, are crucial to population genetics and other genomic invocations of race, explicit and implicit, see Bliss, *Race Decoded*; Fujimura et al., "Race and Ancestry"; Reardon, *Race to the Finish*; Sankar, "Forensic DNA Phenotyping."

127. See Mosley, *The Wave*, 111–12, 123, 129, 131, 201.

128. On the history of Black people being seen as properly belonging to the "tropics," rather than "temperate" spaces such as the United States and Canada, see Asaka. This imagery of the "environment" also resonates with Christina Sharpe's characterization of antiblackness and the afterlives of slavery as like the weather. She writes, "[T]he weather is the totality of our environments; the weather is the total climate; and that climate is antiblack" (*In the Wake*, 104).

129. Ahuja, *Bioinsecurities*, 11.

130. On the ways Anglo-American discourses of race (particularly blackness) emerge out of earlier legal notions of blood taint for crime, see Dayan, *The Law Is a White Dog*, 39–70. The figures of infection in the novel also might be read as implicitly alluding to

the persistence of a smallpox imaginary in which whites fear being subjected to the kinds of mass death endured by Native peoples after contact. On the ways this imaginary played out in the early 2000s, see Ahuja, *Bioinsecurities*, 133–68.

131. Ahmed, *Queer Phenomenology*, 11, 134.

132. Harney and Moten, *The Undercommons*, 97.

133. Brand, *A Map to the Door of No Return*, 35.

134. Hartman, *Lose Your Mother*, 234.

135. Sexton, "The *Vel* of Slavery," 6.

136. Kamugisha, "The Black Experience of New World Coloniality," 129; Newton, "Returns to a Native Land," 109. This line of thought might be traced to Sylvia Wynter's analysis of Jamaican folklore, specifically of marronage and the preservation and refiguration of African social forms within it. See Wynter, "Jonkonnu in Jamaica." For recent discussions of Black indigenization in the Americas, see Boyce Davies, "From Masquerade to *Maskarade*"; Dillon, *New World Drama*; Mackie, "Welcome the Outlaw"; McKittrick, "Plantation Futures"; Posmentier, *Cultivation and Catastrophe*; Roberts, *Freedom as Marronage*. For critique of such a narrative of indigenization, see Byrd, *The Transit of Empire*; Diaz, "Creolization and Indigeneity"; Jackson, *Creole Indigeneity*; Newton, "Returns to a Native Land." See also the discussion of indigenization in chapter 1. I return to this topic in the next chapter.

137. On the question of whether indigeneity is a useful frame in which to think historical or current political formations in Africa (particularly given histories of indirect rule, the construction of forms of "native" identity under colonialism, and the struggles for postcolonial nationhood), see Claassens and Cousins, *Land, Power, and Custom*: Hodgson, *Being Maasai, Becoming Indigenous*; Mamdani, *Citizen and Subject*.

138. For additional discussion of Black conceptions of immersion in the land of the Americas in the eighteenth and nineteenth centuries that are not presented as indigenization, see Allewaert, *Ariel's Ecology*; Ben-zvi, *Native Land Talk*; Ruffin, *Black on Earth*.

139. As Yael Ben-zvi notes of African American claims to "native" status in the United States, "Arrivant self-nativization was a resettlement project that revised the conditions of belonging to colonized land by turning the nativized arrivant into the consequence of an inevitable historical teleology in which native status functioned as reparations for slavery" (*Native Land Talk*, 158).

140. Having hidden the substance of the Wave that remained after the assault on the cave in a lion statute in Golden Gate Park, Errol thinks when he is recaptured by Wheeler, "All of the kicks and punches were reminders that I had defeated mankind and saved the Black God of Earth" (200). See also Mosley, *The Wave*, 175, 178, 194, 222, 226. In addition, during Errol's first time in government captivity, Wheeler reveals that Arthur's grave had been exhumed, and "all that's left in the coffin is fine white sand," and GT says to Errol, "I am your father. I was dead and I have risen" (100), presenting GT/Arthur as Christ-like.

141. In addition, when GT swallows a portion of the "black tar" in order to preserve it, as well as to enable him to transfer his consciousness to another body, Errol notes, "The sounds he made were like the strangulation of a whole herd of bison" (192), linking the Wave to one of the most iconic figures of Indianness.

142. Dery, "Black to the Future," 190–91. Mosley himself observes, "For black people in particular, the future is all we have because the past has been taken away from us and the present is defined in certain ways" (Brady, *Conversations with Walter Mosley*, 108).

143. The novel also presents the connection of the Wave to Farsinger in fairly hetero-patriarchal terms: Farsinger is the Wave's "mate" (70); the human manifestations of the Wave that exist as actual characters are all men; and when the two are united, "the Wave gushed up into the hole presented by Farsinger's light" (225).

144. In this vein, Colson Whitehead's *The Underground Railroad* suggests that collective Black placemaking in the United States either is organized as part of white projects of extraction/exploitation or, if it attempts to move beyond white control, will be subjected to retributional and disintegrative violence; the central, literalized figure of the underground railroad, then, speaks to the significance of perpetual Black fugitivity. However, even as Whitehead gestures at multiple points toward anti-Indian violence and the ways the United States is built on expropriated Native lands, the novel speaks of Indiana, Oklahoma, and California as potential places for Black dwelling with no sense of these as spaces occupied by still existing Native peoples. Moreover, the text repeatedly speaks of "colored" and "European" *tribes* while indicating, "The Great War has always been between the white and the black. It always would be" (*The Underground Railroad*, 395). The frame of Black fugitivity here seems to leave little room for acknowledging ongoing Native territorialities and sovereignties.

4. THE MAROON MATRIX

1. Gottlieb, *The Mother of Us All*, xiii; Sharpe, *Ghosts of Slavery*, 4; Thompson, *Flight to Freedom*, 47. I use the lower-case "maroon" when talking generically, and the upper-case "Maroon" when speaking about particular communities who refer to themselves in this way.

2. Roberts, *Freedom as Marronage*, 4; Thompson, *Flight to Freedom*, 7.

3. McKittrick, *Demonic Grounds*, xxiii.

4. See Harris, "Whiteness as Property"; King, "In the Clearing"; Moreton-Robinson, *The White Possessive*; Sullivan, *Revealing Whiteness*.

5. While various forms of marronage occurred on land now claimed by the United States, the concept rarely gets invoked when speaking of U.S. history and contemporary African American projects of racial justice, and in this way, it offers a Hemispheric frame that can help reorient discussions of Black collectivity and the (geo)politics of Black landedness. On marronage in the U.S. context, see Diouf, *Slavery's Exiles*; Navakas, *Liquid Landscape*, 91–124; Thompson, *Flight to Freedom*.

6. James, "Afrarealism and the Black Matrix," 124, 127; Thomas, "*Marronnons*/Let's Maroon," 71.

7. Roberts, *Freedom as Marronage*, 124.

8. Jackson, *Creole Indigeneity*, 52, 69. See also Ben-zvi, *Native Land Talk*.

9. Yarimar Bonilla argues, "The association of marronage with the nationalist movement was not exclusive to the French Antilles. Throughout the Caribbean, intellectuals during the period began to turn to the figure of the maroon as a protonationalist hero,"

adding, "[T]he representation of marronage that emerged during this period hinged on the celebration of grand marronage [fugitivity on a large-scale] as a form of both ideological and political rupture" (*Non-Sovereign Futures*, 48).

10. See Anderson, *Black and Indigenous*; Engle, *The Elusive Promise of Indigenous Development*; Escobar, *Territories of Difference*; French, *Legalizing Identities*; Greene, "Introduction"; Hooker, "Indigenous Inclusion/Black Exclusion"; Ng'weno, "Can Ethnicity Replace Race?"; Palacio, "Cultural Identity among Rural Garifuna Migrants in Belize City, Belize."

11. For example, Roberts characterizes marronage as "a multidimensional, constant act of flight," juxtaposing it with modes of sovereignty which he describes as "top down instead of bottom up." Flight, then, indexes a kind of permanent revolution "that usher[s] in new orders and refashion[s] society's foundations." See Roberts, *Freedom as Marronage*, 9, 103, 115–16.

12. Lorde, *Sister Outsider*, 115.

13. De la Cadena, *Earth Beings*, xxv, 4.

14. See Barker, *Native Acts*; Engle, *The Elusive Promise of Indigenous Development*; French, *Legalizing Identities*; Garroutte, *Real Indians*; Hooker, "Indigenous Inclusion/ Black Exclusion"; Rifkin, "Making Peoples into Populations."

15. Scott, *Conscripts of Modernity*, 19.

16. Sharpe, *Ghosts of Slavery*, 4. See also Gottlieb, *The Mother of Us All*.

17. Hopkinson, *Midnight Robber*, 18. Hereafter, page numbers from this work are cited in parentheses in the text.

18. See Duke, *Building a Nation*, 55–61.

19. Garvey's plans for mass mobilization came to a more spectacularly disastrous end, with his being imprisoned in 1923 in the Atlanta State Penitentiary for mail fraud and deported back to Jamaica in 1927. On Garvey's career and significance, see Duke, *Building a Nation*, 71–79; Kelley, *Freedom Dreams*, 36–59; Stephens, *Black Empire*, 75–125.

20. See Enteen, "On the Receiving End of the Colonization," 263; Glave, "An Interview with Nalo Hopkinson," 150.

21. Stephens, *Black Empire*, 48.

22. See Alexander, *Pedagogies of Crossing*; Bogues, "Politics, Nation, and PostColony"; Bonilla, *Non-Sovereign Futures*; Clark, "Twenty Preliminary Propositions for a Critical History of International Statecraft in Haiti"; Dubois, *Haiti*; Iton, *In Search of the Black Fantastic*; Kamugisha, "The Coloniality of Citizenship in the Contemporary Anglophone Caribbean"; Scott, *Omens of Adversity*; Thomas, *Exceptional Violence*; Wilder, *Freedom Time*.

23. Kelley, *Freedom Dreams*, 3, 16.

24. See Anatol, "Maternal Discourses in Nalo Hopkinson's *Midnight Robber*"; Crosby, "Black Girlhood Interrupted."

25. Braithwaite, "Connecting to a Future Community," 89.

26. In this way, the novel plays with the Jamaican national slogan "Out of Many, One People": Hanchard, "Black Memory versus State Memory," 58; Thomas, *Exceptional Violence*, 112. This vision of combination, though, differs from the kinds of amalgamation at play in Butler's *Xenogenesis*, as discussed in chapter 2, in that they are combined as part of a situated political community envisioned as primarily Black.

27. The novel, though, does specifically invoke the Middle Passage in relation to the journey beyond the Earth. As part of the Jonakanoo celebration commemorating the Marryshevites' arrival on Toussaint, the first of the Nation Worlds, Tan-Tan receives a hat "woven in the torus shape of a nation ship," but in offering it to her, Ben, a local artisan, observes, "Long time, that hat woulda be make in the shape of a sea ship, not a rocket ship, and them black people inside woulda been lying pack-up head to toe in they own shit, with chains round them ankles. Let the child remember how black people make this crossing as free people this time" (20–21). On the history of slavery in Jamaica, see Brown, *The Reaper's Garden*.

28. Notably, Marcus Garvey claimed to be descended from Jamaican maroons. See Bilby, *True-Born Maroons*, 27.

29. Likely born in the late seventeenth century, Granny Nanny of the Windward Maroons appears only four times in documentary sources, one of which is not the 1739 treaty with British authorities that officially recognized their relative autonomy. The 1740 land grant for the community, though, is made out to her, and the central village of the community was Nanny Town until it was destroyed in 1734, replaced by Moore Town, which itself often is known as New Nanny Town. On Nanny's history and the ways she is taken up by contemporary Maroons, and more broadly in Jamaica, see Bilby, *True-Born Maroons*; Brathwaite, "Nanny, Palmares, and the Caribbean Maroon Connection"; Gottlieb, *The Mother of Us All*; Sharpe, *Ghosts of Slavery*, 1–43; Zips, *Nanny's Asafo Warriors*.

30. Located in what is now Brazil, it had from fifteen thousand to twenty thousand residents in the late seventeenth century and existed as a confederation of numerous towns, with a capital and a king. See Thompson, *Flight to Freedom*, 86, 129, 212, 218. For a futurist reimagining of Palmares, see Amadahy, *The Moons of Palmares*.

31. In an interview with Dianne Glave, Hopkinson indicates her interest in exploring "what stories we'd tell ourselves about our technology—what our paradigms for it might be," adding, "I wondered what metaphors we (Caribbean people) would create for technologies that we had made, how we would think about those technologies" ("An Interview with Nalo Hopkinson," 149).

32. Notably, Nanny's various abilities (including healing, speaking with the dead, capturing bullets fired at her, and prophesying) are referred to by Maroons as "science," suggesting that Hopkinson implicitly draws on Maroon terminology in connecting domains that for most Euro-Americans would be differentiated as the supernatural versus the technological. See Bilby, *True-Born Maroons*, 7; Gottlieb, *The Mother of Us All*, 14; Sharpe, *Ghosts of Slavery*, 3. In this way, the novel draws on African diasporic traditions to contest the popular representation of Black people as technophobic. See Bould, "The Ships Landed Long Ago"; Dery, "Black to the Future"; Everett, *Digital Diaspora*; Nelson, "Introduction"; Rusert, *Fugitive Science*; Williams, "Black Secret Technology"; Womack, *Afrofuturism*.

33. Sharpe, *Ghosts of Slavery*, 6.

34. This figuration of Nanny as facilitating relations in diaspora is particularly notable given the ways maroon communities often are interpreted, particularly in Jamaica, as the bearers of African memory and culture in ways largely lost by other descendants of African slaves. See Bilby, *True-Born Maroons*, 35, 69–87; Mackie, "Welcome the Outlaw"; Sharpe, *Ghosts of Slavery*, 1–43; Zips, *Nanny's Asafo Warriors*.

35. Nelson, "Making the Impossible Possible," 100. Jillana Enteen suggests that Hopkinson "envisions alternative societal configurations that are embedded in different relationships to power, knowledge, and the legacies of slavery and colonialism" than those of the extratextual present, with Granny Nanny enabling "a world that eliminates previous forms of inequity" ("On the Receiving End of the Colonization," 265). Similarly, Erin Fehskens notes that "the Nanny Web and the Marryshow Corporation appear to have successfully relocated a population out of the Caribbean, out of debt, out of labor, and into a fully surveyed, and yet fully egalitarian world" ("The Matter of Bodies," 140). For discussion of Granny Nanny as a semi-totalitarian presence, see Crosby, "Black Girlhood Interrupted"; Smith, *Globalization, Utopia and Postcolonial Science Fiction*, 43–67.

36. Stephens, *Black Empire*, 13. For critiques of the role of respectability and heteropatriarchy within Caribbean political history, see Alexander, *Pedagogies of Crossing*; Bogues, "Politics, Nation, and PostColony"; Kamugisha, "The Coloniality of Citizenship in the Contemporary Anglophone Caribbean"; Sheller, *Citizenship from Below*; Thomas, *Exceptional Violence*.

37. Sharpe, *Ghosts of Slavery*, 17.

38. Bilby, *True-Born Maroons*, xiv. See also Harris, "The True Traditions of My Ancestors"; Sharpe, *Ghosts of Slavery*; Zips, *Nanny's Asafo Warriors*. This tension also arises, albeit in a refracted way, in the novel's portrayal of the pedicab runners, "a new sect" that emerged "about fifty years" before the main plot of the novel begins and who live in separate group households and have their own cooperative form of semi-self-governance (8–10). Readers learn that they are descended from the people who created Nanny— "We was programmer clan" (52)—and that their greater intimacy with "nannysong," the code through which the system operates, allows them to communicate more fluently with the sentient interface and to request things of it. Here we have a disjunction between those who more directly inherit a relation to Nanny and the rest of the population, for which Nanny functions more diffusely as a guide and encompassing presence. Yet, the part of the novel that takes place on Toussaint is set in Cockpit County (4), of which Antonio is the mayor, and in Jamaica, Cockpit County is where the central village of the Leeward Maroons, Accompong, is located. See Clemente, "Tan-Tan's Exile and Odyssey in Nalo Hopkinson's *Midnight Robber*," 13.

39. As Eric D. Smith notes, New Half-Way Tree is "named both for the midpoint between Kingston Harbour and Spanish Town, a customary resting place for newly transported slaves, and the point of intersection between affluent and poor areas of Kingston" (*Globalization, Utopia and Postcolonial Science Fiction*, 52).

40. Critics also compare the violence of this imposition to Antonio's incestuous relationship with Tan-Tan. See Anatol, "Maternal Discourses in Nalo Hopkinson's *Midnight Robber*," 112; Clemente, "Tan-Tan's Exile and Odyssey in Nalo Hopkinson's *Midnight Robber*," 12; Enteen, "On the Receiving End of the Colonization," 272.

41. Forte, "Introduction," 4. Jackson notes of narratives of cultural change in the Caribbean, "[C]reolization processes literally and figuratively clear the ground upon which they place new, indigenous subjects," adding, "This ground clearing is not achieved once in the past . . . [but] remains active and formative in the ongoing production of belonging" (*Creole Indigeneity*, 74). See also Byrd, *The Transit of Empire*, 77–116; Diaz,

"Creolization and Indigeneity"; Forte, *Ruins of Absence, Presence of Caribs*; Newton, "Returns to a Native Land." This way of envisioning the Caribbean is at play in Glissant's distinction between "Root" and "Relation," discussed in chapter 1.

42. In this way, *Midnight Robber* might be contrasted with the vision of marronage at play in Zainab Amadahy's *The Moons of Palmares*. Amadahy's novel turns on the colonial relation between a corporatized Earth and people who have moved to another world that seeks to have its political independence recognized, but that process of creating collective governance has made those originally from Earth into the Indigenous people of this new world, who then serve as the stewards of its natural resources (enacting something of a mash-up of non–Euro-cultural traditions from Earth, including those of Indigenous peoples). On histories of science fiction's settler colonial imaginary of other worlds as terra nullius, see Kilgore, *Astrofuturism*.

43. See Brathwaite, "Nanny, Palmares, and the Caribbean Maroon Connection," 125–31; Escobar, *Territories of Difference*; French, *Legalizing Identities*; Palacio, "Cultural Identity among Rural Garifuna Migrants in Belize City, Belize." Nanny Town has been described as arising where a Native village previously had been located. See Dillon, "Indigenous Scientific Literacies in Nalo Hopkinson's Ceremonial Worlds," 29.

44. On New Half-Way Tree as the past or "unconscious" of Toussaint, see Smith, *Globalization, Utopia and Postcolonial Science Fiction*, 43–67.

45. On the Trinidadian figure of Papa Bois as a creolized version of a Carib figure, see Hernandez and Forte, "In This Place Where I Was Chief," 125. "Papa Bois" also is reminiscent of "the Ceiba or giant silk-cotton or kapok tree considered sacred by the Taino": Dillon, "Indigenous Scientific Literacies in Nalo Hopkinson's Ceremonial Worlds," 38).

46. Bilby, *True-Born Maroons*, 55, 87, 150; Gottlieb, *The Mother of Us All*, 47; Zips, *Nanny's Asafo Warriors*, 108–13. Furthermore, as Mimi Sheller notes, "Trees have long been at the center of social and political struggles in the Caribbean. In Bwa Kayiman, Haiti, a great mapou tree stands where the ceremony was held in 1791 inaugurating the slave uprising that sparked off the Haitian Revolution" (*Citizenship from Below*, 201). After being captured by French forces, Toussaint L'Ouverture declares, "In overthrowing me, you have cut down in Saint-Dominique only the trunk of the tree of the liberty of the blacks; it will grow back from the roots, because they are deep and numerous." See Roberts, *Freedom as Marronage*, 110. Moreover, everything that lies outside of human villages in the novel is referred to simply as the "bush." See Thompson, *Flight to Freedom*, 107, 281. In this way, the novel alludes to the specific resonance of the "bush" within the Caribbean, marking as it does all that exists beyond the control of the plantocracy, especially maroon communities. As Thompson notes, "The term *bush* in relation to runaway Africans was much more than a botanical expression. In the eyes of the planter class, the forest in all its wild magnificence was reduced to 'the bush,' which became associated with everything that was dark, sinister, even unholy," adding, "In the Caribbean the bush was contrasted with the plantation . . . also because Maroons issued forth periodically from it to harass the plantations" (*Flight to Freedom*, 36).

47. After her stepmother has tracked Tan-Tan to the daddy tree in which Chichibud's people dwell, even though the humans are beaten back without actually finding out about the douen village in the tree's branches, the douen reach the conclusion that they

must abandon the site for fear of discovery and conflict. As one douen women argues, "[T]hem will bring more tallpeople back here to hunt we down. Them will fight we with more of them gun and things. We ain't go have no peace from tallpeople again!" (273)

48. Turner, *This Is Not a Peace Pipe*, 7, 57.

49. Coulthard, *Red Skin, White Masks*, 60.

50. Amadahy and Lawrence, "Indigenous Peoples and Black People in Canada," 119, 122.

51. For an effort to think Harriet Tubman's contributions to fugitivity as part of a challenge to the possessive regimes of U.S. settler colonialism, see Vimalassery, "Fugitive Decolonization."

52. While Jonakanoo and Carnival seem to be parallel festivals in the novel, the one refers to a Jamaican celebration at Christmastime and the other to a Trinidadian festival prior to Lent. See Craton, "Decoding Pitchy-Patchy"; Dillon, *New World Drama*, 196–214; Wynter, "Jonkonnu." The novel pairs these two in ways reminiscent of its movement between Jamaican and Trinidadian dialects and its tendency to combine cultural elements from across the Caribbean.

53. This narrative technique is reminiscent of the U.S. frontier romance, in which Native peoples withdraw to an ever-receding western frontier in ways that enable the plot to conclude by reknitting the heretofore divided non-native community/ies. See Cheyfitz, "Savage Law"; Mielke, *Moving Encounters*; Rifkin, *When Did Indians Become Straight?* 99–142; Tawil, *The Making of Racial Sentiment*.

54. Notably, though, queer relationships appear prominently on both Toussaint and New Half-Way Tree in ways that seem completely normalized. See Hopkinson, *Midnight Robber*, 2, 4, 38–39, 48–49, 121. For discussion of the way the novel offers nonheteropatriarchal conceptions of kinship, see Bahng, *Migrant Futures*, 104–18.

55. See Diouf, *Slavery's Exiles*; Thompson, *Flight to Freedom*. On this dynamic in the novel, see Fehskens, "The Matter of Bodies."

56. Clemente, "Tan-Tan's Exile and Odyssey in Nalo Hopkinson's *Midnight Robber*," 19, 23; Hancock, "New Half-Way Tree and the Second World," 102, 104. See also Bahng, *Migrant Futures*, 117; Boyle. "Vanishing Bodies," 190; Braithwaite, "Connecting to a Future Community," 98; Crosby, "Black Girlhood Interrupted," 201; Enteen, "On the Receiving End of the Colonization," 263; Ramraj, "Nalo Hopkinson's Colonial and Dystopic Worlds in *Midnight Robber*," 137; Smith, *Globalization, Utopia and Postcolonial Science Fiction*, 66.

57. Byrd, *The Transit of Empire*, 66, 69.

58. Byrd, *The Transit of Empire*, 39, 112.

59. See Anatol, "Maternal Discourses in Nalo Hopkinson's *Midnight Robber*"; Braithwaite, "Connecting to a Future Community"; Clemente, "Tan-Tan's Exile and Odyssey in Nalo Hopkinson's *Midnight Robber*"; Dillon, "Indigenous Scientific Literacies in Nalo Hopkinson's Ceremonial Worlds"; Fehskens, "The Matter of Bodies"; Lalla, "The Facetiness Factor."

60. The novel does reference the existence of Indigenous peoples in the Caribbean, but they become part of the "one river" into which the racial and ethnic identities of the Marryshevite emigrants "flow" (18). One of the performance spaces in Cockpit County is "the Arawak Theatre" (6); "Taino Carib and Arawak" are listed as among the people

who "toiled and sweated together" (18); in one of the stories that punctuates the main narrative, Tan-Tan is a "queen of the Taino people" who comes to settle on an Earth that itself does not have any people (78, 90); and in her performance during Carnival on New Half-Way Tree, Tan-Tan lists "Taino redeemer" as one of her identities (320). Hopkinson also has characterized herself as of Arawack descent. See Anatol, "Maternal Discourses in Nalo Hopkinson's *Midnight Robber*," 112. On Indigenous peoplehood in Trinidad, see Forte, *Ruins of Absence, Presence of Caribs*.

61. Ahmed, *Queer Phenomenology*, 31, 37–38.

62. This backgrounding of indigeneity also occurs in Hopkinson's earlier novel *Brown Girl in the Ring*. Readers learn that the government abandonment of Toronto, which leaves a Black majority in the city and sets the stage for the events of the novel, is due to the country being bankrupted due to a fictional Native land claim case that also results in international sanctions, but after this enframing (set of) reference(s), Native peoplehood and placemaking plays no role in the unfolding of the novel or its central concerns. See Hopkinson, *Brown Girl in the Ring*, 11, 39.

63. Byrd, *The Transit of Empire*, 17.

64. Carroll, *Roots of Our Renewal*, 173.

65. Zobel, *Oracles*, 52–53, 57. Hereafter, page numbers from this work are cited in parentheses in the text.

66. Moreton-Robinson, *The White Possessive*, 11.

67. Zobel refuses the notion that Yantuck placemaking takes part in a generalized environmental ethos, repeatedly underlining the ways that climate change intrudes on Yantuck experience—including "berserk" weather patterns (15), "triple-digit day[s]" (17), and mounting pollution that affects plan behavior (33), and the melting of the polar ice caps (165)—while also not suggesting that the value of Indigenous place-based knowledge lies in its capacity to save non-natives from their destructive patterns of consumption. Moreover, the text does not cast an unchanging environmental equilibrium as the horizon of Indigenous ethics. Ashneon's mother tells her, "*when you become a woman, you will see that all mothers bleed to give life. Mother Earth is no different. New life, any change in the universe that matters, requires sacrifice*" (82), and later, Tomuck suggests, "Sun could hang on this way a couple more million years before he goes for good. But he is dying. Sputtering, erupting, petering out. Fire and light signal life or death. For some to be born, the universe must eliminate others. In this case, death for ol' Father Sun means life for who knows what" (94).

68. The narrator later notes, "The mice and spiders knew the truth: the museum was really just woods in disguise. They lived there just as anywhere else outdoors" (93).

69. de la Cadena, *Earth Beings*, 43, 102, 207.

70. Zobel has described the novel as a response to the plan to build what became the Mohegan Sun casino. See Suhr-Sytsma, "The View from Crow."

71. For nuanced renderings of the complex relations between tribal sovereignty and capitalism, see Carroll, *Roots of Our Renewal*; Cattelino, *High Stakes*; Dennison, *Colonial Entanglement*; Duarte, *Network Sovereignty*; Powell, *Landscapes of Power*.

72. The Mohegans have a complicated relation to government recognition, given that they did not hold treaties with the federal government, ceased to be officially recognized

by the state of Connecticut in 1872 (apparently by Mohegan request, in order to get out from under the corruptions of previous guardian system), and were not federally recognized again until 1994 (under the guidelines for federal acknowledgment original promulgated by the Bureau of Indian Affairs in 1978). See Mandell, *Tribe, Race, History*; O'Brien, "State Recognition and 'Termination' in Nineteenth-Century New England"; Suhr-Sytsma, "The View from Crow." On the ongoing battle by Connecticut against federal recognition for Native peoples within what it claims as its borders, see Cramer, *Cash, Color, Colonialism*, 137–62; Den Ouden, "Altered State?"; Torres, "How You See Us, Why You Don't."

73. Simpson, *Mohawk Interruptus*, 158.

74. As de la Cadena says of the limits of acknowledging Indigenous entanglements with other-than-human beings in the context of Peruvian national politics, "[W]hile indigenous individuals can now be politicians or even president of a country, the presence of earth-beings in the political sphere is inconceivable and always extremely controversial" (*Earth Beings*, 89).

75. See Den Ouden, *Beyond Conquest*; Justice, "Go Away, Water!"; Mandell, *Tribe, Race, History*; O'Brien, *Firsting and Lasting*.

76. As de la Cadena suggests, "[M]arket recognition of 'Andean culture' does not repair roads or cancel the state's abandonment of runakuna [Indigenous peoples'/peasants'] lives. It intensifies that abandonment—yet it does so nimbly, via benevolent practices that project the sentiment of egalitarianism and even democracy. Different from earlier liberal forms of inclusion via civilization—and its requirement of cultural-racial hierarchies— the late liberal multicultural market (which can also be a political market) offers runakuna appreciation of their 'cultural diversity' and their 'customs,'" adding, "Yet that market is indifferent to the precariousness that conditions runakuna lives," "enact[ing] a difference that makes no difference in the life of runakuna" (*Earth Beings*, 177). On accretive forms of exhaustion from living through and attempting to survive modes of oppression, particularly against Indigenous peoples, see Povinelli, *Economies of Abandonment*.

77. Glissant, *Poetics of Relation*, 189–90.

78. On non-natives' relation to Native peoples as on ongoing process of "primitive accumulation," see Coulthard, *Red Skin, White Masks*.

79. Conversely, as Blake Hausman suggests in *Riding the Trail of Tears*, non-natives also can consume Native trauma (or consume the image of Native peoples as always-already traumatized) in ways that remake such feelings into a vehicle for settler catharsis—the otherness of Native experience as a resource through which to achieve an enlightened reconciliation. The novel also suggests that Natives can be conscripted into such performances, in ways not unlike Zobel's portrayal of the Yantuck casino.

80. Jones, *The Bird Is Gone*, 24. Hereafter, page numbers from this work are cited in parentheses in the text.

81. On the politics of the novel's style, see Dawes, "'Back to Before All This,' He Said."

82. See Gamber, "The End (of the Trail) Is the Beginning," 30–31.

83. A later entry in the glossary notes that within the terms of the Conservation Act "fauna . . . *could* legally entail Indians, as we were still on the books with mountain lions and coyotes as 'varmints,' *bounty*" (173).

84. On the ways culture and race surrogate for each other in determinations of Indianness, see Barker, *Native Acts*; Garroutte, *Real Indians*; Lyons, *X-marks*; TallBear, *Native American DNA*. On the ways "culture" surrogates for "race" more broadly, see Baker, *Anthropology and the Racial Politics of Culture*; Balibar, "Is There a 'Neo-Racism'?"; Chow, *The Protestant Ethnic and The Spirit of Capitalism*; Visweswaran, *Un/common Cultures*. On the history of political negotiation between "full-bloods" and "mixed-bloods" among the Blackfeet, the Native nation to which Jones belongs, see Rosier, *Rebirth of the Blackfeet Nation*. The Blackfeet currently define membership as persons of "Indian blood" on the tribal census of 1935, all children of tribal members living on-reservation born prior to September 1962, and children born to "a blood member of the Blackfeet tribe" with one-quarter or more degree of "Blackfeet Indian blood." For the Blackfeet Constitution, see http://www.narf.org/nill/constitutions/blackfeet/ bfconstitution.pdf.

85. See Gamber, "The End (of the Trail) Is the Beginning," 38–39.

86. On Indianness as simulacrum, see Vizenor, *Manifest Manners*.

87. See Barker, *Native Acts*; Coulthard, *Red Skin, White Masks*; Deloria, *Playing Indian*; Garroutte, *Real Indians*; Goeman, *Mark My Words*; Povinelli, *The Cunning of Recognition*.

88. In this way, the novel might be thought of as exploring the disjunction between versions of the Constitution of the Blackfeet Nation. One, adopted in the 1930s, characterizes the authority of the nation in terms of its having been vested in them under U.S. law (the 1934 Indian Organization Act in particular) and describes Blackfeet territory as defined by an agreement with the U.S. government in 1895, but the other, a redrafting proposed in 2016, has a preamble linking the Blackfeet Nation to the Blackfoot Confederacy as having "survived and thrived from the beginning of time" and defines the nation's territory as including "all Aboriginal Territory and all lands located within the exterior boundaries of the Blackfeet Nation." For both versions of the Blackfeet Nation's Constitution, see https://www.narf.org/nill/constitutions/blackfeet.

89. See Adams, *Education for Extinction*; Hoxie, *A Final Promise*; Pfister, *Individuality Incorporated*.

90. In terms of affective connection to these lands, the novel notes that "exile" from the Territories for "treason" and other serious offences was worse than death (32–33, 177). On the ways the Blackfeet negotiated the legal apparatus of tribal governance prior to and in the wake of the Indian Reorganization Act, see Rosier, *Rebirth of the Blackfeet Nation*.

91. However, conversely, efforts to seize Native lands and to cease legally to acknowledge Native jurisdiction over such lands historically have often been justified through discourses of "emancipation." For examples, see Hoxie, *A Final Promise*; Fixico, *Termination and Relocation*; Mandell, *Tribe, Race, History*; Philp, *Termination Revisited*.

92. Readers do learn, though, that Mary Boy had a hallucinogen-induced vision prior to the passage of the Conservation Act and that he had written out a document "with all the clauses and terminology he'd had used against him over the course of two divorces and a string of misdemeanor hearings—that DC was hereby giving back all the Indian land it ever took, would take, or was presently taking" (20). This episode might be described as a *treaty imaginary* that contrasts sharply with the actual process through which the act was passed and instituted.

93. Starting from the U.S. Supreme Court decision of *United States v. Kagama* (1887), Congress has been recognized as exerting "plenary" authority over Native peoples, which, while interpreted variously, largely has meant that Congress is seen as having potentially unlimited power over Indian affairs. On the character and scope of plenary authority, see Duthu, *American Indians and the Law*; Harring, *Crow Dog's Case*; Wilkins and Lomawaima, *Uneven Ground*.

94. Goeman, *Mark My Words*, 87, 33, 5.

95. Jones gestures toward the kinds of territorial fungibility licensed by the land restoration. The entry for "Huna Deal" explains that there were a series of "controversial land exchanges immediately following the CONSERVATION ACT where the total acreage of the temporarily 'abandoned' reservations was traded for BLM [Bureau of Land Management] land immediately surrounding the Territories, sometimes at the request of the tribe or nation, but, in the case of some of the tribes or nations holding land bordering national parks, without consent, too" (166). Indianness functions as a vehicle of equivalence that makes all lands occupied by Native peoples into somewhat interchangeable units that can be swapped for each other so long as the "total acreage" remains unchanged. See Gamber, "The End (of the Trail) Is the Beginning," 32–34.

96. Coulthard, *Red Skin, White Masks*, 3.

97. For discussion of this section of the novel, see Dawes, "'Back to Before All This,' He Said."

98. When readers first are introduced to LP, the text notes, "On his application for employment, under Tribal Affiliation, he checked Anasazi—a box he had to draw himself" (14), and later Cat Stand observes that when she first met LP while he was working at the booth at the border of the Territories before he came to work at Fool's Hip, "he wasnt even the Anasazi then was just some guy in a brown jumpsuit," adding that in response to questions about it from Naitche she "would say there were not Anasazi anymore which probably wasn't good because he needs lies to believe in" (114). Cat also refers to LP as a "scab" (36), and during a card game at the end of the novel, Chassis describes LP as the "white man sitting at the table with all these red Indians," possibly referring to his role in the game or his identity (156). LP also gets characterized as a "tomato" (156, 178), defined in the glossary as "red on the outside *and* the in-, yet white just the same" (172).

99. On this figure, see also Dawes, "'Back to Before All This,' He Said," 127.

100. See Bruyneel, *The Third Space of Sovereignty*; Byrd, *The Transit of Empire*; Den Ouden, *Beyond Conquest*; O'Brien, *Firsting and Lasting*; Wolfe, "Settler Colonialism and the Elimination of the Native."

101. Watson, "Settled and Unsettled Spaces," 18–19.

102. Cornum, "The Space NDN's Star Map."

103. See Clifford, *Returns*; Goeman, *Mark My Words*; Ramirez, *Native Hubs*; Vizenor, *Fugitive Poses*.

104. Brand, *A Map to the Door of No Return*, 20, 89.

105. Simpson, "The State Is a Man."

106. Hairston, *Mindscape*, 4–5. Hereafter, page numbers from this work are cited in parentheses in the text.

107. See Hairston, *Mindscape*, 35, 87, 248.

108. See Bilby, *True-Born Maroons*; Diouf, *Slavery's Exiles*; Thompson, *Flight to Freedom*.

109. "Sioux" refers to seven allied peoples who fall into three different language groups, Dakota (the eastern four peoples), Nakota (Yankton and Yanktonai peoples), and Lakota (or Teton). The term "Dakota" also has been used to refer to all seven. For a good overview of available nomenclatures and their philologies, see DeMallie, "Sioux until 1850."

110. It does note that the name of the Captain, the official guard for Lawanda, "sound[ed] old Hawaiian" (380).

111. On Wovoka's Ghost Dance and the events leading up to Wounded Knee, see DeMallie, "The Lakota Ghost Dance"; Hittman, *Wovoka and the Ghost Dance*; Kehoe, *The Ghost Dance*; Ostler, *The Plains Sioux and U.S. Colonialism from Lewis and Clark to Wounded Knee*; Pratt, "Wounded Knee and the Prospect of Pluralism"; Smoak, *Ghost Dances and Identity*; Warren, *God's Red Son*.

112. Smoak, *Ghost Dances and Identity*, 191, 2. On the circulation of this narrative, see Deloria, *Indians in Unexpected Places*, 15–51; DeMallie, "The Lakota Ghost Dance"; Pratt, "Wounded Knee and the Prospect of Pluralism"; Tatonetti, "Disrupting a Story of Loss."

113. Smoak, *Ghost Dances and Identity*, 192–93.

114. Quoted in Escobar, *Territories of Difference*, 211. See also Engle, *The Elusive Promise of Indigenous Development*.

115. See French, *Legalizing Identities*; Perry, *Black Women against the Land Grab*.

116. Anderson, "When Afro Becomes (like) Indigenous," 385.

117. Hooker, "Indigenous Inclusion/Black Exclusion," 293, 302.

118. Anderson, *Black and Indigenous*, 134.

119. See also Greene, "Introduction"; Ng'weno, "Can Ethnicity Replace Race?"; Palacio, "Cultural Identity among Rural Garifuna Migrants in Belize City, Belize."

120. Perry, *Black Women against the Land Grab*, 10–11.

121. Ng'weno, "Can Ethnicity Replace Race?" 422, 427.

122. See Dubey, "The Future of Race in Afro-Futurist Fiction," 20–22.

123. Dubey argues, "Significantly, the Throwbacks who thrive in the future world of the novel are described as ethnic rather than racial, with the category of ethnicity enabling Hairston to shed the concept of race," adding, "The ethnic cultural pluralism affirmed in *Mindscape* is identical in every significant respect to the brand of multiculturalism" in the United States in what amounts to a "culturalization of race" ("Future of Race in Afro-Futurist Fiction," 24). However, I would suggest that, rather than translating race as ethnicity or ignoring processes of racialization in order to produce a "multicultural" pluralism, the novel suggests possibilities for collective placemaking for Black people that normally either have been dismissed (due to the ways attributions of placelessness function as part of Black racialization) or discussed under the category of "ethnicity" (rather than understood as a collective territoriality with a political status).

124. Greene, "Introduction," 347.

125. Povinelli, "The Governance of the Prior"; Barker, *Native Acts*, 223.

126. See Hairston, *Mindscape*, 118, 149, 296.

127. On the emergence of new peoples in the context of Euro-conquest, see Andersen, *"Métis"*; Anderson, *Black and Indigenous*; Forte, *Ruins of Absence, Presence of Caribs*;

Lowery, *Lumbee Indians in the Jim Crow South*. On the rejection of such possibilities for emergence in the politics of tribal acknowledgment in the United States, see also Klopotek, *Recognition Odysseys*.

128. The reappearance at the end of the novel of those who had perished in the Barrier transforms the possibilities for engagement among the zones: "Right before the new corridors opened, all these people, dead people . . . people we carry around in our heads, showed up like a waking dream, ghosting across the Barrier . . . [;] they just got bigger and bigger 'til you couldn't make them out anymore, scattering off in every direction, and the Barrier broke open. Corridors to everywhere, everyone welcome" (435).

129. On the hub as a way of conceptualizing contemporary Native modes of placemaking in the contemporary United States, see Ramirez, *Native Hubs*. On the significance of travel to Indigenous territoriality and identity, see Chang, *The World and All the Things upon It*; Clifford, *Returns*; Goeman, *Mark My Words*; Povinelli, *Labor's Lot*; Vizenor, *Fugitive Poses*. The novel continually refers to the Barrier, and information about how to use it to traverse distances, as "the Promised Land," presenting the Barrier's potential for movement and change as the ultimate horizon rather than something like a national homeland. See Hairston, *Mindscape*, 87, 94, 177, 296.

130. In rejecting the Interzonal Treaty, the born-again Sioux "refused to sign away their sovereignty" (12).

131. See the discussion of such indigenization in chapter 3.

132. See Huhndorf, *Going Native*.

133. Simpson, *As We Have Always Done*, 17–18. See also Martineau and Ritskes, "Fugitive Indigeneity."

134. Simpson, *As We Have Always Done*, 50.

135. For an important scholarly account in a very different context that illustrates the reduction of Indigenous peoplehood to flight from state mappings and control, including characterizing it through marronage, see Scott, *The Art of Not Being Governed*.

136. Not all Anglophone settler-states have treaties (Australia being the most prominent example), and doctrines of discovery and terra nullius have been employed even in those states that do have a history of treaty making. See Miller et al., *Discovering Indigenous Lands*. Also, Hispanophone and Lusophone states in the Americas had and have legal means of recognizing Indigenous landedness and forms of self-governance, as discussed earlier in the chapter, but they do not take the form of treaties as such. In addition to the sources cited previously, see Brysk, *From Tribal Village to Global Village*; Nelson, *A Finger in the Wound*; Seed, *American Pentimento*. I do not mean to suggest that treaties as institutionalized within Anglo legal and administrative regimes provide an inherently better means of engaging with Indigenous polities than other forms, especially given the ways that the treaty system in the United States and Canada has functioned as a means of validating largescale expropriation—including a rejuvenation of this process in Canada presented as part of a policy of recognition and reconciliation. See Coulthard, *Red Skin, White Masks*; McCarthy, *In Divided Unity*; Pasternak, *Grounded Authority*; Simpson, *As We Have Always Done*. Rather, I want to take up the figure of the treaty as a way of thinking about modes of relationality with Indigenous peoples that do not replicate the dynamics of dominant forms of settler governance.

137. Calloway, *Pen and Ink Witchcraft*, 97.

138. As Dorothy Jones suggests, "It was only after the repeated failure of attempts to handle Indian affairs as a domestic problem that United States officials were forced to consider relations *with* the Indians, rather than a unilateral policy *for* the Indians," later noting, "The system was to stay in place for the next seventy-five years—expanding, adding secondary functions, but never changing its primary function of transferring land from Indian ownership to ownership by the United States" (*License for Empire*, 147, 186).

139. Calloway, *Pen and Ink Witchcraft*, 243; McCarthy, *In Divided Unity*, 289. See also Allen, "Postcolonial Theory and the Discourse of Treaties"; Lyons, *X-marks*; Simpson, *Dancing on Our Turtle's Back*, 101–18; Williams, *Linking Arms Together*.

140. On such treaties with maroon communities, see Bilby, *True-Born Maroons*; Gottlieb, *The Mother of Us All*; Harris, "The True Traditions of My Ancestors"; Sharpe, *Ghosts of Slavery*; Zips, *Nanny's Asafo Warriors*.

141. Allen, "Postcolonial Theory and the Discourse of Treaties," 72.

142. Mackey, *Unsettled Expectations*, 130, 133.

CODA: DIPLOMACY IN THE UNDERCOMMONS

1. Delany, *Starboard Wine*, 6, xvi–xvii.

2. In a similar vein, Aimee Bahng "highlights the speculative mode of the 'What if?'" (*Migrant Futures*, 13).

3. de la Cadena, *Earth Beings*, 116.

4. Ahmed, *Queer Phenomenology*, 15–16, 117.

5. Harney and Moten, *The Undercommons*, 74–75.

6. Harney and Moten, *The Undercommons*, 20, 37.

7. Tuck and Yang, "Decolonization Is Not a Metaphor," 28, 35.

8. Tuck and Yang, "Decolonization Is Not a Metaphor," 61.

9. See Nguyen, *The Gift of Freedom*; Rifkin, "Debt and the Transnationalization of Hawai'i."

10. On the relation between fugitivity and experimentation, see Rusert, *Fugitive Science*. For a reading of fugitivity in Moten and Harney that foregrounds its potential connection to indigeneity, see Martineau and Ritskes, "Fugitive Indigeneity."

11. Simpson, *As We Have Always Done*, 165.

12. Simpson, *As We Have Always Done*, 230–31.

13. I would distinguish this effort from what Elizabeth Maddock Dillon has described as creating a "performative commons," which involves "articulating relations of mutual belonging in a collective whole," since the effort here does not presume a "whole" to which the parties involved belong (*New World Drama*, 7). Rather, the notion of diplomacy foregrounds a relation among political entities, even when what constitutes such an entity is itself in question and the subject of ongoing negotiation.

14. Harney and Moten, *The Undercommons*, 63, 98.

15. In "Structures and Events," Jodi Byrd observes, "What I hope for my own Chickasaw Nation is that we can come to an expansive understanding of grounded relationality that resists settler-state modes of sovereign power." See Byrd and Leroy, "Structures and Events."

16. Grossman, *Unlikely Alliances*, 22.

17. Harney and Moten, *The Undercommons*, 17.

18. Amadahy and Lawrence, "Indigenous Peoples and Black People in Canada," 130. See also King, "In the Clearing."

19. Yazzie generously agreed to share a copy of her presentation to the 2017 National Women's Studies Association Annual Meeting. Quotations are from this printed copy. See Yazzie, "#NOBANSTOLENLAND."

20. "Alicia Garza Speaks on Building Power to the A[llied] M[edia] C[onference] 2017 Opening Ceremony," blog post, September 5, 2017, accessed June 15, 2018. http://www.alliedmedia.org/news.

21. The vision of accountability I'm suggesting resonates with Julietta Singh's articulation of "becoming sensitive" and of practices of vulnerability. See Singh, *Unthinking Mastery*.

22. Patterson, "There's No Middle Ground."

Bibliography

Abdur-Rahman, Aliyyah I. *Against the Closet: Black Political Longing and the Erotics of Race*. Durham, NC: Duke University Press, 2012.

Adams, David Wallace. *Education for Extinction: American Indians and the Boarding School Experience, 1875–1828*. Lawrence: University Press of Kansas, 1995.

Adams, Mikaëla M. *Who Belongs? Race, Resources, and Tribal Citizenship in the Native South*. New York: Oxford University Press, 2016.

Adare, Sierra S. *"Indian" Stereotypes in TV Science Fiction: First Nations' Voices Speak Out*. Austin: University of Texas Press, 2005.

Adorno, Theodor W. *Negative Dialectics*, trans. E. B. Ashton. New York: Continuum, 1987.

Ahmed, Sara. *Queer Phenomenology: Orientations, Objects, Others*. Durham, NC: Duke University Press, 2006.

Ahuja, Neel. *Bioinsecurities: Disease Interventions, Empire, and the Government of Species*. Durham, NC: Duke University Press, 2016.

Alexander, Michelle. *The New Jim Crow: Mass Incarceration in the Age of Colorblindness*. New York: New Press, 2010.

Alexander, M. Jacqui. *Pedagogies of Crossing: Meditations on Feminism, Sexual Politics, Memory, and the Sacred*. Durham, NC: Duke University Press, 2005.

Alfred, Taiaiake. "Sovereignty." In *Sovereignty Matters: Locations of Contestation and Possibility in Indigenous Struggles for Self-Determination*, ed. Joanne Barker, 33–50. Lincoln: University of Nebraska Press, 2005.

Allen, Chadwick. "Postcolonial Theory and the Discourse of Treaties." *American Quarterly* 52.1 (2000): 59–89.

Allewaert, Monique. *Ariel's Ecology: Plantations, Personhood, and Colonialism in the American Tropics*. Minneapolis: University of Minnesota Press, 2013.

Althusser, Louis, and Étienne Balibar. *Reading Capital*. New York: Verso, 1998.

Amadahy, Zainab. *The Moons of Palmares*. N.p.: Future History, 2013.

Amadahy, Zainab, and Bonita Lawrence. "Indigenous Peoples and Black People in Canada: Settlers or Allies?" In *Breaching the Colonial Contract: Anti-Colonialism in the U.S. and Canada*, ed. Arlo Kempf, 105–36. N.p.: Springer, 2010.

Anatol, Giselle Liza. "Maternal Discourses in Nalo Hopkinson's *Midnight Robber*." *African American Review* 40.1 (2006): 111–24.

Anaya, S. James. *Indigenous Peoples in International Law*. New York: Oxford University Press, 1996.

Andersen, Chris. *"Métis": Race, Recognition, and the Struggle for Indigenous Peoplehood*. Vancouver: University of British Columbia Press, 2014.

Anderson, Mark. *Black and Indigenous: Garifuna Activism and Consumer Culture in Honduras*. Minneapolis: University of Minnesota Press, 2009.

Anderson, Mark. "When Afro Becomes (like) Indigenous: Garifuna and Afro-Indigenous Politics in Honduras." *Journal of Latin American and Caribbean Anthropology* 12.2 (2007): 384–413.

Anghie, Antony. *Imperialism, Sovereignty and the Making of International Law*. New York: Cambridge University Press, 2004.

Asaka, Ikuko. *Tropical Freedom: Climate, Settler Colonialism, and Black Exclusion in the Age of Emancipation*. Durham, NC: Duke University Press, 2017.

Bahng, Aimee. *Migrant Futures: Decolonizing Speculation in Financial Times*. Durham, NC: Duke University Press, 2018.

Bahng, Aimee. "Plasmodial Improprieties: Octavia E. Butler, Slime Molds, and Imagining a Femi-Queer Commons." In *Queer Feminist Science Studies: A Reader*, ed. Cyd Cipolla, Kristina Gupta, David A. Rubin, Angela Willey, 310–26. Seattle: University of Washington Press, 2017.

Bailey, Garrick A. *The Osage and the Invisible World: From the Works of Francis La Flesche*. Norman: University of Oklahoma Press, 1995.

Baker, Lee D. *Anthropology and the Racial Politics of Culture*. Durham, NC: Duke University Press, 2010.

Balibar, Étienne. "Is There a 'Neo-Racism'?" In Étienne Balibar and Immanuel Wallerstein, *Race, Nation, Class: Ambiguous Identities*, trans. Chris Turner, 17–28. New York: Verso, (1988) 1991.

Barker, Joanne. "Choice." Accessed May 27, 2017. http://joannebarkerauthor.com/2017/04/26/choice.

Barker, Joanne. "For Whom Sovereignty Matters," in *Sovereignty Matters: Locations of Contestation and Possibility in Indigenous Struggles for Self-Determination*, ed. Joanne Barker, 1–32. Lincoln: University of Nebraska Press, 2005.

Barker, Joanne. *Native Acts: Law, Recognition, and Cultural Authenticity*. Durham, NC: Duke University Press, 2011.

Barume, Albert. "Responding to the Concerns of the African States." In *Making the Declaration Work: The United Nations Declaration on the Rights of Indigenous Peoples*, ed. Clare Charters and Ruldolfo Stavenhagen, 170–83. Copenhagen: International Work Group for Indigenous Affairs, 2009.

Baucom, Ian. *Specters of the Atlantic: Finance Capital, Slavery, and the Philosophy of History*. Durham, NC: Duke University Press, 2005.

Bederman, Gail. *Manliness and Civilization: A Cultural History of Gender and Race in the United States, 1880–1917*. Chicago: University of Chicago Press, 1995.

Belich, James. *Replenishing the Earth: The Settler Revolution and the Rise of the Anglo-World, 1783–1939*. New York: Oxford University Press, 2009.

Belk, Nolan. "The Certainty of the Flesh: Octavia Butler's Use of the Erotic in the *Xenogenesis* Trilogy." *Utopian Studies* 19.3 (2008): 369–89.

Bellacasa, María Puig de la. *Matters of Care: Speculative Ethics in more than Human Worlds*. Minneapolis: University of Minnesota Press, 2017.

Bentley, Nancy. "The Fourth Dimension: Kinlessness and African American Narrative." *Critical Inquiry* 35.1 (2009): 270–92.

Ben-zvi, Yael. *Native Land Talk: Colliding Birthrights in Early U.S. Culture*. Lebanon, NH: University Press of New England, 2018.

Berlant, Lauren. *Cruel Optimism*. Durham, NC: Duke University Press, 2011.

Berto, Francesco, and Matteo Plebani. *Ontology and Metaontology: A Contemporary Guide*. New York: Bloomsbury, 2015.

Best, Stephen. *The Fugitive's Properties: Law and the Poetics of Possession*. Chicago: University of Chicago Press, 2004.

Best, Stephen, and Saidiya Hartman. "Fugitive Justice." *Representations* 92.1 (2005): 1–15.

Bieder, Robert E. *Science Encounters the Indian, 1820–1880: The Early Years of American Ethnology*. Norman: University of Oklahoma Press, 1986.

Bilby, Kenneth M. *True-Born Maroons*. Gainesville: University Press of Florida, 2005.

Blackhawk, Ned. *Violence over the Land: Indians and Empires in the Early American West*. Cambridge, MA: Harvard University Press, 2006.

Bliss, Catherine. *Race Decoded: The Genomic Fight for Social Justice*. Stanford, CA: Stanford University Press, 2012.

Bogues, Anthony. "Politics, Nation, and PostColony: Caribbean Inflections." *Small Axe* 6.1 (2002): 11–40.

Bonilla, Yarimar. *Non-Sovereign Futures: French Caribbean Politics in the Wake of Disenchantment*. Chicago: University of Chicago Press, 2015.

Bonilla-Silva, Eduardo. *Racism without Racists: Color-Blind Racism and the Persistence of Racial Inequality in America*, 4th ed. New York: Rowman and Littlefield, 2014.

Bould, Mark. "The Ships Landed Long Ago: Afrofuturism and Black SF." *Science Fiction Studies* 34.2 (2007): 177–86.

Boyce Davies, Carole. "From Masquerade to *Maskarade*: Caribbean Cultural Resistance and the Rehumanizing Project." In *Sylvia Wynter: On Being Human as Praxis*, ed. Katherine McKittrick, 203–25. Durham, NC: Duke University Press, 2015.

Boyd, Danah. "White Flight in Networked Publics: How Race and Class Shaped American Teen Engagement with MySpace and Facebook." In *Race after the Internet*, ed. Lisa Nakamura and Peter A. Chow-White, 203–22. New York: Routledge, 2012.

Boyle, Elizabeth. "Vanishing Bodies: 'Race' and Technology in Nalo Hopkinson's *Midnight Robber*." *African Identities* 7.2 (2009): 177–91.

Brady, Owen E., ed. *Conversations with Walter Mosley*. Jackson: University Press of Mississippi, 2011.

Braidotti, Rosi. *The Posthuman*. Malden, MA: Polity, 2013.

Braithwaite, Alisa K. "Connecting to a Future Community: Storytelling, the Database, and Nalo Hopkinson's *Midnight Robber*." In *The Black Imagination: Science Fiction, Futurism, and the Speculative*, ed. Sandra Jackson and Julie E. Moody-Freeman, 81–99. New York: Peter Lang, 2011.

Brand, Dionne. *A Map to the Door of No Return: Notes to Belonging*. Toronto: Vintage Canada, 2001.

Brathwaite, Kamau. "Nanny, Palmares, and the Caribbean Maroon Connection." In *Maroon Heritage: Archaeological and Ethnographic Historical Perspectives*, ed. E. Kofi Agorsah, 119–38. Kingston, Jamaica: Canoe, 1994.

Brooks, James F. *Captives and Cousins: Slavery, Kinship, and Community in the Southwest Borderlands*. Chapel Hill: University of North Carolina Press, 2002.

Brooks, James F., ed. *Confounding the Color Line: The Indian-Black Experience in North America*. Lincoln: University of Nebraska Press, 2002.

Brooks, Lisa. *The Common Pot: The Recovery of Native Space in the Northeast*. Minneapolis: University of Minnesota Press, 2008.

Brown, Vincent. *The Reaper's Garden: Death and Power in the World of Atlantic Slavery*. Cambridge, MA: Harvard University Press, 2008.

Browne, Simon. *Dark Matters: On the Surveillance of Blackness*. Durham, NC: Duke University Press, 2015.

Bruyneel, Kevin. *The Third Space of Sovereignty: The Postcolonial Politics of U.S.-Indigenous Relations*. Minneapolis: University of Minnesota Press, 1997.

Brysk, Alison. *From Tribal Village to Global Village: Indian Rights and International Relations in Latin America*. Stanford, CA: Stanford University Press, 2000.

Burns, Louis F. *A History of the Osage People*. Tuscaloosa: University of Alabama Press, 2004.

Butler, Judith. *Gender Trouble: Feminism and the Subversion of Identity*. New York: Routledge, 1990.

Butler, Octavia E. *Lilith's Brood*. New York: Grand Central, 2000.

Butler, Octavia E. *Parable of the Sower*. New York: Grand Central, (1993) 2000.

Byrd, Jodi. *The Transit of Empire: Indigenous Critiques of Colonialism*. Minneapolis: University of Minnesota Press, 2011.

Byrd, Jodi, and Justin Leroy. "Structures and Events: A Monumental Dialogue." *Bully Bloggers*, September 20, 2017. https://bullybloggers.wordpress.com/2017/09/20/structures-and-events-a-monumental-dialogue/.

Cacho, Lisa Marie. *Social Death: Racialized Rightlessness and the Criminalization of the Unprotected*. New York: New York University Press, 2012.

Calloway, Colin G. *Pen and Ink Witchcraft: Treaties and Treaty Making in American Indian History*. New York: Oxford University Press, 2013.

Carastathis, Anna. *Intersectionality: Origins, Contestations, Horizons*. Lincoln: University of Nebraska Press, 2016.

carrington, andré m. *Speculative Blackness: The Future of Race in Science Fiction*. Minneapolis: University of Minnesota Press, 2016.

Carroll, Clint. *Roots of Our Renewal: Ethnobotany and Cherokee Environmental Governance*. Minneapolis: University of Minnesota Press, 2015.

Cattelino, Jessica. *High Stakes: Florida Seminole Gaming and Sovereignty*. Durham, NC: Duke University Press, 2008.

Cervenak, Sarah Jane. *Wandering: Philosophical Performances of Racial and Sexual Freedom*. Durham, NC: Duke University Press, 2014.

Chakrabarty, Dipesh. *Provincializing Europe: Postcolonial Thought and Historical Difference*. Princeton, NJ: Princeton University Press, 2000.

Chang, David A. *The World and All the Things upon It: Native Hawaiian Geographies of Exploration*. Minneapolis: University of Minnesota Press, 2016.

Chang, David A. *The Color of the Land: Race, Nation, and the Politics of Land Ownership in Oklahoma, 1832–1929*. Chapel Hill: University of North Carolina Press, 2010.

Charters, Clare, and Ruldolfo Stavenhagen, eds. *Making the Declaration Work: The United Nations Declaration on the Rights of Indigenous Peoples*. Copenhagen: International Work Group for Indigenous Affairs, 2009.

Cheah, Pheng. *Inhuman Conditions: On Cosmopolitanism and Human Rights*. Cambridge: Harvard University Press, 2007.

Cheney-Lippold, John. *We Are Data: Algorithms and the Making of Our Digital Selves*. New York: New York University Press, 2017.

Cheyfitz, Eric. *The Poetics of Imperialism: Translation and Colonization from* The Tempest *to* Tarzan, 2d ed. Philadelphia: University of Pennsylvania Press, 1997.

Cheyfitz, Eric. "Savage Law: The Plot against American Indians in *Johnson and Graham's Lessee v. M'Intosh* and *The Pioneers*." In *Cultures of United States Imperialism*, ed. Amy Kaplan and Donald E. Pease, 109–28. Durham, NC: Duke University Press, 1993.

Chow, Rey. *The Protestant Ethnic and The Spirit of Capitalism*. New York: Columbia University Press, 2002.

Chow-White, Peter A. "Data, Code, and Discourses of Difference in Genomics." *Communication Theory* 19 (2009): 219–47.

Claassens, Aninka, and Ben Cousins, eds. *Land, Power, and Custom: Controversies Generated by South Africa's Communal Land Rights Act*. Athens: Ohio University Press, 2008.

Clark, Michael. "Twenty Preliminary Propositions for a Critical History of International Statecraft in Haiti." In *The Latin American Subaltern Studies Reader*, ed. Lleana Rodríguez, 227–40. Durham, NC: Duke University Press, 2001.

Clarno, Andy. *Neoliberal Apartheid: Palestine/Israel and South Africa after 1994*. Chicago: University of Chicago Press, 2017.

Clear, Todd R. *Imprisoning Communities: How Mass Incarceration Makes Disadvantaged Neighborhoods Worse*. New York: Oxford University Press, 2007.

Clech Lâm, Maivân. *At the Edge of the State: Indigenous Peoples and Self-Determination*. Ardsley, NY: Transnational, 2000.

Clemente, Bill. "Tan-Tan's Exile and Odyssey in Nalo Hopkinson's *Midnight Robber*." *Foundation* 91 (Summer 2004): 10–24.

Clifford, James. *Returns: Becoming Indigenous in the Twenty-First Century*. Cambridge, MA: Harvard University Press, 2013.

Cohen, Cathy J. *Boundaries of Blackness: AIDS and the Breakdown of Black Politics*. Chicago: University of Chicago Press, 1999.

Cohen, Cathy J. "Punks, Bulldaggers, and Welfare Queens: The Radical Potential of Queer Politics?". *GLQ* 3.4 (1997): 437–65.

Cohen, Ed. *A Body Worth Defending: Immunity, Biopolitics, and the Apotheosis of the Modern Body*. Durham, NC: Duke University Press, 2009.

Cohen, Matt. *The Networked Wilderness: Communicating in Early New England*. Minneapolis: University of Minnesota Press, 2009.

Collins, Patricia Hill, and Sirma Bilge. *Intersectionality*. Malden, MA: Polity, 2016.

Comack, Elizabeth. *Racialized Policing: Aboriginal People's Encounters with the Police*. Halifax, NS: Fernwood, 2012.

Conn, Steven. *History's Shadow: Native Americans and Historical Consciousness in the Nineteenth Century*. Chicago: University of Chicago Press, 2004.

Cornum, Lou Catherine. "The Space NDN's Star Map." Accessed June 29, 2017. http://thenewinquiry.com/the-space-ndns-star-map.

Coulthard, Glen Sean. *Red Skin, White Masks: Rejecting the Colonial Politics of Recognition*. Minneapolis: University of Minnesota Press, 2014.

Cox, Aimee Meredith. *Shapeshifters: Black Girls and the Choreography of Citizenship*. Durham, NC: Duke University Press, 2015.

Cramer, Renée Ann. *Cash, Color, Colonialism: The Politics of Tribal Acknowledgment*. Norman: University of Oklahoma Press, 2005.

Craton, Michael. "Decoding Pitchy-Patchy: The Roots, Branches and Essence of Junkanoo." *Slavery and Abolition* 16.1 (1995): 14–44.

Crosby, Shelby. "Black Girlhood Interrupted: Race, Gender, and Colonization in Nalo Hopkinson's *Midnight Robber*." In *Contemporary Speculative Fiction*, ed. M. Keith Booker, 187–202. Ipswich, MA: Salem, 2013.

Cruikshank, Julie. *The Social Life of Stories: Narrative and Knowledge in the Yukon Territory*. Lincoln: University of Nebraska Press, 2000.

Davis, Angela. *Are Prisons Obsolete?* New York: Seven Stories, 2003.

Davis, Mike. *City of Quartz: Excavating the Future in Los Angeles* (1990). London: Verso, 2006.

Dawes, Birgit. "'Back to Before All This,' He Said": History, Temporality, and Knowledge in Stephen Graham Jones's *The Bird Is Gone*." In *The Fictions of Stephen Graham Jones: A Critical Companion*, ed. Billy J. Stratton, 111–31. Albuquerque: University of New Mexico Press, 2016.

Day, Iyko. *Alien Capital: Asian Racialization and the Logic of Settler Colonial Capitalism*. Durham, NC: Duke University Press, 2016.

Day, Iyko. "Being or Nothingness: Indigeneity, Antiblackness, and Settler Colonial Critique." *Critical Ethnic Studies* 1.2 (2015): 102–21.

Dayan, Colin. *Haiti, History, and the Gods*. Berkeley: University of California Press, 1995.

Dayan, Colin. *The Law Is a White Dog: How Legal Rituals Make and Unmake Persons*. Princeton, NJ: Princeton University Press, 2011.

de la Cadena, Marisol. *Earth Beings: Ecologies of Practice across Andean Worlds*. Durham, NC: Duke University Press, 2015.

DeLanda, Manuel, and Graham Harman. *The Rise of Realism*. Malden, MA: Polity, 2017.

Delany, Samuel R. *The Jewel-Hinged Jaw: Notes on the Language of Science Fiction*, rev. ed. Middletown, CT: Wesleyan University Press, 2009.

Delany, Samuel R. *Starboard Wine: More Notes on the Language of Science Fiction*, rev. ed. Middletown, CT: Wesleyan University Press, 2012.

Deloria, Philip J. *Indians in Unexpected Places*. Lawrence: University of Kansas Press, 2004.

Deloria, Philip J. *Playing Indian*. New Haven, CT: Yale University Press, 1998.

Deloria, Vine, Jr., and Clifford M. Lytle. *The Nations Within: The Past and Future of American Indian Sovereignty*. Austin: University of Texas Press, 1984.

DeMallie, Raymond J. "The Lakota Ghost Dance: An Ethnohistorical Account." *Pacific Historical Review* 51.4 (1982): 385–405.

DeMallie, Raymond J. "Sioux until 1850." In *Handbook of North American Indians, Volume 13.2: Plains*, ed. Raymond J. DeMallie, 718–60. Washington, DC: Smithsonian Institution, 2001.

Denetdale, Jennifer Nez. "Chairmen, Presidents, and Princesses: The Navajo Nation, Gender, and the Politics of Tradition." *Wičazo Ša Review* 21.1 (2006): 9–28.

Dennison, Jean. *Colonial Entanglement: Constituting a Twenty-First Century Osage Nation*. Chapel Hill: University of North Carolina Press, 2012.

Den Ouden, Amy E. "Altered State? Indian Policy Narratives, Federal Recognition, and the 'New' War on Native Rights in Connecticut." In *Recognition, Sovereignty Struggles, and Indigenous Rights in the United States: A Sourcebook*, ed. Amy E. Den Ouden and Jean M. O'Brien, 149–68. Chapel Hill: University of North Carolina Press, 2013.

Den Ouden, Amy E. *Beyond Conquest: Native Peoples and the Struggle for History in New England*. Lincoln: University of Nebraska Press, 2005.

Den Ouden, Amy E., and Jean M. O'Brien, eds. *Recognition, Sovereignty Struggles, and Indigenous Rights in the United States: A Sourcebook*. Chapel Hill: University of North Carolina Press, 2013.

Dery, Mark. "Black to the Future: Interviews with Samuel R. Delany, Greg Tate, and Tricia Rose." In *Flame Wars: The Discourse of Cyberculture*, ed. Mark Dery, 179–222. Durham, NC: Duke University Press, 1994.

Dhillon, Jaskiran. *Prairie Rising: Indigenous Youth, Decolonization, and the Politics of Intervention*. Toronto: University of Toronto Press, 2017.

Diaz, Vincente M. "Creolization and Indigeneity." *American Ethnologist* 33.4 (2006): 576–78.

Dillon, Elizabeth Maddock. *New World Drama: The Performative Commons in the Atlantic World, 1649–1849*. Durham, NC: Duke University Press, 2014.

Dillon, Grace L. "Beyond the Grim Dust of What *Was* to a Radiant Possibility of What *Could Be*: Two-Spirit Survivance Stories." In *Love beyond Body, Space, and Time: An Indigenous LGBT Sci-Fi Anthology*, ed. Hope Nicholson, 9–11. Winnipeg, MB: Bedside, 2016.

Dillon, Grace L. "Imagining Indigenous Futurisms." In *Walking the Clouds: An Anthology of Indigenous Science Fiction*, ed. Grace L. Dillon, 1–12. Tucson: University of Arizona Press, 2012.

Dillon, Grace L. "Indigenous Scientific Literacies in Nalo Hopkinson's Ceremonial Worlds." *Journal of the Fantastic in the Arts* 18.1 (2007): 23–41.

Dillon, Stephen. *Fugitive Life: The Queer Politics of the Prison State*. Durham, NC: Duke University Press, 2018.

Dimaline, Cherie. "Legends Are Made, Not Born." In *Love beyond Body, Space and Time*, ed. Hope Nicholson, 31–37. Winnipeg, MB: Bedside, 2016.

Diouf, Sylviane A. *Slavery's Exiles: The Story of the American Maroons*. New York: New York University Press, 2014.

Doerfler, Jill. *Those Who Belong: Identity, Family, Blood, and Citizenship among the White Earth Anishinaabeg*. East Lansing: Michigan State University Press, 2015.

Duarte, Marisa Elena. *Network Sovereignty: Building the Internet across Indian Country*. Seattle: University of Washington Press, 2017.

Dubey, Madhu. "The Future of Race in Afro-Futurist Fiction." In *The Black Imagination: Science Fiction, Futurism and the Speculative*, ed. Sandra Jackson and Julie E. Moody-Freeman, 15–31. New York: Peter Lang, 2011.

Dubey, Madhu. "Speculative Fictions of Slavery." *American Literature* 82.4 (2010): 779–805.

Dubois, Laurent. *Haiti: The Aftershocks of History*. New York: Picador, 2012.

Duggan, Lisa. *The Twilight of Equality? Neoliberalism, Cultural Politics, and the Attack on Democracy*. Boston: Beacon Press, 2004.

Duke, Eric D. *Building a Nation: Caribbean Federation in the Black Diaspora*. Tallahassee: University Press of Florida, 2015.

Duster, Troy. "The Combustible Intersection: Genomics, Forensics, and Race." In *Race after the Internet*, ed. Lisa Nakamura and Peter A. Chow-White, 310–27. New York: Routledge, 2012.

Duthu, N. Bruce. *American Indians and the Law*. New York: Penguin, 2008.

Edwards, Brent. *The Practice of Diaspora: Literature, Translation, and the Rise of Black Internationalism*. Cambridge, MA: Harvard University Press, 2003.

Ellis, Nadia. *Territories of the Soul: Queered Belonging in the Black Diaspora*. Durham, NC: Duke University Press, 2015.

Engle, Karen. *The Elusive Promise of Indigenous Development: Rights, Culture, Strategy*. Durham, NC: Duke University Press, 2010.

Enteen, Jillana. "'On the Receiving End of the Colonization': Nalo Hopkinson's 'Nansi Web." *Science Fiction Studies* 34.2 (2007): 262–82.

Escobar, Arturo. *Territories of Difference: Place, Movements, Life,* Redes. Durham, NC: Duke University Press, 2008.

Eshun, Kodwo. "Further Considerations on Afrofuturism." *CR: The New Centennial Review* 3.2 (2003): 287–302.

Estes, Nick. "Fighting for Our Lives: #NoDAPL in Historical Context." Accessed February 25, 2017. https://therednation.org/2016/09/18/fighting-for-our-lives-nodapl-in-context/.

Estes, Nick, and Jaskiran Dhillon. "Introduction: Standing Rock, #NoDAPL, and Mni Wiconi." Hot Spots, *Cultural Anthropology* website, December 22, 2016. Accessed February 25, 2017. https://culanth.org/fieldsights/1010-standing-rock-nodapl-and-mni-wiconi.

Evans, Brad. *Before Cultures: The Ethnographic Imagination in American Literature, 1865–1920*. Chicago: University of Chicago Press, 2005.

Erevelles, Nirmala. *Disability and Difference in Global Contexts: Enabling a Transformative Body Politic*. New York: Palgrave Macmillan, 2011.

Everett, Anna. *Digital Diaspora: A Race for Cyberspace*. Albany: State University of New York Press, 2009.

Federmayer, Éva. "Octavia Butler's Maternal Cyborgs: The Black Female World of the Xenogenesis Trilogy." In *The Anatomy of Science Fiction*, ed. Donald E. Morse, 95–108. Newcastle, UK: Cambridge Scholars, 2006.

Fehskens, Erin M. "The Matter of Bodies: Materiality on Nalo Hopkinson's Cybernetic Planet." *Global South* 4.2 (2010): 136–56.

Feldman, Keith P. *A Shadow over Palestine: The Imperial Life of Race in America*. Minneapolis: University of Minnesota Press, 2015.

Ferguson, Roderick A. *Aberrations in Black: Toward a Queer of Color Critique*. Minneapolis: University of Minnesota Press, 2004.

Ferguson, Roderick A. *The Reorder of Things: The University and Its Pedagogies of Minority Difference*. Minneapolis: University of Minnesota Press, 2012.

Fixico, Donald L. *Termination and Relocation: Federal Indian Policy, 1945–1960*. Albuquerque: University of New Mexico Press, 1986.

Fixico, Donald L. *The Urban Indian Experience in America*. Albuquerque: University of New Mexico Press, 2000.

Forbes, Jack D. *Africans and Native Americans: The Language of Race and the Evolution of Red-Black Peoples*. Urbana: University of Illinois Press, 1993.

Forte, Maximilian C. "Introduction: The Dual Absences of Extinction and Marginality—What Difference Does an Indigenous Presence Make?" In *Indigenous Resurgence in the Contemporary Caribbean*, ed. Maximilian C. Forte. 1–18. New York: Peter Lang.

Forte, Maximilian C. *Ruins of Absence, Presence of Caribs: (Post)Colonial Representations of Aboriginality in Trinidad and Tobago*. Gainesville: University Press of Florida, 2005.

Fortes, Meyer. *Kinship and the Social Order: The Legacy of Lewis Henry Morgan*. New Brunswick: Aldine Transaction, (1969) 2006.

Foucault, Michel. "Governmentality" (1978). In *Michel Foucault: Power: Essential Works of Foucault, 1954–1984*, vol. 3, ed. James D. Faubion, 201–22. New York: New Press, 2000.

Foucault, Michel. *The History of Sexuality*, vol. 1, trans. Robert Hurley. New York: Vintage, (1978) 1990.

Foucault, Michel. *"Society Must Be Defended": Lectures at the Collége de France, 1975–76*, ed. Maura Bertani and Alessandro Fontana, trans. David Macey. New York: Picador, 2003.

Frances, Conseula, ed. *Conversations with Octavia Butler*. Jackson: University Press of Mississippi, 2010.

Franklin, John Hope, and Loren Schweninger. *Runaway Slaves: Rebels on the Plantation*. New York: Oxford University Press, 1999.

French, Jan Hoffman. *Legalizing Identities: Becoming Black or Indian in Brazil's Northeast*. Chapel Hill: University of North Carolina Press, 2009.

Fujimura, Joan H., Ramya Rajagopalan, Pilar N. Ossorio, and Kjell A. Doksum. "Race and Ancestry: Operationalizing Populations in Human Genetic Variation Studies."

In *What's the Use of Race? Modern Governance and the Biology of Difference*, ed. Ian Whitmarsh and David S. Jones, 169–83. Cambridge, MA: MIT Press, 2010.

Gaertner, David. "Indigenous in Cyberspace: CyberPowWow, *God's Lake Narrows*, and the Contours of Online Indigenous Territory." *American Indian Culture and Research Journal* 39.4 (2015): 55–78.

Galloway, Alexander R. "Does the Whatever Speak?" In *Race after the Internet*, ed. Lisa Nakamura and Peter A. Chow-White, 111–27. New York: Routledge, 2012.

Gamber, John. "The End (of the Trail) Is the Beginning: Stephen Graham Jones's *The Bird Is Gone*." *Western American Literature* 49.1 (2014): 29–46.

Gandy, Oscar H., Jr. "Matrix Multiplication and the Digital Divide." In *Race after the Internet*, ed. Lisa Nakamura and Peter A. Chow-White, 128–45. New York: Routledge, 2012.

Garza, Alicia, Opal Tometi, and Patrisse Cullors. "A HerStory of the #BlackLivesMatter Movement." Accessed February 25, 2017. http://blacklivesmatter.com.

Garroutte, Eva Marie. *Real Indians: Identity and the Survival of Native America*. Berkeley: University of California Press, 2003.

Genetin-Pilawa, C. Joseph. *Crooked Paths to Allotment: The Fight over Federal Indian Policy after the Civil War*. Chapel Hill: University of North Carolina Press, 2012.

Gilmore, Ruth Wilson. *Golden Gulag: Prisons, Surplus, Crisis, and Opposition in Globalizing California*. Berkeley: University of California Press, 2007.

Glave, Dianne D. "An Interview with Nalo Hopkinson." *Callaloo* 26.1 (2003): 146–59.

Glissant, Édouard. *Poetics of Relation*, trans. Betsy Wang. Ann Arbor: University of Michigan Press, 2010.

Goeman, Mishuana. *Mark My Words: Native Women Mapping Our Nations*. Minneapolis: University of Minnesota Press, 2013.

Goffman, Alice. *On the Run: Fugitive Life in an American City*. Chicago: University of Chicago Press, 2014.

Goldberg, David Theo. *The Racial State*. Malden, MA: Blackwell, 2002.

Goldstein, Alyosha. "Finance and Foreclosure in the Colonial Present." *Radical History Review* 118 (2014): 42–63.

Gómez, Laura E. *Manifest Destinies: The Making of the Mexican American Race*. New York: New York University Press, 2008.

Gottlieb, Karla. *The Mother of Us All: A History of Queen Nanny, Leader of the Windward Jamaican Maroons*. Trenton, NJ: Africa World Press, 2000.

Gottschalk, Marie. *Caught: The Prison State and the Lockdown of American Politics*. Princeton, NJ: Princeton University Press, 2015.

Graham, Stephen, and David Wood. "Digitalizing Surveillance: Categorization, Space, Inequality." *Critical Social Policy* 23.2 (2003): 227–48.

Grande, Sandy. *Red Pedagogy: Native American Social and Political Thought*, rev. 10th ed. Lanham, MD: Rowman and Littlefield, 2015.

Green, Michael D. *The Politics of Indian Removal: Creek Government and Society in Crisis*. Lincoln: University of Nebraska Press, 1982.

Greene, Shane. "Introduction: One Race, Roots/Routes, and Sovereignty in Latin America's Afro-Indigenous Multiculturalisms." *Journal of Latin American and Caribbean Anthropology* 12.2 (2007): 329–55.

Grewe-Volpp, Christa. "Octavia Butler and the Nature/Culture Divide: An Ecofeminist Approach to the *Xenogenesis* Trilogy." In *Restoring the Connection to the Natural World: Essays on the African American Environmental Imagination*, ed. Sylvia Mayer, 149–73. Münster: LIT, 2003.

Grossman, Zoltán. *Unlikely Alliances: Native Nations and White Communities Join to Defend Rural Lands*. Seattle: University of Washington Press, 2017.

Guidotti-Hernández, Nicole M. *Unspeakable Violence: Remapping U.S. and Mexican National Imaginaries*. Durham, NC: Duke University Press, 2011.

Hairston, Andrea. *Mindscape*. Seattle: Aqueduct, 2006.

Hanchard, Michael. "Black Memory versus State Memory: Notes toward a Method." *Small Axe* 26 (2008): 45–62.

Hancock, Ange-Marie. *Intersectionality: An Intellectual History*. New York: Oxford University Press, 2016.

Hancock, Brecken. "New Half-Way Tree and the Second World: Themes of Nation and Colonization in Nalo Hopkinson's *Midnight Robber*." In *The Canadian Fantastic in Focus: New Perspectives*, ed. Allan Weiss, 95–105. Jefferson, NC: McFarland, 2015.

Harney, Stefano, and Fred Moten. *The Undercommons: Fugitive Planning and Black Study*. New York: Minor Composition, 2013.

Harring, Sidney L. *Crow Dog's Case: American Indian Sovereignty, Tribal Law, and United States Law in the Nineteenth Century*. New York: Cambridge University Press, 1994.

Harris, Cheryl I. "Whiteness as Property." *Harvard Law Review* 106.8 (1993): 1707–91.

Harris, C. L. G. "The True Traditions of My Ancestors." In *Maroon Heritage: Archaeological and Ethnographic Historical Perspectives*, ed. E. Kofi Agorsah, 36–63. Kingston, Jamaica: Canoe, 1994.

Harris-Perry, Melissa V. *Sister Citizen: Shame, Stereotypes, and Black Women in America*. New Haven, CT: Yale University Press, 2011.

Hartman, Saidiya V. *Lose Your Mother: A Journey along the Atlantic Slave Route*. New York: Farrar, Straus and Giroux, 2007.

Hartman, Saidiya V. *Scenes of Subjection: Terror, Slavery, and Self-Making in Nineteenth-Century America*. New York: Oxford University Press, 1997.

Hausman, Blake M. *Riding the Trail of Tears*. Lincoln: University of Nebraska Press, 2011.

Hernandez, Ricardo Bharath, and Maximilian C. Forte. "'In This Place Where I Was Chief': History and Ritual in the Maintenance and Retrieval of Traditions in the Carib Community of Arima, Trinidad." In *Indigenous Resurgence in the Contemporary Caribbean*, ed. Maximilian C. Forte, 107–31. New York: Peter Lang, 2006.

Hesse, Barnor. "Escaping Liberty: Western Hegemony, Black Fugitivity." *Political Theory* 42.3 (2014): 288–313.

Higashida, Cheryl. *Black Internationalist Feminism: Women Writers of the Black Left, 1945–1995*. Urbana: University of Illinois Press, 2011.

Hinton, Elizabeth. *From the War on Poverty to the War on Crime: The Making of Mass Incarceration in America*. Cambridge, MA: Harvard University Press, 2016.

Hittman, Michael. *Wovoka and the Ghost Dance*, rev. ed. Lincoln: University of Nebraska Press, 1997.

Hodgson, Dorothy L. *Being Maasai, Becoming Indigenous: Postcolonial Politics in a Neo-liberal World*. Bloomington: Indiana University Press, 2010.

Holland, Sharon. *The Erotic Life of Racism*. Durham, NC: Duke University Press, 2012.

Hong, Grace Kyungwon. *Death beyond Disavowal: The Impossible Politics of Difference*. Minneapolis: University of Minnesota Press, 2015.

Hooker, Juliet. "Indigenous Inclusion/Black Exclusion: Race, Ethnicity and Multicultural Citizenship in Latin America." *Journal of Latin American Studies* 37.2 (2005): 285–310.

Hopkinson, Nalo. *Brown Girl in the Ring*. New York: Grand Central, 1998.

Hopkinson, Nalo. *Midnight Robber*. New York: Grand Central, 2000.

Hoxie, Frederick E. *A Final Promise: The Campaign to Assimilate the Indians, 1880–1920*. Cambridge: Cambridge University Press, (1984) 1992.

Huhndorf, Shari M. *Going Native: Indians in the American Cultural Imagination*. Ithaca, NY: Cornell University Press, 2001.

Hunt, Linda M., and Mary S. Megyesi. "The Ambiguous Meanings of the Racial/Ethnic Categories Routinely Used in Human Genetics Research." *Social Science and Medicine* 66.2 (2008): 349–61.

Ibrahim, Habiba. *Troubling the Family: The Promise of Personhood and the Rise of Multiculturalism*. Minneapolis: University of Minnesota Press, 2012.

Ingraham, Chrys. "The Heterosexual Imaginary: Feminist Sociology and Theories of Gender." *Sociological Theory* 12.2 (1994): 203–19.

Iton, Richard. *In Search of the Black Fantastic: Politics and Popular Culture in the Post–Civil Rights Era*. New York: Oxford University Press, 2008.

Jackson, Cassandra. "Visualizing Slavery: Photography and the Disabled Subject in the Art of Carrie Mae Weems." In *Blackness and Disability: Critical Examinations and Cultural Interventions*, ed. Christopher M. Bell, 31–46. East Lansing: Michigan State University Press, 2011.

Jackson, Sandra, and Julie Moody-Freeman. "The Black Imagination and the Genres: Science Fiction, Futurism and the Speculative." In *The Black Imagination: Science Fiction, Futurism and the Speculative*, ed. Sandra Jackson and Julie Moody-Freeman, 1–14. New York: Peter Lang, 2011.

Jackson, Shona. *Creole Indigeneity: Between Myth and Nation in the Caribbean*. Minneapolis: University of Minnesota Press, 2012.

Jacobs, Naomi. "Posthuman Bodies and Agency in Octavia Butler's *Xenogensis*." In *Dark Horizons: Science Fiction and the Dystopian Imagination*, ed. Raffaella Baccolini and Tom Moylan, 91–112. New York: Routledge, 2003.

James, Joy. "Afrarealism and the Black Matrix: Maroon Philosophy at Democracy's Border." *Black Scholar* 43.4 (2013): 124–31.

Jameson, Frederic. *Archaeologies of the Future: The Desire Called Utopia and Other Science Fictions*. London: Verso, 2005.

Jarman, Michelle. "Coming Up from Underground: Uneasy Dialogues at the Intersections of Race, Mental Illness, and Disability Studies." In *Blackness and Disability: Critical Examinations and Cultural Interventions*, ed. Christopher M. Bell, 9–30. East Lansing: Michigan State University Press, 2011.

Jemisin, N. K. *The Stone Sky*. New York: Orbit, 2017.

Johns, J. Adam. "Becoming Medusa: Octavia Butler's *Lilith's Brood* and Sociobiology." *Science Fiction Studies* 37.3 (2010): 342–400.

Jones, Dorothy V. *License for Empire: Colonialism by Treaty in Early America*. Chicago: University of Chicago Press, 1982.

Jones, Stephen Graham. *The Bird Is Gone: A ~~Monograph~~ Manifesto*. Tallahassee, FL: FC2, 2003.

Justice, Daniel Heath. "The Boys Who Became the Hummingbirds." In *Love beyond Body, Space and Time*, ed. Hope Nicholson, 54–59. Winnipeg, MB: Bedside, 2016.

Justice, Daniel Heath. "'Go Away, Water!': Kinship Criticism and the Decolonization Imperative." In *Reasoning Together*, ed. Native Critics Collective, 147–68. Norman: University of Oklahoma Press, 2008.

Justice, Daniel Heath. *Our Fire Survives the Storm: A Cherokee Literary History*. Minneapolis: University of Minnesota Press, 2006.

Justice, Daniel Heath. *The Way of Thorn and Thunder: The Kynship Chronicles*. Albuquerque: University of New Mexico Press, 2011.

Kafer, Alison. *Feminist, Queer, Crip*. Bloomington: Indiana University Press, 2013.

Kahn, Jonathan. "What's the Use of Race in Presenting Forensic DNA Evidence in Court?" In *What's the Use of Race? Modern Governance and the Biology of Difference*, ed. Ian Whitmarsh and David S. Jones, 27–48. Cambridge, MA: MIT Press, 2010.

Kamugisha, Aaron. "The Black Experience of New World Coloniality." *Small Axe* 49 (2016): 129–44.

Kamugisha, Aaron. "The Coloniality of Citizenship in the Contemporary Anglophone Caribbean." *Race and Class* 49.2 (2007): 20–40.

Kauanui, J. Kēhaulani. *Hawaiian Blood: Colonialism and the Politics of Sovereignty and Indigeneity*. Durham, NC: Duke University Press, 2008.

Kawash, Samira. *Dislocating the Color Line: Identity, Hybridity, and Singularity in African-American Narrative*. Stanford, CA: Stanford University Press, 1997.

Kazanjian, David. *The Colonizing Trick: National Culture and Imperial Citizenship in Early America*. Minneapolis: University of Minnesota Press, 2003.

Kehoe, Alice Beck. *The Ghost Dance: Ethnohistory and Revitalization*, 2d ed. Long Grove, IL: Waveland, 2006.

Kelley, Robin D. G. *Freedom Dreams: The Black Radical Imagination*. Boston: Beacon Press, 2002.

Kempner, Brandon. "The Unshakeable Intent to Commit Genocide: Walter Mosley's *The Wave*, 9/11 and Politics Out of Context." In *The Black Imagination: Science Fiction, Futurism and the Speculative*, ed. Sandra Jackson and Julie E. Moody-Freeman, 166–86. New York: Peter Lang, 2011.

Khan-Cullors, Patrisse, and asha bandele. *When They Call You a Terrorist: A Black Lives Matter Memoir*. New York: St. Martin's, 2018.

Kilgore, De Witt Douglas. *Astrofuturism: Science, Race, and Visions of Utopia in Space*. Philadelphia: University of Pennsylvania Press, 2003.

King, Tiffany. "In the Clearing: Black Female Bodies, Space, and Settler Colonial Landscapes." Ph.D. diss., University of Maryland, College Park. 2013.

King, Tiffany. "The Labor of (Re)reading Plantation Landscapes Fungible(ly)." *Antipode* 48.4 (2016): 1–18.

Kino-nda-niimi Collective, eds. *The Winter We Danced*. Manitoba: Arbeiter Ring, 2014.

Kipuri, Naomi. "The UN Declaration on the Rights of Indigenous Peoples in the African Context." In *Making the Declaration Work: The United Nations Declaration on the Rights of Indigenous Peoples*, ed. Clare Charters and Ruldolfo Stavenhagen, 252–63. Copenhagen: International Work Group for Indigenous Affairs, 2009.

Klopotek, Brian. *Recognition Odysseys: Indigeneity, Race, and Federal Tribal Recognition Policy in Three Louisiana Indian Communities*. Durham, NC: Duke University Press, 2011.

Kuper, Adam. *The Reinvention of Primitive Society: Transformations of a Myth*. London: Routledge, (1988) 1997.

Kurisato, Mari. "Imposter Syndrome." In *Love beyond Body, Space and Time*, ed. Hope Nicholson, 87–102. Winnipeg, MB: Bedside, 2016.

Lalla, Barbara. "The Facetiness Factor: Theorizing Caribbean Space in Narrative." In *Caribbean Literary Discourse: Voice and Cultural Identity in the Anglophone Caribbean*, ed. Barbara Lalla, Jean D'Costa, and Velma Pollard, 232–49. Tuscaloosa: University of Alabama Press, 2014.

Landzelius, Kyra. "Introduction: Native on the Net." In *Native on the Net: Indigenous and Diasporic Peoples in the Virtual Age*, ed. Kyra Landzelius, 1–42. New York: Routledge, 2006.

Lang, Sabine. *Men as Women, Women as Men: Changing Gender in Native American Cultures*. Austin: University of Texas Press, 1998.

Latour, Bruno. *Reassembling the Social: An Introduction to Actor-Network Theory*. New York: Oxford University Press, 2005.

Latukefu, Alopi S. "Remote Indigenous Communities in Australia: Questions of Access, Information, and Self-Determination." In *Native on the Net: Indigenous and Diasporic Peoples in the Virtual Age*, ed. Kyra Landzelius, 43–60. New York: Routledge, 2006.

Lavender, Isiah, III. *Race in American Science Fiction*. Bloomington: Indiana University Press, 2011.

Lawrence, Bonita. *"Real" Indians and Others: Mixed-Blood Urban Native Peoples and Indigenous Nationhood*. Lincoln: University of Nebraska Press, 2004.

Lee, James Kyung-Jin. *Urban Triage: Race and the Fictions of Multiculturalism*. Minneapolis: University of Minnesota Press, 2004.

Lehmann, Karin. "Aboriginal Title, Indigenous Rights and the Right to Culture." *South African Journal on Human Rights* 20.1 (2004): 86–118.

Lemont, Eric D., ed. *American Indian Constitutional Reform and the Rebuilding of Native Nations*. Austin: University of Texas Press, 2006.

Leroy, Justin. "Black History in Occupied Territory: On the Entanglements of Slavery and Settler Colonialism." *Theory and Event* 19.4 (2016).

Lipsitz, George. *The Possessive Investment in Whiteness: How White People Profit from Identity Politics*, rev. ed. Philadelphia: Temple University Press, 2006.

Little Badger, Darcie. "Né Łe." In *Love beyond Body, Space and Time*, ed. Hope Nicholson, 60–76. Winnipeg, MB; Bedside, 2016.

Lorde, Audre. *Sister Outsider: Essays and Speeches.* Freedom, CA: Crossing, 1984.

Lowe, Lisa. *The Intimacies of Four Continents.* Durham, NC: Duke University Press, 2015.

Lowery, Malinda Maynor. *Lumbee Indians in the Jim Crow South: Race, Identity, and the Making of a Nation.* Chapel Hill: University of North Carolina Press, 2010.

Lowman, Emma Battell, and Adam J. Barker. *Settler: Identity and Colonialism in 21st Century Canada.* Halifax, NS: Fernwood, 2015.

Lyon, David. *Surveillance Studies: An Overview.* Malden, MA: Polity, 2007.

Lyons, Scott Richard. *X-marks: Native Signatures of Assent.* Minneapolis: University of Minnesota Press, 2010.

Mackey, Eva. *Unsettled Expectations: Uncertainty, Land and Settler Decolonization.* Halifax, NS: Fernwood, 2016.

Mackie, Erin. "Welcome the Outlaw: Pirates, Maroons, and Caribbean Countercultures." *Cultural Critique* 59.1 (2005): 24–62.

MacMillan, Ken. *Sovereignty and Possession in the English New World: The Legal Foundations of Empire, 1576–1640.* New York: Cambridge University Press, 2006.

Macpherson, C. B. *The Political Theory of Possessive Individualism: Hobbes to Locke.* New York: Oxford University Press, 1962.

Madden, Paula C. *African Nova Scotian–Mi'kmaw Relations.* Halifax, NS: Fernwood, 2009.

Magnet, Shoshana Amielle. *When Biometrics Fail: Gender, Race, and the Technology of Identity.* Durham, NC: Duke University Press, 2011.

Mamdani, Mahmood. *Citizen and Subject: Contemporary Africa and the Legacy of Late Colonialism.* Princeton, NJ: Princeton University Press, 1996.

Mandell, Daniel R. *Tribe, Race, History: Native Americans in Southern New England, 1780–1880.* Baltimore: Johns Hopkins University Press, 2008.

Manela, Erez. *The Wilsonian Moment: Self-Determination and the International Origins of Anticolonial Nationalism.* New York: Oxford University Press, 2009.

Marez, Curtis. *Farm Worker Futurism: Speculative Technologies of Desire.* Minneapolis: University of Minnesota Press, 2016.

Marriott, David. "Inventions of Existence: Sylvia Wynter, Frantz Fanon, Sociogeny, and 'the Damned.'" *CR: The New Centennial Review* 11.3 (2012): 45–90.

Martineau, Jarett, and Eric Ritskes. "Fugitive Indigeneity: Reclaiming the Terrain of Decolonial Struggle through Indigenous Art." *Decolonization: Indigeneity, Education, and Society* 3.1 (2014): i–xii.

Massey, Douglas S., and Nancy A. Denton. *American Apartheid: Segregation and the Making of the Underclass.* Cambridge, MA: Harvard University Press, 1993.

Mathews, John Joseph. *The Osages: Children of the Middle Waters.* Norman: University of Oklahoma Press, 1961.

Mayer-Schönberger, Viktor, and Kenneth Cukier. *Big Data.* New York: Houghton Mifflin Harcourt, 2013.

Mays, Kyle T. "From Flint to Standing Rock: The Aligned Struggles of Black and Indigenous Peoples." Accessed February 25, 2017. http://culanth.org.

Mbembe, Achille. "Necropolitics," trans. Libby Meintjes. *Public Culture* 15.1 (2003): 11–40.

McCarthy, Theresa. *In Divided Unity: Haudenosaunee Reclamation at Grand River.* Tucson: University of Arizona Press, 2016.

McDonnell, Janet A. *The Dispossession of the American Indian, 1887–1934*. Bloomington: Indiana University Press, 1991.

McKittrick, Katherine. *Demonic Grounds: Black Women and the Cartographies of Struggle*. Minneapolis: University of Minnesota Press, 2006.

McKittrick, Katherine. "Plantation Futures." *Small Axe* 17.3 (2013): 1–15.

McKittrick, Katherine. "Rebellion/Invention/Groove." *Small Axe* 49 (2016): 79–91.

McKittrick, Katherine, ed. *Sylvia Wynter: On Being Human as Praxis*. Durham, NC: Duke University Press, 2015.

McLoughlin, William G. *Cherokee Renascence in the New Republic*. Princeton, NJ: Princeton University Press, 1986.

Melamed, Jodi. *Represent and Destroy: Rationalizing Violence in the New Racial Capitalism*. Minneapolis: University of Minnesota Press, 2011.

Melzer, Patricia. *Alien Constructions: Science Fiction and Feminist Thought*. Austin: University of Texas Press, 2006.

Michaels, Walter Benn. "Political Science Fictions." *New Literary History* 31.4 (2000): 649–64.

Mielke, Laura L. *Moving Encounters: Sympathy and the Indian Question in Antebellum Literature*. Amherst: University of Massachusetts Press, 2008.

Mignolo, Walter D. *The Darker Side of the Renaissance: Literacy, Territoriality, and Colonization*. Ann Arbor: University of Michigan Press, 1995.

Miles, Tiya. *Ties That Bind: The Story of an Afro-Cherokee Family in Slavery and Freedom*. Berkeley: University of California Press, 2006.

Miles, Tiya, and Sharon Holland. *Crossing Waters, Crossing Worlds: The African Diaspora in Indian Country*. Durham, NC: Duke University Press, 2006.

Miller, Bruce Ganville. *Oral History on Trial: Recognizing Aboriginal Narratives in the Courts*. Vancouver: University of British Columbia Press, 2011.

Miller, Jim. "Post-Apocalyptic Hoping: Octavia Butler's Dystopian/Utopian Vision." *Science Fiction Studies* 25.2 (1998): 336–60.

Miller, Robert J., Jacinta Ruru, Larissa Behrendt, and Tracey Lindberg. *Discovering Indigenous Lands: The Doctrine of Discovery in the English Colonies*. New York: Oxford University Press, 2010.

Million, Dian. *Therapeutic Nations: Healing in an Age of Indigenous Human Rights*. Tucson: University of Arizona Press, 2013.

Mithlo, Nancy Marie. *"Our Indian Princess": Subverting the Stereotypes*. Santa Fe, NM: School for Advanced Research Press, 2008.

Moraga, Cherríe, and Gloria Anzaldúa. *This Bridge Called My Back: Writings by Radical Women of Color*, 2d ed. New York: Kitchen Table/Women of Color Press, 1983.

Moreton-Robinson, Aileen. *The White Possessive: Property, Power, and Indigenous Sovereignty*. Minneapolis: University of Minnesota Press, 2015.

Morgan, Lewis Henry. *Ancient Society*. New York: Gordon, (1877) 1977.

Morgan, Lewis Henry. *League of the Ho-dé-no-sau-nee, or Iroquois*, ed. Willian N. Fenton. New York: Corinth, (1851) 1962.

Morgensen, Scott L. *Spaces between Us: Queer Settler Colonialism and Indigenous Decolonization*. Minneapolis: University of Minnesota Press, 2011.

Mosley, Walter. *Futureland: Nine Stories of an Imminent World*. New York: Warner Books, Inc., 2001.

Mosley, Walter. *The Wave*. New York: Warner, 2006.

Mosley, Walter. *What Next: A Memoir toward World Peace*. Baltimore: Black Classic, 2003.

Mosley, Walter. *Workin' on the Chain Gang: Shaking Off the Dead Hand of History*. New York: Ballantine, 2000.

Moten, Fred. "The Case of Blackness." *Criticism* 50.2 (2008): 177–218.

Muhammad, Khalil Gibran. *The Condemnation of Blackness: Race, Crime, and the Making of Modern Urban America*. Cambridge: Harvard University Press, 2010.

Muñoz, José Esteban. *Cruising Utopia: The Then and There of Queer Futurity*. New York: New York University Press, 2009.

Murakawa, Naomi. *The First Civil Right: How Liberals Built Prison America*. New York: Oxford University Press, 2014.

Nanda, Aparajita. "Power, Politics, and Domestic Desire in Octavia Butler's *Lilith's Brood*." *Callaloo* 36.3 (2013): 773–88.

Navakas, Michele Currie. *Liquid Landscape: Geography and Settlement at the Edge of Early America*. Philadelphia: University of Pennsylvania Press, 2018.

Nayar, Pramod K. *Posthumanism*. Malden, MA: Polity, 2014.

Nelson, Alondra. "Introduction: Future Texts." *Social Text* 20.2 (2002): 1–15.

Nelson, Alondra. "'Making the Impossible Possible': An Interview with Nalo Hopkinson." *Social Text* 20.2 (2002): 97–113.

Nelson, Alondra. *The Social Life of DNA: Race, Reparations, and Reconciliation after the Genome*. Boston: Beacon, 2016.

Nelson, Dana. *Commons Democracy: Reading the Politics of Participation in the Early United States*. New York: Fordham University Press, 2016.

Nelson, Diane M. *A Finger in the Wound: Body Politics in Quincentennial Guatemala*. Berkeley: University of California Press, 1999.

Newton, Melanie J. "Returns to a Native Land: Indigeneity and Decolonization in the Anglophone Caribbean." *Small Axe* 17.2 (2013): 108–22.

Nguyen, Mimi Thi. *The Gift of Freedom: War, Debt, and Other Refugee Passages*. Durham, NC: Duke University Press, 2012.

Ng'weno, Bettina. "Can Ethnicity Replace Race? Afro-Colombians, Indigeneity, and the Colombian Multicultural State." *Journal of Latin American and Caribbean Anthropology* 12.2 (2007): 414–40.

Nichols, Robert. "Contract and Usurpation: Enfranchisement and Racial Governance in Settler-Colonial Contexts." In *Theorizing Native Studies*, ed. Audra Simpson and Andrea Smith, 99–121. Durham, NC: Duke University Press, 2014.

Niezen, Ronald. *The Origins of Indigenism: Human Rights and the Politics of Identity*. Berkeley: University of California Press, 2003.

Nixon, Lindsay. "Indigenous Artists and the Dystopian Now." Accessed June 29, 2017. http://gustsmagazine.ca/visual-cultures.

Nyong'o, Tavia. *The Amalgamation Waltz: Race, Performance, and the Ruses of Memory*. Minneapolis: University of Minnesota Press, 2009.

O'Brien, Jean. *Firsting and Lasting: Writing Indians Out of Existence in New England*. Minneapolis: University of Minnesota Press, 2010.

O'Brien, Jean. "State Recognition and 'Termination' in Nineteenth-Century New England." In *Recognition, Sovereignty Struggles, and Indigenous Rights in the United States: A Sourcebook*, ed. Amy E. Den Ouden and Jean M. O'Brien, 149–68. Chapel Hill: University of North Carolina Press, 2013.

Obourn, Megan. "Octavia Butler's Disabled Futures." *Contemporary Literature* 54.1 (2013): 109–38.

Okorafor, Nnedi. *Binti*. New York: Tom Doherty Associates, 2015.

Okorafor, Nnedi. *Binti: Home*. New York: Tom Doherty Associates, 2017.

Okorafor, Nnedi. *Binti: The Night Masquerade*. New York: Tom Doherty Associates, 2018.

Ong, Aiwa. *Neoliberalism as Exception: Mutations in Citizenship and Sovereignty*. Durham, NC: Duke University Press, 2006.

Ostler, Jeffrey. *The Plains Sioux and U.S. Colonialism from Lewis and Clark to Wounded Knee*. New York: Cambridge University Press, 2004.

Pager, Devah. *Marked: Race, Crime, and Finding Work in an Era of Mass Incarceration*. Chicago: University of Chicago Press, 2007.

Palacio, Joseph O. "Cultural Identity among Rural Garifuna Migrants in Belize City, Belize." In *Indigenous Resurgence in the Contemporary Caribbean*, ed. Maximilian C. Forte, 177–96. New York: Peter Lang, 2006.

Papke, Mary E. "Necessary Interventions in the Face of Very Curious Compulsions: Octavia Butler's Naturalist Science Fiction." *Studies in American Naturalism* 8.1 (2013): 79–92.

Pascoe, Peggy. *What Comes Naturally: Miscegenation Law and the Making of Race in America*. New York: Oxford University Press, 2009.

Pasternak, Shiri. *Grounded Authority: The Algonquins of Barriere Lake against the State*. Minneapolis: University of Minnesota Press, 2017.

Patterson, Brandon E. "'There's No Middle Ground': Black Lives Matter Leader Alicia Garza on Charlottesville, Trump, and Democrats." *Mother Jones*, June 15, 2017. Accessed September 8, 2017. http://www.motherjones.com/politics.

Pattillo, Mary. *Black on the Block: The Politics of Race and Class in the City*. Chicago: University of Chicago Press, 2007.

Peppers, Cathy. "Dialogic Origins and Alien Identities in Butler's *Xenogenesis*." *Science Fiction Studies* 22.2 (1995): 47–62.

Perry, Keisha-Khan Y. *Black Women against the Land Grab: The Fight for Racial Justice in Brazil*. Minneapolis: University of Minnesota Press, 2013.

Peters, Evelyn, and Chris Andersen, eds. *Indigenous in the City: Contemporary Identities and Cultural Innovation*. Vancouver: University of British Columbia Press, 2013.

Peterson, Ruth D., and Lauren J. Krivo. *Divergent Social Worlds: Neighborhood Crime and the Racial-Spatial Divide*. New York: Russell Sage Foundation, 2010.

Pettit, Becky. *Invisible Men: Mass Incarceration and the Myth of Black Progress*. New York: Russell Sage Foundation, 2012.

Pfister, Joel. *Individuality Incorporated: Indians and the Multicultural Modern*. Durham, NC: Duke University Press, 2004.

Philp, Kenneth R. *Termination Revisited: American Indians on the Trail to Self-Determination, 1933–1953*. Lincoln: University of Nebraska Press, 1999.

Pinto, Samantha. *Difficult Diasporas: The Transnational Feminist Aesthetic of the Black Atlantic*. New York: New York University Press, 2013.

Posmentier, Sonya. *Cultivation and Catastrophe: The Lyric Ecology of Modern Black Literature*. New York: New York University, 2017.

Povinelli, Elizabeth A. *The Cunning of Recognition: Indigenous Alterities and the Making of Australian Multiculturalism*. Durham, NC: Duke University Press, 2002.

Povinelli, Elizabeth A. *Economies of Abandonment: Social Belonging and Endurance in Late Liberalism*. Durham, NC: Duke University Press, 2011.

Povinelli, Elizabeth A. *The Empire of Love: Toward a Theory of Intimacy, Genealogy, and Carnality*. Durham, NC: Duke University Press, 2006.

Povinelli, Elizabeth A. "The Governance of the Prior." *interventions* 13.1 (2011): 13–30.

Povinelli, Elizabeth A. *Labor's Lot: The Power, History, and Culture of Aboriginal Action*. Chicago: University of Chicago Press, 1993.

Powell, Dana E. *Landscapes of Power: Politics of Energy in the Navajo Nation*. Durham, NC: Duke University Press, 2018.

Pratt, Scott L. "Wounded Knee and the Prospect of Pluralism." *Journal of Speculative Philosophy* 19.2 (2005): 150–66.

Puar, Jasbir K. *Terrorist Assemblages: Homonationalism in Queer Times*. Durham, NC: Duke University Press, 2007.

Quashie, Kevin. *The Sovereignty of Quiet: Beyond Resistance in Black Culture*. New Brunswick, NJ: Rutgers University Press, 2012.

Raheja, Michelle H. *Reservation Reelism: Redfacing, Visual Sovereignty, and Representations of Native Americans in Film*. Lincoln: University of Nebraska Press, 2010.

Raibmon, Paige Sylvia. *Authentic Indians: Episodes of Encounter from the Late-Nineteenth-Century Northwest Coast*. Durham, NC: Duke University Press, 2005.

Ramirez, Renya K. *Native Hubs: Culture, Community, and Belonging in Silicon Valley and Beyond*. Durham, NC: Duke University Press, 2007.

Ramraj, Ruby S. "Nalo Hopkinson's Colonial and Dystopic Worlds in *Midnight Robber*." In *The Influence of Imagination: Essays on Science Fiction and Fantasy as Agents of Social Change*, ed. Lee Easton and Randy Schroeder, 131–38. Jefferson, NC: McFarland, 2008.

Rasmussen, Birgit Brander. *Queequeg's Coffin: Indigenous Literacies and Early American Literature*. Durham, NC: Duke University Press, 2012.

Razack, Sherene H. *Dying from Improvement: Inquests and Inquiries into Indigenous Deaths in Custody*. Toronto: University of Toronto Press, 2015.

Reardon, Jenny. *Race to the Finish: Identity and Governance in an Age of Genomics*. Princeton, NJ: Princeton University Press, 2005.

Reddy, Chandan. *Freedom with Violence: Race, Sexuality, and the U.S. State*. Durham, NC: Duke University Press, 2011.

Richie, Beth E. *Arrested Justice: Black Women, Violence, and America's Prison Nation*. New York: New York University Press, 2012.

Richland, Justin. *Arguing with Tradition: The Language of Law in Hopi Tribal Court*. Chicago: University of Chicago Press, 2008.

Rifkin, Mark. *Beyond Settler Time: Temporal Sovereignty and Indigenous Self-Determination*. Durham, NC: Duke University Press, 2017.

Rifkin, Mark. "Debt and the Transnationalization of Hawai'i." *American Quarterly* 60.1 (2008): 43–66.

Rifkin, Mark. "Making Peoples into Populations: The Racial Limits of Tribal Sovereignty." In *Theorizing Native Studies*, ed. Audra Simpson and Andrea Smith, 149–87. Durham, NC: Duke University Press, 2014.

Rifkin, Mark. *Manifesting America: The Imperial Construction of U.S. National Space*. New York: Oxford University Press, 2009.

Rifkin, Mark. *When Did Indians Become Straight? Kinship, the History of Sexuality, and Native Sovereignty*. New York: Oxford University Press, 2011.

Ritchie, Andrea J. *Invisible No More: Police Violence against Black Women and Women of Color*. Boston: Beacon, 2017.

Roanhorse, Rebecca, Elizabeth LaPensee, Johnnie Jae, and Darcie Little Badger. "Decolonizing Science Fiction and Imagining Futures: An Indigenous Futurisms Roundtable." Accessed June 29, 2017. http://strangehorizons.com/non-fiction/articles/decolonizating-science-fiction-and-imagining-futures-an-indigenous-futurisms-roundtable.

Roberts, Dorothy. *Fatal Invention: How Science, Politics, and Big Business Re-create Race in the Twenty-First Century*. New York: New Press, 2011.

Roberts, Neil. *Freedom as Marronage*. Chicago: University of Chicago Press, 2015.

Rockwell, Stephen J. *Indian Affairs and the Administrative State in the Nineteenth Century*. New York: Cambridge University Press, 2010.

Rodríguez, Dylan. *Forced Passages: Imprisoned Radical Intellectuals and the U.S. Prison Regime*. Minneapolis: University of Minnesota Press, 2006.

Roscoe, Will. *Changing Ones: Third and Fourth Genders in Native North America*. New York: St. Martin's Griffin, 1998.

Rosier, Paul C. *Rebirth of the Blackfeet Nation, 1912–1954*. Lincoln: University of Nebraska Press, 2001.

Ross, Luana. *Inventing the Savage: The Social Construction of Native American Criminality*. Austin: University of Texas Press, 1998.

Rovane, Carol. *The Metaphysics and Ethics of Relativism*. Cambridge, MA: Harvard University Press, 2013.

Ruffin, Kimberly N. *Black on Earth: African American Ecoliterary Traditions*. Athens: University of Georgia Press, 2010.

Rusert, Britt. *Fugitive Science: Empiricism and Freedom in Early African American Culture*. New York: New York University Press, 2017.

Salamon, Gayle. *Assuming a Body: Transgender and Rhetorics of Materiality*. New York: Columbia University Press, 2010.

Saldaña-Portillo, María Josefina. "'How Many Mexicans [Is] a Horse Worth?': The League of United Latin American Citizens, Desegregation Cases, and Chicano Historiography." *South Atlantic Quarterly* 107.4 (2008): 809–32.

Saldaña-Portillo, María Josefina. *Indian Given: Racial Geographies across Mexico and the United States*. Durham, NC: Duke University Press, 2016.

Samuels, Ellen. *Fantasies of Identification: Disability, Gender, Race*. New York: New York University Press, 2014.

Sandvig, Christian. "Connection at Ewiiapaayp Mountain: Indigenous Internet Infrastructure." In *Race after the Internet*, ed. Lisa Nakamura and Peter A. Chow-White, 168–200. New York: Routledge, 2012.

Sankar, Pamela. "Forensic DNA Phenotyping: Reinforce Race in Law Enforcement." In *What's the Use of Race? Modern Governance and the Biology of Difference*, ed. Ian Whitmarsh and David S. Jones, 49–61. Cambridge, MA: MIT Press, 2010.

Saunt, Claudio. *Black, White, and Indian: Race and the Unmaking of an American Family*. New York: Oxford University Press, 2005.

Savage, Echo E. "'We Pair Off! One Man, One Woman': The Heterosexual Imperative in Octavia Butler's *Xenogenesis* Trilogy." In *The Sex Is Out of This World: Essays on the Carnal Side of Science Fiction*, ed. Sherry Ginn and Michael Cornelius, 50–62. Jefferson, NC: McFarland, 2012.

Schalk, Sami. *Bodyminds Reimagined: (Dis)ability, Race, and Gender in Black Women's Speculative Fiction*. Durham, NC: Duke University Press, 2018.

Schneier, Bruce. *Data and Goliath: The Hidden Battles to Collect Your Data and Control Your World*. New York: W. W. Norton, 2015.

Schwab, Gabriele. "Ethnographies of the Future: Personhood, Agency, and Power in Octavia Butler's *Xenogenesis*." In *Accelerating Possession: Global Futures of Property and Personhood*, ed. Bill Maurer and Gabrielle Schwab, 204–28. New York: Columbia University Press, 2006.

Scott, Darieck. *Extravagant Abjection: Blackness, Power, and Sexuality in the African American Literary Imagination*. New York: New York University, 2010.

Scott, David. *Conscripts of Modernity: The Tragedy of Colonial Enlightenment*. Durham, NC: Duke University Press, 2004.

Scott, David. *Omens of Adversity: Tragedy, Time, Memory, Justice*. Durham, NC: Duke University Press, 2014.

Scott, David. "The Re-enchantment of Humanism: An Interview with Sylvia Wynter." *Small Axe* 8 (September 2000): 119–207.

Scott, James C. *The Art of Not Being Governed: An Anarchist History of Upland Southeast Asia*. New Haven, CT: Yale University Press, 2009.

Seed, Patricia. *American Pentimento: The Invention of Indians and the Pursuit of Riches*. Minneapolis: University of Minnesota Press, 2001.

Senier, Siobhan, and Clare Barker. "Introduction." *Journal of Literary and Cultural Disability Studies* 7.2 (2013): 123–40.

Sexton, Jared. *Amalgamation Schemes: Antiblackness and the Critique of Multiracialism*. Minneapolis: University of Minnesota Press, 2008.

Sexton, Jared. "The *Vel* of Slavery: Tracking the Figure of the Unsovereign." *Critical Sociology* (December 2014): 1–15.

Shabazz, Rashad. *Spatializing Blackness: Architectures of Confinement and Black Masculinity in Chicago*. Urbana: University of Illinois Press, 2015.

Sharkey, Patrick. *Stuck in Place: Urban Neighborhoods and the End of Progress toward Racial Equality*. Chicago: University of Chicago Press, 2013.

Sharma, Nandita. "Strategic Anti-Essentialism: Decolonizing Decolonization." In *Sylvia Wynter: On Being Human as Praxis*, ed. Katherine McKittrick, 164–82. Durham, NC: Duke University Press, 2015.

Sharpe, Christina. *In the Wake: On Blackness and Being*. Durham, NC: Duke University Press, 2016.

Sharpe, Christina. *Monstrous Intimacies: Making Post-Slavery Subjects*. Durham, NC: Duke University Press, 2010.

Sharpe, Jenny. *Ghosts of Slavery: A Literary Archaeology of Black Women's Lives*. Minneapolis: University of Minnesota Press, 2003.

Shaviro, Steven. *The Universe of Things: On Speculative Realism*. Minneapolis: University of Minnesota Press, 2014.

Sheller, Mimi. *Citizenship from Below: Erotic Agency and Caribbean Freedom*. Durham, NC: Duke University Press, 2012.

Silva, Denise Ferreira da. *Toward a Global Idea of Race*. Minneapolis: University of Minnesota Press, 2007.

Simon, Jonathan. *Governing through Crime: How the War on Crime Transformed American Democracy and Created a Culture of Fear*. New York: Oxford University Press, 2007.

Simpson, Audra. "From White into Red: Captivity Narratives as Alchemies of Race and Citizenship." *American Quarterly* 60.2 (2008): 251–58.

Simpson, Audra. *Mohawk Interruptus: Political Life across the Borders of Settler States*. Durham, NC: Duke University Press, 2014.

Simpson, Audra. "The State Is a Man: Theresa Spence, Loretta Saunders and the Gender of Settler Sovereignty." *Theory and Event* 19.4 (2016).

Simpson, Leanne Betasamosake. *As We Have Always Done: Indigenous Freedom through Radical Resistance*. Minneapolis: University of Minnesota Press, 2017.

Simpson, Leanne Betasamosake. *Dancing on Our Turtle's Back: Stories of Nishnaabeg Re-Creation, Resurgence, and a New Emergence*. Manitoba: Arbeiter Ring, 2011.

Singh, Julietta. *Unthinking Mastery: Dehumanism and Decolonial Entanglements*. Durham, NC: Duke University Press, 2018.

Singh, Nikhil Pal. *Black Is a Country: Race and the Unfinished Struggle for Democracy*. Cambridge, MA: Harvard University Press, 2004.

Singh, Nikhil Pal. *Race and America's Long War*. Oakland: University of California Press, 2017.

Small, Mario Luis. "Four Reasons to Abandon the Idea of 'the Ghetto.'" *City and Community* 7.4 (2008): 389–98.

Smith, Eric D. *Globalization, Utopia and Postcolonial Science Fiction: New Maps of Hope*. New York: Palgrave Macmillan, 2012.

Smith, Paul Chaat. *Everything You Know about Indians Is Wrong*. Minneapolis: University of Minnesota Press, 2009.

Smith, Rachel Greenwald. "Ecology beyond Ecology: Life after the Accident in Octavia Butler's *Xenogensis* Trilogy." *Modern Fiction Studies* 55.3 (2009): 545–65.

Smoak, Gregory E. *Ghost Dances and Identity: Prophetic Religion and American Indian Ethnogenesis in the Nineteenth Century*. Berkeley: University of California Press, 2006.

Snorton, C. Riley. *Black on Both Sides: A Racial History of Trans Identity*. Minneapolis: University of Minnesota Press, 2017.

Somerville, Siobhan B. "Queer *Loving*." *GLQ* 11.3 (2005): 335–70.

Spillers, Hortense J. "Mama's Baby, Papa's Maybe: An American Grammar Book." In *Black, White, and in Color: Essays on American Literature and Culture*, 203–29. Chicago: University of Chicago Press, 2003.

Srinivasan, Ramesh. "Indigenous, Ethnic and Cultural Articulations of New Media." *International Journal of Cultural Studies*. 9.4 (2006): 497–518.

Stanley, Amy Dru. *From Bondage to Contract: Wage Labor, Marriage, and the Market in the Age of Slave Emancipation*. New York: Cambridge University Press, 1998.

Stephens, Michelle Ann. *Black Empire: The Masculine Global Imaginary of Caribbean Intellectuals in the United States, 1914–1962*. Durham, NC: Duke University Press, 2005.

Stevenson, Lisa. *Life beside Itself: Imagining Care in the Canadian Arctic*. Oakland: University of California Press, 2014.

Sturm, Circe. *Becoming Indian: The Struggle over Cherokee Identity in the Twenty-First Century*. Santa Fe, NM: School for Advanced Research Press, 2010.

Sturm, Circe. *Blood Politics: Race, Culture, and Identity in the Cherokee Nation of Oklahoma*. Berkeley: University of California Press, 2002.

Suhr-Sytsma, Mandy. "The View from Crow Hill: An Interview with Melissa Tantaquidgeon Zobel." *Studies in American Indian Literatures* 27.2 (2015): 80–95.

Sullivan, Shannon. *Revealing Whiteness: The Unconscious Habits of Racial Privilege*. Bloomington: Indiana University Press, 2006.

Tal, Kali. "'That Just Kills Me': Black Militant Near-Future Fiction." *Social Text* 20.2 (2002): 65–91.

TallBear, Kimberly. *Native American DNA: Tribal Belonging and the False Promise of Genetic Science*. Minneapolis: University of Minnesota Press, 2013.

Tatonetti, Lisa. "Disrupting a Story of Loss: Charles Eastman and Nicholas Black Elk Narrate Survivance." *Western American Literature* 39.3 (2004): 279–311.

Tawil, Ezra F. *The Making of Racial Sentiment: Slavery and the Birth of the Frontier Romance*. New York: Cambridge University Press, 2008.

Taylor, Drew Hayden. *Take Us to Your Chief, and Other Stories*. Madeira Park, BC: Douglas and McIntyre, 2016.

Taylor, Keeanga-Yamahtta. *From #BlackLivesMatter to Black Liberation*. Chicago: Haymarket Books, 2016.

Taylor, Keeanga-Yamahtta, ed. *How We Get Free: Black Feminism and the Combahee River Collective*. Chicago: Haymarket Books, 2017.

Teuton, Sean Kicummah. "Disability in Indigenous North America: In Memory of William Sherman Fox." In *The World of Indigenous North America*, ed. Robert Warrior, 569–93. New York: Routledge, 2014.

Thomas, Deborah A. *Exceptional Violence: Embodied Citizenship in Transnational Jamaica*. Durham, NC: Duke University Press, 2011.

Thomas, Greg. "*Marronnons*/Let's Maroon: Sylvia Wynter's 'Black Metamorphosis' as a Species of Marroonage." *Small Axe* 49 (2016): 62–78.

Thompson, Alvin O. *Flight to Freedom: African Runaways and Maroons in the Americas*. Kinsgton, Jamaica: University of the West Indies Press, 2006.

Thrush, Coll. *Native Seattle: Histories from the Crossing-Over Place*. Seattle: University of Washington Press, 2007.

Torres, Ruth Garby. "How You See Us, Why You Don't: Connecticut's Public Policy to Terminate the Schaghticoke Indians." In *Recognition, Sovereignty Struggles, and Indigenous Rights in the United States: A Sourcebook*, ed. Amy E. Den Ouden and Jean M. O'Brien, 195–212. Chapel Hill: University of North Carolina Press, 2013.

Towle, Evan B., and Lynn M. Morgan. "Romancing the Transgender Native: Rethinking the Use of the 'Third Gender' Concept." *GLQ* 8.4 (2002): 469–97.

Trautmann, Thomas R. *Lewis Henry Morgan and the Invention of Kinship*. Berkeley: University of California Press, 1987.

Tuck, Eve, and K. Wayne Yang. "Decolonization Is Not a Metaphor." *Decolonization: Indigeneity, Education, and Society* 1.1 (2012): 1–40.

Tucker, Jeffrey. "'The Human Contradiction': Identity and/as Essence in Octavia E. Butler's *Xenogenesis* Trilogy." *The Yearbook of English Studies* 37.2 (2007): 164–81.

Tully, James. *An Approach to Political Philosophy: Locke in Contexts*. New York: Cambridge University Press, 1993.

Turner, Dale. *This Is Not a Peace Pipe: Towards a Critical Indigenous Philosophy*. Toronto: University of Toronto Press, 2006.

Vimalassery, Manu. "Fugitive Decolonization." *Theory and Event* 19.4 (2016).

Vimalassery, Manu, Juliana Hu Pegues, and Alyosha Goldstein. "On Colonial Unknowing." *Theory and Event* 19.4 (2016).

Vint, Sherryl. *Bodies of Tomorrow: Technology, Subjectivity, Science Fiction*. Toronto: University of Toronto Press, 2007.

Visweswaran, Kamala. *Un/common Cultures: Racism and the Rearticulation of Cultural Difference*. Durham, NC: Duke University Press, 2010.

Vizenor, Gerald. *Fugitive Poses: Native American Indian Scenes of Absence and Presence*. Lincoln: University of Nebraska Press, 1998.

Vizenor, Gerald. *Manifest Manners: Postindian Warriors of Survivance*. Hanover, NH: Wesleyan University Press, 1994.

Vizenor, Gerald. *Treaty Shirts: October 2034—A Familiar Treatise on the White Earth Nation*. Middletown, CT: Wesleyan University Press, 2016.

Von Eschen, Penny M. *Race against Empire: Black Americans and Anticolonialism, 1937–1957*, rev. ed. Ithaca, NY: Cornell University Press, 1997.

Wacquant, Loïc. *Punishing the Poor: The Neoliberal Government of Social Insecurity*. Durham, NC: Duke University Press, 2009.

Wagner, Bryan. *Disturbing the Peace: Black Culture and the Police Power after Slavery*. Cambridge, MA: Harvard University Press, 2009.

Walcott, Rinaldo. "Genres of Human: Multiculturalism, Cosmo-politics, and the Caribbean Basin." In *Sylvia Wynter: On Being Human as Praxis*, ed. Katherine McKittrick, 183–202. Durham, NC: Duke University Press, 2015.

Walcott, Rinaldo. *Queer Returns: Essays on Multiculturalism, Diaspora, and Black Studies.* London, ON: Insomniac, 2016.

Walker, David. *Appeal to the Coloured Citizens of the World, but in Particular, and Very Expressly, to Those of the United States of America.* New York: Hill and Wang, (1829) 1995.

Wallace, Molly. "Reading Octavia Butler's *Xenogenesis* after Seattle." *Contemporary Literature* 50.1 (2009): 94–128.

Warren, Kenneth. *What Was African American Literature?* Cambridge, MA: Harvard University Press, 2011.

Warren, Louis S. *God's Red Son: The Ghost Dance Religion and the Making of Modern America.* New York: Basic, 2017.

Waters, Anne. "Language Matters: Nondiscrete Nonbinary Dualism." In *American Indian Thought: Philosophical Essays*, ed. Anne Waters, 97–115. Malden, MA: Blackwell, 2004.

Watson, Irene. "Settled and Unsettled Spaces: Are We Free to Roam?" In *Sovereign Subjects: Indigenous Sovereignty Matters*, ed. Aileen Moreton-Robinson, 15–32. Crows Nest, Australia: Allen and Unwin, 2008.

Weheliye, Alexander G. *Habeas Viscus: Racializing Assemblages, Biopolitics, and Black Feminist Theories of the Human.* Durham, NC: Duke University Press, 2014.

Whitehead, Colson. *The Underground Railroad.* Large print ed. New York: Random House, 2016.

Wiegman, Robyn. *American Anatomies: Theorizing Race and Gender.* Durham, NC: Duke University Press, 1995.

Wilder, Gary. *Freedom Time: Negritude, Decolonization, and the Future of the World.* Durham, NC: Duke University Press, 2015.

Wilderson, Frank B., III. *Red, White, and Black: Cinema and the Structure of U.S. Antagonisms.* Durham, NC: Duke University Press, 2010.

Wilkins, David E. *American Indian Sovereignty and the U.S. Supreme Court: The Masking of Justice.* Austin: University of Texas Press, 1997.

Wilkins, David E., and K. Tsianina Lomawaima. *Uneven Ground: American Indian Sovereignty and Federal Law.* Norman: University of Oklahoma Press, 2001.

Wilkins, David E., and Shelly Hulse Wilkins. *Dismembered: Native Disenrollment and the Battle for Human Rights.* Seattle: University of Washington Press, 2017.

Williams, Ben. "Black Secret Technology: Detroit Techno and the Information Age." In *Technicolor: Race, Technology, and Everyday Life*, ed. Alondra Nelson and Thuy Linh N. Tu, with Alicia Headlam Hines, 154–76. New York: New York University Press, 2001.

Williams, Robert A. *Linking Arms Together: American Indian Treaty Visions of Law and Peace, 1600–1800.* New York: Oxford University Press, 1997.

Wilson, Charles E., Jr. *Walter Mosley: A Critical Companion.* Westport, CT: Greenwood Press, 2003.

Wilson, Daniel H. *Robogenesis.* New York: Simon and Schuster, 2014.

Wilson, Daniel H. *Robopocalypse.* New York: Vintage, 2011.

Wilson, Terry P. *The Underground Reservation: Osage Oil.* Lincoln: University of Nebraska Press, 1985.

Wolfe, Patrick. "Settler Colonialism and the Elimination of the Native." *Journal of Genocide Research* 8.4 (2000): 387–409.

Womack, Ytasha L. *Afrofuturism: The World of Black Sci-Fi and Fantasy Culture.* Chicago: Lawrence Hill, 2013.

Wright, Michelle. *Physics of Blackness: Beyond the Middle Passage Epistemology.* Minneapolis: University of Minnesota Press, 2015.

Wynter, Sylvia. "1492: A New World View." In *Race, Discourse, and the Origin of the Americas*, ed. Vera Lawrence Hyatt and Rex Nettleford, 5–57. Washington, DC: Smithsonian Institution Press, 1995.

Wynter, Sylvia. "Jonkonnu in Jamaica." *Jamaica Journal* 4.2 (1970): 37–45.

Wynter, Sylvia. "On How We Mistook the Map for the Territory, and Reimprisoned Ourselves in Our Unbearable Wrongness of Being, of *Désêtre*: Black Studies toward the Human Project." In *Not Only the Master's Tools: African-American Studies in Theory and Practice*, ed. Lewis R. Gordon and Jane Anna Gordon, 107–72. Boulder, CO: Paradigm, 2006.

Wynter, Sylvia. "Unsettling the Coloniality of Being/Power/Truth/Freedom: Towards the Human, after Man, Its Overrepresentation—An Argument." *CR: The New Centennial Review* 3.3 (2003): 257–337.

Yaszek, Lisa. "Afrofuturism, Science Fiction, and the History of the Future." *Socialism and Democracy* 20.3 (2006): 41–60.

Yazzie, Melanie. "#NOBANSTOLENLAND: Towards a Politics of Radical Relationality." Presentation at the National Women's Studies Association Annual Meeting. Baltimore, MD, November 17, 2017.

Yirush, Craig. *Settlers, Liberty, and Empire: The Roots of Early American Political Theory, 1675–1775.* New York: Cambridge University Press, 2011.

Young, Cynthia A. *Soul Power: Culture, Radicalism, and the Making of a U.S. Third World Left.* Durham, NC: Duke University Press, 2006.

Zaki, Hoda M. "Utopia, Dystopia, and Ideology in the Science Fiction of Octavia Butler." *Science Fiction Studies* 17.2 (1990): 239–51.

Zips, Werner. *Nanny's Asafo Warriors: The Jamaican Maroons' African Experience.* Kingston, Jamaica: Ian Randle, 2011.

Zobel, Melissa Tantaquidgeon. *Oracles.* Albuquerque: University of New Mexico Press, 2004.

Index

"Afrarealism and the Black Matrix" (James), 169

African Americans: Black-Indigenous difference and, 18–19, 33–37; incarceration rates for, 11–12, 117–22, 126–27, 259n4; indigeneity for, 151–65, 272n139; indigenous sovereignty and, 59–61; placemaking by, 151–65, 263n38; as settlers, 52–61; tribal denial of citizenship to, 50–52; unemployment and imprisonment for, 263n43. *See also* Black-Indigenous difference

African descent: in Hopkinson's *Midnight Robber,* 175–86; Indigenous peoples of, 18–19; in Jamaican culture, 275n34; Latin American marronage and peoples of, 207–11

Afrofuturism, 248n193; Black-Indigenous relations and, 8–9, 61–72

Ahmed, Sara, 4; on background and fugitivity, 185–86; on Black-Indigenous struggles, 16–17, 19; on collective identity, 34, 69, 230; on indigeneity, 207, 221; Native sovereignty and, 43; racial embodiment and, 158, 221; territoriality framework and, 27

Ahuja, Neel, 157

Alexander, Michelle, 119–20

Alfred, Taiaiake, 50

alienation, blackness and, 151–65

alien-human difference, in Butler's *Xenogenesis,* 107–14

Allewaert, Monique, 249n12, 269n98

Allied Media Conference, 229

allotment, 51, 101, 104, 196, 267n78

Althusser, Louis, 235n13

Amadahy, Zainab, 28, 44, 54–55, 182, 277n42

amalgamation: in Butler's *Xenogenesis,* 92–116, 274n6; in Hopkinson's *Midnight Robber,* 176–86, 274n6; racial embodiment and, 76–78; species similarity and, 107–14

Ancient Society (Morgan), 87

Anderson, Mark, 208

"Angel's Island" (Mosley), 123–26, 260n16, 266n67

Anishinaabe culture, 42, 65–66, 92, 101, 224–25, 229, 241n88; *biskaabiiyang* narratives in, 65–66

antiblackness: carceral space and, 123–37; in futurist narratives, 62; Indigenous sovereignty and, 53–61. *See also* blackness

anticolonialism, Wynter's discussion of, 21–25

anti-immigration policies, Indigenous self-determination and, 227

antiracism: in Butler's fiction, 11, 122; Wynter's discussion of, 21–25

antiterrorism initiatives: "categorical suspicion" and, 262n33; in Mosley's *The Wave,* 155, 165–67

Archaeologies of the Future (Jameson), 66

astrofuturism, 65

As We Have Always Done (Simpson), 213, 224

bad debt relations, Harney and Moten's discussion of, 223–26

Bahng, Aimee, 64

Barker, Adam J., 55–56, 243n116

Barker, Joanne, 39–40, 42, 89

"Being or Nothingness" (Day), 29
Bellacasa, María Puig de la, 248n194
Ben-zvi, Yael, 244n131, 272n139
Best, Stephen, 4–5, 49
Big Data (Mayer-Schönberger and Cukier), 127, 261n27, 262n29
Bilby, Kenneth M., 177–78
Bilge, Sirma, 34
Bioinsecurities (Ahuja), 157
biopolitics: governance and, 96–99, 102–3, 254n74, 256n86; in Mosley's *The Wave*, 156–57
Bird Is Gone: A ~~Monograph~~ Manifesto, The (Jones), 13–14, 172, 187, 192–201, 213
biskaabiiyang narratives, 65–66
Black and Indigenous (Anderson), 208
Blackfeet Nation, 281n84, 281n88
Black feminist theory: Black internationalist feminism and, 60; difference perspectives in, 20, 30–37; intersectionality and, 244n136; politics of difference and, 9–10
"Black History in Occupied Territory" (Leroy), 28–29
Black-Indigenous relations: African Americans and, 18–19, 33–37; in Afrofuturist fiction, 8–9, 61–72; in Hairston's *Mindscape*, 201–19; in Hopkinson's *Midnight Robber*, 173–86; Latin American policies and, 207–11; marronage and, 170; in Mosley's *The Wave*, 151–65; undercommons and, 220–31
Black Is a Country (Singh), 58
Black Lives Matter movement: organization and structure of, 233n6; response to state-sanctioned violence by, 3–4, 228–29; solidarity in Dakota Access Pipeline protest with, 1–3
"Black Metamorphosis" (Wynter), 236n28
blackness: as aberrance and anomaly, framing of, 4–5; alienation and, 151–65; commensuration with indigeneity and, 30–37; diaspora and, 43–44, 136–37, 241n94; fungibility and, 8–11, 39, 49–52, 73–78; futurist fiction and Black-Indigenous relations, 8–9, 61–72; Latin American marronage policies and, 207–11; Native identity and, 18–19, 33–37; political movements and principles of, 9–10, 173–86; racialization of mass

incarceration and, 11–12, 117–22, 126–27, 259n4; as reduction to flesh, 5, 10–11, 73–78; settler colonialism and, 52–61; slavery and settler colonialism and, 15–19; sociopolitical dynamics of, 233n5; sovereignty concepts and, 38–52; unemployment and, 263n43; urban space as zones of, 44–45, 241n97; in Mosley's *The Wave*, 122; Wynter's discussion of, 22–25. *See also* antiblackness
Bonilla, Yarimar, 46–47, 242n106, 273n9
Bonilla-Silva, Eduardo, 265n52
Braidotti, Rosi, 78
Brand, Dionne, 43–46, 59–60, 135–37, 159, 241n94, 242n102
Brazil, maroon communities in, 207–8; Palmares settlement, 177, 275n30, 277n42
Brown Girl in the Ring (Hopkinson), 279n62
Butler, Octavia: biopolitics in work of, 96–97; collective self-determination in work of, 181–82; critical analysis of works by, 254n69; on difference, 225; on genetics, 91, 93; on human genre, 75–78, 110–14, 140; indigeneity in work of, 87; Mosley and, 122, 246n161; on race and incarceration, 11, 254n71; racial embodiment and work of, 81; on species similarity, 106–14; on territoriality and self-determination, 98–99, 101–6; *Xenogenesis* trilogy, 11, 75–116, 121, 181–82, 213, 249n9, 251n40, 251n42, 254n69, 255n76, 255n81, 256n85. See also *Xenogenesis* trilogy (Butler)
Byrd, Jodi, 5, 28, 57, 142, 184, 285n15

Cacho, Lisa Marie, 118, 259n10
Calloway, Colin, 215
Canada: claims of Native nations in, 25–28, 279n62; Native sovereignty and governance in, 40–41, 182; settler colonialism in, 55–56
capacity, in Butler's *Xenogenesis*, 93–106
capital, oppression and, 64–72
Carastathis, Anna, 33, 238n58, 239n69
carceral space: gender and, 135–37; in Mosley's *Futureland*, 119–22, 150–51, 165–66, 222; in Mosley's *The Wave*, 161–67, 222; neoliberal apartheid and, 122–37; private interests and, 263n37; racialization of, 117–22; in Wilson's *Robopocalypse* series, 138–51; state-sanctioned containment and, 11–12

Caribbean: African indigeneity in, 160; Black communal landedness in, 52; Creole indigeneity in, 57, 213, 276n41, 278n60; decolonization and self-governance in, 46–52; erasure of Indigenous peoples from, 49, 160; in Hopkinson's *Midnight Robber,* 173–86; marronage and maroon identity in, 170–71, 215–17, 273n9, 278n60

Carroll, Clint, 41–42, 188

"The Case of Blackness" (Moten), 5

Cervenak, Sarah Jane, 137

Césaire, Aimé, 242n106

Chakrabarty, Dipesh, 2–3, 19–20

Chandler, Nahum Dimitri, 48

Cheney-Lippold, John, 127–28

Cherokee Nation, 41–42, 267n78, 267n80

citizenship: blackness and concepts of, 43–52; indigeneity and, 87; in Mosley's *Future-land,* 132–34; tribal denial to African Americans of, 50–52

civilization, in Butler's *Xenogenesis,* 108–14

Clarno, Andy, 260n14

Clemente, Bill, 184

Cohen, Cathy, 239n65

Collins, Patricia Hill, 34

Colombia: Law 70 in, 207–8

colonialism. *See* settler colonialism

Combahee River Collective, 244n136

comparison: translation *vs.,* 239n68

conscientious misrepresentation, 220

Conscripts of Modernity (Scott), 18, 235n11

Cornum, Lou, 63–64, 248n193, 256n94

Coulthard, Glen: on grounded normativity, 143–44, 146, 161, 197; on land practices and sovereignty, 166–67, 182; on politics of recognition, 197; on settler colonialism, 25–28, 42; on structural violence, 20

creativity, difference and, 32

Creole Indigeneity (Jackson), 57

criminal justice system: carceral space and, 118–22, 259n4; employment regulations and, 263n43; legal status and, 259nn10–11; in Mosley's *The Wave,* 155–65

Cukier, Kenneth, 127, 261n27, 262n29

Cullors, Patrisse, 3–4

Dakota Access Pipeline, racial and ethnic solidarity in protest against, 1–3

Dancing on Our Turtle's Back (Simpson), 42

data: on criminal justice, 259n4; in Hopkinson's *Midnight Robber,* 176–86; in Mosley's *The Wave,* 165–67; racial identity and, 127–37, 264n46; in Wilson's *Robopocalypse* series, 137–51

Davis, Angela, 58

Dawes Rolls, 51

Day, Iyko, 29–30

Dayan, Colin, 154, 271n122

decolonization: in Caribbean, 175–86; self-determination and, 23–25; sovereignty and, 46–52

"Decolonization Is Not a Metaphor" (Tuck and Wayne), 23–24, 245n141

dehumanization, blackness and dynamics of, 22–25

de la Cadena, Marisol: Andean indigenous peoples and, 6, 8, 17, 189, 280n74, 280n76; on equivocation and difference, 30, 37, 78, 143; on onto-epistemic formations, 93, 172; on speculation, 70

Delany, Samuel, 62–63, 67–69, 164, 193, 201, 220, 247n182, 249n16; *Starboard Wine,* 67, 220

Demonic Grounds (McKittrick), 21, 60, 242n101, 243n115

Dennison, Jean, 40–41

Denton, Nancy A., 45

Dery, Mark, 62

Dhillon, Jaskiran, 2

difference: commensuration and, 30–37; fungibility and, 75–78; in futurist narratives, 61–72; racial embodiment and, 88–92; women of color feminist perspectives on, 20, 30–37; in Butler's *Xenogenesis,* 107–15

Dillon, Elizabeth Maddock, 285n13

Dillon, Grace L., 65–66, 70

diplomacy: debt and, 223–26; undercommons and, 220–31, 285n13. *See also* treaties

disability, in Butler's *Xenogenesis,* 93–106, 256n85

"Doctor Kismet" (Mosley), 126, 133

Douglass, Frederick, 152

Drums along the Mohawk (Edmonds), 226

Dubey, Madhu, 283n123

Du Bois, W. E. B., 59–60

Edwards, Brent, 58

"The Electric Eye" (Mosley), 125–26

Ellis, Nadia, 46, 136–37

Empire of Love, The (Povinelli), 86

Engle, Karen, 86

"En Masse" (Mosley), 126

Enteen, Jillana, 276n35

environmental devastation: in Butler's *Xenogenesis* trilogy, 106–14; in Jones's *Bird Is
Gone,* 193–201; in Mosley's *The Wave,* 157,
163–65; race and ethnicity and vulnerability
to, 1–2, 271n128, 279n67; in Zobel's *Oracles,*
187–93

equivocation: Black and Indigenous imaginaries and, 6; science fiction and ethics of, 10

Eshun, Kodwo, 64–65

Estes, Nick, 2

ethnology: in Hopkinson's *Midnight Robber,*
176–86; indigeneity and, 87, 283n123

Eurocentric perspectives, well-being in context
of, 20–25

Everett, Anna, 62

Fanon, Frantz, 235n25

Federmayer, Éva, 79–80

female body, blackness and, 79–80

Five Tribes, 50–52

Forte, Maximilian, 179

"For Whom Sovereignty Matters" (Barker),
39–40

Foucault, Michel, 96, 254n74

"1492: A New World View" (Wynter), 22–25,
236n26

Freedom Dreams (Kelley), 66

"From Flint to Standing Rock" (May), 34

frontier romance literature, Indigenous
peoples in, 278n53

"Fugitive Justice" (Best), 4–5

fugitivity: African American locatedness and,
151–65, 265n59, 273n144; criminal justice
system and, 266n61; gender and, 135–37; in
Hairston's *Mindscape,* 201–19; in Hopkinson's *Midnight Robber,* 176–86; marronage
and maroon identity and, 168–69, 274n11;
in Mosley's *Futureland,* 122, 133–38, 161,
266n68; in Mosley's *The Wave,* 161–62,
166–67; in Wilson's *Robopocalypse* series,
146–51; sovereignty and, 43–52

fungibility: blackness and, 8–11, 39, 49–52,
73–78; dehumanization through, 4; settler
colonialism and, 54–55, 60–61; slavery and,
43; sovereignty and, 48–49; in Butler's
Xenogenesis, 93–106

*Futureland: Nine Stories of an Imminent
World* (Mosley), 12, 259n8; carceral space
in, 119–22, 150–51, 165–66; fugitivity
in, 122, 133–38, 161; neoliberal apartheid
in, 122–37, 156, 260n14; territoriality in,
121–22, 137, 143

futurist fiction: carceral space in, 122–37; by
Indigenous peoples, 8–9, 11, 61–72, 137–51,
187–201, 256n94, 270n110. *See also* Afrofru-
turism; Indigenous futurism; speculation

Garifuna communities (Honduras), 207–8

Garvey, Marcus, 175, 274n19

Garza, Alicia, 3–4, 228–30

gender: carceral space and, 135–37; difference
and, 20, 30–37; racial embodiment and,
79–80, 83–84

genetics: carceral space and, 127–37; in Mosley's *Futureland,* 134–37; racial categorization and, 262n36; repudiation of hierarchy
and, 109–14; in Butler's *Xenogenesis,*
93–106, 257n108

geography: African American placemaking
and, 151–65; black landlessness and, 60–61;
in Hairston's *Mindscape,* 201–19; Indigenous placemaking and, 50–52; in Jones's
Bird Is Gone, 196–201; marronage and, 170;
of mass incarceration, 122–37; in Mosley's
Futureland, 130–37; in Mosley's *The Wave,*
156–57; in Wilson's *Robopocalypse* series,
139–51; slavery as rupture of, 43; space of
refusal and, 102–6. *See also* land use and
landedness; placemaking

Ghost Dance, in Hairston's *Mindscape,* 203–19

Gilmore, Ruth Wilson, 263n43

Glave, Dianne, 275n31

Glissant, Édouard, 35–36, 49, 95, 107, 143, 191

Goeman, Mishuana, 50, 91–92, 149–50,
197–98

Goffman, Alice, 118

Gottschalk, Marie, 263n43

governance: biopolitics and, 96–99; in Black
and Indigenous political imaginaries, 5–6,

265n54; in Butler's *Xenogenesis* trilogy, 107–14, 213; corporations and, 262n31; decolonization and, 46–52; in Hairston's *Mindscape,* 202–19; in Hopkinson's *Midnight Robber,* 176–86; Indigenous modes of, 229–31; in Jones's *Bird Is Gone,* 194–201; Native sovereignty and, 40–41, 50–52, 284n135; self-determination and, 25–28

Grande, Sandy, 24, 26

Granny Nanny, 176–77, 275n29, 275n32, 275n34, 276n35, 276n38

Great Migration, 45

Greene, Shane, 211

Grossman, Zoltán, 226

grounded normativity, 25–28, 143–45

Hairston, Andrea, 13, 170–71, 201–19; *Mindscape,* 13, 170–73, 201–19, 225

Haiti, 170, 277n46

Hancock, Ange-Marie, 33–35, 239n69

Harney, Stefano, 14, 134–36, 159, 221–23, 225–26, 230, 266n64, 267n73; *The Undercommons* (Harney and Moten), 14, 221–31

Hartman, Saidiya: on aberrance of blackness, 4–5; fungibility of blackness and, 49; on geography and diaspora, 43, 159; on nationhood, 59–60, 242n104; on racial embodiment, 81–82; on urban segregation, 45–46

Hausman, Blake, 270n110, 280n79

"A HerStory of the #BlackLivesMatter Movement," 3–4

Higashida, Cheryl, 60, 245n156

Hill, Susan, 216

Himes, Chester, 220

Hinton, Elizabeth, 259n4

History of Sexuality, The (Foucault), 96

Hobbes, Thomas, 106, 113–14

Honduras, maroon communities in, 208

Hong, Grace Kyungwon, 18, 30, 61, 256n86

Hooker, Juliet, 208

Hopkinson, Nalo, 13, 170–71, 173–86, 217–19, 229, 275n31, 276n35; *Midnight Robber,* 13, 170–86, 217–19, 229

human genres: disability and, 93–106; Eurocentric concepts of, 20–21; fungibility of, in Butler's *Xenogenesis,* 75–78, 110–14; indigeneity and, 78–92; in Wilson's *Robopocalypse* series, 140–51; species similarity

in Butler's *Xenogenesis* trilogy and, 106–14; Wynter's perspective on, 20–25, 235n25. *See also* nonhuman entities

hybridity: in Hopkinson's *Midnight Robber,* 184–86; racial embodiment and, 75–78

Ibrahim, Habiba, 44–45, 248n3

"Imposter Syndrome" (Kurisato), 103–4

incarceration. *See* carceral space; mass incarceration

INCITE Toronto, 54

Indianness. *See* indigeneity

Indian Organization Act, 281n88

indigeneity: in Africa, 272n137; African Americans and, 151–65, 272n139; Black Native peoples and boundaries of, 51–52, 242n102; blackness and, 18–19, 33–37; carceral space and, 121–22; commensuration with blackness, 30–37; as global phenomenon, 233n5; in Hairston's *Mindscape,* 201–19; in Hopkinson's *Midnight Robber,* 192; in Jones's *Bird Is Gone,* 192–201; marronage and, 13, 169–73; in Mosley's *The Wave,* 202; placemaking and, 165–67; political movements and principles of, 9–10, 173–86; problem-spaces and, 85–86; racial embodiment and, 78–92; in Wilson's *Robopocalypse* series, 143–51; slavery and settler colonialism and, 15–19, 200–201; sovereignty and self-determination and, 11; in Butler's *Xenogenesis* trilogy, 78–92, 115–16, 251n40, 251n42; in Zobel's *Oracles,* 189–92, 200–201

Indigenous futurism, 8–9, 61–72, 137–51, 186–201, 256n94, 270n110

Indigenous peoples: Andean intellectuals, 17; Black-Indigenous relations, 8–9, 61–72; Black Lives Matter and, 228–29; capitalization of, 233n2; categorization of, 18–19; definitions of difference for, 31–37; erasure in Caribbean of, 49; futurist fiction by, 8–9, 61–72, 137–51, 256n94, 270n110; in Hopkinson's *Midnight Robber,* 173–86, 207; place-making and, 166–67; post-Apocalypse visions of, 65–66; separateness of, 187–201; settler colonialism and, 13, 25–28; solidarity with other ethnic groups, 1–5; sovereignty concepts and, 13, 38–52;

Indigenous peoples (continued)
  treaties and non-state sovereignty for,
  213–17, 284n136; tribal denial of citizenship to African Americans by, 50–52; U.S.
  detribalization efforts and, 101; Wynter's
  discussion of, 22–25
individuality: in Butler's *Xenogenesis* trilogy,
  106–16; indigeneity and, 86–87. *See also*
  personhood
insurance industry, slavery and rise of, 64–65
internet, in Hopkinson's *Midnight Robber,*
  176–86
interracial families, 74–78, 248n3, 249n4
"In the Clearing" (King), 53–54
"in the last instance" effects, 20
Inuit, youth suicide epidemic among, 98–99
Iton, Richard, 243n109, 247n178

Jackson, Sandra, 63
Jackson, Shona, 57, 170, 276n41
Jacobs, Naomi, 81, 84–85
James, Joy, 169
Jameson, Frederic, 66
Jemisin, N. K., 254n72
Jewel-Hinged Jaw, The (Delany), 67
Johns, J. Adam, 84–85, 257n108
Jones, Dorothy, 285n138
Jones, Stephen Graham, 13–14, 172, 187,
  192–202, 207, 218–19, 222, 282n95; *The Bird
  is Gone,* 13–14, 172, 187, 192–201, 213

Kafer, Alison, 98
Kahnawà:ke Mohawk identity, 42–43
Kelley, Robin D. G., 66
Kempner, Brandon, 155–56
Kennedy, Adrienne, 44
Kilgore, De Witt Douglas, 65
King, Tiffany, 53–54, 73, 80, 93, 144
kinship, indigeneity and, 86–87, 253n54
Kurisato, Mari, 11, 103–4

Lacks, Henrietta, 255n81
Lakota tribe, 206
land use and landedness: Black collective
  land claims, 52, 208, 217–19; blackness and,
  60–61, 151–65, 264n46, 264n48, 272n138,
  273n144; in Hairston's *Mindscape,* 202–19;

indigeneity and, 14, 85–86, 166–67,
  170, 172–73, 182; in Jones's *Bird Is Gone,*
  193–201, 282n95; marronage and, 168–69,
  217–19; non-native presence and, 207–8,
  229; in Wilson's *Robopocalypse* series,
  139–51; settler colonialism and, 38–52,
  187–201, 222, 245n141; treaties and non-
  state sovereignty and, 213–17, 284n136; in
  Zobel's *Oracles,* 188–92. *See also* geography;
  placemaking; problem-spaces
Latin America: Black communal landedness
  in, 52; marronage in, 13, 172–73, 201–2,
  207–11, 215–17; non-state sovereignty in,
  213–17, 284n136
Latour, Bruno, 240n70
Lavender, Isaiah, 75–76
Law 70 (Colombia), 207–8
Law Is a White Dog, The (Dayan), 154
Lawrence, Bonita, 28, 44, 54–55, 182
Leroy, Justin, 28–30, 57
liberal multiculturalism: interracial familialism
  and, 248n3; state violence and, 29, 237n49
Little Badger, Darcie, 64
"Little Brother" (Mosley), 129, 264n44
Lorde, Audre, 18, 30–33, 35, 60, 72, 171–72,
  245n156
Lose Your Mother (Hartman), 43
L'Ouverture, Toussaint, 277n46
Loving v. Virginia, 74, 248n3
Lowe, Lisa, 237n49, 240n70
Lowman, Emma Battell, 55–56, 243n116
Lyon, David, 120

Mackey, Eva, 216
A Map to the Door of No Return (Brand),
  43–44
marronage and maroon identity: Black communal landedness and, 52, 208, 217–19; colonialism and, 13; in Hairston's *Mindscape,*
  201–19; in Hopkinson's *Midnight Robber,*
  173–86; indigeneity and, 13, 169–73,
  201–19; terminology of, 168–69, 176–77,
  275n29, 275n32; in the United States, 273n5
Marryshow, T. A., 175, 278n60
Marvin, Trayvon, 3
Massey, Douglas S., 45
mass incarceration: as coercive mobility,
  266n61; data on, 259n4, 259nn10–11;

Mosley's portrayal of, 261n22; as neoliberal apartheid, 122–37, 260n14; racialization of, 11–12, 117–22, 126–27, 259n4; unemployment and, 263n43

maternity, racial embodiment and, 79–80, 83–84

Mayer-Schönberger, Viktor, 127, 261n27, 262n29

Mays, Kyle T., 34

McKittrick, Katherine, 21, 60, 151, 155, 169, 210, 218, 236n28, 243n115

Michaels, Walter Benn, 109

Midnight Robber (Hopkinson), 13, 170–86, 217–19, 229

Migrant Futures (Bahng), 64

Mindscape (Hairston), 13, 170–73, 201–19, 225

miscegenation, 74–78, 248n3. *See also* racial mixture, fungibility and

modernity, Wynter on global character of, 235n14

Mohegans, 179n72

Moody-Freeman, Julie, 63

Moons of Palmares, The (Amadahy), 277n42

Moreton-Robinson, Aileen, 143–44, 146, 188

Morgan, Lewis Henry, 87, 253n54

Mosley, Walter, 12, 246n161; on blackness and the future, 273n142; carceral space in works of, 119–22, 222; *Futureland,* 12, 119–38, 143, 150–51, 156, 161, 165–66, 259n8, 260n14; indigeneity in works of, 151–65, 202, 225, 272n139; mass incarceration in work of, 261nn22–24; neoliberal apartheid in work of, 122–37, 144; *The Wave* (Mosley), 12, 122, 151–67, 202, 225, 272nn140–41, 273n143; *Workin' on the Chain Gang,* 261n24

Moten, Fred: bad debt concept of, 223; on blackness, 5, 159; on fugitivity, 134–36; *The Undercommons* (Harney and Moten), 14, 221–31, 266n64, 267n73

Mother Jones, 229–30

Moynihan Report, 248n3

multiplicity, in Hopkinson's *Midnight Robber,* 184–86

Muñoz, José Esteban, 66, 247n181

Murakawa, Naomi, 118, 132

nationalist movements, marronage and, 171–73, 273n9

nationhood: Hartman's discussion of, 59–60, 242n104

nation-state model: Black intellectual critique of, 57–61; Indigenous peoples formulation of, 43–52; in Wilson's *Robopocalypse* series, 141–51; sovereignty concepts and, 38–52

Native peoples. *See* Indigenous peoples

Nelson, Alonda, 62

neoliberal apartheid: corporations as governance and, 262n31; mass incarceration and, 260n14; in Mosley's *Futureland,* 122–37; in Mosley's *The Wave,* 155–65

Ng'weno, Bettina, 209–10

Nichols, Robert, 114–15

Niezen, Ronald, 85–86

"The Nig in Me" (Mosley), 125–26, 134

Nishnaabeg, sovereignty of, 42, 92, 224–25, 241n88

Nixon, Lindsay, 247n177

#nobanonstolenlands, 14, 227, 230–31

nonhuman entities: in Hopkinson's *Midnight Robber,* 176–86; in Jones's *Bird Is Gone,* 194–201; national politics and, 280n74; in Native fiction, 187–92; in Wilson's *Robopocalypse* series, 147–51, 269n98; in Butler's *Xenogenesis,* 106–14, 255n76, 257n106; in Zobel's *Oracles,* 187–92

Nyong'o, Tavia, 75–77

Obourn, Megan, 102

O'Brien, Jean, 63

Oceti Sakowin (The Great Sioux Nation), sovereignty and self-determination of, 2

Office of Federal Acknowledgment, 51

"On How We Mistook the Map for the Territory" (Wynter), 21–22, 24, 237n35

opacity: difference and, 35–36, 72, 107, 192, 216; marronage and, 184; settler colonialism and, 181; speculation and, 61, 199

oppression: sovereignty and collective identity of, 59–61; in Butler's *Xenogenesis* trilogy, 114–16

Oracles (Tantaquidgeon Zobel), 13–14, 172, 187–93, 200–201, 213

Osage Nation, Wilson's portrayal of, 138–51, 267n78, 267n80

Palmares maroon settlement, 177, 275n30, 277n42

Papa Bois (Trinidadian cultural figure), 277nn45–46

Papke, Mary E., 257n108

Parable of the Sower (Butler), 252n45

Parker, Sharon, 34

peoplehood: Black feminism and, 244n136; Brand's discussion of, 41–43, 242n102; Butler's discussion of, 78, 93; fugitivity and, 213; fungibility and, 171–72; in futurist fiction, 103, 105–6, 110–11, 116, 121, 149–51, 166, 187; Ghost Dance and, 205–7, 212; marronage and, 172, 201, 205–9; in Mosley's fiction, 137–38; Native concepts of, 1, 5, 99, 138–43, 149, 160; non-native recognition and, 218–19; placemaking and, 11, 22–24, 28, 47–50, 169–71, 182, 187, 189–91, 221; self-determination and, 8–9, 23, 99; settler colonialism and, 192, 197, 200; sovereignty and, 113–15, 202–3, 218; treaties and, 213–14

Perry, Keisha-Khan Y., 208

personhood: Allewaert's discussion of, 249n12, 269n98; in Butler's *Xenogenesis* trilogy, 106–16; in Hairston's *Mindscape*, 204–19; in Hopkinson's *Midnight Robber*, 173–86, 207; in Mosley's *Futureland*, 131–37; in Mosley's *The Wave*, 154–65; in Wilson's *Robopocalypse* series, 139–51. *See also* identity; individuality; self-determination

Pinto, Samantha, 44

placemaking: Black projects of, 14, 273n144; in Hairston's *Mindscape*, 209–19; in Hopkinson's *Midnight Robber*, 176–86; indigeneity and, 165–67; in Jones's *Bird Is Gone*, 192–201, 194–201; Latin American marronage and, 207–11; marronage and maroon identity and, 13, 169–73; in Mosley's *The Wave*, 151–65; in Native fiction, 187–201; in Zobel's *Oracles*, 187–93, 279n67. *See also* geography; land use and landedness; problem-spaces; sovereignty

Poetics of Relation (Glissant), 35–36, 49

political entities: carceral space and, 122–37; disability and capacity and, 97–106; indigeneity and marronage and, 217–19; Native peoples as, 43–52; species similarity in Butler's *Xenogenesis* trilogy and, 106–14

"Political Science Fiction" (Michaels), 109

postcolonial states, sovereignty concepts and, 38–52

Povinelli, Elizabeth, 86, 89, 211

prison-industrial complex, 261nn22–23, 263n43

problem-spaces: for African Americans, 137–51, 263n38, 273n144; of Black and Indigenous identity, 18–19, 235n11; carceral space as, 123–37; in Hopkinson's *Midnight Robber*, 180–86; indigeneity and, 85–86, 256n94; in Jones's *Bird Is Gone*, 194–201; in Mosley's *Futureland*, 122, 150–51; in Native fiction, 187–201; in Wilson's *Robopocalypse* series, 137–51; undercommons and, 231. *See also* placemaking

Provincializing Europe (Chakrabarty), 3

Puar, Jasbir, 97, 128, 264n50

Queer Phenomenology (Ahmed), 158, 185–86

racial embodiment: blackness and, 5, 10–11; collective place making and, 243n115; indigeneity and, 78–92; in Jones's *Bird Is Gone*, 194–201; reproduction and, 79–80; Sharpe's discussion of, 84, 251n38; slavery and, 249n6; sovereignty and citizenship and, 43–52; in U.S. political imaginary, 73–78. *See also* disability

racial/ethnic binaries, settler colonialism and, 25–37

racialization: in Butler's *Xenogenesis*, 108–14; of carceral space, 117–22; carceral space and, 117–22, 122–37; culture and, 281n84; futurist destabilization of, 69–72; global politics of, 21–25; humanness and, 114–15; indigeneity and, 84–92; in Jones's *Bird Is Gone*, 194–201; in Latin American marronage policies, 208–11; in Mosley's *The Wave*, 156–57; technology and, 128–37, 262n36

racial mixture, fungibility and, 74–78. *See also* miscegenation

rationality, Eurocentric concepts of, 20–25

Reardon, Jenny, 262n36

Red, White, and Black (Wilderson), 48–49

Red Pegagogy (Grande), 24

Red Skin, White Masks (Coulthard), 25–28

refusal, space of, in Butler's *Xenogenesis*, 93–106

relativism, truth claims and, 246n159
reproduction, racial embodiment and, 79–80, 83–84
Riding the Trail of Tears (Hausman), 270n110, 280n79
Roberts, Dorothy, 128
Roberts, Neil, 168, 170, 274n11
Robogenesis (Wilson), 146–49, 166–67, 268n82, 268n86
Robopocalypse (Wilson), 12, 121, 137–51; indigeneity in, 137–51, 187; nonhuman entities in, 147–51, 269n98, 270n113; place as being and becoming in, 166–67
Rodríguez, Dylan, 264n50
Rovane, Carol, 246n159

Sartre, Jean-Paul, 193
Schwab, Gabriele, 251n42
science fiction: Delany's discussion of, 67–69, 220, 249n16; equivocation and, 10
Scott, David, 18, 61, 235n11
segregation: African American literature and, 131–32; Black political movements and, 57–61; racial mixture and, 74–78; urban geography and, 44–45, 241n97
self-determination: African diaspora and Indigenous concepts of, 52–61; Black settlers and Native concepts of, 53–61; in Butler's *Xenogenesis* trilogy and, 107–14, 213; decolonization and, 23–25; in Hopkinson's *Midnight Robber,* 173–86; Indigenous projects of, 2, 5–6, 9, 14, 86–87; in Jones's *Bird Is Gone,* 194–201; marronage and, 168–69, 171–73, 284n135; post-slavery concepts of, 82; in Wilson's *Robopocalypse* series, 146–51; settler colonialism and, 25–28; sovereignty and, 42–52, 98–106; U.S. anti-immigration policy and, 227; in Zobel's *Oracles,* 189–92. *See also* peoplehood; personhood; sovereignty
Senghor, Léopold, 242n106
"Settled and Unsettled Spaces" (Watson), 150
settler colonialism: blackness and indigeneity and, 10, 15–19; Black people as settlers and, 52–61; in futurist narratives, 62, 69–72, 277n42; in Hopkinson's *Midnight Robber,* 173–86; in Jones's *Bird Is Gone,* 192–201, 222; liberalism and, 29, 237n49; limits of

research on, 245n139; Native placemaking and, 187–201; population classifications under, 24–25; in Wilson's *Robopocalypse* series, 139–51; self-determination and, 98–106; sovereignty of Indigenous peoples and, 38–52, 187–201, 222, 245n141; territoriality and, 25–28, 98–106; treaties and non-state sovereignty and, 213–17, 284n136; Wynter's discussion of, 21–25; in Zobel's *Oracles,* 189–92, 222
Settler: Identity and Colonialism in 21st Century Canada, 55–56
Sexton, Jared, 48, 54, 59, 74–77, 159–60
Sharkey, Patrick, 242n100
Sharma, Nandita, 236n28
Sharpe, Christina, 84, 249n4, 251n38, 271n128
Sharpe, Jenny, 173, 177
Sheller, Mimi, 277n46
Simon, Jonathan, 259n11
Simpson, Audra, 5, 31, 42–43, 93–106, 190; *As We Have Always Done,* 213, 224
Simpson, Leanne, 9, 42, 213, 224–25; *Dancing on Our Turtle's Back,* 42
Singh, Nikhil Pal, 58–60, 244n133
Sioux peoples, 205–6, 283n109
slavery: blackness and indigeneity and, 15–19; concepts of belonging and, 43–52; in futurist narratives, 62–63; Hopkinson's *Midnight Robber* and, 275n27; indigeneity and, 15–19, 200–201; insurance industry and economies of, 64; marronage and maroon identity and, 168–69; in Mosley's *The Wave,* 153–54, 163–65; politics and legacy of, 4–5; prison labor as, 126, 261nn22–23; settler colonialism and, 52–61; weather and, 271n128
Smith, Rachel Greenwald, 257n96
Smoak, Gregory, 209
Snorton, C. Riley, 84
sociogenic: Fanon's concept of, 235n25; Wynter's discussion of, 24–25
sovereignty: Black and Indigenous concepts of, 38–52; blackness and indigeneity and, 10, 28–30; Black settlers and, 53–61; bodily/racial purity and, 93–94; in Butler's *Xenogenesis* trilogy, 113–14; in Hairston's *Mindscape,* 211–17; in Hopkinson's *Midnight Robber,* 177–86; in Mosley's work, 137; Native concepts of, 50–52; post-Westphalian

sovereignty (continued)
concepts of, 38; in Wilson's *Robopocalypse*
series, 140–51; settler colonialism and,
26–28; treaties and non-state sovereignty,
213–17, 284n136; undercommons and,
223–31; in Mosley's *The Wave*, 122, 161–65;
Wynter's discussion of, 22–25; in Zobel's
Oracles, 188–92
speculation: in Butler's *Xenogenesis,* 77–78; in
Hairston's *Mindscape,* 201–19; in Mosley's
The Wave, 153–65; in Native fiction,
187–201; oppression and, 61–72, 246n158
Spillers, Hortense, 249n6
Standing Rock Sioux reservation, 1–2
Starboard Wine (Delany), 67, 220
statelessness, blackness and, 47–52
state-sanctioned violence: Black Lives Matter
as response to, 3–4; Black *vs.* Native experi-
ence of, 15–19; in Hairston's *Mindscape,*
208–17; indigenous land use and, 85–86;
liberal multiculturalism and, 29, 237n49;
mass incarceration and, 118–19; in Mosley's
Futureland, 125–37; in Mosley's *The Wave,*
155–65; in Wilson's *Robopocalypse* series,
138–51
"The State Is a Man" (Simpson), 5
Stephens, Michelle Ann, 47–48, 175
Stevenson, Lisa, 98–99
Stone Sky, The (Jemisin), 254n72
straight time, in futurist narratives, 66–67
"Strategic Anti-Essentialism: Decolonizing
Decolonization" (Sharma), 236n28
structural violence, systemic analysis of, 20–36
subjectivity, in futurist narratives, 67–69,
249n16
system modeling, Black and Native identity
and, 19–37, 231

Tal, Kali, 265n54
Tate, Greg, 70
Taylor, Drew Hayden, 11, 64
technology: carceral space and, 122–37; in
Hopkinson's *Midnight Robber,* 176–86;
oppression and, 64–65; racialization and,
128–37, 262n36; in Wilson's *Robopocalypse*
series, 137–51, 268n84
territoriality: blackness and, 159; carceral space
and, 121–22, 137, 143; in futurist fiction,

12, 14; in Hairston's *Mindscape,* 209–17;
in Hopkinson's *Midnight Robber,* 176–86;
indigeneity and, 5–6, 90–92, 209–11; in
Jones's *Bird Is Gone,* 193–201, 282n95; marronage and, 171–73; in Wilson's *Robopocalypse* series, 143–51; settler colonialism and,
25–28, 237n35; sovereignty and, 39
Third World Left, 59
Thirteenth Amendment, 261n23
Thomas, Greg, 169
Thompson, Alvin O., 168, 277n46
Tometi, Opal, 3–4
Transit of Empire, The (Byrd), 142
translation: Black and Indigenous imaginaries and, 17–19, 237n45; difference and,
30–31, 37, 231; equivocation and, 6, 143;
fugitivity and, 152; of marronage, 202, 207;
non-identical movements and, 9, 16, 25,
228; political imaginaries and, 7, 17–20;
settler colonialism and, 53–54, 56–57, 61;
in speculative fiction, 71, 167, 208; system
modeling and, 20
transnational affiliation: African American political movements and, 58–61; in
Hopkinson's *Midnight Robber,* 175–76;
sovereignty and, 46–52
treaties: geographies of colonialism and,
224–25; Indigenous non-state sovereignty
and, 213–17, 279n72, 281n92, 284n136;
285n138; marronage and, 170–71
Treaty Shirts (Vizenor), 270n110
tree imagery, in Hopkinson's *Midnight Robber,*
181, 277nn45–46
Tuck, Eve, 23, 36, 55–56, 223, 231
Tucker, Jeffrey, 109
Turner, Dale, 40–41, 182, 191–92

uncommonality, Black and Indigenous movements and, 36
undercommons, Black-Indigenous difference
and, 220–31
Undercommons, The (Harney and Moten), 14,
221–31
Underground Railroad, The (Whitehead),
273n144
unemployment, imprisonment and, 263n43
United Nations Declaration on the Rights of
Indigenous Peoples, 100

United States: Black political movements in, 57–61, 97; detribalization program in, 101; marronage in, 273n5; Native sovereignty and governance in, 40–41, 50–52; "plenary" authority over Native peoples in, 196–98, 282n93; racial embodiment in politics of, 73–78; treaties and non-state sovereignty and, 213–17, 285n138

United States v. Kagama, 282n93

Universal Negro Improvement Association, 175

unknowing, among oppositional movements, 238n54

"Unsettling the Coloniality of Being/Power/Truth/Freedom" (Wynter), 20, 22–23

urban geography: blackness and, 44–45, 241n97, 263n38; marronage and, 170–71; mass incarceration and, 117–22, 130–37; in Wilson's *Robopocalypse* series, 141–51

utopia, in futurist narratives, 66–67

"The *Vel* of Slavery" (Sexton), 48, 159

Vizenor, Gerald, 270n110

Wacquant, Loïc, 130–31, 260n14

Walcott, Rinaldo, 22

Walking the Clouds (Dillon), 65

Wallace, Molly, 102, 252n44

Warren, Kenneth, 131–32

Watson, Irene, 150, 200

Wave, The (Mosley), 12, 122, 151–67, 202, 225, 272nn140–41, 273n143

weblining, 264n46

Weheliye, Alexander, 48, 75, 110, 114, 236n31, 239n68

"What to a Slave Is the Fourth of July?" (Douglass), 152

What Was African American Literature? (Warren), 131–32

"Whispers in the Dark" (Mosley), 133, 135

Whitehead, Colson, 273n144

whiteness: Black and Indigenous political imaginaries in context of, 6–7; state power and, 126–37, 264n50

Wilder, Gary, 46–47, 242n106

Wilderson, Frank, 48–49, 54

Williams, Raymond, 67

Wilson, Daniel, 12, 121, 137–51, 166–67, 182, 210, 267n78, 268n84; *Robogenesis,* 146–49, 166–67, 268n82, 268n86; *Robopocalypse,* 12, 121, 137–51, 166–67, 187, 269n98, 270n113

Wilson, Jack (Wovoka), 206

Windward Maroons, 176–77, 275n29

Wolfe, Patrick, 25

Workin' on the Chain Gang (Mosley), 261n24

Wounded Knee massacre, 206–7, 212

Wright, Richard, 220

Wynter, Sylvia: biopolitics and work of, 97; on blackness, 236n26, 236n28, 236nn30–31; on difference and humanity, 20–25, 140, 235n25; on indigeneity, 57; on modernity and globalization, 235n14; on selfhood, 110, 114; on sovereignty, 48

Xenogenesis trilogy (Butler): capacity, disability, and refusal in, 92–106, 256n85; collective self-determination in, 181–82, 213; critical analysis of, 254n69; indigeneity in, 78–92, 115–16, 251n40, 251n42; Mosley's *Futureland* and, 121; publication of, 249n9; racial embodiment in, 75–78, 106–14, 255n81; racialization and, 11; species similarity in, 106–14, 255n76

Yang, K. Wayne, 23, 36, 55–56, 223, 231

Yaszek, Lisa, 65

Yazzie, Melanie, 14, 227, 230–31

Young, Cynthia, 58–59

Zaki, Hoda M., 109–10

Zimmerman, George, 3

Zobel, Melissa Tantaquidgeon, 13–14, 172, 187–93, 200–202, 207, 218–19, 222, 279n67; *Oracles,* 13–14, 172, 187–93, 200–201, 213